"When I commanded U.S. military forces in Latin America and NATO forces in Europe, I observed first-hand how transnational human security challenges have become national security priorities. From poverty and piracy to illicit trafficking, climate change, and cyber attacks, this exceptional text provides a roadmap for integrating human security challenges into national security calculations. The collaborative approach explored here offers the only sensible way forward for states and communities to protect and promote security in our globalized world."

—*Admiral James Stavridis, USN (ret.) and former Dean, Fletcher School of Law and Diplomacy, U.S.*

"Given the changes in the international security environment, the co-authors have made a compelling case why focusing exclusively on traditional state-centered national security threats is no longer a viable analytical paradigm. It has to be supplemented by a new organizing concept of human security, predicated on how people are impacted and focusing in particular on such subnational and transnational challenges as health, environment, poverty, and crime, among others. The book makes an important contribution to the national security literature by detailing thoroughly why these challenges, if ignored, will be at one's own peril. It is a must read for policy-makers, academics, and civil society."

—*Ambassador Paula J. Dobriansky, Harvard University, U.S.*

"*Human and National Security* is an outstanding book offering a comprehensive examination of what elements are necessary for meaningful security in the contemporary world. This book provides a significant and forward-looking appraisal of the security environment, situating human security concerns as vital in the pursuit of national security. Written in an engaging and accessible style, it is an excellent and immensely important read for students, scholars, and practitioners of national security."

—*Anna Hayes, James Cook University, Australia*

"Since the publication of the first edition, I have used the textbook numerous times in my courses with great success. Students have appreciated the well-written and straightforward approach, as well as the book's rich theoretical and substantive material on human security. The second edition continues in this exceptional tradition with its up-to-date examples, and emphasis on understanding and preparing for the transformative forces shaping the world that pose a threat to human security."

—*Mary Pettenger, Western Oregon University, U.S.*

Human and National Security

Deliberately challenging the traditional, state-centric analysis of security, this book focuses on subnational and transnational forces—religious and ethnic conflict, climate change, pandemic diseases, poverty, terrorism, criminal networks, and cyber attacks—that threaten human beings and their communities across state borders. Examining threats related to human security in the modern era of globalization, Reveron and Mahoney-Norris argue that human security is national security today, even for great powers.

This fully updated second edition of *Human and National Security: Understanding Transnational Challenges* builds on the foundation of the first (published as *Human Security in a Borderless World*) while also incorporating new discussions of the rise of identity politics in an increasingly connected world, an expanded account of the actors, institutions, and approaches to security today, and the ways diverse global actors protect and promote human security.

An essential text for security studies and international relations students, *Human and National Security* not only presents human security challenges and their policy implications, it also highlights how governments, societies, and international forces can, and do, take advantage of possibilities in the contemporary era to develop a more stable and secure world for all.

Dr. Derek S. Reveron is Professor and Chair of National Security Affairs at the U.S. Naval War College in Newport, Rhode Island.

Dr. Kathleen A. Mahoney-Norris is Professor Emeritus, USAF Air Command and Staff College, Air University, Alabama.

Human and National Security
Understanding Transnational Challenges

SECOND EDITION

Derek S. Reveron and
Kathleen A. Mahoney-Norris

Routledge
Taylor & Francis Group
NEW YORK AND LONDON

Second edition published 2019
by Routledge
711 Third Avenue, New York, NY 10017

and by Routledge
2 Park Square, Milton Park, Abingdon, Oxon, OX14 4RN

Routledge is an imprint of the Taylor & Francis Group, an informa business

First edition published by Westview 2011

Library of Congress Cataloging-in-Publication Data
Names: Reveron, Derek S., author. | Mahoney-Norris, Kathleen, author.
Title: Human and national security : understanding transnational challenges / Derek Reveron and Kathleen Mahoney-Norris.
Other titles: Human security in a borderless world
Description: Second edition. | New York : Routledge, 2018. | First edition published: Human security in a borderless world. Philadelphia, PA : Westview Press, c2011. | Includes bibliographical references and index.
Identifiers: LCCN 2018004316 | ISBN 9781138587755 (Hardback) | ISBN 9780813350905 (Paperback) | ISBN 9780429503726 (E-book)
Subjects: LCSH: Security, International. | National security. | National security—United States.
Classification: LCC JZ5588 .R496 2018 | DDC 355/.033—dc23
LC record available at https://lccn.loc.gov/2018004316

ISBN: 9781138587755 (hbk)
ISBN: 9780813350905 (pbk)
ISBN: 9780429503726 (ebk)

Typeset in Sabon
by Apex CoVantage, LLC

I am convinced that the creation of open, equitable, inclusive and pluralist societies, based on the full respect of human rights and with economic opportunities for all, represents the most tangible and meaningful alternative to violent extremism.

—United Nations Secretary-General António Guterres, Preface to "Journey to Extremism in Africa," UNDP, 2017

Contents

Illustrations

Boxes

Figures

Images

Maps

Tables

About the Authors

Dr. Derek S. Reveron is Professor and Chair of National Security Affairs at the U.S. Naval War College in Newport, Rhode Island, and is a faculty affiliate at the Belfer Center for Science and International Affairs at Harvard Kennedy School. He has authored or edited thirteen books, and specializes in strategy development, non-state security challenges, and defense policy. He teaches courses on human security, international security, grand strategy, foreign policy analysis, and cybersecurity.

Dr. Kathleen A. Mahoney-Norris is Professor Emeritus, USAF Air Command and Staff College, Air University, Alabama. She teaches and consults for online academic programs, and develops international relations and national security-focused curricula for military officers and civilian professionals. She has also co-edited *Democratization and the Protection of Human Rights: Challenges and Contradictions*, and has contributed articles and chapters to various journals and books, including *The International Studies Encyclopedia*.

Preface

Collectively, the authors have been thinking about or promoting U.S. national security for more than sixty years as military officers and educators focused on security studies. In both professions, we have continually confronted biases oriented toward studying great powers and big wars. That logic made more sense during the Cold War when Soviet and U.S. foreign policies under the shadow of nuclear exchange kept both countries on the verge of World War III. But, as we commemorate the thirty-year anniversary of Soviet collapse in 2021, both professions need to move beyond a doomsday scenario to fully understand the new (albeit thirty-year-old) security environment where subnational and transnational challenges stymie government efforts to improve international peace and security. While great power tensions are visible among the United States, Russia, China, India, and Japan, all countries have economic incentives and political institutions to avoid war. While the U.S. and China may be competitors, they are also partners addressing challenges such as climate change, transnational organized crime, and pandemic diseases. Blindfolding ourselves to this increasingly complicated and ambiguous contemporary world will only delay our ability to address today's security issues, where human security is truly national security.

Human Security and National Security: Understanding Transnational Challenges is designed to be a textbook for those students, researchers, and practitioners thinking about international and national security. While this work is developed from a U.S.- informed security perspective, we believe that the analysis stands on its own. We offer a detailed examination of the challenges that threaten most human beings, their societies, and their governments today, along with an alternative approach to thinking about national security, encapsulated in the concept of *human security*. As the influential United Nations Development Programme has phrased it, "Security is a child who did not die, a disease that did not spread, a job that was not cut, an ethnic tension that did not explode in violence, a dissident who was not silenced."

Instead of protecting against the most catastrophic possibilities (rogue states and nuclear attack), we think it is important to think about the most likely threats (non-state actors and transnational challenges). International institutions, norms, and diplomacy are proving able to prevent interstate war. Consequently, we must educate ourselves about the many issues that have often been decades in the making and are now demonstrating their capability to threaten all human beings. These include issues such as climate change, pandemic diseases, endemic poverty, weak and failing states, transnational narcotics trafficking and criminal gangs, and vulnerable information systems. Engaging in critical thinking now will enable governments, militaries, nongovernmental groups, and individual citizens to improve national and human security, while improving good governance and social and economic prosperity for all.

Acknowledgments

We are both grateful to Toby Wahl for his confidence in the first edition, and Katie Moore, Kathryn Lindquist, Grace Fujimoto, Claire Maloney, Maria Anson and Richard Kemp for their energy to make this second edition possible. They all gave us an important opportunity to share our vision for rethinking national security, which is not only essential but also long overdue.

We also thank the editorial and marketing staffs of Routledge, Westview, PublicAffairs, and the Perseus Books Group who turned our ideas into this textbook. For generous use of images, we thank Jennifer Doyle and Babak Parviz.

Individually, Derek would like to acknowledge the support of his colleagues at the Naval War College who research national security and develop future strategic leaders for sixty-five countries. In particular, Derek is grateful to David Polatty, Hank Brightman, Chris Fettweis, Jeffrey Murer, Mike Miner, and Scott Cheney-Peters. Tanna Wise also provided important research support.

Individually, Kathleen expresses appreciation to her colleagues within Air University who have been supportive and stimulated her thinking about national security along non-traditional lines, especially Chuck Costanzo, Mary Hampton, Bart Kessler, David Sorenson, and Ryan Wadle. Additionally, Kathleen thanks John Ackerman, Jack Miller, Lewis Ware, Giacomo Chiozza, and especially Carol Atkinson for her exceptional insights and assistance. On a personal note, Kathleen acknowledges the unwavering support and encouragement of David Norris.

These views are their own and do not represent the views of the Department of Defense.

Chapter 1

Human and National Security

Concepts, Theories, and History

Chapter contents

No matter where our men and women are serving, the security environment they face is unlike any we've seen before:

- Violent non-state actors can, and do, challenge the sovereignty of our nations, the integrity of our institutions, and the safety of our citizens.
- Border security has fundamentally changed. What was once confined to enforcing trade and immigration laws has been joined by an expanding new series of threats like criminal and extremist networks.
- For many nations, the line between internal defense and domestic security is blurring.[1]

—Admiral Kurt Tidd, U.S. Southern Command

What U.S. Navy Admiral Kurt Tidd noted for much of the Western Hemisphere is increasingly true across the globe; non-traditional or human security challenges are increasingly relevant for countries throughout the international system—including the United States. It appears that traditional war as a way of settling grievances between states or advancing national interests is actually disappearing.[2] At the end of 2017, the Uppsala Conflict Data Program tracked one interstate conflict (e.g. Russia-Ukraine) and about fifty intrastate conflicts (e.g. Sudan and Nigeria), many of which are internationalized internal conflicts (e.g. Congo and Afghanistan).[3] With few exceptions, conflict rarely results in more than 1,000 battle deaths, which is often considered the threshold for war. Interstate rivalry remains (e.g. North Korea and Japan or Israel and Iran) but the data reinforce well-known scholar John Mueller's conclusion that war among great powers has almost ceased to exist.[4]

Of course, the potential for major conflict cannot be disregarded as tensions persist between the U.S. and Russia, India and Pakistan, South Korea and North Korea, and Israel and Iran. Yet incidents such as the Saudi intervention in Yemen in 2015, Russia's invasion of Ukraine in 2014, or the U.S. invasion of Iraq in 2003 are rare. The absence of major war is also evident in the proliferation of United Nations peacekeeping missions around the world. In 2018, about 100,000 "blue helmets" separated former warring factions and development agencies and nongovernmental organizations (NGOs) worked to ameliorate underlying conditions to prevent future conflicts between states. Further, militaries that were once trained and equipped solely to defend their countries' borders are increasingly used in ways to promote peace, provide disaster relief, and improve human development as Admiral Tidd suggested in the epigraph above, blurring "the line between internal defense and domestic security."[5] Instead, illegally armed criminal and terrorist groups, pandemic disease, malevolent cyber actors, and environmental degradation occupy the concerns of many national security professionals as they seek to improve security for their citizens.[6]

The implications of a changed security landscape are profound for every human being. In retrospect, security concerns over the past thirty years have been increasingly focusing on human-centered security issues such as disease, poverty, and crime. These security concerns often entail contrasting views about actors, threats, and issues, which are reflected in the diversity of ways in which the United States protects its national security today (see Table 1.1 for highlights of contrasting views on national versus human security). Although there are remnants of Cold War conflicts on the Korean Peninsula and in the Persian Gulf region—and nuclear weapons still pose strategic threats—these are largely the exception. Instead, the U.S. military no longer has a singular emphasis on defending the United States from other countries and preparing for major combat, but also focuses on providing security and other types of assistance to more than 150 countries ranging from Afghanistan to Zambia. It does so not out of imperial ambition but as a means to protect the United States from transnational challenges by addressing what are known as security deficits.[7]

Thus, with a few exceptions (primarily counterterrorism operations), American military forces usually do not engage in combat today; instead, they train and equip partners'

Table 1.1 Contrasting Forms of Security

	National Security	Human Security
Primary Actor	States	Individuals
Primary Concerns	Regime stability and security	Economic status, health, personal security, and liberties
Primary Threats	Forms of economic, military, or diplomatic coercion	Disease, poverty, and crime
Origin of Threats	Unfriendly states, weak states, and rival states	Non-state actors, transnational issues (e.g., climate change), repressive regimes, and illegally armed groups
Measure of Strength	Military power, economic productivity, control of borders, and appeal of values	Human development index that captures quality of life, educational opportunities, and life expectancy
Basis	National interests	Universal human needs and values
Ultimate Endstate	National sovereignty, territorial integrity, vitality of government, institutions, and society	Freedom from want, freedom from fear, freedom of expression, and freedom of beliefs
Legal Basis	United Nations Charter and International Law	Universal Declaration of Human Rights and Responsibility to Protect (R2P) doctrine

militaries, lead civil engineering projects, and provide medical assistance. All of these activities are designed to strengthen partner nations' capabilities, sovereignty, and stability, which are increasingly threatened by subnational and transnational actors. Yet significantly, these challenges are not entirely new. The 9/11 terrorist attacks occurred almost 20 years ago and, in spite of robust U.S.-led global counterterrorism operations, terrorism shows no sign of abating, but continues to evolve. As the U.S. National Intelligence Council forecast in 2017,

> The US and Soviet proxy wars, especially in Vietnam and Afghanistan, were a harbinger of the post-Cold War conflicts and today's fights in the Middle East, Africa, and South Asia in which less powerful adversaries deny victory through asymmetric strategies, ideology, and societal tensions. The threat from terrorism will expand in the coming decades as the growing prominence of small groups and individuals use new technologies, ideas, and relationships to their advantage.[8]

Technological changes spurring increased information flows and networking have helped to stimulate not only terrorism but also new transnational challenges that are creating widespread insecurity across the civic, economic, environmental, maritime, health, and cyberspace realms. Examples are numerous and diverse. The proliferation of small arms and light weapons, often linked to narco-trafficking and criminal gangs, undermines government legitimacy and social stability in Latin America and the Caribbean, as individual citizens do not feel secure. International migrant smuggling and trafficking in persons challenge traditional notions of sovereignty and human rights in West and North Africa. Development inequities, systemic corruption, and persecution of certain groups foster unrest within, and between, societies in Europe and Asia alike. In many of these cases, the insecurity triggers human migration by sea as families seek a better life in Europe or North America. At the same time, through malicious code cyber criminals, foreign intelligence services, and hacktivists threaten information and cyber security for governments, businesses, and consumers throughout the world. Clearly the interconnected world has brought benefits, but it also enables threats to move freely throughout the world, weakening governments and communities, and challenging democracy. In this regard, noted commentator Francis Fukuyama sees "The biggest single problem in societies aspiring to be democratic has been their failure to provide the substance of what people want from government: personal security, shared economic growth and the basic public services (especially education, health care and infrastructure) that are needed to achieve individual opportunity."[9]

Fukuyama's observation reflects the fact that today most governments face destabilizing threats from within their borders rather than from neighboring states that challenge their sovereignty. We have not only observed increases in civil conflicts, terrorism, and pandemic diseases, but also the rise of populism that threatens liberal democracies in response to migrations triggered by human insecurity issues in the Middle East, Central Asia, Latin America, and Africa.

Traditional analyses that focus on challenges to U.S. national security in the form of competitor states like China fail to take into account these growing security challenges at the subnational and transnational levels. While existing international institutions were designed to prevent conflict among states, these subnational and transnational forces challenge conventional ideas about power and security. Because of this, the United States now finds itself engaged around the world in military operations and initiatives that have little to do with warfighting but everything to do with providing humanitarian assistance (such as depicted in Image 1.1), training foreign militaries, and building security, justice, and law

Image 1.1 Humanitarian Assistance in Nepal. Photo: U.S. Department of Defense

enforcement institutions to improve domestic stability. Yet narrow conceptions of national security cannot account for this phenomenon of assistance, while influential perspectives on world politics such as realism, which focuses on the preeminent role of states, offer little insight into the growing American preoccupation with transnational issues.

Likewise, traditional conceptions of security are severely strained to explain today's security environment, where potential peer competitors or possible adversaries like the United States and China are transforming into cooperative partners to combat common transnational challenges such as pandemic diseases, maritime piracy, and climate change. Neither can state-based conceptions of security make sense of the growing influence of nongovernmental groups and activists who form social movements that work across state boundaries to tackle human rights abuses, poverty, the spread of HIV/AIDS, and climate change.

Perspectives on the New Security Environment

To ensure national security in a world characterized by these threats without borders requires new ways of conceptualizing security beyond the dominant international relations paradigm of realism or its near competitor, international liberalism. We argue here that the factors and issues fueling conflict and a pervasive sense of insecurity over the past thirty years will only accelerate in the next twenty years, requiring an increasingly nuanced understanding of these issues beyond and below the nation-state. The long-established realist and liberal perspectives of international relations are too narrowly focused on states (especially realism) and institutions that contain states (particularly liberalism), and their policies. These dominant perspectives can still offer valuable insights for national security professionals on certain aspects of the international system, but they are not very useful for assessing and responding to the evolution (some might say transformation) of human security issues occurring at the subnational and transnational levels.

Indeed, realism and liberalism often seem to be lacking even when considering the actions of major states in the twenty-first century. For example, given the preeminent military position of the United States, adherents of realism would predict that a new power must emerge to balance the United States. This reflects the realist school's emphasis on the vulnerable position of the state in an anarchic international system, where the state can rely only on its own power for survival, and thus must constantly accrue more power and "balance" against other rival states. In fact, from 1945 to 1991 the Soviet Union filled this role, as persuasively demonstrated by prominent (neo)realist scholar Kenneth Waltz.[10] But, contrary to realist expectations, since 1991 no new country has emerged to effectively challenge the United States. In fact, empirical work on the origins of war suggests very few rivalries result in war after 1945.[11] Countries with sufficient economic resources like the United Kingdom, Germany, and Japan are allies of the United States and spend too little on national defense. Powerful emerging economies like India lack the strategic rationale to balance the United States. Finally, competitors like Russia and China lack the economic independence and conventional military might that the former Soviet Union once possessed. Prominent political scientist Graham Allison believes the United States and China can avoid the realist-centric "Thucydides Trap" that would predict that the rising power (China) would challenge the status quo power (the U.S.)—but this requires accommodation of each others' interests.[12]

Significantly, instead of increased international (military) competition among states, this new era of globalization is also characterized by economic interdependence that makes traditional war costly for the major powers. Many assume that the increasingly prevalent phenomenon of contemporary globalization—characterized by high levels of worldwide economic trade, the movement of people, and information exchange—is a critical factor in ameliorating conflict in our contemporary age. Journalist and Pulitzer Prize-winner Thomas Friedman is well known for having popularized this concept of globalization, proposing in the late 1990s that the dynamic phenomenon "has replaced the Cold War as the defining international system."[13] For Friedman and other observers, globalization has appeared on balance to be a positive development, as it arguably fosters innovation, integration and even similar cultural values. Thus, disputes are arguably more likely to be resolved peacefully, either bilaterally or through multilateral organizations like the World Trade Organization (WTO) and the International Court of Justice (ICJ).

This positive assessment of globalization is generally shared by the international relations school of liberalism, the major competing worldview to realism.[14] For international liberals, whether scholars like Anne Marie Slaughter and G. John Ikenberry, or policymakers such as former presidents Bill Clinton and Barack Obama, the forces of globalization are projected to lead to beneficial economic development for all peoples, along with the spread of democratic and human rights ideals—all of which should translate to a more peaceful international system.[15]

At the same time as great power conflict has not occurred, this new era of globalization has also brought together many of the world's countries that face similar security challenges such as climate change, illicit trafficking of drugs and people, and computer viruses. Given the transnational character of these challenges, international liberals would argue that states obviously realize that international cooperation is essential to resolve these issues, and thus cooperation is bound to increase even further. (Table 1.2 contrasts the perspectives of the major international relations schools of realism and liberalism; constructivism is introduced below and explored in more detail in Chapter 2.)

Admittedly the prevailing international liberal order among states is being threatened as we write these words; great power politics are gaining attention again with China's hegemonic rise in East Asia and Russia is seeking to re-litigate the end of the Cold War in Europe. The U.S. National Intelligence Council has somberly forecast that "the decline in the number and intensity of conflicts during the past 20 years appears to be reversing: conflict levels are increasing and battle-related deaths and other human costs of conflict are up sharply since 2011."[16] But interstate conflict is not pre-ordained. While there remains normal friction among key states, bilateral diplomacy and international institutions have successfully prevented war between the traditional dyadic rivals of the United States. The major powers have vested interests in preserving many of the advances made by globalization, which continue to contribute to their prosperity and favorable position. This book reflects our own view that the increasing urgency of transnational human security issues and challenges will motivate states (and other actors) to continue to work together on a number of issues, as prominently represented by the near-universally endorsed 2015 Paris Accords to address climate change.

Globalization: Challenges to State and Human Security

Overall, international liberals and most U.S. policymakers alike have seen globalization on balance as a positive force in terms of both national and human security, and this viewpoint has been clearly represented in the national security strategies issued by every administration—Republican or Democrat—since the end of the Cold War.[17] The growing

Table 1.2 International Relations Theories: Perspectives on Security

Theory	Realism and Its Neovariants	Liberalism and Its Neovariants	Constructivism
Principal Concern	Power where the strong dominate the weak	Order and justice regardless of relative position in the international system	Shared ideas continuously shape interactions between humans and institutions
Theorists	Thomas Hobbes Niccolò Machiavelli Kenneth Waltz John Mearsheimer	Immanuel Kant John Locke Joseph S. Nye G. John Ikenberry	Sigmund Freud Michel Foucault Alexander Wendt Martha Finnemore
View of Human Nature	Individuals are greedy, aggressive, and will seek power	Individuals are social and perfectible through learning, and will seek cooperation	Individuals are thinking, adaptable, and will create environments to suit their needs
Goal for Foreign Policy	Maximize national security	International peace and justice (or prosperity)	Mutually determined by society
Means to Survival	Military and economic power used to reward or coerce other states	International order through non-coercive diplomacy and economic cooperation	Shared values to enhance the well-being of all
Primary Actors	States	States in intergovernmental organizations (e.g., United Nations) and non-state actors	Individuals and groups
Antagonists	Great powers (regardless of type of government)	Non-democracies (according to "the Democratic Peace Theory")	Policy entrepreneurs who shape norms
Measures of Power	Hard power: military capabilities and economic resources	Hard and Soft power: appeal of political, economic, and cultural norms	Pervasiveness and acceptance of ideas
Worldview Metaphor	Jungle: international system is anarchic; strong governments make the rules and dominate weak governments	Country club: international system is constrained by rules so strong and weak governments have more equal access	Blogosphere: density of connections and prevalence of transnational ideas matter
Causes of War	Anarchic international system; all states amass power as they fear for their survival. For Thucydides, causes are fear, honor, and interests	Misperception among states; the absence of enforceable international law to punish aggressor states and wrongdoers. Democracies do not go to war with each other	Enabling security discourse where government leaders can manipulate populace to adopt aggressive behavior toward other peoples
Path to Peace	Balance of power; powerful states constrain one another from going to war	Collective security, international law, democracy, and economic interdependence	Liberalization of thought; shared human rights and values and peaceful norms

integration of the world community has been applauded. And, up until quite recently, Americans and citizens of developed countries tended to view globalization as a beneficial force, too. Yet as we approach the next decade, we have been witnessing a populist, often nationalist, backlash against the international order that threatens to roll back the integration and cooperation that has been fueled in large part by globalization. For instance, the United Kingdom voted by popular referendum in 2016 to abandon the supranational European Union (EU). Later that same year the United States elected Donald Trump, who had frequently proclaimed his antipathy for free trade, large-scale immigration into the country, and international cooperation on issues like climate change. (In fact, the Trump administration's national security strategy of December 2017 did reflect a more cautious view on interdependence, globalization, and integration of the international system, stressing the competitive nature of the system.) Analyst Michael Mazarr voices a representative analysis, that the populist uprisings in many areas of the world "have been spurred on by outrage at increasing economic inequality, uneasiness with cultural and demographic changes, and anger at a perceived loss of national sovereignty"; furthermore, "the populist surge has featured outbursts in Europe and the United States against the perceived intrusions of a globalizing order."[18]

Yet even before these recent events, cautions had been raised about the potential dangers and concerns in this age of globalization where some societies were not well situated to benefit from rapid change, and where this type of change may be viewed as destabilizing to communities (an issue addressed further in Chapter 3). Additionally, it should not be surprising to find that developed states have tended to be more immune than developing states to negative aspects of issues propelled by globalization. As the 2009–2010 influenza pandemic illustrated, the United States has the resources to manufacture vaccines, stockpile antiviral medicines, and inoculate tens of millions of people in a short period of time. Developing countries are not so well equipped. The same is true when it comes to illegally armed, violent groups or criminal gangs. In the United States these gangs are a problem for law enforcement. But in Central America gangs outnumber and overwhelm law enforcement and even militaries. In that region gangs are a serious national security threat; they have benefited from globalization through easy weapons procurement and new markets, enabling them to compete with traditional state institutions and security forces.

Unfortunately, in almost every country of the world, transnational actors beyond the control of the state have been steadily waging "wars of globalization," which leading thinker Moisés Naím encapsulates as the illegal trafficking of drugs, small arms, and humans; violations of intellectual property; and money laundering.[19] Svante Cornell and Niklas Swanström argue that, among transnational criminal activities, illegal drug production and trafficking pose a full-spectrum threat to both state and human security. For example, narcotics trafficking affects societies through addiction, crime, and disease.[20] Drug production also undermines or weakens effective governance by fostering corruption and powerful criminal networks, and it may provide financial support to terrorist and insurgent groups. Prominent examples include: the resurgence of the Taliban in Afghanistan, enabled by profits from the heroin trade; the FARC insurgent movement in Colombia, which had sustained itself through cocaine trafficking until a landmark peace deal was reached; and competing drug trafficking organizations challenging the Mexican state's ability to govern. The issue of drug trafficking also highlights the fact that traditional distinctions between foreign and domestic policies are fading when it comes to many transnational concerns. Clearly, Mexico's violent internal battle with its drug cartels spills over into the border regions of the United States, affecting the security of U.S. citizens and the demands on local law enforcement officials there. In turn, this affects U.S. foreign policy toward Mexico and U.S. willingness to become involved in Mexico's domestic campaign against its drug cartel problem, while equally motivating the United States to expand physical barriers between the two countries.

Unfortunately for developed countries like the United States, weak states are assessed to have a comparative advantage in generating international crime, terrorism, and violence that tend to spill over into developed regions like North America and Europe.[21] Because of this, transnational security issues have emerged as key challenges for all states and their citizens in the twenty-first century. Paul Smith has defined these challenges as "non-military threats that cross borders and either threaten the political and social integrity of a nation or the health of that nation's inhabitants."[22] These threats are very different from conventional threats. In many cases non-state actors such as terrorist groups or criminal enterprises cause these threats, and they find either sanctuary or support within weak states. For example, most law enforcement agencies regard West African criminal networks as dangerous adversaries with global reach.[23] Similarly, the transnational gang Mara Salvatrucha (MS-13) challenges the viability of Central American governments, even as it has links to sister gangs in cities like Los Angeles. Or witness the meteoric rise of Somali piracy that has since forced dozens of countries to deploy warships to the Gulf of Aden and the Indian Ocean.[24] These transnational security issues often represent the "dark side" of globalization, where individuals and groups compete with governments on a regional or global scale.

Turning specifically to Africa, many of the continent's fifty-three countries have been plagued by famine, disease, natural disasters, internal conflict, and population displacement that then crosses national borders to generate further security destabilization on that continent, and even further afield. For instance, in response to a 2014 Ebola outbreak in West Africa that seems triggered in part by loss of habitat for wild animals, the United States felt compelled to deploy over 3,000 military personnel to build public health facilities and support national medical systems in the region. Even the once-isolated trans-Saharan arc is increasingly seen as a breeding ground for violent conflict, terrorism, and regional instability. To respond to these complex security challenges, the United States created a military command to assist African governments in developing their security institutions, including capabilities against threatening subnational groups or violent transnational networks. Ironically, these non-state actors have demonstrated some inherent advantages, especially over weak governments. Small private groups can more readily harness off-the-shelf technology such as satellite phones, encryption, and transportation technology. In Nigeria, for example, organized criminal groups illegally trade 100,000 barrels of stolen oil every day, which requires an elaborate system of transportation and financing. Whether they are local, transnational, narco-terrorist, radical Islamist, or neo-communist, these groups have access to a variety of underground economies, suspect religious charities, and often illicit and corrupt government sponsorship.

With so many nongovernmental and illegal groups operating at a subnational level, many police forces in developing countries from Africa to Latin America are under-equipped to effectively confront them, and too frequently are co-opted through corruption. Further, military forces largely lack the capabilities, doctrine, and culture to confront these transnational security challenges. Militaries tend to prepare for defending their borders from invading forces, and not for improving how they work with police or enforce domestic law and order. However, this is changing, as military forces in many countries are beginning to think beyond warfare as they develop core competencies to meet the challenges of subnational and transnational threats to better address nontraditional human security concerns.

From the U.S. perspective, formerly distant internal security concerns have now been elevated to the status of international security concerns, as they threaten national unity, stability, and internal peace within states—but also have much larger implications for regional and global security. Given these transformational changes in the security environment, we contend that traditional notions of security focused solely at the interstate level have little to offer in terms of understanding threats without borders. Instead, a human security construct is necessary to make sense of these transnational challenges and to develop viable policy options.

The Construct of Human Security

In this book we propose that the only effective way to grapple with U.S. security concerns—and indeed, global security concerns—is to move beyond the traditional state-centric focus of *national security* to the organizing concept of *human security*, which is a people-centered approach focused on individual human beings and their rights and needs. In this we agree with the UN Commission on Human Security's assessment that we are "moving away from traditional, state-centric conceptions of security that focused primarily on the safety of states from military aggression, to one that concentrates on the security of the individuals, their protection and empowerment."[25] We also believe that the Commission's slogan—"Freedom from fear, freedom from want, freedom to live in dignity"—is a useful way to conceptualize human security, which we parse in greater detail in the next chapter and throughout the book.

In point of fact, the national security of states cannot be achieved without first achieving human security. There is an excellent argument for adding a codicil to the well-known scholarly and policy proposition on the democratic peace; that democracies do not fight one another. This codicil would include scholar Laura Neack's conclusion, that "there is also empirical evidence that democratic states are internally secure and better international neighbors . . . and that human security . . . is enhanced in democracies."[26] Arguably, this belief is reflected in the steady shift in U.S. foreign policy, increasingly focused on combating threats without borders and placing development on an equal footing with the traditional tools of diplomacy and defense. This was already acknowledged under the George W. Bush administration, progressed rapidly with the Obama administration, and has received some support in the Trump administration. As then-Secretary of State Rex Tillerson acknowledged in his confirmation hearing in January 2017:

> Our approach to human rights begins by acknowledging that American leadership requires moral clarity. We do not face an "either or" choice on defending global human rights. Our values are our interests when it comes to human rights and humanitarian assistance . . . our leadership demands action specifically focused on improving the conditions of people the world over, utilizing both aid and economic sanctions as instruments of foreign policy when appropriate.[27]

We believe that there is ample evidence that human security concerns have become an integral component of U.S. foreign policy.

Reflecting this changing view of foreign policy, we are convinced that it is essential to understand contemporary challenges through a more interdisciplinary, inclusive approach focused on human security that "equates security with people rather than territories, with development rather than arms."[28] The dynamic forces transforming human interactions at the international, transnational, regional, and domestic levels all have profound implications for the (human) insecurity perceived by individuals, groups, and states. Indeed, much of this dynamism is fueled by the process of globalization noted above, which is constantly accelerating change. And, in spite of his generally positive view of globalization noted above, Thomas Friedman has also acknowledged that this type of rapid change can "breed enormous insecurity as well as enormous prosperity. [It] can breed in people a powerful sense that their lives are now controlled by forces they cannot see or touch."[29] Therefore, examining globalization as an ongoing process affecting human security is essential to our analysis throughout this work.

While we deal in large part with the negative aspects of globalization—for example, how it contributes to the growth of transnational threats—it is equally important to consider the positive, cooperative aspects of globalization referenced briefly above. Thus, in Chapter 2 we review the growth of the transnational human rights movement with its many facets, and in Chapter 10 the recognition of such human-centered international norms as the Responsibility to Protect (R2P). Only with this broader perspective can the human security construct be properly understood, along with the role of forces such as globalization. In fact, the increasingly influential constructivist school of international relations scholars (see Table 1.2) would argue that the type of broader perspective reflected in the human security construct is necessary to appropriately analyze and make sense of the changing international system. For constructivists, people's views and beliefs on trends such as globalization are formed through mutual give-and-take as human beings and societies adapt their ideas and build new norms of behavior. Not surprisingly, these ideas and norms are equally influenced by cultural and religious values and traditions. The evolving perspective of constructivism is addressed further in Chapter 2, and we are convinced that this newer international relations perspective deserves equal, if not predominant, consideration when assessing human security—along with the long-established perspectives of realism and international liberalism.

Human Security as National Security

In the twenty-first century, it seems fair to conclude that human security concerns have gained currency in U.S. national security circles and have now become the basis for more nuanced thinking about security. In our view this is particularly significant because if the most powerful state in the international system acknowledges the importance of these concerns, then the human security construct will continue to gain increased traction. To be sure, the Pentagon still largely trains and equips military forces for major war, but, as noted above, the U.S. military increasingly finds itself operating in non-war-fighting environments—frequently attempting to alleviate human suffering brought on by natural disaster, civil war, or insurgency. And these types of operations seem likely to increase in the wake of climate change. As the influential National Intelligence Council proposed in 2016:

> Climate change and its resulting effects are likely to pose wide-ranging national security challenges for the United States and other countries over the next 20 years through the following pathways: threats to the stability of countries, heightened social and political tensions, adverse effects on food prices and availability, increased risks to human health, negative impacts on investments and economic competitiveness, and potential climate discontinuities and secondary surprises.[30]

The connection between climate change and military intervention is based in part on the assumption that extremists can gain sanctuary where governments are weak, and that climate change will further weaken fragile states that already lack capacity to provide basic services and security for their populations. Additionally, climate change will spur mass human migrations, challenging the ability of more stable regions to absorb increasing populations—a trend we are already witnessing as desperate migrants from Africa and the Middle East attempt to reach Europe. Unfortunately, this does not necessarily mean that developed countries or the U.S. government will act in sufficient time. Three retired senior officers made this point well before Donald Trump was elected in 2016: "Military leaders see a direct connection between addressing the effects of climate change and succeeding in its mission to protect the United States. In short, the military gets it. But until our politicians get it too, we run the risk of fulfilling MacArthur's admonishment of being 'too late.'"[31] In other words, while proactively addressing threats to human security can help prevent future military interventions, there is no guarantee that U.S. policymakers will be willing to commit sufficient resources to address those threats.

On the other hand, since at least the 1990s the United Nations has been at the forefront of promoting human security concerns, as part of the vision of a "new world order" as the Cold War concluded. In 1992 then Secretary-General of the United Nations, Boutros Boutros-Ghali, set forth a widely heralded agenda for peace, "to enhance respect for human rights and fundamental freedoms, to promote sustainable economic and social development for wider prosperity, to alleviate distress and to curtail the existence and use of massively destructive weapons."[32] Unprecedented levels of UN peacekeeping operations accompanied this strategic outlook. And in the wake of continuing internal and regional conflicts and violence against civilians—including the tragedy of genocide in Rwanda—the United Nations formalized its prevention activities on behalf of individual groups and populations, appointing a special adviser on the prevention of genocide in 2004. Soon afterward, in 2009, UN Secretary-General Ban Ki-moon outlined three key elements of a recently acknowledged *responsibility to protect* doctrine (R2P) for civilian populations that has gained increasing international support. The R2P construct clearly rests on the primacy of human security needs, but still weighs a government's ability to provide security for its own citizens, as examined further in Chapter 10.

Based on these converging trends and assessments, we believe that it is clearly not possible to understand the complex threats to U.S. national security—or how to develop effective strategies and policies to deal with those threats—without a deeper understanding of the component issues that underlie human security. Thus, in this work we consider how best to attain human security for states, groups, and individuals by examining the continuum of interrelated issue areas that we conceptualize in specific chapters as identity security, civic security, economic security, environmental security, maritime security, health security, and information security. Figure 1.1 portrays these interrelated seam issues graphically, in relationship to traditional security issues (such as nuclear and conventional attack) and specific instances of human security challenges (poverty, crime, corruption). Also portrayed are the types of capabilities and actors most prevalent in each type of issue.

It is important to acknowledge here that the seven issue areas we highlight throughout this work are modified from the initial human security issues laid out in the foundational United Nations Development Programme's (UNDP) *Human Development Report 1994*. In that document the UNDP identified "seven main categories" as threats to human security: economic security, food security, health security, environmental security, personal security, community security, and political security.[33] But, as influential and useful as that initial construct has been, we believe it is more appropriate almost twenty-five years later to adjust the parameters of the issues, especially in terms of our focus on human security as national security. Thus, for instance, we consider food security as part of economic security, and combine personal and political security into "civic" security. This also allows us to bring in the newer human security challenges of "maritime" and "information"

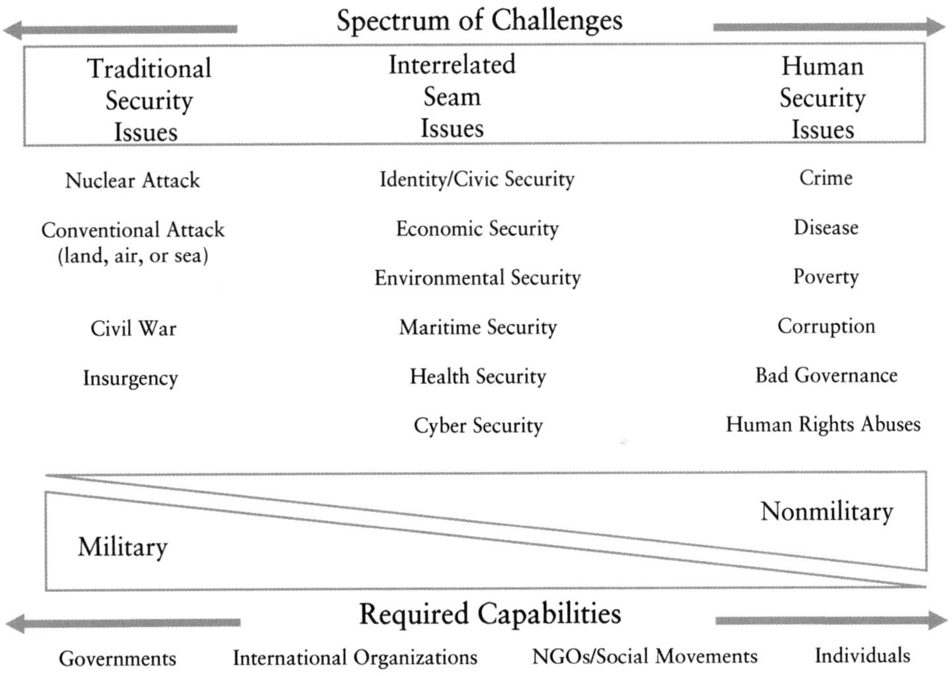

Figure 1.1 Spectrum of Challenges

security; these domains affect and enable all other human security interests. In fact, the United Nations and its many agencies have continued to evolve their understanding of what human security encompasses. In 2000 the UNDP spearheaded the formulation of eight "Millennium Development Goals" (MDGs) essential for human security; in 2015 these eight goals were expanded to seventeen "Sustainable Development Goals" (SDGs) that have now been endorsed by essentially all UN member states (these important goals are explored further in Chapters 2 and 5).[34]

In every chapter devoted to these issues we explore each area to provide a basis for understanding the problem and its challenges for human security; and the issue's relevance for the international community as a whole and for U.S. national security in particular, and for individual citizens. We also consider key policy recommendations. Fundamentally, we believe that states and their inhabitants are most threatened by subnational or transnational actors; that domestic instability can quickly develop into regional or global instability; and that international and transnational cooperation are essential to strengthening efforts at every level to improve human security. We advocate for no specific international relations paradigm in this analysis, but propose that aspects of realism, liberalism, and especially constructivism can be usefully applied depending upon the particular issue—and that is the approach we apply here.

Chapter Outline

We begin Chapter 2 by providing some important context on the historical development of the *human security construct*, which is integrally linked to the founding and evolution of the United Nations system of agencies. But even prior to the United Nations, we note the genesis of the concept in President Franklin Delano Roosevelt's famous "Four Freedoms" speech of 1941. We trace how these ideas evolve in tandem in the twentieth century with a progressively influential human rights movement, and with a concerted effort to advance economic and social development for the less advantaged. The chapter examines how globalization has served as an enabler for both intergovernmental and nongovernmental organizations and movements to promote these ideas, which place the individual and local communities at the center of their analysis and concern. We briefly consider how the traditional international relations paradigms of realism and liberalism are less helpful to understand this new thinking than the newer paradigm of constructivism. Finally, in the last section of this chapter we essentially come full circle as we describe how human security in the twenty-first century has come to be perceived as a critical element in supporting the national security interests of states. We conclude that the experiences, and lessons learned, of the U.S. military during interventions and peacekeeping missions have played an important role in changing U.S. perspectives on human security.

Chapter 3 addresses what might be considered the most basic human security interest, or need—that of *identity security*. In this chapter we first define identity security, along with the important intertwined concepts of culture and community. In fact, much of the focus here is on the component aspects of culture that are central to defining human identity, especially nationalism and religion, and the consequences for human security. Unfortunately, in this globalized age radical extremist leaders and groups—including radical or nationalist populists—can use these crucial aspects to their benefit, to strengthen certain communities at the expense of others, or even to circumscribe the role of women. While one's gender is clearly a fundamental biological characteristic that exists apart from culture, it is mainly cultural and often religious beliefs and practices that affect women's security concerns, as we summarize here. Finally, in this chapter we pay particular attention to indigenous peoples because these vulnerable groups around the world share a common experience of persecution as they seek recognition of their unique identities and traditions.

In addition to one's identity and sense of self, probably the most basic of other human security interests is to feel secure in one's person. Traditional national security perspectives have long focused on the security threats posed by states to one another as they engage in conflict or war. Implicit in this type of analysis is recognition that individual citizens of those states will be endangered, but individuals are not the main concern—unlike in the human security construct. Thus, in Chapter 4 we are concerned with the type of threats to individuals that may be caused by repressive and authoritarian governments, or, conversely, by ineffective and failing governments, both of which threaten the *civic security* of citizens in those societies. In the first case an individual's physical security and integrity may be threatened because the government is actually abusing his or her human rights—including their political and civil rights—whereas in the second case the government is incapable of providing public security and protecting the physical integrity and way of life or cultural values of each citizen. The latter problem is attaining increasing importance as globalization empowers domestic and transnational criminal gangs, drug traffickers, human traffickers, smugglers, and others who flourish in weak and poorly governed societies to prey upon ordinary citizens. The gravity of this issue is reflected in the fact that, globally, three times as many people die from homicide each year as do from conflict or war. We focus first on the Latin American region to illustrate the complexity and interrelated nature of security threats ranging from transnational criminal gangs to weak, corrupt governments who cannot, or will not, protect their citizens' security, or political and civil rights. This situation continues to have a direct impact on U.S. human, and national security, interests. Chapter 4 then concludes with an examination of the

"Arab Spring" protest movement that began in 2011, to further illustrate how repressive and corrupt governance may lead to increased violence and instability which eventually threatens entire regions.

Most would probably consider *economic security*, in the sense of being able to provide food and shelter for oneself and one's family, as critically essential to human security. Thus, in Chapter 5 we explore the grim reality of unsustainable and inequitable development, and severe poverty, that predominate in so much of the world today. Extensive studies by the UNDP highlight the staggering differences in life expectancy and other development indicators around the world, and how women are particularly disadvantaged (and overburdened with the tasks of daily life, as depicted in Image 1.2). These statistics provide the context for the importance of achieving the global SDGs outlined in this chapter. But the SDGs also support national security interests because poverty and lack of opportunity have the clear potential to stoke instability, violence, and conflict; and this clearly motivates the many millions of displaced persons and migrants in the world who seek a better life. Many scholars would further argue that it is socioeconomic factors and inequities that first fuel insecurity and conflict between different groups of people, and not identity differences. Thus, Chapter 5 asks how lesser developed countries can achieve the necessary economic growth to overcome poverty, especially when so many countries are dependent upon agriculture and commodities for export to the global market. Can the free trade system work for these countries, and are free trade schemes a useful tool? Is foreign aid from countries like the United States, and assistance from intergovernmental institutions such as the World Bank, of any lasting value?

Image 1.2 Women in Uganda Wash Clothes in the Nile River. Photo: Derek S. Reveron

In Chapter 6, we take up *environmental security*. There is strong and growing worldwide consensus that climate change is real and will have profound effects on international security. According to the conclusions of the UN Intergovernmental Panel on Climate Change (IPCC) in 2009:

> By the end of the century, sea levels may rise twice as much as was predicted two years ago . . . [which] means that the lives of some 600 million people living on low-lying islands, as well as those living in Southeast Asia's populous delta areas, will be put at serious risk.[35]

Although there are climate change skeptics, the implications of relocating literally millions of human beings in areas threatened by climate change are staggering, and people are already moving internally from low-lying areas in Bangladesh and the Philippines. For some island countries, like Kiribati and the Maldives, abandoning low-lying areas is not an option, as their entire countries may become uninhabitable. Clearly, "ecomigration" is a growing trend, one triggered not only by rising seas but also by desertification and a lack of fresh water in areas like the African Sahel region bordering the Sahara.[36]

Whereas the United States may have the resources to at least mitigate the effects of climate changes such as this in the future, developing countries and their populations will obviously be most at risk, as they lack adequate resources. Climate change will weaken already feeble states, contributing further to regional and global insecurity. And as populations are further stressed, the potential for instability, conflict, and even resource wars grows, especially where traditional societies may be already prone to clash with Western modes of development and modernity.

Key among resource wars are those that may take place in the maritime domain, which is the subject of Chapter 7. Considering this domain is essential, since 70 percent of the earth's surface is covered by water, 80 percent of the world's population lives on or near a coast, and the majority of international commerce travels by sea. Thus, it is important to increase awareness of the many dangers to *maritime security*. Illegal, unreported, and underreported fishing devastates fish stocks and undermines developing countries' food supplies. Piracy costs international shipping millions of dollars and threatens key shipping lanes connecting Europe and Asia. And pollution at sea—unintentionally through oil spills like the one in 2010 in the Gulf of Mexico or intentionally through toxic-waste dumping—threatens sustaining oceans as a vital resource. Finally, illicit groups increasingly benefit from maritime insecurity by exploiting trade routes to traffic drugs, people, and weapons. And as new maritime routes open because of the retreating Arctic ice sheets, countries must resolve competing claims for these new routes and the natural resources that likely exist in the "High North." To consider these issues, Chapter 7 explores new legal agreements, international conventions, and initiatives to improve maritime security.

As the 2014–2015 Ebola outbreak made clear, disease knows no boundaries, making the United States vulnerable to chronic and infectious diseases prevalent in many parts of the world. These include HIV/AIDS, malaria, hepatitis, tuberculosis, and influenza. On average, three pandemics per century have been documented since the sixteenth century, occurring at intervals of ten to fifty years. If an influenza pandemic virus were to appear similar to the one that struck in 1918 (killing an estimated 40 million people), there would be serious consequences for international and human security. Air travel and international commerce would stop. Disease outbreaks could trigger massive human migrations, disrupting social orders. Chapter 8 on *health security* discusses the security aspects and lessons to be learned from past outbreaks of other epidemics and the challenges of preparing for the next pandemic. It also provides a brief overview of other widespread diseases such as HIV/AIDS and malaria, which multiply the already serious development problems in many weak states in sub-Saharan Africa.

The previous chapters explore security in the material world, yet citizens in developed countries like the United States increasingly inhabit the virtual world. Thus, Chapter 9 deals with the constantly accelerating issue of *information security*. Within just the past decade, human beings, along with their governments and militaries, have become as dependent on the virtual world for their daily activities as they are on the physical world for human activities. The International Telecommunications Union of the United Nations has found that more than one-quarter of the world's 6.7 billion people use the Internet, while more than half of the world's population pay for mobile phone access.[37] This interconnection of the world's population within and across societies holds tremendous implications for economic growth and development, particularly for impoverished areas. For example, global fiber-optic networks have enabled communication in an unprecedented manner, propelling the emergence of India as the world's "back office." On the other hand, just as with globalization generally, there is a dark side of the information age wherein hackers, phishing scam artists, and transnational criminal groups harness the technology, too. Through Trojan horses, criminals and spies gain access to government and private computer networks. Through viruses and denial-of-service attacks, individuals and groups can bring down government and corporate websites. And through spyware and influence operations, the cherished civil liberty of privacy is subverted. Ultimately, cyberspace may prove to be the arena for future military conflicts, too. Recent conflicts in Europe and the Middle East included cyber operations, and the U.S. military is focused on developing cyber warfare capabilities, as are other countries.

In the concluding chapter, we first explain how protection of individuals and communities has come to be considered an international obligation that may transcend state sovereignty in certain situations, through the R2P construct. This is an instance where human security concerns may actually trump national security concerns, as in the case of the UN-sanctioned intervention in Libya in 2011, which is assessed here. We then examine the increasingly accelerating trend of tens of millions of refugees, internally displaced persons, migrants, and stateless persons in the world. These people often flee due to domestic human security concerns, but in turn their presence often causes human security issues in host nations and regions. The resulting instability may trigger national security concerns and generate conflict between states. Concluding our text with the example of these desperate groups of people is a fitting, if tragic, way to highlight the nexus between human and national security threats and challenges in today's interconnected world.

This issue, and the others we examine in succeeding chapters, leads us to reiterate that exclusively state-based approaches to understanding national security are no longer viable in an era marked by globalization, a revolution in information technologies, economic integration of states and regions, and a host of transnational challenges and threats. Instead, a new conceptual framework is necessary to understand the spectrum of challenges and the variety of actors and capabilities necessary to address the needs of individuals, communities, and states.

The human security-centered framework places the individual citizen at the heart of national security not only to protect him- or herself, but also because individuals are literally on the front lines fighting disease, hunger, and malicious software. Further, this framework explains the rationale for growing American preoccupation with non-state actors ranging from pirates and terrorists to criminal gangs and drug traffickers. Formerly considered a nuisance or footnote for national security professionals, non-state actors have emerged over the past two decades as the principal challengers to U.S. national security, and help explain much of contemporary U.S. foreign policy. As our human security construct predicts, U.S. foreign policy is prominently focused on subnational and transnational groups, which operate in and across weak states. Consequently, the United States has been seeking to bolster the security capacity of nearly every developing country in the world. Although this approach is a step in the right direction, we believe that it is still too state- and government-centric, and does not adequately address the underlying challenges ranging from civic security to cyber security. Ultimately, as examined throughout this book, any plan to advance human security on a global level must equally account for the transnational actors and forces that are shaping the international community, for better or worse. The Commission on Human Security eloquently warns us of the dangers ahead if we refuse to deal with these issues:

> Today's global flows of goods, services, finance, people, and images spotlight the many interlinkages in the security of all people. We share a planet, a biosphere, a technological arsenal, a social fabric. The security of one person, one community, one nation rests on the decisions of many others—sometimes fortuitously, sometimes precariously.[38]

Notes

1 Kurt Tidd, "Remarks at Central American Regional Leaders Conference at U.S. Army South," March 2017. www.southcom.mil/Media/Speeches-Transcripts/Article/1127277/adm-tidd-prepared-remarks-central-american-regional-leaders-conference/.

2 Ted Robert Gurr and Monty Marshall, *Peace and Conflict* (College Park, MD: Center for International Development, 2005).

3 Uppsala codes "internationalized internal armed conflict" as conflict "between the government of a state and one or more internal opposition group(s) without intervention from other states." Uppsala Conflict Data Program (Date of retrieval: 18/03/17) UCDP Conflict Encyclopedia: www.ucdp.uu.se, Uppsala University.

4 John Mueller, "War Has Almost Ceased to Exist: An Assessment," *Political Science Quarterly* (Summer 2009): 297–322.

5 Tidd, "Remarks at Central American Regional Leaders Conference."

6 U.S. Commission on National Security/21st Century, *New World Coming: American Security in the 21st Century* (Washington, DC: U.S. Government Printing Office, 1999), 5, available at www.au.af.mil/au/awc/awc gate/nssg/. The U.S. Commission on National Security is also known as the Hart-Rudman Commission for its two principal authors, Gary Hart and Warren B. Rudman.

7 See Derek S. Reveron, *Exporting Security: International Engagement, Security Cooperation, and the Changing Face of the U.S. Military*, 2nd edn (Washington, DC: Georgetown University Press, 2016).

8 National Intelligence Council, *Global Trends: Paradox of Progress* (Washington, DC: National Intelligence Council, 2017), ix-x. Available at www.dni.gov/index.php/global-trends-home.

9 "At the 'End of History' Still Stands Democracy," *Wall Street Journal*, June 7–8, 2014.

10 The core principles of neorealism (also known as structural realism) are laid out in the classic work by Kenneth N. Waltz, *Theory of International Politics* (New York: McGraw-Hill, 1977).

11 Gennady Rudkevich, Konstantinos Travlos, and Paul F. Diehl, "Terminated or Just Interrupted? How the End of a Rivalry Plants the Seeds for Future Conflict," *Social Science Quarterly* vol. 94, no. 1 (2013): 158–174; Paul D. Senese and John A. Vasquez, *The Steps to War: An Empirical Study* (Princeton, NJ: Princeton University Press, 2008); John A. Vasquez, *The War Puzzle Revisited* (New York: Cambridge University Press, 2009).

12 Graham T. Allison, *Destined for War: Can America and China Escape Thucydides's Trap?* (New York: Houghton Mifflin, 2017).

13 Thomas L. Friedman, *The Lexus and the Olive Tree* (New York: Farrar, Straus, and Giroux, 1999), 7.

14 In their 1977 pathbreaking work, *Power and Interdependence: World Politics in Transition* (Boston, MA: Little, Brown), Robert O. Keohane and Joseph S. Nye provided the foundational analysis for

what would come to be known as the "transnational relations" approach and "complex interdependence," broadening the restrictive lens of realism.

15 Jonathan Kirshner, "Globalization, American Power, and International Security," *Political Science Quarterly* vol. 123, no. 3 (2008): 363–389.

16 National Intelligence Council, *Global Trends*, 20.

17 Among many other provisions, the monumental Goldwater-Nichols Department of Defense Reorganization Act of 1986 required that, under "SEC.104. (a)(1) The President shall transmit to Congress each year a comprehensive report on the national security strategy of the United States." That report is required to address "(1) The worldwide interests, goals, and objectives of the United States that are vital to the national security of the United States." Cited in Public Law 99–433, Goldwater-Nichols Department of Defense Reorganization Act of 1986 October 1, 1986, 100 STAT 1075. Of note, this requirement has been fulfilled only sketchily by each administration, never producing the strategy every year and rarely in a timely manner. But the unclassified strategies are useful for highlighting the themes and priorities of an administration, both to the American people and to the world at large. At: http://history.defense.gov/Portals/70/Documents/dod_reforms/Goldwater-NicholsDoDReordAct1986.pdf.

18 Michael J. Mazarr, "The Once and Future Order: What Comes after Hegemony," *Foreign Affairs* vol. 96, no. 1 (2017): 25–32, 28–29.

19 Moisés Naím, "Five Wars of Globalization," *Foreign Policy*, November 3, 2009. At: https://foreignpolicy.com/2009/11/03/five-wars-of-globalization/.

20 National Intelligence Council, *Mapping the Global Future: Report of the National Intelligence Council's 2020 Project* (Washington, DC: National Intelligence Council, 2004), 14, available at www.cia.gov/ nic/NIC_globaltrend2020_es.html.

21 Paul Collier, *The Bottom Billion: Why the Poorest Countries Are Failing and What Can Be Done About It* (Oxford: Oxford University Press, 2007).

22 Paul J. Smith, "Transnational Security Threats and State Survival: A Role for the Military," *Parameters* vol 30, no. 3 (2000): 78.

23 Gail Wannenburg, "Organised Crime in West Africa," *African Security Review* vol. 14, no. 4 (2005): 5–16.

24 J. Peter Pham, "The Challenge of Somali Piracy," *New Atlanticist*, September 29, 2008.

25 United Nations Trust Fund for Human Security, "Human Security in Theory and Practice: An Overview of the Human Security Concept," www.un.org/humansecurity/sites/www.un.org.humansecurity/files/human_security_in_theory_and_practice_english.pdf.

26 Laura Neack, *National, International, and Human Security: A Comparative Introduction* (New York: Rowman & Littlefield, 2017), 191.

27 Rex Tillerson, "Senate Confirmation Hearing Opening Statement," January 11, 2017. www.foreign.senate.gov/imo/media/doc/011117_Tillerson_Opening_Statement.pdf.

28 UNDP, "Human Development Report 1994". At: http://hdr.undp.org/en/content/human-development-report-1994.

29 Friedman, *Lexus and the Olive Tree*, 336.

30 National Intelligence Council, "Implications for US National Security of Anticipated Climate Change." NIC WP 2016-01, Washington, DC, September 21, 2016.

31 Anthony Zinni, Ronald Keys, and Frank Bowman, "Opinion: Pentagon Weighs in on the Threat of Climate Change," October 28, 2104. http://archive.northjersey.com/opinion/opinion-pentagon-weighs-in-on-the-threat-of-climate-change-1.1120024.

32 UN General Assembly, *Implementing the Responsibility to Protect: Report of the Secretary-General* (New York: UN, 2009), 2.

33 UNDP, *Human Development Report 1994* (New York: Oxford University Press, 1994), 24–25. At: http://hdr.undp.org/sites/default/files/reports/255/hdr_1994_en_complete_nostats.pdf.

34 UNDP, "Sustainable Development Goals." At: www.undp.org/content/undp/en/home/sustainable-development-goals.html.

35 Jean-Marie Macabrey, "Researchers: Sea Levels May Rise Faster than Expected," *New York Times*, March 11, 2009.

36 Shankar Vedantam, "Climate Fears Are Driving 'Ecomigration' across Globe," *Washington Post*, February 23, 2009, A1.

37 Chris Tryhorn, "Nice Talking to You . . . Mobile Phone Use Passes Milestone," *The Guardian*, March 3, 2009, available at www.guardian.co.uk/technology/ 2009/mar/03/mobile-phones1/.

38 Commission on Human Security, *Human Security Now: Protecting and Empowering People* (New York: Commission on Human Security, 2003), 2, available at www.humansecurity-chs.org.

To Learn More

In 2003 the highly regarded, independent Commission on Human Security published its landmark report, *Human Security Now: Protecting and Empowering People* (New York: Commission on Human Security, 2003), at www.human security-chs.org.

The National Intelligence Council is composed of varied government experts who focus on longer-term, objective strategic thinking and forecasts for the United States as reflected in periodic reports like *Global Trends*; the council also consults regularly with outside academics and the private sector to inform their assessments. View their unclassified reports at: www.dni.gov/.

Scan the reader, *International Security Studies: Theory and Practice*, by Peter Hough, Shahin Malik, Andrew Moran, and Bruce Pilbeam (New York: Routledge, 2015), to get an excellent overview and sense of the complex international/national/human security environment.

Mary Kaldor reconsiders war and the transformation of political violence in *New and Old Wars: Organized Violence in a Global Era*, 3rd edn (Stanford, CA: Stanford University Press, 2012). Paul Collier analyzes the challenges of promoting sustainable human security in *The Bottom Billion: Why the Poorest Countries Are Failing and What Can Be Done about It* (Oxford: Oxford University Press, 2008).

Roland Paris challenges the value of human security in "Human Security: Paradigm Shift or Hot Air?" *International Security* vol. 26, no. 2 (2001): 87–102.

Derek S. Reveron explores how the changed international security environment is impacting the U.S. military in *Exporting Security: International Engagement, Security Cooperation, and the Changing Face of the U.S. Military*, 2nd edn (Washington, DC: Georgetown University Press, 2016).

John Mueller sees the end of war but the inadequacy of governments to provide for human security in *The Remnants of War* (Ithaca: Cornell University Press, 2007).

Chapter 2

Actors, Institutions, and Approaches to Human Security

Chapter contents

> The international community urgently needs a new paradigm of security. Why? Because the security debate has changed dramatically since the inception of state security advocated in the 17th century. According to that traditional idea, the state would monopolize the rights and means to protect its citizens. State power and state security would be established and expanded to sustain order and peace. But in the 21st century, both the challenges to security and its protectors have become more complex. The state remains the fundamental purveyor of security. Yet it often fails to fulfil its security obligations—and at times has even become a source of threat to its own people. That is why attention must now shift from the security of the state to the security of the people—to human security.
>
> Commission on Human Security, *Human Security Now* (2003)

As the Commission on Human Security—which was supported by the United Nations, governments, foundations, and policy experts and scholars—makes clear, human security is a complex, multifaceted concept. It should come as no surprise, then, to find a wide variety of approaches employed for assessing human security concerns, along with a correspondingly large number of diverse actors and institutions. Recognition of human security as an analytical frame or construct did not happen overnight, but rather grew slowly beginning in the latter part of the twentieth century. The slow acceptance of the human security concept could be compared to the gradual, and incremental, acceptance of human rights as a legitimate, albeit still contested, international security concern. Both of these concepts (human security and human rights) have achieved wider acceptance as the state's ability to serve as the sole provider and protector of security and rights for human beings has diminished. The gradual acceptance of the concept of human security developed in tandem with the founding of the United Nations, and then with the growth in numbers and scope of intergovernmental organizations (IGOs) and nongovernmental organizations (NGOs) that have served as advocates for human security and purveyors of development programs. The accelerating forces of the information age have also been instrumental in magnifying the influence of non-state groups as well as the ability of individuals to threaten both state security and the security of individuals, as noted in the preceding chapter.

In this chapter, we review key developments in the evolution of the concept of human security within the context of international security events and evolving policy. We describe how and why human security has come to achieve increasing legitimacy as a national security concern of states. The chapter is divided into four sections. The first section begins our analysis by looking at how the idea of human security is rooted in President Franklin D. Roosevelt's vision of "Four Freedoms" and in the founding principles of the United Nations after the carnage of World War II. The second section links ideas on the rights of individuals with their need for social and economic development. It emphasizes that our ability to be "humanly secure" is inextricably linked to recognition of basic human rights, along with economic prosperity that provides access to basic necessities such as food, clean water, shelter, health care, and education. The United Nations has played the central role in developing and expanding these ideas. The third section of the chapter provides examples of how regional and nongovernmental organizations, as well as individuals, have contributed to human security, human rights, and development goals. In this process globalization has been an extremely important enabler. The fourth section of the chapter considers how the international relations perspectives introduced in the preceding chapter contribute to our understanding of why advancing human security concerns supports the national security interests of states. This final section of the chapter also notes how and why the U.S. military has accepted its role of aiding human security needs during interventions; a theme explored further in the book.

Defining Human Security: Genesis and Evolution

Most scholars and policy experts would probably agree that an important shift in thinking beyond the traditional notion of exclusive state sovereignty and national security occurred in the mid-twentieth century, when the United Nations came into formal existence in October 1945, as the world concluded fighting the most destructive conflict in history. Yet, even prior to that occasion, the Declaration by United Nations of January 1, 1942 (proclaimed by the Allied powers fighting the Axis powers) had endorsed the principles of the earlier Atlantic Charter of August 14, 1941, signed by President Franklin Roosevelt of the United States and Prime Minister Winston Churchill of the United Kingdom. Both declarations, and the newly formed United Nations, espoused the goal of working together to ensure "freedom from fear" and "freedom from want" for all peoples. The concepts of freedom from fear and want link back to Roosevelt's well-known State of the Union Address on January 6, 1941 (see Image 2.1), in which he proclaimed the importance of the "Four Freedoms": freedom of speech, freedom of worship, freedom from want, and freedom from fear. While freedom of speech and freedom of worship were already guaranteed to U.S. citizens by the U.S. Constitution, Roosevelt was reacting to significant change in the international system that had led to World War II when he developed the two concepts of freedom from want and fear. He saw these four freedoms as a "definite basis for a kind of world attainable in our own time."[1]

Image 2.1 President Franklin D. Roosevelt delivers the 1941 State of the Union Address[2]

This broadening of scope in terms of how many and which rights human beings should be accorded would be reflected in the new UN Charter in 1945. Not only does the charter acknowledge as its key purpose "to maintain international peace and security" but, equally, "to achieve international co-operation in solving international problems of an economic, social, cultural, or humanitarian character, and in promoting and encouraging respect for human rights and for fundamental freedoms for all without distinction as to race, sex, language, or religion."[3] This broader perspective has been carried forward into the twenty-first century; the motto of the UN Secretariat's Human Security Unit (founded in 2004) largely reflects Roosevelt's 1941 vision: "Freedom from fear, freedom from want, freedom to live in dignity."

Thus, there is a direct linkage between today's human security construct to U.S. ideas in the 1940s. But that does not mean the evolution of the concept took a direct, continuous route as there has always been a tension in U.S. foreign policy between short-term threats and long-term development programs. This might seem surprising considering that as early as 1948 the bedrock Universal Declaration of Human Rights (UDHR) was passed by the newly formed United Nations General Assembly. This declaration, inspired in large part by the horrors of World War II, was very comprehensive in scope, acknowledging not only civil and political rights commonly found in democracies, but also economic and social rights such as found in Article 25, that "everyone has the right to a standard of living adequate for the health and well-being of himself and of his family."[4] For most human rights advocates, achieving true human security for all citizens of the world would be the ultimate realization of human rights.

In the decades after the UDHR was passed, there was often intense disagreement about the universality of certain rights and the obligations of governments to provide certain rights—or to even acknowledge a concept such as human security—considering the centrality of state sovereignty under international law and the United Nations itself. So even though the UDHR declared the catalog of human rights to be globally applicable to all people, some governments, national and religious leaders, and scholars and policy experts have continued to disagree about the applicability of certain rights.

The United States has long prioritized what are often termed the "first generation" of political and civil rights, which protect the individual from government abuses such as torture, arbitrary arrest, and limitations on freedom of speech and the press.[5] These rights are clearly integral to democratic governance, and are central U.S. values. By contrast, for many years Americans were prone to discount a "second generation" of economic and social rights, such as the "right" to a job, housing, and medical care—provided by the state, if necessary. This dichotomy was particularly marked during the Cold War era of the twentieth century when the United States and its "Free World" democratic allies waged an ideological battle on behalf of free enterprise and individual liberties, while the communist and socialist world under the Soviet Union and China discounted individual rights and promoted government-directed economies and collective economic and social benefits. Viewpoints on human rights became even more complicated and contested in the 1970s–1980s as the developing, or "Third World," countries that were emerging out of decolonization began to press the case for a proposed "third generation" of people's collective, or group, rights to development. This focus on development and the concerted use of UN agencies by developing countries—such as the United Nations Conference on Trade and Development (UNCTAD) and the UN Development Programme (UNDP)—would prove central to laying the groundwork for the human security concept.

With the end of the Cold War in the 1990s the United States began to publicly acknowledge the importance of economic and social development to sustain democratic governance and freedoms.[6] At the same time the democratization trends of the 1990s and early twenty-first century in many regions strengthened cooperation in peace and security matters at the international level, as represented by the UN Security Council-endorsed Persian Gulf War of 1990–1991. Then, in 1992 UN Secretary-General Boutros Boutros-Ghali set forth his agenda for peace, as noted in the preceding chapter, "to enhance respect for human rights and fundamental freedoms, to promote sustainable economic and social development for wider prosperity, to alleviate distress and to curtail the existence and use of massively destructive weapons."[7] A renewed emphasis on economic and social development programs was in evidence, and this was the context in which the UNDP published its landmark *Human Development Report, 1994*, which set out the concept of human security.

The UN, Human Security, and Sustainable Development

The "Foreword" to the UNDP report of 1994 was quite explicit in proclaiming that "sustainable human development" was essential to promoting peace and security in the world; and that this meant "development that not only generates economic growth but distributes its benefits equitably; that regenerates the environment rather than destroying it; that empowers people rather than marginalizing them." The authors of the report were determined to "explore . . . new frontiers of human security in the daily lives of people . . . [and to] outline . . . a new design for development cooperation in the post-cold war era." They saw their conceptions of human security as building on past models and ideas about development promulgated by the UNDP. Even more profoundly, the 1994 report declared that "it will not be possible for the community of nations to achieve any of its major goals—not peace, not environmental protection, not human rights or democratization, not fertility reduction, not social integration—except in the context of sustainable development that leads to human security."[8]

Sustainable development became a central core of UN efforts—and key to human security efforts. Any cursory review of UN issues or agencies and programs cannot escape this concept, whether considering environmental issues, peace, agricultural concerns, children, or refugees. Significantly, at the UN Millennium Summit in 2000—held to reconsider the purposes of the United Nations at the onset of the twenty-first century—189 heads of state agreed upon a global partnership to achieve eight Millennium Development Goals (MDGs) by 2015 to address the world's main development challenges, ranging from poverty to HIV and other major diseases. The comprehensive approach of the MDGs was an accurate reflection of the consensus that had emerged about the interrelated, complex nature of generating development, especially on a sustained basis. While important progress had been made in all the goal areas by 2015, as reflected in Table 2.1, and many lessons had been learned, there was much more to accomplish. Thus, UN member states agreed to replace and expand these original goals to 17 even more comprehensive Sustainable Development Goals (SDGs), beginning in 2016; these goals constitute a "universal call to action to end poverty, protect the planet, and ensure that all people enjoy peace and prosperity" by 2030.[9] Measuring achievements in meeting the earlier MDGs and now the SDGs is the central approach for assessing the progress of human security today. The critical and complex topic of development and its central role in human security, along with the SDGs, is addressed in more detail in Chapter 5, as part of economic security.

While ideas about human security have long been part of the discussion on human development, it was not until the twenty-first century that the concept received wider

Table 2.1 Millennium Development Goals (2000–2015) and Key Accomplishments

1. Eradicate extreme poverty and hunger	Number of people living in extreme poverty reduced by half (nearly 1 billion people removed from extreme poverty; 836 million remain in extreme poverty) Proportion of undernourished people in developing regions reduced by half
2. Achieve universal primary education	Number of out-of-school children dropped by more than half (since 1990) Primary-school enrollment rate in developing countries at 91%
3. Promote gender equality and empower women	Gender parity in primary schools achieved in majority of countries
4. Reduce child mortality	Child mortality reduced by half (since 1990)
5. Improve maternal health	Maternal mortality down 45% worldwide
6. Combat HIV/AIDS, malaria, and other diseases	HIV/AIDS infections fell by almost 40% Over 6 million malaria deaths averted
7. Ensure environmental sustainability	Over 2 billion people gained access to better sanitation 147 countries met MDG drinking water target
8. Develop a global partnership for development	Official development assistance from developed countries increased 66% in real terms from 2000 and 2014, to $135 billion

Sources: UNDP, "Background on the Sustainable Development Goals," at: www.undp.org/content/undp/en/home/sustainable-development-goals/background.html; UNDP, "Millennium Development Goals," at: www.undp.org/content/undp/en/home/sdgoverview/mdg_goals.html.

attention and adherents. This is evident from the quotation noted at the beginning of this chapter from the independent Commission on Human Security, which published its *Human Security Now* report in 2003. After producing this very influential report, the governmental, policy, and subject matter expert members of the Commission effectively closed up shop. But in the Commission's wake the United Nations officially established the "Human Security Unit" in 2004 to support discussions on human security at the UN and to manage the UN Trust Fund for Human Security. As the Human Security Unit's website declares, their specific goals are to "Underscore the importance of human security for all"; "Respond to different situations of human insecurity"; "Develop practical tools"; and "Disseminate lessons learned and foster collaboration."[10] Yet the assumption that this particular organization within the UN exercises the main responsibility for human security would be a huge oversimplification. In fact, the concept of human security is now firmly embedded and prevalent throughout the UN's six principal organs, numerous agencies, and programs. The UN Secretary-General's 2013 report on human security noted that "many organizations of the United Nations system have highlighted the added value of the human security approach in fostering overall coherence of policies across different entities of the United Nations system."[11] This prevalence of human security concerns in major UN agencies is evident with just a cursory overview of those agencies.

It might seem obvious that between the main UN organs the Economic and Social Council (ECOSOC) would be particularly concerned with issues related to human security. Indeed, this is reflected in the functional commissions of ECOSOC, from "Crime Prevention and Criminal Justice" to "Narcotic Drugs" to "Population and Development" to "Status of Women." Additionally, the names of many specialized agencies of the UN ("autonomous organizations whose work is coordinated through ECOSOC") read like a typology of human security concerns: Food and Agriculture Organization of the United Nations, International Fund for Agricultural Development, International Labour Organization, United Nations Educational, Scientific and Cultural Organization (UNESCO), and World Health Organization. However, the UN Security Council, which is the principal authority for matters related to peace and security, has a Counter-Terrorism Committee as a subsidiary organ, and its related organizations include the International Criminal Court, the International Organization for Migration, and the International Tribunal for the Law of the Sea—all of which deal directly with human security-related issues. The UN General Assembly's subsidiary organs include the UN Human Rights Council, programs such as the UN Environment Program, and funds such as those dealing with population (UNFPA) and children (UNICEF). Also affiliated is the continuously busy Office of the United Nations High Commissioner for Refugees (UNHCR). Finally, under the UN Secretariat is located the United Nations Office on Drugs and Crime, the Department of Peacekeeping Operations, and the Office for the Coordination of Humanitarian Affairs—the latter two of which inevitably involve interrelated human security issues.[12]

The increasingly central role of human security within the United Nations is reflected in the General Assembly's resolution 66/290 (adopted in September 2012), which provides "a common understanding of human security" to include "the right of people to live in freedom and dignity, free from poverty and despair. All individuals, in particular vulnerable people, are entitled to freedom from fear and freedom from want, with an equal opportunity to enjoy all their rights and fully develop their human potential." However, important as this consensus on human security may be at the international level, the resolution also encompasses seven other aspects that are revealing in terms of the equally important consensus on the national security of states. For instance, the resolution includes the points that: "human security is distinct from the responsibility to protect and its implementation"; that "it does not replace State security"; and that "human security must be implemented with . . . full respect for the sovereignty of States, territorial integrity and non-interference in matters that are essentially within the domestic jurisdiction of States."[13] Thus, while agreement on the centrality of the human security of human beings is near universal, so is agreement that individual state (national) security interests remain central and at least on par with human security. This seeming paradox is a prominent theme within the book, as is our contention that both types of security tend to be mutually reinforcing and cannot be realistically separated as security among states and security within states. Figure 2.1 depicts a timeline highlighting major milestones in the development of the human security construct.

Perhaps no single issue demonstrates the human security–national security conundrum more prominently than the Responsibility to Protect (R2P) doctrine. As noted in

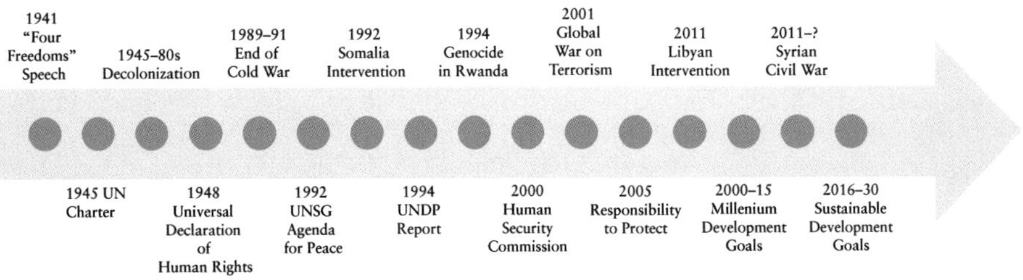

Figure 2.1 Human Security Timeline

the previous chapter, the key to prevention in R2P lies in identifying states at risk and developing appropriate responses to aid governments' efforts to promote development and improve standards of living; or conversely, to intervene on behalf of a civilian population which is being deliberately abused by its own government. These concerns are at the core of human security, and the R2P construct clearly rests on a human security approach. The desperate human security situation in Syria would seem to be tailor-made for a full-scale R2P intervention, as described in 2017 by the respected NGO Human Rights Watch:

> According to the Syrian Center for Policy Research, an independent Syrian research organization, the death toll from the [Syrian] conflict as of February 2016 was 470,000. The spread and intensification of fighting has led to a dire humanitarian crisis, with 6.1 million internally displaced people and 4.8 million seeking refuge abroad, according to the UN Office for the Coordination of Humanitarian Affairs. By mid-2016, an estimated 1 million people were living in besieged areas and denied life-saving assistance and humanitarian aid. More than 117,000 have been detained or disappeared since 2011, the vast majority by government forces.[14]

The Syrian case demonstrates that national security concerns may compete with human security concerns, and that it is often difficult at the international level to reach agreement on when the demands of individuals' human security might require that the sovereignty of a particular state be discounted. This is especially relevant when major external powers have competing security interests in the area, as with the United States, Russia, Turkey, and Iran—a point reflected in the UN General Assembly resolution of 2012 cited above. Also reflected is that the United Nations was founded based upon the cardinal principle of state sovereignty, and it has often been successful in ending conflict and keeping the peace *between* member states. But it has been struggling to enhance security *within* states and for communities, a struggle that is all too familiar to U.S. policymakers and the U.S. military in the twenty-first century. This vexing issue is discussed further in Chapter 10, where we consider the practicalities and limitations of efforts to protect human security, including the R2P construct.

Globalization: Human Security and Human Rights Enabler

The analysis to this point has stressed the role of the United Nations and its extensive family of agencies and programs; but other intergovernmental organizations also play important roles with regard to human security concerns, particularly regional organizations. These range from the African Union to the Pacific Islands Forum, to the Inter-American Commission on Human Rights to the Organization for Security and Cooperation in Europe. Major powers like the U.S. and China, for example, have directed significant amounts of development assistance to support the African Union in a multilateral way, in addition to the bilateral aid these countries also provide. In fact, under Article 52, the UN Charter specifically states that:

> Nothing in the present Charter precludes the existence of regional arrangements or agencies for dealing with such matters relating to the maintenance of international peace and security as are appropriate for regional action provided that such arrangements or agencies and their activities are consistent with the Purposes and Principles of the United Nations.[15]

And prominent scholar and policymaker Anne-Marie Slaughter has argued that in our increasingly networked world where faster, more flexible responses are often required to respond to security issues, "flattening the hierarchy between the UN and regional organizations, so the latter can act more autonomously" could be quite useful.[16]

Equally significant in advancing certain human security concerns—if not more so in some respects—are private, non-state actors. Shifting from a traditional state-based territorial definition of security to a human-centric view of security requires recognizing the importance of these non-state actors, most commonly termed nongovernmental organizations (NGOs). Often these groups form components of larger national and transnational social movements or networks composed of diverse actors ranging from domestic and international NGOs to foundations to individual activists—and in some instances states and state-based organizations, as in the case of human rights. The groups arise out of civil society—that sector unconnected to governments and with generally altruistic motives (thus, civil society does not encompass private but for-profit organizations such as multinational corporations and banking institutions).[17] These decentralized movements are usually motivated by perceived injustices, ranging from abuse of human rights, corrupt governments, and the prostitution and trafficking of women and children to the unfair labor practices of multinational corporations and environmental degradation. These groups raise funds from private donors and governments (some of our readers have doubtless contributed to various NGOs). Prominent examples today include the human rights movement/network and the environmental or green movement/network. Unfortunately, as highlighted in Chapter 1, there are also non-state networks of actors that seek to actively harm the human security of many individuals, as exemplified by criminal, drug trafficking, and terrorist groups.

The word "network" is crucial to understanding how and why these non-state actors have been so influential in terms of human security. Already beginning at the end of the twentieth century and clearly in the twenty-first century, the informational and technological advances propelled by globalization have empowered non-state actors in ways that were not possible prior to the leveling effects of the networked world. For example, consider that even though an abolitionist, anti-slavery movement expanded worldwide in the eighteenth and especially nineteenth centuries, its reach and influence was limited by the slow transmission of information and the expense of dissemination of information, plus the lack of literacy in many sectors. Thus, while an anti-slavery norm might actually have had broader international support earlier, there was no quick, inexpensive way to link groups (and states) agitating against slavery.

Contrast those limitations to the ability today to near-instantaneously, and cheaply, disseminate news and images of human rights and ultimately human security violations on a worldwide basis. As scholars and policymakers Kishore Mahbubani and Lawrence Summers noted, "the vast majority of humanity is literate, at least somewhat mobile, and has access to the world's store of existing knowledge. Around half of the adults in the world own a smartphone and there are now more connected mobile devices in total than there are people on the planet."[18] U.S. Air Force intelligence and satellite expert Sean Larkin has argued that "commercial satellite imagery has proved particularly effective in empowering groups to monitor and publicize developments in areas where access is otherwise denied" (such as China reclaiming and building up reefs in the South China Sea). Larkin also points out that:

> the surge of satellite imagery will benefit even those who cannot pay for it directly. Already, journalist, bloggers, and think tanks use satellite imagery to contextualize events, such as Russia's military deployments to Syria . . . [and] the commercial satellite industry is also

expanding the free services it provides to NGOs and the UN for environmental, humanitarian, and disaster-relief purposes."[19]

Nongovernmental groups like the Carter Center (in partnership with Emory University) and Harvard's Humanitarian Initiative (an academic and research center) have brought these specific capabilities to bear in mapping Syria's humanitarian crisis.

Globalization has even made it possible for private citizens—philanthropists like Bill and Melinda Gates and individual activists like Jody Williams, Malala Yousafzai, and Kailash Satyarthi—to act as catalysts to change government policies, improve people's lives, and incrementally transform the international system. In the case of Jody Williams, she successfully organized a diverse network of people around the world against landmines and was the spokesperson for the International Committee to Ban Landmines. With the knowledge that more than 100 million landmines are scattered across the developing world, the group fought to change how militaries and governments behave with respect to their indiscriminate use. Jody Williams's efforts brought together more than 1,000 different groups networked in sixty countries to pressure governments to adopt a ban on landmines, known as the Ottawa Treaty. The Nobel Peace Prize was awarded in 1997 to Jody Williams and the coalition of groups' contributions to international security. The Nobel Committee specifically recognized the power of NGOs and expressed hope for similar models in the future for disarmament and peace. This example illustrates how governments can benefit from individuals' and civil society's efforts to improve international security, or, conversely, see their own perceived national security efforts constrained, as the United States has found with its use of

Image 2.2 Cleared Ground Demining Operations on Peleliu Island, Palau, 2013. Photo: DFAT[21]

antipersonnel landmines on the Korean Peninsula continuing to be called into question by NGOs and other actors.[20]

The more recent examples of Malala Yousafzai and Kailash Satyarthi demonstrate how individuals can make a difference at the most basic level of meeting human security needs and protecting human rights. In this case the Norwegian Nobel Committee recognized each of the 2014 Peace Prize recipients for their individual work to protect the rights of children and their access to education. Malala Yousafzai was recognized specifically for her concerted campaign in her native Pakistan to insist on the rights of girls to be educated, at great personal risk to herself (including being shot). Indian Kailash Satyarthi, a former teacher, founded an NGO which has assisted thousands of children to leave slave-like labor conditions and attend school, in addition to helping to build international agreements on the rights of children. While these Nobel laureates are justly recognized for their individual (and group) efforts, human security needs have also been advanced by a private institution—the Nobel Foundation. But while it is a non-state group, it wields immense influence in this globalized information age, as Nobel Prizes are considered to be among the most prestigious awards in the world.

The United Nations also helps to empower non-state groups, with more than 4,500 nongovernmental groups now possessing consultative status with the UN's Economic and Social Council.[22] Consultative status means these NGOs can directly influence UN member states and the deliberations of the United Nations on important policymaking issues. And these are just the nongovernmental groups that have official consultative status; experts on NGOs worldwide estimate their numbers in the millions. Slaughter is just one of many who advocate for increased recognition and involvement of these groups, because:

> for every nongovernmental organization that has been granted hard-won observer status at a UN meeting, thousands more have been shut out by the state gatekeepers of the current international system . . . [yet] those organizations must flatten. They have to open up their hierarchies and formalized routines to allow for more flexible arrangements among their members and to allow for interactions with a mix of citizen, corporate, and civic networks.[23]

These non-state groups are incredibly diverse and work in all areas of human security. For example, consider Transparency International (TI), which is a nongovernmental group of experts that was formed in 1993 specifically to publicize and to reduce corruption within governmental and other sectors. The group's work is potentially very significant for enhancing the good governance that is so central to ensuring human security (as discussed in Chapter 4), and their reports are widely cited by various governments, organizations, and scholars and policymakers.

As another illustration, indigenous tribal groups in Brazil and Ecuador have received financial, moral, and legal support and advice from many outside groups as they vociferously protest—often linked to indigenous groups in other countries—and in some cases wage legal proceedings against their ancestral lands being threatened and exploited by developers and multinational oil companies. Finally, perhaps the most prominent example of how globalization has aided in improving human security for individuals, groups, and even nations is represented by the successes of the international, and transnational, human rights movement. The human rights movement also demonstrates that human security issues seem likely to progress most successfully through a concerted effort that involves governments and IGOs at the international (state) level, and NGOs and individual activists at the transnational (nongovernmental) level.

❖ BOX 2.1 THINK AGAIN: ISN'T HUMAN SECURITY JUST HUMAN RIGHTS?

It is not surprising that the concept of human security has been criticized as being so general and inclusive of any and all needs so as to not be useful for theory, measurement, or policy purposes (as noted in the first chapter). Some observers further argue that human security is essentially human rights, so why not focus on the now well-established canon of human rights rather than divert attention and dilute resources on a competing and fuzzy framework. To support this position, consider the very general nature of the seven human security areas first laid out by the UNDP in 1994—economic security, food security, health security, environmental security, personal security, community security, and political security. Each of these conceptual areas achieves necessary clarity and the possibility of formulating appropriate legislation and policy development when fleshed out into enumerated human rights. For example, political security translates into many specific rights widely acknowledged as fundamental human rights, such as the right to freedom of thought and religion, and the right not to be arbitrarily detained or tortured. Violations of each of these rights can be, and have been, widely adopted in instruments of international law and in domestic legislation in a way that is not possible with the concept of political security.

In fact, many human security critics would argue that the human rights movement has been able to achieve much of its record of success because it is grounded in the Universal Declaration of Human Rights (1948) and corresponding international legal treaties which reflect those rights—particularly the Covenant on Civil and Political Rights and the Covenant on Economic, Social, and Cultural Rights (both of which entered into force in 1976). These agreements have helped to enable the purposeful application of international law to advance the enumerated rights, and this use of a legalistic framework has been very fruitful. There has been demonstrable progress in recognition, and enforcement, of various human rights both in international venues (within the United Nations system and in regional institutions such as the Inter-American Court of Human Rights) and under domestic law, within individual countries.

This type of approach is generally missing from the human security construct. Rather, the emphasis is on a preemptive approach, recognizing and addressing the root causes of human insecurity by employing a wide variety of actors (international, transnational, and domestic) and methods to enable each individual to have a life of dignity, free from fear or want. But, unlike fundamental human rights that are universal and cannot be derogated (such as the right not to be tortured or executed extrajudicially), a human security approach acknowledges that the concept will vary in its policies and in any definition of success depending upon individuals and their communities. In that sense the human security approach more closely resembles the concept of development that is quite malleable, and has attracted some similar criticisms but also praise.

Over the decades certain states (such as the United States), intergovernmental organizations (such as the Inter-American Commission on Human Rights), and progressively more and more nongovernmental groups (such as Amnesty International) and individual activists (such as Holocaust survivor Elie Wiesel) have established an influential transnational human rights movement in an attempt to realize the UDHR goals. For many, the fact that almost all governments now find it necessary to at least publicly proclaim support for human rights is a signal victory, regardless of the abuses that many of those governments still carry out. United Nations members affirmed the UDHR in 2008 with these words at a sixtieth anniversary celebration:

> Many things can be said about the Universal Declaration of Human Rights (UDHR). It is the foundation of international human rights law, the first universal statement on the basic principles of inalienable human rights, and a common standard of achievement for all peoples and all nations. . . . Drafted by representatives of all regions and legal traditions, the UDHR has stood the test of time and resisted attacks based on "relativism." The Declaration and its core values, including non-discrimination, equality, fairness and universality, apply to everyone, everywhere and always.[24]

The goals have essentially been endorsed by all countries, which marks a huge shift in international and national thinking to now view human rights as requiring both "positive" implementation policies from governments, institutions, and communities—in addition to "negative" policies where governments refrain from abusing their citizens' political and civil rights. The recognition that governments may need to take positive actions on behalf of human rights and related human security needs receives its most far-reaching expression in the Responsibility to Protect doctrine introduced above. In this case the long-established principle of state sovereignty may have to give way to the importance of protecting the basic rights and lives of human beings. And significantly, as pointed out by Anne-Marie Slaughter, "the principle of sovereign equality enshrined in the Peace of Westphalia [and the UN Charter] took hundreds of years to implement. Yet R2P has managed to take hold remarkably fast: the UN Security Council has already invoked the doctrine 50 times in the past decade [2005–2015]." Thus, Slaughter gives the human rights movement credit as the catalyst for a more open international order where "international law is recognizing states and citizens at the same time" as having certain rights.[25] Of course this notion of individuals possessing rights in and of themselves is essential in advancing the case for a construct like human security.

More on (IR) Perspectives on Human Security

The recognition that international law is a significant component of international order would not be surprising for those applying a liberal international perspective to analyze international relations (IR). After all, as noted in the previous chapter, this IR perspective gives due weight to the influence of international institutions other than states. Yet at the same time, in this perspective states are still considered to be the key actors, although they often cooperate through intergovernmental organizations (and to some extent with non-state organizations), through which process states may modify their policies. On the other hand, those applying a realist IR perspective would downplay the importance of international law—and international institutions—by virtue of viewing states as the only actors of consequence in the international system. For realists, if states respect international law and the rights of human beings, this would normally be for temporary, instrumental reasons that are seen to benefit a particular state.

Yet even applying a realist perspective and privileging a national security focus, there are arguments to be made that supporting human rights—and human security—is in the national interest of states. One of the conditions viewed as most important for enhancing national security is stability among, and between, states. This is why realists devote so much attention to the question of order in the international system, and a stable "balance of power" between states. Thus, events that threaten that stability and lead to uncertainty and disorder are of concern. But as examination of many human security issues in this book makes clear, these are exactly the types of issues that are most prone to lead to disorder, not only in a particular state but also among that state's neighbors and within a larger region. Relevant examples include identity issues—especially ethnicity/race and religion—which are causing intense conflict, and refugees fleeing conflict in many areas of Africa and the Middle East to escape to Europe, which in turn has caused political and societal unrest in Europe. Also of note is climate change, the effects of which are impoverishing already weak states and causing communities to flee to areas where they can obtain access to water (in the case of desertification), or where they can escape too much water for those living in areas of flooding. Other migrants flee violence perpetrated by their own governments, as with Syria; or by criminal gangs, as the flood of Central American children to the United States in 2015–2016 illustrated, with consequences for U.S. immigration policies and domestic political and societal discord.

The United States has long held itself out to be an exemplar not only for modeling democracy, human rights, and humanitarian behavior, but also for actively promoting those norms within the international system. In this regard William F. Schulz provides a useful viewpoint in his work *In Our Own Best Interest: How Defending Human Rights Benefits Us All.* The then executive director of a major human rights group, Amnesty International USA, sets out several arguments as to why U.S. foreign policies incorporating respect for human rights and humanitarian behavior support U.S. national interests. One of those arguments relates to the well-established democratic peace theory ("democracies do not fight one another"), where Schulz argues that democratic peace only works where there is also a culture of human rights. Thus:

> the bottom line is that even based on a "realist" analysis of the relationship between peace and democracy, the conclusion is inescapable that the more respect for human rights we can help engender in a country, the less likely that country is to go to war with us or other like communities.

Additionally, as Schulz points out, "autocracies" that do not respect the human security needs of their citizens are unstable in the long run, and a stable world order is in the national interest of the United States—not to mention a cardinal objective of realists. Yet, as Schulz warns:

> what is indisputably true, however, is that whenever the United States allies itself or its interests with a regime that disparages democracy and human rights, it takes a huge risk of residual resentment in future years, of being aligned with a government whose repression breeds terrorism that could be redirected at the United States, of striking deals with those most likely to renege on commitments.

Note that Schulz made this argument in 2001, prior to the 9–11 attacks on the United States and the accumulating threats of terrorism that have multiplied in the turbulent Middle East and southwest Asian regions. And even some fifteen years ago, already seeing the changes propelled by globalization, Schulz asked, "on a globe as interdependent as ours, how can American interests possibly be divorced from those of our trading partners, our cyberspace neighbors, and indeed even our would-be adversaries?" Finally, while Schulz acknowledges that U.S. "military intervention should always be a last resort" for humanitarian purposes, he emphasizes the close relationship between U.S. national security interests, U.S. economic welfare interests, and our moral interests in making the hard choices about intervention.[26]

It is not surprising that a leading human rights group figure like Schulz would seek to rationalize human rights and humanitarian action; but it may be surprising to find that the U.S. military has recognized that meeting human security needs often serves national interests by stabilizing conflicted areas, reducing large-scale refugee flows, and forestalling even more violent and protracted warfare. The military has also realized that these actions help to reduce the availability of ungoverned, lawless areas where terrorist and criminal groups could multiply. In general, the record of U.S. military interventions in the post-Cold War period—from Somalia to Bosnia to Kosovo to Haiti to Afghanistan—can be framed as both supporting U.S. national security interests and humanitarian needs (the one clear exception based purely on humanitarian motives is the 1992–1993 Somali intervention).

The U.S. military's growing acceptance of a humanitarian ethos can be traced to obvious factors such as the post-Cold War focus on fighting peacekeeping and humanitarian intervention operations, as opposed to conventional warfighting missions. This came to be the "new normal" for many military establishments around the globe. But it was not an easy transition to make for the world's most powerful military, and, as some experts have noted, the Department of Defense "experienced revolutionary change in its perception of its role in stability operations and more particularly, nation-state building." An important factor in influencing this changed perception was that the U.S. military eventually realized cessation of hostilities alone did not bring peace in East Africa, the Middle East, and Central Asia; consequently, the military had to work at the community level to restore electricity and water, rebuild schools, and support economic development. Thus, while traditional national interests may have motivated intervention in Afghanistan (2001) and Iraq (2003), the military operations there soon shifted from a predominantly national security focus to encompass human security interests in order to stabilize communities and forestall the reemergence of conflict and threats to U.S. interests. U.S. military doctrine was rewritten to reflect this changed mindset, to include U.S. Army Field Manual 3–07, *Stability Operations Doctrine*, in 2008. This doctrine identifies five component areas as being necessary for a stable environment: "security, justice, and reconciliation; humanitarian assistance and social well-being; participatory governance; and economic stabilization and infrastructure"—all areas of concern within the human security construct.[27] Further underscoring the continuing concern with non-traditional security issues, the Chairman of the Joint Chiefs of Staff directed in January 2018 that all joint professional military education for the U.S. military must include "Non-Traditional Threats to Security and Stability," to include environmental risk factors which could "destabilize human security by reducing the availability of food, water, or energy supplies . . . [which] can lead to social unrest or migration, which in turn increases the risk of instability and conflict."[28]

We see that interests and norms can converge in the case of humanitarian intervention and, more broadly speaking, in terms of human security concerns. As the essay on "Humanitarian Intervention and International Security" in the *International Studies Encyclopedia* points out, "Humanitarian intervention lies at the intersection of realism and liberalism, where power and the material interests of states meet human rights and the responsibilities of sovereignty."[29] This underscores one of our central points in the book: that U.S national security interests and human security interests not only coincide frequently, but they are also increasingly converging and being recognized as such in foreign policy efforts.

Unfortunately, the perspectives of realism and liberalism are not very helpful in explaining why and how new norms and policies supporting human security have originated and are gaining traction in the international system (although international liberalism's recognition of the key role that institutions may play—both state and non-state—is an important aspect). Additionally, while the importance of globalization as an enabler is emphasized in this work, the process of globalization does not answer the how and why question of changing norms related to human beings, either. Here is where the constructivist perspective, noted briefly in the previous chapter as a third major IR perspective (see Table 1.2), may offer some of the most useful tools for human security purposes.

Simply put, norms matter for constructivists. This is because people's identities and interests—and their views and beliefs on specific ideas such as globalization or human security—are formed through mutual give-and-take as human beings and their societies adapt ideas and build new norms of behavior. This viewpoint helps to explain why states are instrumental in formulating and recognizing human security as a legitimate concept, but equally why an intergovernmental institution like the United Nations is just as instrumental; and furthermore, why these two types of actors interact with one another to influence one another's ideas. For instance, recall the initial part of this chapter that described Franklin Roosevelt's conception of the "Four Freedoms" that clearly influenced other states' viewpoints, along with the newly formed United Nations. In turn, the evolving United Nations steadily influenced thinking among countries like the United States and other international actors on human rights, development, and eventually human security. Constructivists hold that this "social learning" process also involves transnational, non-state actors whose ability to influence other (state and intergovernmental) actors has only been magnified by the process of globalization in recent years. This learning process was referenced above in the discussion on the progress made by the international and transnational human rights movement.

We argue that the social learning process has also occurred among U.S. military forces as they have been deployed in many unstable areas to provide security assistance and eventually reconstruction activities, and have come to understand the importance of meeting basic human needs to achieve stability (as reflected in Image 2.3). Scholar Julie Mertus's detailed analysis of U.S. foreign policy related to human rights provides additional support for our thesis. Applying a constructivist lens, she finds that "the identity of the U.S. military has changed the most in casting off the traditional warrior image and adopting an identity of professionalism and humanitarianism . . . the military does indeed play an important role in framing the debate about international problems and in making human rights arguments more socially available." Mertus concludes that "the [U.S.] military has indirectly bolstered human rights norms by framing their operations in human rights terms. [And] the military has also supported human rights norms directly."[30]

Furthermore, it is not just the U.S. military that has been influenced by human security considerations. These norms have clearly influenced how the international community thinks about humanitarian intervention in general. To guide approaches to humanitarian intervention, the UN General Assembly has endorsed principles of humanity, neutrality, impartiality, and independence.[32] The UN sees the goal as protecting life and health and ensuring respect for all human beings. To remain neutral, humanitarian actors must not take sides in hostilities or engage in controversies of a political, racial, religious, or ideological nature. Humanitarian action must be carried out on the basis of need alone, giving priority to the most urgent cases of distress and making no distinctions on the basis of nationality, race, gender, religious belief, class, or political opinions. Finally, humanitarian action must be autonomous from the political, economic, military, or other objectives that any actor may hold with regard to areas where humanitarian action is being implemented.

Image 2.3 U.S. Military Tests Water Samples at Caritas Djibouti, a mission providing humanitarian aid and education to Djiboutian children living on the streets, 2017. Photo: Air Force Tech. Sgt. Andria Allmond[31]

There are other perspectives that can be extremely useful in assessing human security concerns. It seems obvious why feminist, or gendered, analyses of international relations would be critical to fully understand the link between national and human security issues, and in order to arrive at viable policy options. As many chapters of this work demonstrate, understanding the key role that women play in so many human security issues is central to achieve progress. Prominent feminist scholar Cynthia Enloe has argued that:

> How one thinks about national security not only affects global relations but determines who is even allowed to sit at the table to take part in the security conversation. The more militarized the understanding of what national security is . . . the more likely it will be that the conversation about national security—and international security—will be a largely masculinized affair.[33]

If that occurs, the central role of women in the family and within their communities and greater society is either neglected or misinterpreted, either of which is inimical to advance sustainable development and to achieve human security needs. These points are expanded upon in this book, especially in Chapters 3 and 5.

We note in passing that there are obviously numerous other perspectives that may provide useful insights into aspects of human security. These range from cosmopolitanism, dependency, and world-systems theory to development economics, foreign policy analysis, international law and ethics, and neoliberal economics, to name just a representative sampling. In this text we include pertinent observations, as it is not our intent to neglect any viewpoint that might be helpful in understanding human security issues and how policies might be improved. In fact, it would be surprising to conclude that any one framework, or even several frameworks, could adequately encompass such a complex construct as human security, which focuses on addressing challenges to individuals' identity, economic security, and personal security.

Conclusion

As this chapter demonstrates, the animating principles undergirding human security have had a major impact in building consensus on policies affecting human beings since Franklin Roosevelt first advanced his vision of the "Four Freedoms." The founding charter of the United Nations recognized these principles while also acknowledging the tension that may occur with the central principle of state sovereignty. The end of the twentieth century saw the first "official" declaration of human security norms in the landmark UNDP report of 1994. These norms and related indicators have expanded rapidly in the twenty-first century, propelled by a variety of institutions and non-state actors concerned with human security. In part this has occurred in tandem with the growth of the transnational human rights movement and the efforts of the international development community to elevate sustainable development as a cardinal goal of the United Nations. The informational and technological revolutions enabled by globalization have been critical in achieving much of this progress—even empowering individuals to orchestrate successful transnational campaigns to protect and enhance human lives.

This chapter also assessed how the international relations perspectives introduced in Chapter 1 can assist our understanding of human security and its current status. International liberalism—with its emphasis on institutions, reason, and the possibility of human progress—seems able to most comfortably accommodate human security. The constructivist approach, which focuses on how ideas and norms evolve among actors as they interact and learn from one another, provides another useful lens for understanding the appearance, and evolution, of human security norms. Finally, we have also argued here that there is no necessary contradiction between the realist perspective privileging national security interests as those interests are often best served by supporting human security needs. This point is particularly evident when examining many (humanitarian) intervention cases, where stability and peace can only be achieved by addressing the basic human needs of the communities involved—both short and long term.

Yet, in spite of the generally positive tenor of this chapter in assessing the evolution and progress made in advancing human security needs, there are still many factors and trends that may derail this progress. That becomes evident as we turn to the next chapter on "identity security." While all human beings understandably identify with a particular community—linked by such factors as ethnicity/race, religion, historical tradition, and values—at times these factors, and particular communities, can exhibit not only discrimination but also xenophobic nationalism or extremism toward communities that are perceived as different from them. This can occur domestically within a state, or more widely within a region, between states. As we shall see in Chapter 3, in the worst cases these perceptions can trigger conflict, violence, and even genocide, as the destruction historically of so many indigenous peoples reminds us; and as the Balkan conflicts of the 1990s and the Rwandan genocide of 1994 demonstrate. These reactions can also motivate the type of radical terrorist groups we have witnessed in the twenty-first century.

While this chapter has reflected a mainly positive view of globalization as an enabler to advance human security concerns, the next chapter considers how globalization can trigger adverse reactions from communities who feel threatened by many of the changes that globalization helps to propel. The informational and technological advances can also empower criminal groups and terrorist networks, especially in areas that lack strong governments and societal institutions. Finally, within the advanced industrial democracies of the West, we observe how globalization is perceived to be unfairly benefiting some groups over others, thus serving to empower populist nationalist groups—even within the United States. Chapter 3 assesses how these trends affect and, almost inevitably, retard progress in meeting human security needs.

Notes

1 Franklin D. Roosevelt, "State of the Union Address," January 6, 1941. www.presidency.ucsb.edu/ws/?pid=16092.
2 The image is in the public domain, taken from www.fdrlibrary.marist.edu/archives/collections/franklin/?p=digitallibrary/digitalcontent&id=4190.
3 United Nations Charter, Chapter 1. At www.un.org.
4 Universal Declaration of Human Rights. At: www.un.org/en/universal-declaration-human-rights/index.html.
5 The International Covenant on Civil and Political Rights entered into force in 1976, along with the International Covenant on Economic, Social, and Cultural Rights. These two covenants, along with the UDHR, are known as the International Bill of Human Rights. See Office of the High Commissioner for Human Rights, "Fact Sheet No. 2 (Rev. 1), The International Bill of Human Rights," (n.d.). At: www.ohchr.org/Documents/Publications/FactSheet2Rev.1en.pdf. Other landmark human rights agreements include the Convention on the Elimination of All Forms of Discrimination Against Women (1979); the United Nations Convention Against Torture and Other Cruel, Inhuman, or Degrading Treatment or Punishment (1984); the Convention on the Rights of the Child (1989); and the United Nations Declaration on the Rights of Indigenous Peoples (2006).
6 Most recently, under the Obama administration there was an explicit recognition that economic opportunity is a human right, as equitable economic and social development is crucial to effective democracy and its freedoms. See Barack Obama, *National Security Strategy 2010* (Washington, DC: Office of the President, 2010).
7 UN General Assembly, *Implementing the Responsibility to Protect: Report of the Secretary-General* (New York: UN, 2009), 2.
8 UNDP, *Human Development Report, 1994* (New York: Oxford University Press, 1994), 3, 1.
9 UNDP, "Sustainable Development Goals."
10 UN Human Security Unit. At: www.un.org/humansecurity/human-security-unit/about-human-security-unit-0.
11 UN General Assembly A/68/685, "Follow-up to General Assembly Resolution 66/290 on Human Security," 23 December 2013, 9.
12 UN, "The United Nations System: UN Principal Organs." At: www.un.org/en/aboutun/structure/pdfs/17-00023e_UN%20System%20Chart_8.5x11_4c_EN_web.pdf.
13 Cited in UN General Assembly A/68/685, 2.2, 3.
14 Human Rights Watch, "Syria: Events of 2016," in *World Report 2017* (New York: HRW, 2017). At www.hrw.org/world-report/2017.
15 UN Charter, Article 52. At: www.un.org/en/sections/un-charter/un-charter-full-text/.
16 Anne-Marie Slaughter, "How to Succeed in the Networked World: A Grand Strategy for the Digital Age," *Foreign Affairs* vol. 95, no. 6 (2016): 76–89, 85.
17 A U.S. government fact sheet noted in 2016 "approximately 1.5 million NGOs operate in the United States." The publication further noted that "civil society is the collection of social organizations [NGOs], formed voluntarily by citizens to advance shared goals or interests. This includes independent public policy research organizations, advocacy organizations,

organizations that defend human rights and promote democracy, humanitarian organizations, private foundations and funds, charitable trusts, societies, associations and non-profit corporations. It does not include political parties." U.S. Department of State, Bureau of Democracy, Human Rights and Labor, "Fact Sheet: Non-Governmental Organizations (NGOs) in the United States," January 16, 2016, 1. At: www.humanrights.gov/pdf/fact-sheet-ngo-201603.pdf.

18 Kishore Mahbubani and Lawrence H. Summers, "The Fusion of Civilizations: The Case for Global Optimism," *Foreign Affairs* vol. 95, no. 3 (2016): 126–135, 127.

19 Sean P. Larkin, "The Age of Transparency: International Relations without Secrets," *Foreign Affairs* vol. 95, no. 3 (2016): 136–146, 140.

20 While the United States declared in 2014 that it was aligning its policy in accordance with the 1997 treaty banning landmines, it continues to make an exception for the use of anti-personnel mines on the Korean Peninsula. See Human Rights Watch, "United States Landmine Policy: Questions and Answers," October 3, 2014. At: www.hrw.org/news/2014/10/03/united-states-landmine-policy-questions-and-answers.

21 Full title: "Cleared Ground Demining Operations Director, Steve Ballinger (left) with DFAT representatives Caroline Adams, Lucinda Kaval and Erin Magee at the opening of the Australian-funded Regional Explosive Ordnance Disposal Training School on Peleliu Island, Palau, April 2013." Originally released by DFAT Flickr stream, at www.flickr.com/photos/106853342@N04/13252777395. Image is in the public domain as released by Department of Foreign Affairs and Trade, Australia (found at Wikimedia Commons [CC BY 2.0 (http://creativecommons.org/licenses/by/2.0)].

22 UN Department of Economic and Social Affairs, "NGO Branch." At: http://csonet.org/index.php?menu=14.

23 Slaughter, "How to Succeed in the Networked World," 76–89, 86.

24 UN Human Rights, at www.un.org/events/human-rights/2007/udhr.shtml.

25 Slaughter, "How to Succeed in the Networked World," 89.

26 William F. Schulz, *In Our Own Best Interest: How Defending Human Rights Benefits Us All* (Boston, MA: Beacon, 2001), 51, 62–63, 190, 189–190.

27 Derick W. Brinkerhoff, Ronald W. Johnson, and Richard Hill, *Guide to Rebuilding Governance in Stability Operations: A Role for the Military?* (Carlisle, PA: U.S. Army War College Strategic Studies Institute, 2009), v, vii.

28 General Joseph F. Dunford, Jr., Memorandum for Military Education Coordination Council (CM-0016-18). Academic Year 2018–2019 Joint Professional Military Education Special Areas of Emphasis List, 25 January 2018.

29 Taylor B. Sebolt, "Humanitarian Intervention and International Security," in *The International Studies Encyclopedia*, ed. Robert A. Denemark and Renee Marlin-Bennett (Malden, MA: Wiley-Blackwell, 2017). At: www.oxfordreference.com/view/10.1093/acref/9780191842665.001.0001/acref-9780191842665-e-0190?rskey=4IESuO&result=205.

30 Julie A. Mertus, *Bait and Switch: Human Rights and U.S. Foreign Policy* (New York: Routledge, 2004), 16–17, 129.

31 Image is in the public domain—U.S. Department of Defense photo. Full caption: Water Test: Navy Petty Officer 1st Class Samantha Ward, center, assigned to the Camp Lemonnier Emergency Medical Facility, and Army Maj. Donald Dais, 443rd Civil Affairs Battalion Functional Specialty Team Environmental Health officer in charge, test water samples at Caritas Djibouti, a mission providing humanitarian aid and education to Djiboutian children living on the streets, in Djibouti City, Djibouti, Aug. 23, 2017. The team checked for chlorine levels and retrieved samples to test for bacteria, in addition to conducting a food handling and sanitation tutorial. Air National Guard photo by Air Force Tech. Sgt. Andria Allmond." At: www.defense.gov/Photos/Photo-Gallery/igphoto/2001799289/.

32 General Assembly Resolution 46/182 in 1991. The principle of independence was added in 2004 under General Assembly Resolution 58/114.

33 Cynthia Enloe, *Globalization and Militarism: Feminists Make the Link* (Lanham, MD: Rowman & Littlefield, 2007), 40.

To Learn More

In 2003 the highly regarded, independent Commission on Human Security published its landmark report, *Human Security Now: Protecting and Empowering People* (New York: Commission on Human Security, 2003), available at www.human security-chs.org.

The United Nations website (www.un.org) provides a wealth of information on almost every issue affecting human beings—including human security—as the universal organization has evolved to meet the needs of both states and individual citizens. While the UN hosts a specific "Human Security Unit" (at www.un.org/humansecurity/human-security-unit/), almost every UN agency or program deals with aspects of human security issues.

One of the most well-known scholars of human rights is David P. Forsythe; scan the fourth edition of his influential textbook on human rights, *Human Rights in International Relations* (New York: Cambridge University Press, 2017).

William F. Schulz, executive director of Amnesty International USA, provides a compelling pragmatic and moral case on the value of considering human rights in foreign policy decisions; see *In Our Own Best Interest: How Defending Human Rights Benefits Us All* (Boston: Beacon Press, 2001).

In addition to Amnesty International (at www.amnestyusa.org), Human Rights Watch may be the most well known of the international human rights organizations, issuing well-researched annual and specific reports on various human rights violations (at www.hrw.org).

In *Military Soft Power: Public Diplomacy through Military Educational Exchanges* (Lanham, MD: Rowman & Littlefield, 2014), Carol Atkinson provides an essentially constructivist argument for how and why ideas and norms about democracy and human rights are shared between international military networks and educational programs.

Cynthia Enloe argues that accurate understanding of the militarized nature of national security is impossible without considering a feminist perspective and the role of women in *Globalization and Militarism: Feminists Make the Link* (Lanham, MD: Rowman & Littlefield, 2007).

Chapter 3

Identity Security

Chapter contents

> Globalization has engendered a myriad of identity-based political formations, including Hindu majoritarianism in India, settler Zionism in Israel, and xenophobic nationalism in Austria, China, Japan, Hungary, Poland, Russia, and the United States. Hate-mongering against immigrants, refugees, minorities, and various other outsiders has gone mainstream . . . Lynch mobs and mass shooters thrive in a climate where many people think of others only in terms of friends and foes and where sectarian loyalty or nativist hatred override civic bonds.
>
> Pankaj Mishra, Indian essayist and novelist[1]

Reading Mishra's quote, one might think that this description must apply to the world order of some decades ago, assuming one could substitute "modernization" for "globalization." After all, has contemporary globalization not been a positive process for human beings around the world? Certainly the vast majority of U.S. policymakers and U.S. citizens have long believed that globalization, and particularly the worldwide information revolution, has promoted greater understanding and tolerance of people's differences, thus contributing to peaceful relations, democratization, and protection of everyone's security. President George W. Bush spoke for the majority of his countrymen when he published his administration's first national security strategy in 2002, declaring:

> America's experience as a great multi-ethnic democracy affirms our conviction that people of many heritages and faiths can live and proposer in peace . . . When we see democratic processes take hold among our friends in Taiwan or in the Republic of Korea, and see elected leaders replace generals in Latin America and Africa, we see examples of how authoritarian systems can evolve, marrying local history and traditions with the principles we all cherish.[2]

Significantly, globalization proponent Thomas Friedman has gone further to argue that the dominant and homogenizing culture of globalization *is* Americanization.[3] Although recognizing there might be some disagreement about the desirability of spreading all facets of American popular culture (especially as portrayed in certain controversial Hollywood movies, television shows, and popular songs), Friedman and most U.S. citizens have viewed the spread of American values such as democracy and respect for individual freedoms and human rights as entirely beneficial for all human beings. They would find it hard to imagine that these cherished American ideals might exacerbate divisions and conflict within certain regions of the world, except perhaps among fanatical religious extremist groups such as al Qaeda or ISIS.

This positive perspective on globalization and American values was clearly in evidence during the Obama administration. In President Obama's speech to the United Nations General Assembly on September 23, 2009, he expressed his firm belief that the basic security needs of every human being can best be, or perhaps can only be, protected under a democratic government (this theme is explored in the next chapter). But even at that time he acknowledged the continuing relevance of cultural factors when he warned that there was no one-size-fits-all democratic model that could be imposed; each country has to follow its own path that would reflect its people's values and traditions. And when the president gave his farewell speech to the United Nations in fall 2016, the *New York Times* analysis of the speech contrasted "the soaring ambition of 2009" to the darker tone of the later speech, where President Obama issued a warning: "At this moment, we all face a choice . . . We can choose to press forward with a better model of cooperation and integration, or we can retreat into a world sharply divided and ultimately in conflict along age-old lines of nation and tribe and race and religion."[4]

By 2016 President Obama had ample reason to be discouraged about the continuing appeal of nation, tribe, race, and religion—whether spurred by divisions between nations and religions, such as the targeted persecution of the Rohingya ethnic Muslim community by the dominant Burmese Buddhists; or the tribal, interethnic violence that has wracked South Sudan since its independence in 2011; or the centuries-old conflict between sects of the same religion, as with the Sunni–Shiite divide in Islam which continues to spark immense loss of life in the Middle East. President Obama might have been further discouraged by how existing ethnic- or religious-based cultural traditions continue to be manipulated by authoritarian governmental or religious leaders such as Robert Mugabe of Zimbabwe and Ayatollah Ali Khaminei in Iran in order to maintain their grip on power. Equally disheartening are the instances of extremist groups within a society that use culture or religion as a rallying call to rebel against a perceived unjust, corrupt, or ineffective government, such as the Taliban in Afghanistan or ISIS in Iraq and Syria. And in the most egregious cases, hatred and violence fostered against others perceived as being "different" or illegitimate can result in mass violations of human security amounting to genocide, as demonstrated in Rwanda in 1994.

How is it that personal affiliation with a collective identity remains such a powerful trigger that can fuel xenophobic nationalism and religious extremism in the twenty-first century—with such catastrophic results for human beings? And why is it that radical and nationalist populism has been gaining strength, even in the developed countries of Europe and the United States? The short answer is that identity matters to all human beings, even in—or especially in—the era of globalization. Thus, in this chapter we unpack a set of interrelated challenges to each human being's most basic identity concerns. We first define identity security, along with the important intertwined concepts of culture and community. In fact, much of the focus here is on the component aspects of culture that are central to defining human identity, especially nationalism and religion, and the consequences for human security. We explore how in this globalized age radical extremist leaders and groups can use these crucial aspects to their benefit, to strengthen certain communities at the expense of others. And in that context we then consider key issues related to gender—*women's* security issues. While one's gender is clearly a fundamental biological characteristic that exists apart from culture, it is mainly cultural and often religious beliefs and practices that affect women's security concerns. Finally, we pay particular attention to indigenous peoples because these vulnerable groups around the world share a common experience of persecution as they seek recognition of their unique identities and traditions. These examples illustrate how the pursuit of what are perceived to be legitimate identity security interests can help generate cascading challenges in many human security areas, from poverty to natural disasters to outright violence—in turn spurring internal displacement of peoples and mass migrations across borders. Ultimately, the resulting conflict and instability from these divisions may threaten the national security interests of neighboring countries and of major powers with interests in an affected region.

Defining Identity Security

As the landmark 1994 UNDP report on human development observed when it proposed the concept of human security: "Most people derive security from their membership in a group—a family, a community, an organization, a racial or ethnic group that can provide a cultural identity and a reassuring set of values. Such groups also offer practical support."[5] In terms of the seven categories of human security proposed by the UNDP in their report, it is evident that "community" security corresponds closely to the concept of "identity" security. This is because human security concerns about an individual's identity arise in conjunction with that individual's perceived relationship, or identification, with a larger group or community. Thus, while the entry on "Identity in International Relations" in the *International Studies Encyclopedia* notes that "the nature of the [individual] Self and the meaning of personhood have occupied philosophers since Plato, the concept of *identity* entered the social sciences only in the 1950s . . . [and] in the IR literature in the late 1980s and early 1990s."[6] As Felix Berenskoetter further explains, this was in conjunction with the rise of constructivism as an IR perspective, which held that the state was a socially constructed entity, with its own collective or national identity. At the same time:

> the dissolution of seemingly stable political entities such as the Soviet Union and Yugoslavia raised questions about the volatility of borders, loyalties, nationalism(s), and the ability to manipulate them. Simultaneously, the phenomenon of "globalization" and processes of European integration undermined the conception of the Westphalian state as the fixed/dominant entity in world politics.[7]

New ways of theorizing and world events reinforced the conclusion that communities, or nations, were again—or indeed, always had been—critical to understand issues of conflict, war, and peace. In turn, this deeper understanding is necessary to assess the national security concerns of states and the human security needs of individuals and their communities.

It is important to acknowledge that identity is a very complex, multilayered concept for individuals, communities, and states. But in this work we can only sketch key parameters related to human (and national) security concerns. Therefore, we simply conceptualize identity security as respect for a human being's personal beliefs and dignity. And as those beliefs and dignity are derived from, or attached to, a particular community, we focus here on major aspects of culture that inform one's beliefs and sense of belonging related to various communities. By culture we mean the commonly understood sense of that concept, which includes the beliefs, values, norms, and practices that a society holds as meaningful to define itself through generations. Finally, ethnicity, religion, language, and common history and traditions or values are normally considered to be the defining aspects of culture which are employed in this chapter.

Culture and Globalization

The first two chapters of this book address how the processes of globalization can be viewed both positively and/or negatively in terms of the impact upon human security concerns. It should not be surprising to find that globalization has clearly affected communities and their cultural values and practices both positively and negatively, too. As noted earlier, the predominant U.S. perspective on globalization has been favorable. Besides the long-held belief that the democratic model of governance should be spread throughout the world, Americans have viewed an open international system with the free exchange of ideas, goods, and education as benefiting all groups and countries. This is clearly the perspective of international liberalism, reflecting the roots of liberal ideas in the Enlightenment era (eighteenth century), with its very positive view of human progress, individual freedom, and liberal free trade. This perspective can be seen, too, in the founding documents of the United States, from the Declaration of Independence to the Constitution, which constitute fundamental values and traditions for American society. And these ideals also underlay the open international economic and political order that the United States helped to establish and support after World War II; ideals that globalization trends have spread throughout the world. Yet in spite of this seemingly entrenched U.S. consensus on the importance of an open and democratic international order, at the time of this writing the Trump administration was taking a number of policy actions that indicated fundamental disagreement with some tenets of this consensus (e.g. restrictions on immigration and tariffs on imports). Beyond the United States, it has also become increasingly clear that numerous communities and cultures do not share the optimistic viewpoint or types of values traditionally proclaimed by U.S. policymakers and citizens.

Pankaj Mishra argues that the freedoms engendered by the processes of globalization can be overwhelming as many "find life outside traditional communities to be burdened with fear, uncertainty, and unfulfillable fantasies of self-aggrandizement . . . [and] social isolation."[8] He traces the growth of "identity-based political formations" to globalization, too; specifically to the fact that globalization "has weakened traditional forms of authority everywhere," which has left space for "an array of unpredictable new international actors that have seized on the sense of alienation and dashed expectations that defines the political mood in many places."[9] Actors that have been empowered range from fundamentalist religious, quasi-state groups like ISIS in the Middle East and Al-Shabaab in eastern Africa, to nationalist authoritarian leaders like Turkish President Recep Tayyip Erdoğan and President Vladimir Putin of Russia. Yet this phenomenon is not restricted to developing countries or non-Western countries; most recently, these feelings of alienation and lack of optimism have appeared in the guise of populism in the industrialized democracies of Europe and the United States.

A Word on Populism

Of note, when we published the first edition of this book in 2011, there had been signs of discontent and rejection of globalization trends for some time, especially when those trends were perceived as weakening or even belittling long-established cultural and community values in more traditional societies. However, what was not as clear at the time was how widespread was the increasing anger over economic inequality, economic displacement, and discontent in industrialized democracies, along with the sense that both domestic elites and especially outsiders (often foreigners) were benefiting more from the international economic system—especially in the wake of the global recession beginning in 2008. In hindsight, the strong populist reaction to globalization was clearly in the making in much of Europe and the United States.

When considering populism, it is important to understand that it occurs predominantly in democracies as a protest of the "common people" against the perceived privileges and injustices of the elites in society. As populism is a fairly generic concept and does not correlate to a specific political ideology, it appears in many different versions, from left-wing to right-wing, and it may motivate peaceful protests or more violent actions. Recent U.S. examples include the "Occupy Wall Street" movement on the left, which flourished in 2011 under a slogan "We are the 99%." On the right the "Tea Party" movement within the Republican Party began in 2009 to rally against many of the policies of the new Obama administration, including concerns about taxation and the national debt. Many would characterize the 2016 presidential campaigns of Republican Donald Trump and Democrat Bernie Sanders as populist in nature, albeit at different ends of the political spectrum. But, as well-known commentator Fareed Zakaria notes about populism, "all versions share a suspicion of and hostility toward elites, mainstream politics, and established institutions. Populism sees itself as speaking for the forgotten 'ordinary' person and often imagines itself as the voice of genuine patriotism."[10]

Populism is important to take into account, as the respected policy journal *Foreign Affairs* has forecast that populism will not disappear any time soon. This was the near-unanimous conclusion of its 2017 survey of authorities on the subject. *Foreign Affairs* asked 26 experts with broad and specialized expertise related to the topic of populism to agree or disagree with the following statement: "The populist surge in industrial democracies will continue to grow stronger over the next decade." Six respondents marked "strongly agree," 18 marked "agree," and two were "neutral." Notably, not one expert surveyed disagreed with this statement.[11]

Clearly much of the fuel for populism comes from the documented rise in inequality in industrialized democracies, which in turn is often perceived to be caused by a globalized international economy that relies on free trade. (Of note, while free trade does appear to be a contributing cause to inequality in some sectors, most studies point to a number of factors, such as automation and government policies favoring corporations and the wealthy.) This perception often ties to additional beliefs: that other countries are benefiting from the global economy at the expense of one's own nation, and that immigrants (legal or illegal) within one's own country are taking jobs away from citizens and unfairly receiving privileges. This belief tends to be particularly strong where immigrants come from different races and cultures than the existing society. This fits with populism, too, as populism is essentially about dividing people and not uniting them.

In fact, commentators such as Zakaria believe that the key, underlying motivation for populism actually lies in cultural values.[12] Indeed, for some scholars, "[populism's] crucial identifying mark is the belief that each country has an authentic 'people' who are held back by the collusion of foreign forces and self-serving elites at home."[13] It is at this juncture where populism intersects with issues of identity and may become radical, or national, populism, with significant consequences for both human and national security concerns.

Nationalism

Unfortunately, nationalism as a precipitating cause of violence and ensuing violations of human security—whether within a state or between states—is so common historically as to be almost routine. We define nationalism very simply here, as "the idea that people sharing a significant heritage such as a language should live in a single state."[14] But the implications of that idea are anything but simple, or benign. Nationalism has been extremely important for contemporary world history and the making and unmaking of states, with World War I being an epic example of both tendencies. As Cathie Carmichael observes, "Nationalist movements to change or revise boundaries by either negotiation, stealth, or force have been one of the most fundamental causes of both international and internal conflict in the modern epoch."[15] It hardly needs saying that these types of conflict tend to involve violence, and thus have enormously harmful effects on the human security of individuals and communities.

Today violent conflicts inspired at least in part by nationalism are most prevalent in developing regions, which European countries had colonized in the eighteenth and nineteenth centuries. When decolonization processes occurred in the wake of World War II, the artificial boundaries that European colonizers had established to encompass different national communities, or that had separated longstanding national communities, were generally kept in place. It was assumed that to deconstruct these new states would lead to unending secessions, violence, and instability. Whether this reasoning may have been justified at the time, it is the case that many of those boundaries are still being contested today: in the Middle East, whether in Iraq (and Syria, Turkey, and Iran), with the Kurdish people demanding an autonomous homeland, or the well-known

Israeli–Palestinian conflict; in Africa, where tribal differences help fuel the struggle for political power between groups in the newly independent South Sudan and with contested elections and violence in the long-established democracy of Kenya; or in Asia, with India and Pakistan still at odds over the territory and people of Kashmir. In human security terms, these conflicts have tragic consequences for many civilians—as in South Sudan where in 2017 close to 2 million people were internally displaced, hundreds of thousands were seeking refuge in neighboring African countries, and some 7.5 million were in need of humanitarian assistance.

In national security terms, these conflicts also increase the chances of broadening the conflict as they bring in regional and major powers that may see their interests threatened by instability in key areas. The United States, for example, has long-established interests in the Middle East, whether in ensuring a stable Iraq, facilitating the free flow of oil through the Persian Gulf, guaranteeing the existence of the state of Israel—or, most recently, combating radical and extremist terrorist groups. At the same time the United States has attempted to balance communal violence between India and Pakistan, both of which have nuclear weapons.

Yet it is important to acknowledge that nationalism is not just a characteristic of the developing world, but that it has been used as an appeal to inspire restrictive domestic policies and violence against minority communities in European countries. Thus, in Hungary, not only has an authoritarian democracy been incrementally established, but the government has also been aggressively clamping down on refugees trying to get through Hungary to claim asylum elsewhere. As Human Rights Watch reported in late 2016, the Hungarian government was not only not fulfilling its responsibilities as a European Union member to treat refugees appropriately, but it was also treating those refugees brutally and placing them in terrible camp conditions. According to Human Rights Watch during 2015–2016:

> The Hungarian government has stirred up xenophobic sentiments against refugees and migrants and has gone to great lengths, and cost, to spew hateful messages nationwide. Along with restrictive new laws making life difficult for asylum seekers and refugees, anti-migrant rhetoric by decision makers and high-ranking politicians is commonplace. Asylum seekers and refugees are called, "intruders," and "potential terrorists," all bent on destroying Western civilization, burying Christianity and the Western culture.[16]

Unfortunately, Hungary has not been alone in these policies. Largely in reaction to the flood of refugees from Africa, South Asia, and the Middle East seeking asylum within the European Union (well over 1 million in 2015 alone), Central and Eastern European countries have been clamping down, too. This more radical, nationalist extremism in Europe is expressed well by Andrea Mammone:

> today's European right wing identifies Europe as a white bastion of civilization. For it, globalization, immigration, and Islam anywhere in Europe threaten the whole of it. Globalization destroys tradition, African immigrants assault European borders, and Muslims promote terrorism and hate. In sum, they are all enemies because they challenge the "pure" identity and culture of the old continent.[17]

While this type of reaction to seemingly uncontrolled immigration from other regions might be more understandable, nearly all European countries have put in place restrictive policies, or at least tolerated discrimination and actual violence against fellow

Europeans—the nearly 10 million Roma, or Gypsies. These people constitute "Europe's largest and most consistently shunned indigenous minority." In fact, some anthropologists argue "that the central problem is that European societies have 'ethnicized' the Roma, making their ethnicity their primary identifying feature, thereby highlighting differences between them and others that otherwise might have remained invisible."[18]

Clearly nationalism can be used in a deliberate way to vilify and persecute individuals and communities within society that are perceived to be different and to possess a different identity. In some cases this can be the occasion for conflict and war between states, to include drawing in major powers from outside a region. Most recently in Europe the Bosnian (and Kosovo) wars of the 1990s stand out for the number of neighboring states and external powers and groups involved, to include the United States through the NATO alliance and Russia through its Slavic allies. This complex conflict that emerged with the breakup of Yugoslavia led to perhaps 100,000 lives lost and, most significant for purposes of the discussion here, involved conflict between ethnic groups who also adhered to different religions—Serbs (Orthodox Christian), Croats (Catholic), and Bosnian Muslims. Prior to the war (and during the socialist period of Yugoslavia's history), intermarriage among ethnic groups was common, but post-Cold War leaders used ethnicity politically to achieve independent countries, which led to civil war in the Balkans. The Bosnian war revealed that in the worst case interethnic conflict may devolve into targeted "ethnic cleansing" which occurred there, primarily waged by Bosnian Serbs against the Muslim Bosniaks. The single most horrific example was the 1995 massacre (or genocide, according to the International Court of Justice) of over 8,000 Bosniak men and boys by Bosnian Serb forces in Srebrenica. The Bosnian war thus provides a tragic example demonstrating how nationalism can cause human security and national security concerns to converge.

Nationalism may also be used by a state to exert what it perceives to be its legitimate interests in safeguarding the rights of its perceived national community residing within another state's borders. This actually occurred during the Bosnian and Kosovo wars when the Russians felt compelled to support a community they perceived to be their fellow (Orthodox) Slavs—the Serbs. Another contemporary example can be found in Russia's 2014 annexation of the Crimean Peninsula from Ukraine. While Russia clearly had national security interests in securing a port on the Black Sea, along with the Black Sea Fleet residing there, arguably Russian nationalism was equally influential in the decision. Not only is the majority of Crimea's population Russian, but also Russia continues to see itself as an exceptional historical nation—partly due to its role as the pan-Slavic and Russian Orthodox protector in Eurasia. As of 2018 Russia was also continuing to support pro-Russian separatists in eastern Ukraine. While there are clear national security interests for Russian involvement in Ukraine—to have friendly states on its borders—it is worth noting that Russian President Putin also did not recognize the Ukrainians to be a separate people, or nation, apart from Russia.[19] In this case not only do Russian actions reveal the nexus between their perceived human security (identity) and national security interests, but equally their actions have increased U.S. and NATO national security concerns.

Most Americans still tend to find evidence of this type of cultural-nationalist conflict and ethnic hatred disconcerting and unfamiliar, preferring to believe that political ideology has been the main dividing force among groups in the United States. This is in spite of the fact that there have been periods where the United States pursued less-than-admirable policies against certain domestic ethnic groups, most notably American Indian tribal nations (many would argue discriminatory practices have never ended), mistreatment of Irish settlers (and many other immigrant groups), and the decision to intern Japanese-Americans in detention camps during World War II. Of course, it would be disingenuous not to recognize that these examples can also be used to demonstrate that race specifically may play an important role in dividing people and influencing perceptions of threats. The most egregious example of this in American history is the institution of slavery based upon race, which still has ramifications in our contemporary era—as the persistence of the white supremacy movement reminds us. But important as this issue remains, we do not focus on race separately in this work, but consider it in conjunction with ethnicity and nationalism to focus on themes related to human and national security.

In any case, the fact that Americans would generally not be inclined to give as much credence to the importance of nationalism, or ethnic identity, triggering security threats is not surprising to historian Jerry Muller. As he observes:

> projecting their own experience onto the rest of the world, Americans generally belittle the role of ethnic nationalism in politics. After all, in the United States people of varying ethnic origins live cheek-by-jowl in relative peace (Table 3.1 lists the most current U.S. Census-derived breakout of ethnicity and race). Within two or three generations of immigration, their ethnic identities are attenuated by cultural assimilation and intermarriage. Surely, things cannot be so different elsewhere.[20]

While the recent appeal of populism and concerns about illegal immigration may have dampened some Americans' belief in easy assimilation, it is important to understand that these types of optimistic assumptions have undergirded much of U.S. foreign policy and its international assistance policy geared toward promoting elections and building modern, inclusive democratic societies and economies. The question is whether these optimistic assumptions are still relevant today, a point explored further in the book.

Notwithstanding conventional U.S. perceptions, most scholars and regional experts do not find it surprising that different cultures—whether distinguished by such factors as ethnicity (and race), religion, language, or common history and traditions—are prone to

Table 3.1 U.S. Population Race/Ethnicity, 2016 (self-reported)

Race and Hispanic Origin	% of Population (323 million estimate)
White alone	76.9
Black/African American alone	13.3
American Indian/Alaska Native alone	1.3
Asian alone	5.7
Native Hawaiian/other Pacific Islander alone	0.2
Two or more races	2.6
Hispanic or Latino*	17.8
White alone, not Hispanic or Latino*	61.3

Source: U.S. Census Bureau, "Quick Facts," at www.census.gov/quickfacts/fact/table/US/PST045216.

Notes:

* Hispanics may be of any race, so are also included in applicable race categories.

While the Census Bureau lists a date of July 2016 for this data, the last full census of the U.S. population was in 2010 (a full census has been conducted every 10 years since 1790, a requirement of the Constitution in order to apportion congressional representative seats among the states). Of note, the census reported that for 2011–2015, the number of "Foreign Born Persons" was 13.2%.

fear one another and will often experience misunderstanding and conflict. History is replete with relevant examples. Renowned U.S. political scientist Samuel Huntington provided probably the most well-known (and controversial) arguments related to reasons for this proclivity, although he envisioned entire "civilizations" clashing, placing primary emphasis on religious differences. (See "Think Again" box on "Clash of Civilizations?")

❖ BOX 3.1 THINK AGAIN: CLASH OF CIVILIZATIONS?

In 1993 renowned U.S. political scientist Samuel Huntington provided probably the most well-known (and still controversial) arguments setting out why different cultures may come into conflict with one another. However, Huntington envisioned what he termed entire "civilizations" clashing, arguing that "a civilization is a cultural entity . . . the highest cultural grouping of people and the broadest level of cultural identity people have . . . defined by common objective elements, such as language, history, religion, customs, institutions, and by the subjective self-identification of a people."[1] He viewed religion as being the single most important identifier among the seven or eight major civilizations he differentiated: Western, Confucian, Japanese, Islamic, Hindu, Slavic-Orthodox, Latin American, and potentially African. For Huntington, the differences between these civilizations were much more important than any political or ideological divisions (such as the communist–democracy divide during the Cold War).

Huntington predicted at the time that these incidences of conflict would increase as cultures inevitably interacted and became more aware of their differences because of accelerating globalization trends. In other words, contrary to prevailing wisdom, modernization and even democratization and integration of the world economy and international community would actually have detrimental effects, including increasing the feelings of insecurity for many human beings and their desire to remain, or to become assimilated, with their own cultural communities. Huntington further predicted the phenomenon of "kin-country" syndrome, where states and communities from one civilization would tend to support their fellow states engaged in war with another civilization—citing the widespread Arab and Muslim popular support for the Iraqi government in spite of the U.S.-led coalition war against Iraq in 1991. Contrarily, he believed that any conflicts within civilizations would be less violent and prolonged.

It should be noted that many scholars have disputed Huntington's argument on both theoretical and historical grounds, and via detailed case studies of various conflicts that seem to contradict his thesis.[2] In this regard it is telling to note that Huntington cited the case of Ukrainian–Russian relations in 1991–1992 as supporting his thesis because, despite the fact that the two countries had reasons to fight over Crimea and the Black Sea fleet, they were negotiating. According to Huntington, "if civilization is what counts, however, the likelihood of violence between Ukrainians and Russians should be low. They are two Slavic, primarily Orthodox peoples who have had close relationships with each other for centuries." Yet what might be seen as confirmatory in 1993 seems quite mistaken in 2017 as Russia and the Ukraine are carrying out at least a low-level war between one another in the wake of Russian annexation of the Crimea and intervention in eastern Ukraine. On the other hand, it is significant that Huntington published his analysis in the midst of the "afterglow" of the end of the Cold War, when democratization and liberal, free market trends were receiving near-universal endorsement by scholars and policymakers alike, and Francis Fukuyama argued that liberal, democratic capitalism had triumphed. Certainly the scale and scope of ethnic- and religious-motivated violence in the twenty-first century could encourage further consideration of Huntington's 1993 thesis.

1 Samuel Huntington, "The Clash of Civilizations?" *Foreign Affairs* vol. 72, no. 3 (1993): 22–49.
2 For example, Reveron and Murer's detailed studies of numerous conflicts concluded that: "The conflicts often 'linked' [by culture] do not represent any global struggle against the West and their connections to one another are spurious at best. There are real economic and political reasons for the conflicts." Derek S. Reveron and Jeffrey Stevenson Murer, *Flashpoints in the War on Terrorism* (New York: Routledge, 2006), xiv.

Huntington and others predicted that incidences of conflict between communities and groups would increase as cultures inevitably interacted and became more aware of their differences because of accelerating globalization trends. On the other hand, many U.S. and international policymakers continue to believe that closer connections between different groups is a desirable trend, as demonstrated in a *Foreign Affairs* article that appeared some twenty years after Huntington's seminal essay, deliberately entitled "The Fusion of Civilizations: The Case for Global Optimism." Here the authors argue, "The great world civilizations, which used to have detached and separate identities, now have increasingly overlapping areas of commonality. Most people around the world now have the same aspirations . . . the West should be celebrating its phenomenal success at injecting the key elements of its worldview into other great civilizations."[21] It is unclear at this juncture whether these authors or Huntington's predictions are more accurate, and it is prudent to conclude that we probably will not know the answer for the foreseeable future.

Regardless of one's opinion on the effects of globalization, it is evident that cultural appeals can be deliberately manipulated not only by warring groups within or outside a state, but also by authoritarian leaders who may use them to attain, or keep, governmental power. Unfortunately, what Thomas Friedman has termed the "globalization backlash" makes it even easier for these "backlash demagogues" to offer traditional, if unworkable, solutions to societal problems because these types of solutions tend to appeal to those who feel most insecure and threatened by the changes fostered by globalization.[22] In turn, individuals and groups from different cultural communities who refuse to support authoritarian leaders and their policies tend to be deliberately discriminated against by state officials. At worst, they may be singled out for violation of their most basic human rights, up to and including imprisonment, torture, rape, and death. This certainly is the case in Sudan, where Sudanese leader Omar al-Bashir is the first sitting president to be indicted by the International Criminal Court, specifically for directing interethnic, tribal, and religiously motivated rape and murder in his country, especially in the Darfur region. Estimates (2017) are that at least several hundred thousand have died in Darfur since 2003, with some 2 million displaced or refugees in neighboring Chad.[23]

Religion

Many of the examples cited above about the proclivity for nationalism to trigger, or intensify, conflict between groups and countries should have sparked recognition of another contributing factor that often accompanies ethnic differences—religion. Historically, nationalism has often been most potent when allied to a particular religion. Consider, for example, that initially Islam was spread extremely quickly and widely by Arab tribes who shared a common ethnic background, values, and traditions. And for hundreds of years Confucianism was intimately associated with the Chinese empire and its society. The conception of "the West" referenced above has as much to do with a Judeo-Christian heritage as it does with certain national or ethnic groups.

It should not be surprising to find that in the twenty-first century most Americans perceive that religion as a motivating factor represents the gravest threats to U.S. national security, primarily in the guise of terrorist groups manifesting extremist religious ideologies. In fact, a representative Gallup poll from 2016 shows that U.S. citizens continued to rank the threat of international terrorism first (79 percent) in their concerns as a "critical threat," followed closely by concerns about Iran's potential nuclear-related capabilities (surely it is not coincidental that Iran is an Islamic regime that also funds Islamic terrorist groups). And in public opinion polls, terrorism and immigration are both perceived to be serious problems by the mainly Western European citizens polled, with Gallup analysts noting that it was the dual fears of terrorism and immigration that had helped contribute to the rise of nationalist parties in Europe beginning in 2016.[24]

It is clear that the ideologies of transnational terrorist groups in the twenty-first century tend to be linked to fundamentalist, frequently intolerant perspectives rooted in ethnic, and especially religious, cultural factors. These ideologies are typically found within the developing, non-Western regions of the world. This includes certain regions and areas that contain unstable or failing states, or even ungoverned areas, not only in Southwest Asia (Afghanistan, Pakistan) and the Middle East (Iraq, Iran, Syria, Yemen) but also in Africa (Somalia in the Horn of Africa, parts of Sudan, Chad, and Nigeria). In the chapters that follow we consider further the problem of weak or failing states, which encompass almost every human security concern.

Religion and nationalism can also motivate conflict, instability, and threats to American security as well as in more developed and putatively Western areas of the world, such as the Balkans in Europe or with the Ukrainian–Russian conflict (western Ukraine is primarily Roman Catholic, whereas eastern Ukraine and Russia are primarily Orthodox Christian). Furthermore, extremist, religious-inspired threats can actually develop within the United States itself and among U.S. citizens, as a number of well-publicized cases after the devastating attacks of September 11, 2001 have demonstrated. These range from U.S. Army major Nidal Malik Hasan being convicted for shooting thirteen individuals at Fort Hood, Texas, for religious reasons; to two Chechen Muslim immigrant brothers launching twin bomb blasts at the Boston Marathon in April 2013, killing three; to a radicalized Muslim killing four Marines and one sailor in Chattanooga, Tennessee in 2015; to a self-radicalized married couple killing fourteen people at a holiday party in December 2015, in San Bernardino, California. These incidents reflect a concern among many counterterrorism experts about whether radicalization of Americans will accelerate, fueled in part by the continuing U.S. involvement in certain Muslim countries and by the ability of U.S. citizens to receive indoctrination and training from terrorist groups in venues ranging from Yemen to Pakistan to Somalia.[25] Significantly, as the Fort Hood case demonstrates, it is not even necessary to travel outside the United States to receive indoctrination in view of the ability of extremist groups to reach out via cyberspace to attract recruits worldwide.

For most Americans, it is shocking to accept that someone raised within the United States could be won over to a fundamentalist, intolerant ideology that challenges the core principles of U.S. democratic and pluralist ideology. Yet it is important to acknowledge that there is a threat not only from radical Islam, but also from domestic anti-Islamic hate groups and other violent radical groups in the United States (who may or may not be religiously motivated). For example, "the Council on American-Islamic Relations released a report that found that, nationally, 'the number of hate crimes [against Muslims] in the first half of 2017 spiked 91% compared to the same period in 2016,' which had previously been a record-breaking year."[26] In terms of violent incidents, the first half of 2017 saw mosques being bombed and set on fire; and three civilians who intervened to protect two Muslim girls from being harassed by a white nationalist in Portland, Oregon, were stabbed to death by that individual. If one includes all recent terrorist actions by domestic extremists (often white nationalists) in the United States, the number of incidents would substantially increase, to include the death and injuries of peaceful protestors in Charlottesville, Virginia, against white supremacists in 2017; to the nine African-American church worshipers in Charleston, South Carolina, shot to death in 2015 by a white supremacist.

The Pew Research Center's representative poll of American Muslims in 2017 (who totaled some 3.3 million out of a U.S. population of 325 million when the poll was conducted) found that 75 percent believed there was "a lot of discrimination against Muslims in the U.S." In terms of specifics, the Pew Center analysis found that, of those polled:

> about one-third (32%) say that others have acted suspicious because they are Muslim, one-fifth say they had been called offensive names, and 18% say airport security had singled them out. One-in-ten (10%) say they had been singled out by other law enforcement officers and 6% say they have been physically threatened or attacked.[27]

While these individual experiences are troubling, in terms of societal cohesion what may be more disconcerting is the finding that "most Muslims (62%) say Americans do not view Islam as part of mainstream American society. In fact, a plurality of U.S. adults (50%) say they don't see Islam as part of mainstream society."[28]

These findings are important because if the United States is to protect its national interests around the globe and the security of U.S. citizens, the country must improve its ability to understand other cultures, including how and why insecurity may fuel diverse individuals and groups to turn to culturally based extremism. Regardless of one's opinion about how large a role culture may play in particular situations, there is little doubt that it can be a decisive factor in setting the stage for, or providing the proximate cause of, human insecurities, violence, and war. Whereas in the past the United States might not have seemed to be that threatened by interethnic and religious conflicts in faraway states or regions, in today's globalized society the danger has been clearly evident since at least September 11, 2001.

Failing states that may form after years of conflict and instability can offer enabling conditions for ideologically driven non-state actors such as terrorist groups to find support, expand their operations, and launch attacks—as shown by the deadly mix of the Taliban government and al Qaeda in Afghanistan and the mixture of terrorist, extremist groups such as ISIS that have been destabilizing Syria, Yemen, and Somalia. Table 3.2 depicts the top twenty fragile states at most risk of actual failure, many of which have been on the list continuously for some years. Of note is that almost every one of these states (except for Haiti) is in this precarious situation—to a greater or lesser extent—because of interethnic, racial, and/or religious conflict. And this situation is aggravated, or sometimes caused, by poor governance, as discussed in the next chapter.

Conflict within a state is also of greater concern because it may easily spread to neighboring states, particularly where ethnic and religious communities are not confined by recognized state borders (Afghanistan and Pakistan provide sobering examples). Refugees may flee from one state to another, seeking security, as has been the case with hundreds of thousands of Syrians. In turn, this may generate further instability in the state now housing those refugees, especially if there are different national and religious groups who

Table 3.2 Top 20 Most At-Risk States, 2016

1. Somalia*	11. Iraq*
2. South Sudan*	12. Guinea*
3. Central African Republic*	13. Nigeria*
4. Sudan*	14. Pakistan*
5. Yemen*	15. Burundi*
6. Syria*	16. Zimbabwe*
7. Chad*	17. Guinea-Bissau*
8. Democratic Republic of Congo*	18. Eritrea
9. Afghanistan*	19. Niger*
10. Haiti*	20. Kenya

Source: Fund for Peace, "Fragile States Index 2016," at http://fsi.fundforpeace.org/

Note: * Countries in the top 20 since 2015.

are already at odds within the host state. This phenomenon has occurred numerous times in areas of Africa, particularly in the Great Lakes region (Rwanda, Burundi, and the Democratic Republic of the Congo). Finally, the existence of culturally based grievances among groups within a particular state may skew access to, and control over, government power and resources, thus negating the possibility of equitable development and the chances of creating a viable, stable state. In the worst case this can lead to massive human rights abuses, targeted killings, and war, as the breakup of Yugoslavia and the genocide in Rwanda in the 1990s demonstrate. Tragically, even now internal wars continue in Afghanistan, Sudan, Yemen, and Syria, and Islamic extremist groups such as Boko Haram perpetrate killings and kidnappings of young girls in Nigeria and Chad.

It would be entirely too easy, and mistaken, to attribute most of this conflict or terrorism to religious differences—especially to radical Islam. First, many of the recent conflicts have been fueled primarily by ethnic and not religious differences. Rwanda's genocide, led by its majority Hutu ethnic government, killed some 800,000 Tutsi ethnic minority members (and some Hutu moderates). Even in the Yugoslav conflicts of the 1990s, it would be difficult to conclude whether religious (Muslim–Christian) or ethnic (Serb–Croat–Bosnian) differences were most responsible for those persecuted and killed. Additionally, interethnic and not religious conflict often poses the greatest threat in terms of generating instability and terrorist threats within the Muslim world, whether these originate from Afghanistan, Pakistan, Somalia, or Yemen. Thus, while all four of these countries are overwhelmingly Muslim in religion, they feature different ethnic, tribal, or clan groups that have traditionally been in conflict with one another. Finally, it is significant that the widespread protests beginning in 2010 across numerous Arab nations such as Tunisia and Egypt—the so-called "Arab Spring—were not primarily religious or ethnic in nature, but were political and reformist movements. That is why this important development is explored in the next chapter on civic security, which focuses on topics like good governance, governmental corruption, and criminal violence.

Women's Human Security

Regardless of which cultural attribute one examines—whether ethnicity, religion, or historical tradition—it is striking to find the nearly universal practice of discrimination and violence based upon gender. In other words, it is difficult to find a culture that has not delegated women and their human security needs to second place. Where efforts to achieve more gender equality have progressed in the contemporary era, it has been mainly in the industrialized, developed countries, and many would attribute the changes to women being incorporated into the national economy. Additionally, recall that the preceding chapter described how the recognition of human rights evolved since the mid-twentieth century, a process that accelerated in the 1990s with the end of the Cold War. This included women's rights as part of changing conceptions.

Yet this clearly does not mean that every country in the world agrees with the conception that all human rights are universal and equal in importance. In fact, an important perspective argues that human rights are "relativistic"—that is, human rights are legitimately culturally constrained, whether by religion or ethnic or historical traditions. And even though the Universal Declaration of Human Rights was unanimously proclaimed by the new United Nations in 1948, it should be noted that in 1948 most developing states in Africa and Asia were still colonies, and thus were not represented at the United Nations to formulate and sign the declaration. Thus, some developing states have argued that the UDHR is really a "Western" perspective on human rights and that it marginalizes non-Western views, so it cannot be considered universal.

This argument still resonates in the human rights literature, and admittedly developing countries have expressed some legitimate concerns related to cultural values and the difficulties in importing Western traditions and values without considering all the societal ramifications. Yet one of the problems with arguing that human rights are culturally bound is that this claim can be used by a group holding power as a pretext for denying rights to some peoples and privileging certain groups over others. Nowhere is this tendency more evident, and systematic in nature, than in the case of women's rights. (Image 3.1 depicts just one of the international programs sponsored by the United States in an attempt to improve women's rights.)

While most U.S. citizens are familiar with the abuse of Afghan women under the extremist version of Islam practiced by the Taliban, the number of ways in which culture has been used to stymie women's human rights and human security is legion. Discrimination and abuse may be based on national and ethnic values, religious beliefs and norms, or traditional practices—ranging from prohibiting women to work outside the home, inherit property on their own, vote, or run for office, to even female genital mutilation. Probably the most egregious violation of women's rights, however, occurs in conjunction with practices such as human trafficking and the use of sexual violence against women as a deliberate policy in conflict situations. As for human trafficking, UN reporting cited a number of 63,251 victims located in 106 countries between 2012 and 2014; 70 percent of those victims were women or girls. These victims are trafficked for sexual exploitation, forced labor, and servitude—to include actual slavery—and for the purpose of removal of organs.[30] It is important to note that these are only the cases that were detected and reported, and that the true incidence of human trafficking is undoubtedly larger, especially in areas of instability or actual conflict.

The statistics on the deliberate practice of sexual violence against women in conflict situations are staggering. According to the United Nations, "in Rwanda, up to half a million women were raped during the 1994 genocide. The numbers were approximately 60,000 in the Balkans conflicts of the 1990s; in Sierra Leone, the number of incidents of war-related sexual violence among internally displaced women from 1991 to 2001 was approximately 64,000."[31] This tactic has expanded and intensified in the twenty-first century in war-torn areas. For example, during her 2009 visit to the Democratic Republic of the Congo then Secretary of State Hillary Clinton met with representatives of an estimated 200,000 victims of sexual violence in that conflicted country; in the conflicts in the Sudan

Image 3.1 Women's Empowerment Program Sponsored by the U.S. Government, Pakistan. Photo: USAID Pakistan[29]

and neighboring South Sudan rape continued as a preferred tactic by all warring parties through 2017; and ISIS used the practice of rape, abduction, and forcible marriage of girls from the Yezidi ethnic minority group. While this practice is obviously abhorrent in terms of violations of individuals' human rights and security, it is significant to note that the UN Security Council passed a resolution in 2008 specifically declaring rape to be a tactic of war and a threat to international security. Additionally, the International Criminal Court's definition of crimes against humanity for which it can prosecute offenders includes "offences such as murder, rape, imprisonment, enforced disappearances, enslavement—particularly of women and children, sexual slavery, torture, apartheid and deportation."[32] As with the practices of ethnic cleansing and genocide, rape is used as a specific tactic because it destroys a community and its identity.

Considering just these few specific examples of violations of women's human rights, it should not be surprising to find that as early as 1979 the United Nations General Assembly found it necessary to adopt the Convention on the Elimination of All Forms of Discrimination Against Women. The convention aims to achieve "equality between women and men through ensuring women's equal access to, and equal opportunities in, political and public life . . . The Convention is the only human rights treaty which affirms the reproductive rights of women and targets culture and tradition as influential forces shaping gender roles and family relations."[33] Further affirming the importance of women's particular human security needs, in 2010 the General Assembly unanimously approved the creation of UN Women (the United Nations Entity for Gender Equality and the Empowerment of Women), a new umbrella organization to consolidate and strengthen the efforts of several smaller, often fragmented UN agencies dealing with women's issues. And it is notable that the UN's Sustainable Development Goals for 2030 not only cite gender equality as a specific goal, but also many of the other goals related to poverty, hunger, good health, education, clean water, and economic growth are only possible with the full participation of women. This aspect is of great significance because of increasing evidence documenting that women are the key to successful development and to overcoming poverty (see Image 3.2), as it is generally women who ensure food, education, and health care for the children in a family (this critical aspect is considered further in Chapter 5).

Clearly, women's access to political and public life is essential to effective governance and public policy, and there has been progress toward that goal in most societies. For example, the United States Senate passed the Women, Peace, and Security Act of 2017 to express the sense of the U.S. Congress that "the United States should be a global leader in promoting the participation of women in conflict prevention, management, and resolution and post-conflict relief and recovery operations" because of the recognition that women play a crucial role in building and sustaining democratic societies in the aftermath of conflict.[35] In very conservative Saudi Arabia women were allowed to vote in 2015 and stand for office in municipal elections for the first time, and in 2018 women were permitted to drive themselves. However, it is probably fair to say that cultural practices and expectations concerning a woman's role in the family and society continue to be much more resistant to change. Yet even here, surprising examples of change continue to appear in every corner of the world, to include a female heavy metal group in conservative, rural West Java, Indonesia. The three members of the group come from poor families and attend a madrasa, or Muslim school. According to one of the teenage band members in 2017, "'I'm a different musician because I'm a woman, and I play metal music but I'm wearing hijab . . . Hijab is my identity, OK?"[36] Examples such as this demonstrate that key aspects of identity can be retained even with change.

Image 3.2 Let Girls Learn: Bangladesh Horticulture Project. Photo: USAID[34]

Indigenous Groups' Human Security

It is appropriate to end this consideration of identity security by briefly surveying the situation of groups who share fundamental identities and characteristics, and who by choice have sought to remain distinct from the dominant societies around them. United Nations data suggest there are some 370 million indigenous peoples located in 70 different countries. Yet, as Cher Weixia Chen notes in the *International Studies Encyclopedia*, the definition of "indigenous peoples" remains controversial, and some indigenous groups disdain the term itself. Nevertheless, "scholars generally agree that indigenous societies are vastly heterogeneous but they endure remarkably similar experiences such as lack of statehood, economic and political marginalization, and cultural and racial discrimination."[37] As the UN has further noted, "Indigenous peoples have sought recognition of their identities, way of life and their right to traditional lands, territories and natural resources for years, yet throughout history, their rights have always been violated."[38]

However, the situation for indigenous groups has shown some improvement as contemporary conceptions of human rights have evolved to include the specific recognition of certain communal, collective, or solidarity rights. Thus, while indigenous people's rights are still contested, it is worth noting that the UN General Assembly passed the United Nations Declaration on the Rights of Indigenous Peoples in 2007.[39] Furthermore, just as UN agencies have been instrumental in furthering the overall concept of human security, as described in Chapter 2, they have also been extremely important in advancing the concept of indigenous people's rights. But, as Chen highlights:

> the emergence of indigenous rights within the UN was not an accident. Instead, it was a purposeful undertaking by a large number of indigenous NGOs . . . the first international indigenous NGOs emerged in the 1950s . . . [and] in 1975, the World Council of Indigenous Peoples commenced a global framework that interconnects the national and international networks of indigenous groups.[40]

But while the category of indigenous peoples has received at least some political and legal recognition of their communal status, the basic notion of "collective" rights attaining to these groups has continued to remain a difficult fit for international law, which is predicated on "individual" rights—i.e., the rights of an individual human being or an individual state. Even more complicated is the concept of self-determination for indigenous peoples. It is noteworthy that the UN Declaration recognizes that:

- Indigenous peoples have the right to self-determination. By virtue of that right they freely determine their political status and freely pursue their economic, social and cultural development (Article 3).
- They have the right to autonomy or self-government in matters relating to their internal and local affairs, as well as ways and means for financing their autonomous functions (Article 4).
- They shall not be forcibly removed from their lands or territories (Article 10).
- They have the right to own, use, develop and control the lands, territories and resources that they possess by reason of traditional ownership or other traditional occupation or use (Article 26)
- States shall consult and cooperate in good faith with the indigenous peoples concerned through their own representative institutions in order to obtain their free and informed consent prior to the approval of any project affecting their lands or territories and other resources, particularly in connection with the development, utilization or exploitation of mineral, water or other resources (Article 32).

Yet in spite of these encouraging provisions, it is critical to highlight that, according to Article 46, "Nothing in this Declaration may be . . . construed as authorizing or encouraging any action which would dismember or impair, totally or in part, the territorial integrity or political unity of sovereign and independent States."[41] As noted earlier with reference to the UN Charter itself, a clear dichotomy is established—the right of self-determination for communities exists, but not at the sacrifice of state sovereignty.

Thus, indigenous people's rights provide a near-perfect textbook case of how the human security needs of a community and the national security needs of a state may clash. In point of fact, this is not a textbook or hypothetical situation. Numerous real-world conflicts exist in many regions of the world, often linked to disputes over the control, or use, of land. One UN expert has noted that in spite of the UN Declaration's Article 26—that indigenous communities should be consulted over development projects in their territories—a study from 2016 of fifty companies showed a mere 10 percent were considering that principle when dealing with communities.[42]

Of greater consequence is that indigenous activists trying to monitor and protect what they perceive to be their lands are not only harassed but also killed. For example, in Latin American countries like Nicaragua, Ecuador, Peru, Colombia, and Brazil, indigenous communities have frequently clashed with multinational corporations trying to extract resources and minerals (Image 3.3 depicts one of the indigenous groups of Panama). These companies have their own security forces, but government forces may provide security for those companies, too. The government itself may be the primary threat to its own citizens when it constructs hydropower dams without adequate consultation

Image 3.3 Embera Indians in Panama. Photo: Kathleen A. Mahoney-Norris[43]

of traditional communities, who are almost inevitably displaced by the dams. One of the most infamous cases in 2016 involved the murder of Honduran indigenous activist Berta Cáceres, undoubtedly for her protests against a huge hydropower dam complex which would displace her indigenous community. According to the international NGO Global Witness, which tracks attacks against environmental and land activists, attacks have been increasing worldwide. Their report for 2016 documented 200 killings in 27 countries versus 185 killings in 16 countries in 2015, with 40 percent of those killed being indigenous individuals. It is no surprise that the large country of Brazil, where struggle continues over its vast Amazon resources, has the most killings.[44]

These types of conflict may directly, or indirectly, involve U.S. national security interests, such as when a U.S. multinational corporation is involved in extracting strategic minerals of interest to the U.S. government in a contested area. In a larger sense, the United States is always concerned when there is instability in any of its neighbors to the south. And the United States has witnessed its own domestic conflict with American Indian groups protesting certain projects they view as being harmful to their communities and lands. For example, in 2017 the controversial Keystone XL Pipeline project—to carry tar sands oil from Canada through a number of U.S. states and eventually as far south as Houston, Texas—was still being challenged by indigenous communities in Canada and the United States, along with private citizens and other groups in some states. As indigenous communities in numerous instances are receiving public support, and may even collaborate with non-indigenous groups, some may view this as a promising advance for human security interests.

Conclusion

The fact that human beings identify themselves in a number of ways beyond their official citizenship in a particular state is a critically important piece of understanding of why so many security challenges today are international, and transnational, in scope. Whether one examines ethnicity/race, religion, or gender, it is impossible to dispute the fact that, historically, these community and individual traits have mattered, and they matter today. As this chapter has underscored, the fundamental attachment that we all have to our cultural identity and traditions must be acknowledged in order to comprehend why change can be viewed as so threatening, and where it might actually enhance the possibilities for conflict, terrorism, and human rights abuses. Of additional concern is that these types of identity issues may be deliberately exploited by extremist groups to further destabilize weak governments, or by a government's leaders to legitimize the use of repression and violence against opposition or minority groups so as to remain in power—an issue which is addressed further in the next chapter. These issues may also be used by regional neighboring states or external powers to further their perceived security interests.

It is clear that the processes of globalization can be viewed as both helpful and harmful in terms of identity security. It can be harmful if we believe that Samuel Huntington's argument that bringing different cultural (civilizational) groups closer together actually makes them more aware of their differences and more antagonistic toward one another; and if we presume that Thomas Friedman's "globalization backlash" is a potent threat. These types of argument seem to have gained more traction in 2017 with the strength of nationalist populism in many countries of the world, to include the United States. On the other hand, if we agree with Kishore Mahbubani and Lawrence Summer that globalization makes it possible to recognize the commonalities, or fusion, between different cultures, then a more positive assessment of globalization can be made.

Certainly the record of human rights successes and changing norms over the past sixty years—especially with regard to women, indigenous communities, and other persecuted minority groups—has been possible only through the ability to link a transnational community of individual citizens and activists, scholars and lawyers, domestic human rights groups, international human rights organizations, foundations, key states, and the United Nations. The capability to share information and strategies with concerned actors literally across the globe, and to instantly publicize violations of communities' human security interests, was not available to the indigenous populations being decimated in the Western Hemisphere beginning in the fifteenth century; to those enslaved and the anti-slavery movement of the eighteenth and nineteenth centuries; to the ethnic communities persecuted by their colonizers and empires of the nineteenth and twentieth centuries; or to the early women's rights campaigners of those two centuries. In this sense one can make the case that the information technologies that propel globalization support human security interests, often in the face of governmental opposition.

Unfortunately, as the next chapter demonstrates, weak, authoritarian, or corrupt governments can violate the human security needs of human beings. Chapter 4 addresses a set of interrelated challenges to each human being's most basic civic security concerns, which include their rights to life, liberty, and participation as citizens in their society. Even where there are no serious identity issues between communities to cause conflict and human rights violations, a bad government can weaken or even negate the rights of citizens within and between communities. The reality is that governments are simultaneously the principal protectors and the principal abusers of human beings, and the processes of globalization clearly affect governments' abilities to both protect and to abuse.

As explored in the next chapter, globalization may empower governments when it assists their development efforts and strengthens their abilities to institutionalize democratic government and to rule humanely and justly—often aided by other governments, international organizations, and activist groups. Yet globalization can also empower authoritarian, often corrupt, leaders to persecute targeted opposition groups more easily and to use information technologies to incite culturally based dissension to remain in power and prevent change. Globalization can foster, too, the illegal actions of transnational criminal networks and gangs who use violence as a tactic as they seek to undermine public security and even rival the authority of governments within certain communities. This problem has been endemic in much of Central America and parts of Mexico, and the resulting human security issues continue to directly affect U.S. national security interests.

Notes

1 Pankaj Mishra, "The Globalization of Rage: Why Today's Extremism Looks Familiar," *Foreign Affairs* vol. 95, no. 6 (2016): 46–54, 48–49.

2 George W. Bush, *The National Security Strategy of the United States of America* (Washington, DC: Office of the President, 2002).

3 Friedman, *The Lexus and the Olive Tree*, 9.

4 Mark Landler, "Obama, in Farewell to U.N., Paints Stark Choices for Unsettled World," *New York Times*, September 19, 2016. At www.nytimes.com/2016/09/21/world/barack-obama-unga-2016-united-nations.html.

5 UNDP, *Human Development Report 1994*, 31.

6 Felix Berenskoetter, "Identity in International Relations," in *The International Studies Encyclopedia*, emphasis added. At: www.oxfordreference.com/view/10.1093/acref/9780191842665.001.0001/acref-9780191842665-e-0192?rskey=F7k63T&result=214.

7 Ibid.

8 Mishra, "Globalization of Rage," 53.
9 Ibid., 48.
10 Fareed Zakaria, "Populism on the March: Why the West Is in Trouble," *Foreign Affairs* vol. 95, no. 6 (2016): 9–15, 9.
11 "Is Populism Here to Stay?," *Foreign Affairs*, August 9, 2017. At: www.foreignaffairs.com/articles/2016-10-19/populism-here-stay.
12 Zakaria, "Populism on the March," 13.
13 Jeff D. Colgan and Robert O. Keohane, "The Liberal Order Is Rigged: Fix It Now or Watch It Wither," *Foreign Affairs* vol. 96, no. 3 (2017): 36–44, 36.
14 Cathie Carmichael, "Nationalisms in International Conflict," in *The International Studies Encyclopedia*. At: www.oxfordreference.com/view/10.1093/acref/9780191842665.001.0001/acref-9780191842665-e-0282?rskey=omlhoq&result=319.
15 Ibid.
16 Lydia Gall, "Hungary's War on Refugees," *Human Rights Watch*, September 16, 2016. At: www.hrw.org/news/2016/09/16/hungarys-war-refugees.
17 Andrea Mammone, "The Future of Europe's Radical Right: Why the Politics of Race Are Here to Stay," *Foreign Affairs*, September 20, 2011. At: www.foreignaffairs.com/articles/europe/2011-09-20/future-europes-radical-right.
18 Andrew Moravcsik, "The Gypsy 'Menace': Populism and the New Anti-Gypsy Politics," (book review), *Foreign Affairs* vol. 93, no. 3 (2014). At: www.foreignaffairs.com/reviews/capsule-review/2014-04-21/gypsy-menace-populism-and-new-anti-gypsy-politics.
19 Stephen Kotkin, "Russia's Perpetual Geopolitics: Putin Returns to the Historical Pattern," *Foreign Affairs* vol. 95, no. 3 (2016): 2–9.
20 Jerry Z. Muller, "Us and Them: The Enduring Power of Ethnic Nationalism," *Foreign Affairs* vol. 87, no. 2 (2008): 18.
21 Samuel Huntington, "The Clash of Civilizations?" *Foreign Affairs* vol. 72, no. 3 (1993): 22–49; Kishore Mahbubani and Lawrence H. Summers, "The Fusion of Civilizations: The Case for Global Optimism," *Foreign Affairs* vol. 95, no. 3 (2016), 126–135, 126.
22 Friedman, *Lexus and the Olive Tree*, 336.
23 Human Rights Watch, "Human Rights Benchmarks for Sudan: Eight Ways to Measure Progress," May 3, 2017. At: www.hrw.org/news/2017/05/03/human-rights-benchmarks-sudan.
24 Justin McCarthy, "Americans Cite Cyberterrorism among Top Three Threats to U.S.," *Gallup Politics*, February 10, 2016. At: www.gallup.com/poll/189161/americans-cite-cyberterrorism-among-top-three-threats.aspx?g_source=global+terrorism&g_medium=search&g_campaign=tiles. Also Steve Crabtree and Sophia Kluch, "Terrorism, Migration Trouble Many in Europe," *Gallup World*, June 15, 2017. At: www.gallup.com/poll/212405/terrorism-migration-trouble-europe.aspx?g_source=position5&g_medium=related&g_campaign=tiles.
25 On the concerns about Somali American youths disappearing from their homes in Minnesota to go fight with al Qaeda elements in Somalia and then potentially return to launch attacks in the United States, see Dina Temple-Raston, "FBI Sheds Light on Missing Somali-Americans," on *All Things Considered*, National Public Radio (NPR), March 11, 2009. At; www.npr.org/templates/story/story.php?storyId=101751571.
26 Moustafa Bayoumi, "Trump Is Ignoring the Minnesota Mosque Bombing: We Know Why," *The Guardian*, August 10, 2017. At: www.theguardian.com/commentisfree/2017/aug/10/minnesota-mosque-bombing-donald-trump-silence?
27 Jeff Diamant, "American Muslims Are Concerned: But Also Satisfied with Their Lives," Pew Research Center, July 26, 2017. At: www.pewresearch.org/fact-tank/2017/07/26/american-muslims-are-concerned-but-also-satisfied-with-their-lives/.
28 Ibid.
29 Photo in the public domain, "Gender Empowerment in Pakistan: Gender Equity Program (Celebrating International Women's day through hand raising ceremony)", at: www.usaid.gov/news-information/photo-gallery/gender-empowerment-pakistan.
30 UN Office on Drugs and Crime, *2016 Global Report on Trafficking* (Vienna: UNODC, 2016), 23, 26. At: www.unodc.org/documents/data-and-analysis/glotip/2016_Global_Report_on_Trafficking_in_Persons.pdf.

31 U.S. Department of State, "United Nations Security Council to Adopt Resolution to Protect Women in Conflict Situations." Press release, September 30, 2009. At: www.state.gov/r/pa/prs/ps/2009/sept/129997.htm.
32 International Criminal Court, "How the Court Works." At: www.icc-cpi.int/about/how-the-court-works.
33 UN Division for the Advancement of Women, Department of Economic and Social Affairs, "Convention on the Elimination of All Forms of Discrimination Against Women." At: www.un.org/womenwatch/daw/cedaw/.
34 Photo in public domain, "Let Girls Learn—Bangladesh: Horticulture Project." Full caption: "USAID's Horticulture Project increases students' awareness of the nutrition in Bangladesh, including the value of orange-fleshed sweet potatoes and different vegetables. The project encourages positive family behavior change and vegetables in schools." At: www.usaid.gov/news-information/photo-gallery/let-girls-learn-bangladesh#slideshow-0.
35 S.1141–115th Congress, "Women, Peace, and Security Act of 2017," Library of Congress. At: www.congress.gov/bill/115th-congress/senate-bill/1141?q=%7B%22search%22%3A%5B%22S1141%22%5D%7D&r=1.
36 Ashley Westerman, "Meet Voice of Bracepot, the All-Girl Metal Band Making Waves in Indonesia," Music Interviews, NPR, August 9, 2017. At: www.npr.org/2017/08/09/542238928/meet-voice-of-baceprot-the-all-girl-metal-band-making-waves-in-indonesia.
37 Cher Weixia Chen, "Indigenous Peoples and International Law," in *The International Studies Encyclopedia*, ed. Robert A. Denemark and Renee Marlin-Bennett (Malden, MA: Wiley-Blackwell, 2017). At: www.oxfordreference.com/view/10.1093/acref/9780191842665.001.0001/acref-9780191842665-e-0426?rskey=Rgekzv&result=218.
38 United Nations Division for Social Policy and Development-Indigenous Peoples, "Indigenous Peoples at the UN." At: www.un.org/development/desa/indigenouspeoples/about-us.html. See also Umberto Bacchi, "Interview: Engaging with Indigenous People Benefits Business, Environment—U.N. Expert," Thomson Reuters Foundation, August 8, 2017. At: http://news.trust.org/item/20170808173218-c51tn/; and United Nations Division for Social Policy and Development-Indigenous Peoples, "Indigenous Peoples at the UN." At: www.un.org/development/desa/indigenouspeoples/about-us.html.
39 "United Nations Declaration on the Rights of Indigenous Peoples," 2008). At: www.un.org/esa/socdev/unpfii/documents/DRIPS_en.pdf.
40 Chen, "Indigenous Peoples and International Law."
41 "UN Declaration on the Rights of Indigenous Peoples."
42 Bacchi, "Interview."
43 Personal photo taken by co-author Mahoney-Norris while visiting Panama in May 2011.
44 Global Witness, "Defenders of the Earth Report," July 13, 2017. At: www.globalwitness.org/.

To Learn More

Examine the website of the International Criminal Court in the Hague, the Netherlands, which investigates and tries individuals for genocide, war crimes, and crimes against humanity, at www.icc-cpi.int.

To view eminent political scientist Samuel P. Huntington's argument about what makes for American identity, see his rather controversial book, *Who Are We? The Challenges to America's National Identity* (New York: Simon & Schuster, 2005).

Psychoanalyst Vamık Volkan examines how different national, ethnic, and religions groups perceive world affairs in *Enemies on the Couch: A Psychopolitical Journey through War and Peace* (Durham, NC: Pitchstone, 2013).

To examine Francis Fukuyama's influential argument about the end of history, which forecast the "universalization of Western liberal democracy as the final form of human government" due to the triumph of the Western idea, see his article "The End of History" in *The National Interest*, vol. 16 (Summer 1989): 3–18.

The U.S. Congress requires the Department of State to analyze trafficking in persons and evaluate countries' practices to reduce human trafficking. See www.state.gov/j/tip/.

To examine the identity-based labels that the United States employs to categorize the American population, go to the United States Census Bureau site, at www.census.gov/.

To gain a better understanding of populism, see the accessible, enjoyable, and *short* book, *Populism: A Very Short Introduction*, by Cas Mudde and Cristóbal Rovira Kaltwasser (New York: Oxford University Press, 2017).

Examine the rationale for the 12 indicators and related data behind compiling an annual list of the top at-risk states by the respected Fund for Peace at "Fragile States Index," available at http://fsi.fundforpeace.org/.

To view representative statistics and reports about the status of women around the world, go to the intergovernmental site, UN Women, at www.unwomen.org.

Consider the "United Nations Declaration on the Rights of Indigenous Peoples" (New York: United Nations, 2008), at www.un.org/esa/socdev/unpfii/documents/DRIPS_en.pdf.

Check out data and personal stories of murdered environmental activists—including indigenous groups—at the United Kingdom-based NGO Global Witness, whose mission is to investigate and publicize "the hidden links between demand for natural resources, corruption, armed conflict and environmental destruction." At www.globalwitness.org/.

Chapter 4

Civic Security

Chapter contents

> Effective rule of law reduces corruption, combats poverty and disease, and protects people from injustices large and small. It is the foundation for communities of equity, opportunity, and peace—underpinning development, accountable government, and respect for fundamental rights. Traditionally, the rule of law has been viewed as the domain of lawyers and judges. But everyday issues of safety, rights, justice, and governance affect us all; everyone is a stakeholder in the rule of law.
>
> The World Justice Project[1]

Traditionally most citizens have feared threats to their lives and individual security arising from enemy countries in the case of war or invasion, or perhaps from extremist groups in their own country who may become motivated by ethnic or religious hatred. However, the reality in the contemporary world is that individuals in states that do not possess good governance and the rule of law are usually most threatened by terrorist groups, mercenaries, and criminal networks and gangs; or, sadly, by their own state's security forces—to include the military, law enforcement, and paramilitary groups. Note that an estimated 180,000 civilians and military personnel were killed in war or conflict situations in 2014, whereas The *Global Study on Homicide 2013* assembled by the UN's authoritative Office on Drugs and Crime (UNODC) documented that "intentional homicide caused the deaths of almost half a million people (437,000) across the world." Additionally, the World Health Organization's (WHO) analysis of data on violence and injuries has found that "3 times more people die each year from homicide than from war-related injury."[2] In other words, as we highlighted in the first chapter, the predominant threats to a human being's fundamental right to live today most often arise out of related threats, or security deficits, in human security areas, and not from military conflict or warfare.

In this chapter we examine a set of interrelated challenges to each human being's most basic civic security concerns, conceptualized here as protection of one's physical safety and integrity, and equally respect for one's rights as a citizen—the right to be a political participant in decisions about how one will be governed. Thus, in the first section, we outline the concept of civic security as we explain how it integrates the UNDP concepts of physical security and political security. We also make some general observations about the role of globalization processes with regard to civic security.

In the second section the challenge of criminal violence (primarily transnational organized crime) and its key toxic aspects are assessed, ranging from drug trafficking (the primary focus), arms trafficking, and migrant smuggling to money laundering. Particular attention is paid to the drug trade and Latin America and the clear link these interrelated challenges pose to national security interests in the Western Hemisphere. Powerful criminal networks are one factor contributing to the widespread problem of weak and failing states and the lack of good, or even minimally functioning, governments who are able to protect their citizens' physical security or respect their political rights. Frequently these governmental deficits are magnified by entrenched practices of corruption at many levels. This issue is examined with regard to a number of countries, to include Afghanistan, which serves as a case in point.

In the last section the chapter considers the critical need for good governance and the rule of law to protect civic security interests, and we examine these concepts in the context of African states. We conclude by briefly surveying "the Arab Spring" protest movement that began in 2011 to underscore the importance of good governance in every region of the world to advance civic security interests. As that movement demonstrates, the participation of ordinary citizens in civil society is crucial—and has been enabled by globalization processes—but it is often not sufficient to sustain reform efforts, at least in the short term.

Defining Civic Security

The original UNDP conception of human security in 1994 listed the areas of personal security and political security separately. In this work we combine these two areas within the concept of civic security as they are complementary and, we believe, inextricably linked. Consider that in order for one to be secure from physical violence the state must be capable enough to protect citizens from threats from other states and hostile armed groups such as militias or terrorists; and from transnational or domestic groups, to include criminal groups and ethnic/religious groups that may be motivated to conflict by the identity concerns explored in the preceding chapter.

At the same time the state may pose a threat of violence to its own citizens, as highlighted in the UNDP report. This type of threat to personal security is often linked to the abuse of political security rights, where the authoritarian state is seeking to repress the political opposition, and may censor, intimidate, imprison, torture, "disappear," or even execute individuals perceived as a threat to the governing regime. Governments can also label groups as the "enemy" and use that label to repress, imprison, or deport particular groups of people. Political security rights are clearly fundamental to ensuring the most basic of human rights to life, liberty, and security from physical violence.[3] It does not make sense that a government abusing its citizens' rights and negating their full participation in society would be associated with a positive record of protecting human security concerns.

The fact is that governments are simultaneously the principal protectors and the principal abusers of human beings' civic security rights, and the processes of globalization outlined in this text clearly affect governments' abilities to protect or abuse. On the positive side, globalization may empower governments when it strengthens their abilities to institutionalize democratic government and to rule humanely and justly—often aided by other governments, international organizations, and activist groups. At the same time, the worldwide availability of information and transnational networks has made it possible for citizens to hold their governments more accountable, to uncover evidence of corruption, and to publicize human rights violations on a truly international scale. However, globalization can also empower authoritarian leaders to persecute targeted opposition groups more easily and to use information technologies to incite dissension among communities in order to remain in power and prevent change. And globalization can enable terrorist groups based in weak or failing states to spread their extremist ideologies and incite violence with relative ease and few resources as these groups can network with actors dispersed around the world.

Globalization also enables criminal gangs and cartels to operate more easily and to coordinate together to further co-opt and corrupt countries with weak institutions; and to spread their illicit activities, such as drug trafficking, transnationally across borders to work with other criminal elements—as demonstrated between the United States and some of its Latin American and Caribbean neighbors. Furthermore, the web of international financial systems enabled by globalization technologies allows criminal enterprises (and terrorist groups) to commit fraud, launder money, and hide assets in order to support their illegal and violent activities.

The Challenge of Criminal Violence

It bears repeating that for many human beings in the world the most serious, proximate threat to their daily lives and physical safety arises not from warfare or even ethnic conflict (as discussed in Chapter 3), but from common criminal violence—often associated with illegal drug trafficking, arms trafficking, smuggling of migrants and wildlife, and other illicit activities (including the human trafficking of women and children noted in the previous chapter). Globalization has empowered not only terrorist groups and authoritarian leaders who may use violence and engage in criminal activities to support themselves, but also transnational *criminal* networks of non-state actors who are primarily motivated by financial gain and not ideology.[4] UN law enforcement and drug control officials consider the problem of transnational organized crime (TOC) to be one of the major threats to human security, declaring: "Organized crime threatens peace and human security, violates human rights and undermines economic, social, cultural, political and civil development of societies around the world."[5] The scope and scale is so enormous that we can only address aspects here that are most fundamental to human security values—the right to not only live, but the right to a life free of violence or coercion. For that reason we focus on drug trafficking below, although that discussion clearly reveals that this criminal activity is almost invariably linked to other criminal ventures such as human trafficking, arms trafficking, smuggling, and money laundering.[6]

Drug Trafficking

Not surprisingly, international drug trafficking is usually viewed as the most serious illicit activity linked to criminal violence. It has been recognized as a major concern for most states and there are three major international drug control treaties, with the first (Single Convention on Narcotic Drugs) dating to 1961, followed by the Convention on Psychotropic Substances of 1971, and the United Nations Convention against Illicit Traffic in Narcotic Drugs and Psychotropic Substances of 1988. The UN Convention focuses on measures to combat illegal drug trafficking and what is seen as the closely related concern of money laundering of drug profits.[7] Global Financial Integrity (GFI), a well-respected non-profit research organization, found that the global drug trafficking trade for 2014 was worth between $426 billion and $652 billion, which was about one-third of the total transnational crime revenues—estimated to fall between $1.6 trillion and $2.2 trillion.[8] Cannabis makes up the largest sector of the drug trade, followed by cocaine, opiates, and amphetamine substances.

With profits such as this, it is no wonder that human life is considered to have so little value relative to the drug trade. Many would argue that violence is actually intrinsic to the drug trade, a practical tool to settle disputes and important for maintaining discipline and an effective system, as routinely seen in some U.S. cities.[9] In other instances violence or its threat is employed when individuals are pressed to become members of violent gangs or else be executed; or when law enforcement officials and border control officials choose to accept bribes and look the other way for gangs rather than be killed; or when farmers attempting to grow alternative crops rather than coca or poppies soon abandon that practice in order to avoid being killed by groups who want them to support the drug trade. Violence clearly permeates all aspects of drug trafficking.

These common practices of violence associated with the drug trade do not include the human security costs to individual drug users. According to the UNODC's *World Drug Report* of 2016:

> it is estimated that 1 in 20 adults, or a quarter of a billion people aged 15–64 years, used at least one drug in 2014 . . . Almost 12 per cent of the total number of people who use drugs, or over 29 million people, are estimated to suffer from drug use disorders.

More alarming is that "with an estimated 207,400 drug-related deaths in 2014, corresponding to 43.5 deaths per million people aged 15–64, the number of drug-related deaths worldwide has also remained stable."[10]

Incredibly, this number surpasses the number of civilians and military killed in war and conflict worldwide (estimated 180,000). With regard to the United States specifically, the State Department's Bureau of International Narcotics and Law Enforcement concluded in 2017:

> The most urgent drug-related public health crisis within the United States remains the ongoing opioid epidemic. This long-developing epidemic, spurred originally by misuse of prescription opioids within the United States, is now increasingly fueled by heroin and synthetic opioids, such as fentanyl, trafficked into the United States by *transnational criminal networks*. Public health officials have called the current opioid epidemic the worst drug crisis in U.S. history, costing the lives of more than 33,000 people in 2015. In 2015, for the first time, deaths from heroin alone surpassed gun homicides. *Transnational crime's* role in fueling this public health crisis underscores the importance of international engagement to reduce the production of illegal drugs at their source and disrupt the movement of drugs in transit.[11]

The fact that as early as 1969 U.S. President Richard Nixon declared a "war on drugs" demonstrates the longstanding public health and law enforcement concerns about illegal drug use in the United States and some recognition of its consequences for individuals and their families and communities, regardless of the type of substance. But more than a human security, public health, or law enforcement concern, the several cases we discuss below demonstrate how transnational drug trafficking may translate into perceived national security threats. Colombia, Mexico-Central America, and Afghanistan all illustrate various aspects of national security concerns beyond the obvious human security costs of loss of life or serious injuries and abuse.

The Latin American Region

The drug trade increasingly became seen as a *national security* threat by the United States with the rise of the powerful and violent Medellín and Cali cartels in Colombia in the 1980s and 1990s, and their near-monopoly on the cocaine trade. These groups—especially the Medellín cartel under the leadership of Pablo Escobar—posed serious threats to the stability and viability of the important South American country of Colombia as they used massive bribery of officials and routinely assassinated law enforcement and judicial officials who opposed them. The instability and violence from the drug trade were compounded by the existing legacy of violence in Colombia, exemplified by a period of virtual civil war in the 1940s-1950s known as *la violencia*. The Marxist-fueled insurgency that originated in the 1960s, represented most prominently by the "Revolutionary Armed Forces of Colombia" (FARC), added to the violence, as did opposing paramilitary groups on the right. And even when the Colombian government had effectively decimated the Medellín and Cali cartels with U.S. help, the FARC and other armed groups became involved in the drug trade as a way to support their struggle against the Colombian government.

Regardless of whether the insurgent groups' primary motive was not self-enrichment, unlike the cartels, the results were often the same for ordinary Colombians caught up in the unending conflict. Estimates are that insurgents, government forces, paramilitary forces, and drug trafficking forces have killed some 220,000 Colombians in the last sixty years, in addition to millions of people being displaced in areas of conflict. Colombia illustrates the truth of analysis by UNODC: that the immense profits from illicit activities such as the drug trade "have played a role in complicating and extending armed conflict, often increasing their overall lethality."[12]

Even without internal armed conflict, a state that cannot effectively control all its territory, has weak institutions, ineffective rule of law, and inequitable development is prime territory for organized criminal groups to operate, commit violence, and to corrupt governmental and financial institutions. While it might not be surprising to find that this description applies to many of the small, weak countries in Central America and the Caribbean, it also applies in good measure to the larger and more developed country of Mexico, with its population of 125 million people. Mexico has become a particular source of concern for the U.S. government as Mexican drug trafficking organizations (DTOs) have multiplied and become more powerful, and are now the major wholesalers of drugs in the United States; plus they are increasingly involved in retail distribution of the drugs in alliance with U.S. gangs (see Image 4.1).[13] In large part their growth has coincided with the weakening of the Colombian drug cartels. This point highlights a well-known, unfortunate trend with drug trafficking that is often referred to as the "balloon effect," whereby interdicting drug cultivation and smuggling routes in one area causes the trade to relocate, or "balloon" into another region or country. Similarly, some analysts believe that successful interdiction efforts against the drug trade and better border security may be part of the reason that Mexican drug trafficking organizations have evolved into "poly-criminal organizations" that are involved in more varied types of criminal activities.[14]

In the very visible and violent drug war being waged between the Mexican government and the DTOs since 2006 under then newly elected President Felipe Calderón, well over 100,000 persons are believed to have died, including many civilians. Although it is unknown how many were specifically linked to the drug trade, reputable studies have estimated that organized crime groups carry out one-third to one-half of the homicides, along

Image 4.1 U.S. Coast Guard Member Offloads Cocaine Interdicted in 2017 in Florida. Photo: U.S. SOUTHCOM, Petty Officer 1st Class Michael De Nyse[15]

with many instances of kidnapping and extortion.[16] Some of these killings reflect intra-gang competition and warfare; other killings have been carried out by vigilante groups fighting drug traffickers in more remote areas of Mexico. Of particular concern in terms of human security is the fact that increasingly DTOs have been targeting government and law enforcement officials, journalists, students, and others within civil society.[17]

Equally disconcerting are numerous cases where governmental security forces have been suspected of extrajudicial killings of civilians (along with torture and other abuses) in the course of battling organized crime. As with the Colombian government, the Mexican government has a long record of violating the physical security needs of its citizens, first through omission—not protecting civilians from the widespread criminal violence associated with drug trafficking (and related crimes such as human trafficking and arms trafficking). Second, the Mexican government is criticized for commission—not controlling governmental security forces that abuse and kill civilians, and not ensuring honest and effective governmental institutions to prosecute the guilty and protect citizens' rights. Consider that U.S. government studies have found that "Violence and criminality have overwhelmed Mexico's law enforcement and judicial institutions, with record numbers of arrests rarely resulting in successful convictions. With impunity rates averaging 78.6% nationally for homicide and even higher for other crimes."[18] Incredibly, this means that nearly 80 percent of homicides and many other types of criminal activity go unpunished.

Almost all countries perceive their national security interests to require stable and friendly neighbors in their region, so it is not surprising that the United States is concerned about its nearly 2,000-mile long border with Mexico and the effectiveness of governance within that country (and within Colombia for the reasons explained above). The realization that the problem of criminal violence was not just a Mexican one but was also of more personal concern to many U.S. citizens became glaringly apparent by at least 2009, as the media publicized the upsurge in criminal violence in Mexico. In fact, a Gallup poll in the spring of 2009 indicated that not only were 51 percent of Americans "very concerned" about drug violence in Mexico (with 28 percent being "somewhat concerned"), but also that the violence in Mexico was rated on a par with concerns over the international threat of North Korean nuclear capabilities, and only a few points below Iran's nuclear capabilities and international terrorism. The U.S. State Department began issuing travel advisories against Americans visiting the border regions of Mexico, and in 2017–2018 advisories were still being routinely issued for certain parts of Mexico because of the threat of criminal organizations in those areas. While not deliberately targeted by these groups, U.S. citizens have been the victims of homicide, kidnapping, carjacking, and robbery within Mexico.[19]

U.S. national security concerns about Mexican criminal violence only increased as larger numbers of Mexican immigrants fled to the United States, specifically to escape that criminal violence. The U.S. government also became more concerned that potential terrorists might be infiltrating with Mexican immigrants. But the true extent of the issue of regional criminal violence became indisputable in 2015–2016 when over 180,000 children (and some families) primarily from El Salvador, Honduras, and Guatemala were apprehended at the U.S.–Mexico border. Although the lack of economic opportunity at home has motivated some of these Central American youth, it is the pervasive crime and violence within their communities that fuels the insecurity and their justification for claiming asylum and refugee status. The record is staggering. As the respected nongovernmental Washington Office on Latin America (WOLA) has documented with reference to El Salvador, in 2015 the murder rate in that small country of some 6 million people reached a level not seen since the country's decade-long civil war ended in 1992, with over 5,000 murders. But, similarly to Mexico, the "impunity rate" (lack of accountability) for homicides in all three Central American countries was estimated to be an astounding 95 percent!

According to WOLA, drug smuggling operations tied to transnational crime cartels contribute to the violence and insecurity, as do local street gangs or *maras* that "impact every aspect of life in the neighborhoods and communities they control."[20] Probably most well known among these gangs is Mara Salvatrucha ("MS-13"), which also has a strong presence in U.S. cities. A 2016 analysis by well-known crime expert Douglas Farah finds that it is the growing involvement of Central American gangs like MS-13 (with "tens of thousands of members") in the global cocaine trade, and the huge revenues that have been generated for these gangs, that has propelled increases in crime, allowed them to control territory and communities and to take on the trappings of almost nonexistent or ineffective governmental institutions.[21]

What might be of particular concern in terms of national security for the United States and other regional countries is Farah's reporting that MS-13 was found to have literature related to radical Islamic terrorist group tactics. While he does not claim that there are linkages between these groups and terrorist organizations (although some evidence has been found of linkages between criminal gangs and terrorist organizations within certain areas of Africa), Farah does point to some similarities between MS-13 and Islamic State (ISIS) behavior, in terms of recruiting young men with few opportunities, socializing them into violence, and reinforcing the belief that their existing, weak, and corrupted country and government has little to offer them, and is powerless to stop their activities.

We highlight this point because it bears on the critical question of what policies might effectively address transnational crime, particularly the drug trafficking issue, and protect individuals' physical security. It is true that a stable, wealthy, and functioning government and society like the United States has the capacity to confront these types of challenges and to control their most pernicious effects on civilians, so that transnational crime is generally considered to be a *law enforcement* issue. Yet equally true is that even with all of its resources, the United States has been unable to control illegal drug consumption, stop criminal organizations from operating domestically, or prevent transnational crime across U.S. borders. It should not be surprising, then, that the still-developing countries of Colombia and Mexico have been experiencing even more severe problems—not to mention the very poor Central American countries. Organized and wealthy criminal networks may easily overwhelm fragile governments and threaten civic security in entire regions, making it a true national security threat for these countries. In recognition of this, and in support of its own interests, the United States has developed bilateral assistance programs for Colombia (Plan Colombia, beginning in 2000, now transitioned to Peace Colombia), Mexico (the Mérida Initiative, first implemented in 2008), and Central America as a whole (the Central American Regional Security Initiative, in 2010).

The initial focus and funding of U.S. programs was to strengthen each country's security forces' capabilities to defeat major criminal organizations (and in Colombia to also defeat insurgency forces) with equipment, technical assistance, and training. In this regard Colombia has made progress in both weakening the large, hierarchical criminal trafficking networks and in establishing a peace process with demobilized FARC and other insurgent elements; meanwhile Mexico has successfully targeted many major drug figures, which has reduced criminal violence in some areas. But prominent Latin American expert Bruce Bagley argues that this has led to many decentralized, dispersed criminal networks that are actually more difficult for security forces to target and attack, even if they pose a lesser threat to the overall survival of the Colombian or Mexican state. The "cockroach effect," meaning "the displacement of criminal networks from one city/state/region to another within a given country or from one country to another in search of safer havens and more pliable state authorities," is clearly evident when considering the movement of Mexican drug gangs into Guatemala and Honduras—a trend that has only increased violence and instability in these already weakly governed, struggling countries.[22] As Human Rights Watch noted with regard to Honduras in 2017: "Rampant crime and impunity for human rights abuses remain the norm in Honduras . . . Efforts to reform the institutions responsible for providing public security have made little progress. Marred by corruption and abuse, the judiciary and police remain largely ineffective."[23]

The evidence from these assistance programs demonstrates that while it is critical to have capable security forces, without effective and accountable governmental institutions ordinary citizens cannot be—and will not be—protected from criminal organizations and their associated violence. It is equally important that citizens actually trust their governmental institutions and believe that the government can protect them if criminal gangs are not able to recruit new members or to receive at least tacit community support. At least some analysts contend that with regard to Mexico, "the most important tools for managing the problem include long-term institutional reform to replace a culture of illegality and corruption with one of rule of law and respect for lawful authority."[24] U.S. assistance programs have shown more recognition of this point with increased funding devoted to building the rule of law, as with the Mérida Initiative shifting from its main focus of strengthening security forces to encompass institution building and justice sector reform, economic development, community-based social programs, and even attempts to uncover "the root causes of violence."[25]

As emphasized throughout this text, we contend that the root causes of violence lie in the failure to meet even basic human security needs. There are numerous historical, cultural, and economic reasons why this might occur, but below we consider the major problem of corruption, defined simply as "the abuse of entrusted power for private gain."[26] It is the enormous profits available in transnational drug trafficking and related criminal activity that have enabled levels of corruption within weak states today that make it extremely difficult for governmental reform efforts that would improve citizens' civic security, regardless of which region of the world we assess, to succeed. (See Box 4.1 to consider arguments for decriminalizing individual use of drugs in order to greatly reduce transnational criminal violence and strengthen weak states.)

❖ BOX 4.1 THINK AGAIN: DRUG USE SHOULD BE DECRIMINALIZED

When it comes to illicit drugs, most countries have vacillated between the poles of being "tough on crime" with little sympathy for drug users versus distinguishing between drug users and drug traffickers, and offering rehabilitation programs to the former. Lately the picture has been clouded even further by the move to legalize or at least decriminalize individual use of cannabis (marijuana). At the time of writing, a growing number of countries and states in the United States had legalized the use of recreational cannabis, and others had decriminalized possessing small amounts of marijuana (still others allow for medical marijuana usage). While many argue in favor of legalizing the use of some drugs based upon individual rights and public health, our concern here is with arguments that support legalizing drugs based upon the belief that this would reduce transnational crime, violence, and corruption, and better protect human security interests.

Latin Americans have long contended, with good reason, that it is the U.S. demand for illicit drugs such as cannabis, cocaine, and heroin that has fueled the drug trade with its large-scale criminal violence and corruption in their societies. Noted security expert Bruce Bagley is sympathetic to this argument, criticizing the U.S. government and the

United Nations' unquestioned backing for the "war on drugs" regardless of the harmful consequences. Bagley observes that this war has not only failed but has actually been "counterproductive" for both the United States and Latin American countries as it has not reduced demand for drugs; rather, it has magnified crime and violence throughout the region while empowering and enriching criminal organizations, and it has further weakened and corrupted already fragile state institutions. Bagley documents how the war has been especially "high in both blood and treasure" for Colombia and Mexico.[1]

The Global Commission on Drug Policy conducts perhaps the most authoritative campaign being waged to legalize personal drug use, producing "technical and political reports to ground evidence-based policy recommendations." The organization's commissioners represent an extremely prominent group of world leaders and experts in drug policy, to include five past presidents of major Latin American countries from Brazil to Colombia to Chile to Mexico (among U.S. commissioners is George Schultz, former Secretary of State). The organization's 2016 report, "Advancing Drug Policy Reform: A New Approach to Decriminalization," advocates ending all penalties for individual drug use and focusing on drug policies "with a greater emphasis on justice, dignity, and human rights [and] the implementation of alternatives to punishment for all low-level, non-violent actors in the drug trade." They believe prohibition has failed and that market regulation of drugs should be considered as the next logical step.[2]

As former UN Secretary-General, Nobel Peace Prize-winner, and Commissioner Kofi Annan points out, drug use does represent a health risk, and thus should be regulated. Annan compares this type of policy to the successful regulation of addictive tobacco, which, along with education and a public health campaign, has reduced smoking in many countries.[3] It is worth noting that in Portugal individual drug use is treated as a disease, not a crime. The country decriminalized all drug use in 2001, in conjunction with a major public health campaign. By 2017 Portugal's drug mortality rate was the lowest in Western Europe, and it had an estimated 25,000 users of heroin, down from 100,000 users prior to decriminalization and the public health focus.[4]

1 Bruce Bagley, "Drug-Trafficking and Organized Crime in the Americas: Major Trends in the 21st Century," Woodrow Wilson Center Update on the Americas, August 2012, 13–14. At: www.wilsoncenter.org/sites/default/files/BB%20Final.pdf.
2 Global Commission on Drug Policy, "Advancing Drug Policy Reform: A New Approach to Decriminalization," 2016. At: www.globalcommissionondrugs.org/reports/advancing-drug-policy-reform/.
3 Kofi Annan, "Lift the Ban! Kofi Annan on Why It's Time to Legalize Drugs," *Spiegel Online*, February 22, 2016. At: www.spiegel.de/international/world/kofi-annan-on-why-drug-bans-are-ineffective-a-1078402.html.
4 Nicholas Kristof, "How to Win a War on Drugs: Portugal Treats Addiction as a Disease, Not a Crime," *New York Times*, September 22, 2017. At: www.nytimes.com/2017/09/22/opinion/sunday/portugal-drug-decriminalization.html?emc=edit_nk_20170922&nl=nickkristof&nlid=67183949&te=1.

Corruption

As the United Nations has recognized, "corruption is a complex social, political and economic phenomenon that affects all countries. Corruption undermines democratic institutions, slows economic development and contributes to governmental instability." In 2005 the United Nations Convention against Corruption came into force—"the only legally binding universal anti-corruption instrument"—and almost all UN member states are signatories.[27] While any level of corruption is unacceptable, we are not concerned here with localized instances of graft or bribery, or conflicts of interest, which exist even in established democracies like the United States. What we are concerned with is corruption on a scale that is entrenched and pervasive throughout a country's public sector—to include the judiciary and law enforcement—and within the business community, so that citizens are routinely denied government services, accountability, and opportunity. Stable economic growth benefiting the majority of citizens is stunted. In the worst cases citizens cannot receive justice against criminals or state agents as impunity predominates—and citizens may even face extrajudicial execution, as noted with certain Latin American countries.

The respected independent global organization Transparency International (TI) publishes the widely cited "Corruption Perceptions Index" (CPI) annually to provide assessments of state corruption. According to Transparency International, for 2016 "the global average score is a paltry 43, indicating endemic corruption in a country's public sector." All of the Latin American countries assessed above score below this average, with Colombia being the "least worst" of the group with a score of 37 (and ranking 90 out of 176 countries in total); and Guatemala being the absolute worst with a score of 28 and ranking 136 (Mexico did scarcely better with a score of 30 and ranking 123).[28] Yet the Latin American region is not the most corrupt in the world.

Table 4.1 lists the states perceived to be the most corrupt in the world in the public sector. It should come as no surprise that fourteen of the twenty most highly corrupt states depicted in this index are also on the list of the top twenty most at-risk states in 2016 (see Table 3.2). Where corruption is at such extreme levels state institutions are essentially a mere facade, being tightly controlled by authoritarian leaders (such as in North Korea, Sudan), barely functioning due to civil war (Syria, South Sudan, Yemen), or hollow shells run by powerful figures to enrich themselves and their small group of supporters (Afghanistan, Angola).

It is useful to highlight the case of Afghanistan, which still ranks as a major national security concern for the United States and other countries, features a very dismal human security profile, and shares some important and unfortunate characteristics with the Latin American countries assessed in this chapter. Afghanistan was ranked as the eighth most corrupt country in 2016 by Transparency International, and has been singled out for its prevalent, pervasive corruption by the U.S. government itself. At the same time, Afghanistan

Table 4.1 States Perceived as Most Highly Corrupt

1. Somalia*	11. Iraq*
2. South Sudan*	12. Eritrea*
3. North Korea*	13. Angola*
4. Syria*	14. Republic of Congo
5. Yemen*	15. Haiti*
6. Sudan*	16. Chad
7. Libya*	17. Central African Republic
8. Afghanistan*	18. Burundi*
9. Guinea-Bissau*	19. Uzbekistan*
10. Venezuela*	20. Democratic Republic of Congo

Source: Adapted from Transparency International, "Corruption Perceptions Index 2015" and "Corruption Perceptions Index 2016," licensed under CC BY 4.0 DE. For more information, visit www.transparency.org.

Note: *State was in top 20 most corrupt for 2015.

is also assessed to be one of the fragile states most at risk of failure (see Table 3.2). Additionally, the country is a major actor in the world drug trade, "accounting for some 70 per cent (3,300 tons) of global opium production"; and "the total value of the [Afghan] illicit opiate economy was $2.8 billion in 2014—equivalent to 13 per cent of the country's gross domestic product."[29] Other UNODC studies devoted to Afghanistan have documented the individual human security costs of opium, with one of the highest opiate addiction rates in the world, and estimating that "almost 10 percent of Afghans aged between 15 and 64 were drug users."[30]

This disastrous situation is not surprising considering the cash that farmers may obtain from growing opium poppies with few other viable alternatives; the lack of governmental control or real security in much of the country; and the large-scale presence of not only drug traffickers but also anti-government and insurgent or terrorist groups (the Taliban and al Qaeda factions such as the Haqqani network). Unsurprisingly, insurgent groups may garner significant revenue by taxing drug-related operations in areas they control, as occurred with insurgent groups and the cocaine traffickers in Colombia. The U.S. government's own 2017 International Narcotics Control Strategy found with reference to Afghanistan: "A symbiotic relationship exists between the insurgency and narcotics trafficking. Traffickers provide weapons, funding, and material support to the insurgency in exchange for protection. Some insurgent commanders traffic drugs to finance operations . . . the narcotics trade undermines governance and rule of law throughout Afghanistan."[31]

Image 4.2 Women Serving in the Afghan National Police. Photo: U.S. DOD, Lt. Charity Edgar[32]

These issues all persist despite the fact that by 2016 Afghanistan had received over 100 billion dollars in aid from the United States since 2002—with well over $4 billion planned for 2017 (as a point of comparison, close U.S. ally Israel ranked second after Afghanistan for receiving the most U.S. foreign aid). The majority of this aid has continued to go to build Afghanistan's security forces, and for counternarcotics efforts (see Image 4.2 illustrating the inclusion of women in the Afghan security forces). Almost a quarter of the aid has been dedicated to improving Afghan governmental agencies and their capacity to function and provide services, the development of key infrastructure and public institutions such as schools and hospitals, and to develop the agricultural sector.[33] It is actually more accurate to say *redevelop* the agricultural sector because agriculture had been the mainstay of the Afghan economy, and the country's fruit and nut crops had a worldwide reputation before the country entered into near-continuous civil war and foreign occupation (the disastrous Soviet intervention of the 1980s).

Many other countries, especially within much of Africa and the Middle East, share the multifaceted security issues Afghanistan confronts. Note that African states and several Middle Eastern states predominate in the top twenty states most at risk of failing (see Table 3.2), and are also the states perceived as most highly corrupt (see Table 4.1). Additionally, in a 2016 assessment, the UNODC commented that while Africa traditionally had served as a transit region for drugs moving into Europe:

> drug trafficking and organized crime increasingly pose a multifaceted challenge to health, the rule of law and development within the continent itself . . . drug traffickers, insurgent groups and terrorists all thrive in parts of Africa where there is minimal legitimate government authority, which in turn poses a wider threat to security and development across the continent.[34]

This assessment highlights a theme that has been both implicit and explicit here in considering the magnitude of transnational criminal violence—particularly associated with the drug trade—and the corruption it fuels. That theme is the absolutely critical role that good governance and effective rule of law plays in defeating, or at least controlling, these challenges so that citizens' lives are respected. As the 1994 UNDP report noted with regard to the concept of political security, "One of the most important aspects of human security is that people should be able to live in a society that honours their basic human rights." Respect for basic human rights, in turn, is only possible in a country possessing good governance and effective rule of law.

The Challenge of Good Governance and the Rule of Law

Two independent, interdisciplinary organizations—the Mo Ibrahim Foundation and the World Justice Project (WJP)—are engaged in some of the most useful and comprehensive analysis in this area. While the Mo Ibrahim Foundation focuses on Africa, its definition of governance is widely applicable: "the provision of the political, social and economic goods that a citizen has the right to expect from his or her state, and that a state has the responsibility to deliver to its citizens." The foundation relates this definition to four conceptual categories—safety and rule of law, participation and human rights, sustainable economic opportunity, and human development.[35]

The World Justice Project takes a somewhat different approach in singling out the rule of law as the essential quality of (good) governance, relying on "two main ideas pertaining to the relationship between the state and the governed":

> first, that the law imposes limits on the exercise of power by the state and its agents, as well as individuals and private entities . . . Second, that the state limits the actions of members of society and fulfills its basic duties towards its population, so that the public interest is served, people are protected from violence and members of society have access to mechanisms to settle disputes and redress grievances.

(Note that these ideas effectively capture the concept of civic security.) The project further relies on what it views as four universal principles of accountability—just laws, open government, and accessible and impartial dispute resolution.[36]

This emphasis on open, accountable government that protects the rights of its citizens, encourages civic participation, and provides impartial justice is shared in both definitions. The fact that the Mo Ibrahim Foundation also considers sustainable economic development and opportunity to be central to governing responsibilities is not surprising in view of its African lens, as achieving sustainable development in African countries has long been integral for progress there, and governments are central to that process (as the next chapter on economic security examines).

These two groups provide annual indices examining and ranking good governance and the rule of law in countries based upon data, expert opinions, and surveys of citizens and certain groups, similarly to Transparency International and its CPI. It is worth observing here that even though the earlier part of this chapter could be interpreted as a negative view of globalization in terms of how it has enabled transnational criminals, drug trafficking, money laundering, and corruption, without the informational and technological advantages provided by globalization these nongovernmental groups would be very hampered in their ability to gather information, network, and publicize their extremely important findings about governments.

The Mo Ibrahim Foundation has been publishing and refining the annual "Ibrahim Index of African Governance" (IIAG) since 2007, and the World Justice Project has published its "Rule of Law Index" since 2008. The IIAG considers over 90 indicators in its assessment of governance of 54 African countries, ranking each indicator separately.

Table 4.2 African States Ranked as Most Poorly Governed

1. Somalia	11. Guinea-Bissau
2. South Sudan	12. Burundi
3. Central African Republic	13. Congo
4. Libya	14. Guinea
5. Eritrea	15. Mauritania
6. Sudan	16. Zimbabwe
7. Chad	17. Cameroon
8. Equatorial Guinea	18. Nigeria
9. Democratic Republic of Congo	19. Djibouti
10. Angola	20. Gambia

Source: Mo Ibrahim Foundation, *A Decade of African Governance 2006–2015*, 2016 Ibrahim Index of African Governance, Index Report, available at http://mo.ibrahim.foundation/.

Table 4.2 depicts the African states ranked as most poorly governed in 2015. Twelve of these states also appear in Table 4.1 (which lists the most highly corrupt states) and twelve of them (the large majority the same states) appear in Table 3.2, which lists the states most at risk of failing. These findings should not be surprising as there is increasingly widespread agreement on what is essential to good governance and which countries are the most deficient. On the other hand, it is important to keep in mind that the Mo Ibrahim Foundation considers governmental policies on development and opportunity to be an essential part of good governance, so some African states may rank higher on their overall score than one might otherwise expect if they are considered to be performing well on development indicators.[37]

The World Justice Project's Rule of Law Index for 2016 assesses eight factors: "constraints on government powers, absence of corruption, open government, fundamental rights, order and security, regulatory enforcement, civil justice, and criminal justice." It evaluates 113 countries at this point, and most African countries are not assessed; nor are countries that are experiencing armed conflict—such as Syria, Yemen, and South Sudan—or have few governmental institutions, such as Somalia and Libya. But countries that are assessed as having very weak rule of law do show up as being among the most corrupt (Afghanistan, Venezuela, Uzbekistan) and as states at most risk of failing (Afghanistan, Pakistan, Kenya, Nigeria, Zimbabwe). Afghanistan is actually ranked 111 in the Rule of Law Index (coming in last is Venezuela at 113), in large part due to the presence of corruption. Finally, in view of their own problems with corruption, along with transnational crime, violence, and impunity, it should not be surprising to find that the Latin American countries examined above do not rank very well in the Rule of Law Index. Colombia is the "best," ranked at 71 out of 113 countries, followed by El Salvador at 75, Mexico at 88, Guatemala at 97, and Honduras at 102.[38]

Democracy and the "Arab Spring"

We have consciously focused on good governance and the rule of law as being foundational to human security interests rather than the concept of "democracy." Doubtless these characteristics should normally coincide, as citizens and policymakers of established liberal democracies would believe. However, the term democracy is problematic and easily abused, going back to at least the Cold War era when authoritarian states on both the left and the right would hold very circumscribed elections in order to claim they were democracies (for example, North Korea's official name is the Democratic People's Republic of Korea). Furthermore, noted scholar Paul Collier has convincingly argued in *War, Guns, and Votes: Democracy in Dangerous Places* that the superficial-type elections now held by many of the poorest states have "'increased political violence instead of reducing it.' Without rules, traditions, and checks and balances to protect minorities, distribute resources fairly, and subject officials to the law, these governments lack the accountability and legitimacy to discourage rebellion." Furthermore, Collier demonstrates that when elections are fraudulently won, these democracies-in-name-only promote bad governance because the types of policies required for these leaders to remain in power and reward their followers—e.g., corrupt practices—are not the same ones that would lead to good governance. Larry Diamond, a renowned scholar of democracy, terms these electoral democracies "predatory states," which epitomize bad governance, as in these states a government's purpose is not to provide public goods for its citizens but to enrich the ruling officials and their cronies with the wealth of the nation.[39]

We believe it is important to make these points about democracy and good governance because perceptions are critical when assessing what are arguably important turning points in advancing human security interests. An important question in that regard is whether, and how much, the political and social protests and ensuing reforms made in numerous Arab states beginning in 2011 may have improved their citizens' civic security needs. That is a different question than asking whether these states are democracies. In fact, Samuel Huntington argued in 1993 that because of increased levels of economic and social development, "some openings in Arab political systems have already occurred. The principal beneficiaries of these openings have been Islamist movements. In the Arab world, in short, Western democracy strengthens anti-Western political forces."[40] Whether or not Huntington's argument was valid in the 1990s, or even today, it has continued to be used to justify authoritarian rule rather than risk the supposed (Islamist) extremists that would take over. We contend that regardless of what type of political system emerges, it is good governance and the rule of law that is the key for furthering Arab citizens' human security interests, as in any other region of the world. Furthermore, it has been because of failures in governance that these societies have continued to undergo such turmoil.

The events commonly known in the Western world as "the Arab Spring" (or "Jasmine Revolution")—but within Tunisia as the "Dignity Revolution," a revealing term—began with just one poor Tunisian vendor. After refusing to pay the normal bribe to local officials and being denied justice by government offices, Mohamed Bouazizi set himself on fire as a protest on December 17, 2010 and died a few days later. In the past this may have received little attention elsewhere, but the globalization-enhanced power of the Internet and social media soon made it a national cause in Tunisia, and within a month of swelling protests (see Image 4.3 illustrating a typical protest) the nearly twenty-five-year reign of corrupt and authoritarian leader Ben Ali was over as he fled office. The Tunisian model spread with amazing speed in 2011 throughout most Arab states ranging from Egypt to Jordan to Yemen to Syria to Libya, with citizens demanding reforms and opportunity long denied from their authoritarian governments. Respected journalist Robin Wright argues that while no one could have foreseen the speed with which the primarily peaceful and secular uprisings occurred, challenges to the old order were "inevitable," attributing the rebellions to "a confluence of at least four factors: education, raised expectations, demographics, and communication technology." The majority youth population in all these countries had some degree of education and literacy, and many had access to the Internet and social media, but lacked economic opportunity or meaningful political participation. Wright quotes one young Egyptian actor: "People are asking that the state be in their service . . . and that the state not be allowed to terrorize them."[41] In other words, the people were demanding good governance.

Unfortunately, as this text was being finalized, the Arab reform movements had achieved a very mixed record of success in terms of achieving good governance and, more importantly, in sustaining reforms. The most promising case remains Tunisia, which has an elected unity government and has minimized violence as it attempts to use consensus to decide difficult political, economic, and social issues. For example, the original issue of governmental corruption that sparked the immolation of Mohamed Bouazizi cannot be fixed quickly or easily, even though one expert views it as the leading threat to the new democracy. In 2017 the government had launched "a total war against corruption," and for 2016 Transparency International did note some slight improvements with anti-corruption steps taken, but Tunisia's score barely changed from earlier years. The Ibrahim Index did acknowledge positive advances in governance in Tunisia since 2010, ranking the country 7th out of 54 African nations, while the World Justice Project ranked Tunisia at number 58 in the world (the lower the number, the better the rule of law). Human Rights Watch also commented favorably on

Image 4.3 Tunisia Unrest, January 14, 2011. Photo: Voice of America (VOA)[42]

the improvements on human rights protection that were being implemented, in spite of continuing, serious human rights violations.[43]

On the other side of the spectrum, Egypt quickly reverted to authoritarian rule after a short period of uncertainty and democratic rule (June 2012–July 2013) under elected Muslim Brotherhood leader Mohamed Morsi, who was soon deposed in a military coup. Morsi remains imprisoned, although his initial death sentence was overturned by an Egyptian court and he was ordered to be retried for those charges. While President Abdel Fattah el-Sisi was elected to that office in 2014, it must be noted that it was General (Field Marshall) Sisi who removed Morsi as president and then ran for office himself. Although Sisi was democratically elected, this was after much of the opposition had been imprisoned or killed—among them the Muslim Brotherhood—and under his rule the military has virtually unchecked powers. This recalls our point above about the problematic nature of associating elections with democratic, or good, governance. The Human Rights Watch report on Egypt for 2016 is extremely critical for almost all areas of Egyptian governance, ranging from banning public criticism of the government and public protest, to the regular use of torture by security forces and enforced disappearances. The World Justice Project ranked Egypt 110th in the world out of the 113 countries ranked; the Ibrahim Index ranked Egypt 24th out of the 54 African states. This latter ranking might seem surprisingly good, but recall that the Ibrahim Foundation also considers human and economic development indicators in its assessment (in which it saw progress in Egypt), and unfortunately there are numerous other, very poorly governed states in Africa.[44]

In the wake of the Arab reform movements the most tragic cases for all aspects of human security are undoubtedly Syria and Yemen, which remain mired in civil wars—abetted by outside powers and extremist groups. In a previous chapter we discussed the startling loss of life and dire humanitarian situation in much of Syria, and Human Rights Watch's assessment of the Syrian government's illegal and inhumane actions against its own citizens in 2016 (which continue unabated) reinforces the importance of civic security for all human beings. The Yemeni government's actions and treatment of the civilian population are also assessed very negatively by Human Rights Watch, as are the actions of various warring factions in the country and extremist groups linked to al Qaeda and ISIS (although with a population of some 27 million—about 10 million more than Syria—far fewer Yemenis have been killed or abused relative to Syria).[45]

What these examples from the Arab uprisings and their aftermath demonstrate is the extreme difficulty of moving toward good governance where a legacy of authoritarian, often military-dominated, governance exists, usually strengthened by corrupt practices within the public and business sectors. Yet, as these protests also illustrate, the abuses of authoritarian rule and personal enrichment at the expense of the public are increasingly difficult to hide in the information age. Dedicated individuals and groups arising out of civil society have been willing and able to network both locally and globally to expose abuses, protest, and demand citizens' rights, all enabled by technology. This is true whether we consider the actions of just one individual like Egyptian Wael Ghonim, the creator of a "We Are All Kahled Said" Facebook page to commemorate a young Egyptian whom authorities had beaten to death in 2010; the page gained more than 350,000 followers in just a few months and Ghonim was able to inspire tens of thousands to agree to show up to protest.[46] This is true when we consider the multiplication of truly global, independent groups of experts and citizens like Transparency International, the Global Justice Project, the Mo Ibrahim Foundation, and Human Rights Watch—who network with local and intergovernmental groups and cooperate to document and assess government actions while insisting on better governance.

Conclusion

Civic security is a multifaceted concept that has both negative and positive aspects. On the one hand, governments are supposed to protect their citizens from violent criminals and other extremist groups, whether domestic or transnational, and to provide justice where feasible. At the same time the government itself cannot be the abuser of a citizen's right to life and to meaningful participation in their community. Furthermore, public officials have a positive duty to protect exercise of those rights and participation in the political process—without expecting to be enriched in the process.

In some ways this chapter could lead well-meaning individuals to be inclined to throw up their hands and conclude that the prevalence of transnational crime and accompanying violence—especially when fueled by illicit drugs and corruption—is simply too enormous to surmount, particularly for governments that do not have the resources or capabilities to be effective. Yet progress is possible. It is worth acknowledging the slow progress that Colombia (and within Mexico, to a more limited extent) is making toward peace and improved governance after decades of criminal and insurgent violence. While clearly it took governmental commitment to make this happen, it would not have been possible without the equally important role played by individual Colombian citizens and nongovernmental groups, often in conjunction with concerned outside groups and countries. The informational advances of globalization have enhanced this type of coordinated effort.

The ability to connect even economically disadvantaged people in society was also crucial to the Arab protest movement, and for the model to spread so quickly within the region. And, as noted above, the fact that a significant part of society in key Arab countries is now educated, including to university level, has also added to the willingness and ability to engineer protests and demand reforms. This is an important ingredient that is missing from El Salvador, Honduras, and Guatemala; from the rural parts of Mexico where the drug trade and gangs often flourish; and from Afghanistan with its egregious record of misrule and corruption. Given the importance of economic development to complement reform efforts in the political and public sphere, we address this in the next chapter. As explored there, the issue of global poverty and rising inequality has serious implications for issues such as criminality, corruption, and societal unrest and conflict—and, ultimately, for the good governance essential to protecting human security needs.

Notes

1 World Justice Project, "About Us," at https://worldjusticeproject.org/.

2 International Security Studies Institute, "Armed Conflict Database," at https://acd.iiss.org/en; UN Office and Drugs and Crime, *Global Study on Homicide 2013: Trends, Contexts, Data* (Vienna: UNODC, 2013), at www.unodc.org/documents/gsh/pdfs/2014_GLOBAL_HOMICIDE_BOOK_web.pdf; and World Health Organization, "Injuries and Violence: The Facts" (Geneva: World Health Organization, 2010), at http://apps.who.int/iris/bitstream/10665/44288/1/9789241599375_eng.pdf.

3 UNDP, *Human Development Report, 1994*, 30–33. The practice of "disappearing" a perceived opponent to an authoritarian regime to increase uncertainty and anxiety in civil society became infamous in much of Latin America during the period of military dictatorships, which began in the 1960s, and in some cases lasted through the 1980s.

4 Note that at least some of these groups are seeking profits in order to fund an ethnic-based struggle for independence, such as the Wa and Kachin ethnic armies in Myanmar who cultivate and traffic opium for heroin. Others, such as the Taliban in Afghanistan, have become involved in opium poppies and heroin at least in part to fund their religiously based struggle against the government.

5 UNODC, "Transnational Organized Crime," at www.unodc.org/unodc/en/organized-crime/index.html.

6 Note that while arms trafficking (small arms and light weapons) is one of the less profitable transnational crimes, Global Financial Integrity emphasizes that "it is also one of the most consequential [i.e., deadly] for human security in developing countries. This market was worth US$1.7 billion to $3.5 billion in 2014, which represents 10 to 20 percent of the legal arms trade. Three main factors drive prices: an area's level of conflict, political unrest, and political tension; the distance over which the items are smuggled; and, the levels of enforcement traffickers must overcome." Channing May, *Transnational Crime and the Developing World* (Washington, DC: Global Financial Integrity, 2017), xi.

7 UNODC, "Legal Framework for Drug Trafficking," at www.unodc.org/unodc/en/drug-trafficking/legal-framework.html.

8 May, *Transnational Crime and the Developing World*, xi. GFI based its estimates upon a wide range of governmental, intergovernmental, and nongovernmental sources related to eleven types of transnational crime: drug trafficking; small arms and light weapons trafficking; human trafficking; organ trafficking; trafficking in cultural property; counterfeiting; illegal wildlife trade; illegal, unreported, and unregulated fishing (IUU); illegal logging; illegal mining; and crude oil theft.

9 June S. Beittel, "Mexico: Organized Crime and Drug Trafficking Organizations," Congressional Research Service (CRS) Report R41576, Washington, DC, April 25, 2017), 2. At: https://fas.org/sgp/crs/row/R41576.pdf.

10 UNODC, *World Drug Report 2016* (New York: United Nations, 2016), 1, ix. At: www.unodc.org/doc/wdr2016/WORLD_DRUG_REPORT_2016_web.pdf.

11 U.S. Department of State Bureau for International Narcotics and Law Enforcement Affairs (INL), *International Narcotics Control Strategy Report, Volume I: Drug and Chemical Control* (Washington, DC: INL, 2017), 18 (emphasis added). At: www.state.gov/documents/organization/268025.pdf.
12 UNODC, *World Drug Report 2016*, xix.
13 Beittel, "Mexico: Organized Crime and Drug Trafficking Organizations."
14 Claire Ribando Seelke and Kristin Finklea, "U.S.-Mexican Security Cooperation: The Mérida Initiative and Beyond," CRS Report R41349, Washington, DC, June 29, 2017), 14. At: https://fas.org/sgp/crs/row/R41349.pdf.
15 In the public domain. Full caption: "St. Petersburg—A crew member from Coast Guard Cutter Tarpon, an 87-foot Coast Patrol Boat homeported in St. Petersburg, Florida, and his crew offload 1,735 kilograms of cocaine, an estimated wholesale value of $56 million, Wednesday, May 3, 2017 at Coast Guard Sector St. Petersburg, Florida. At: www.southcom.mil/MEDIA/IMAGERY/igphoto/2001742050/.
16 Brianna Lee and Danielle Renwick, "Mexico's Drug War," Council on Foreign Relations, May 25, 2017. At: www.cfr.org/backgrounder/mexicos-drug-war. Justice in Mexico, *Drug Violence in Mexico: Data and Analysis through 2016* (San Diego, CA: Justice in Mexico, 2017). At: https://justiceinmexico.org/drug-violence-mexico-data-analysis-2016/. Justice in Mexico is a research and public policy program based at the University of San Diego.
17 Beittel, "Mexico: Organized Crime and Drug Trafficking Organizations," 2.
18 Ribando Seelke and Finklea, "U.S.-Mexican Security Cooperation," 15.
19 Gallup, "Most Americans Concerned about Mexico's Drug Violence," April 3, 2009. At: www.gallup.com/poll/117271/Americans-Concerned-Mexico-Drug-Violence.aspx; U.S. Department of State, "Mexico Travel Warning," August 22, 2017. At: https://travel.state.gov/content/passports/en/alertswarnings/mexico-travel-warning.html.
20 Adriana Beltrán, "Children and Families Fleeing Violence in Central America," *Beyond the Wall: Migration, Rights, and Border Security,* Washington Office on Latin America (WOLA) Report (Washington, DC: WOLA, 2017), 5–6. With an immensely larger population of some 320 million, according to FBI statistics the U.S. recorded some 15,000 homicides for 2015.
21 Douglas Farah, "Central America's Gangs Are All Grown Up," *Foreign Policy*, January 19, 2016. At: http://foreignpolicy.com/2016/01/19/central-americas-gangs-are-all-grown-up/.
22 Bruce Bagley, "Drug-Trafficking and Organized Crime in the Americas: Major Trends in the 21st Century," Woodrow Wilson Center Update on the Americas, August 2012. At: www.wilsoncenter.org/sites/default/files/BB%20Final.pdf.
23 Human Rights Watch, "Honduras: Events of 2016," in *World Report 2017*. At: www.hrw.org/world-report/2017/country-chapters/honduras.
24 Beittel, "Mexico: Organized Crime and Drug Trafficking Organizations," 28.
25 Ribando Seelke and Finklea, "U.S.-Mexican Security Cooperation," 10.
26 Transparency International, "What Is Corruption?" At: www.transparency.org/what-is-corruption/.
27 UNODC, "UNODC's Action against Corruption and Economic Crime" and "United Nations Convention against Corruption." At: www.unodc.org/unodc/en/corruption/uncac.html.
28 Transparency International, "Corruption Perceptions Index 2016," At: www.transparency.org/news/feature/corruption_perceptions_index_2016. Of interest, the United States had a score of 74 and was ranked 18, just below Austria and right above Ireland. The organization aggregates data from a number of reputable sources based upon the perceptions of country experts and business people about the level of corruption in the public sector within a particular country.
29 UNODC, *World Drug Report 2016*, 27, xx.
30 UNODC, *Impacts of Drug Use on Users and Their Families in Afghanistan* (Vienna: UNODC, 2014). At: www.unodc.org/documents/data-and-analysis/Studies/Impacts_Study_2014_web.pdf.
31 INL, *International Narcotics Control Strategy Report*, 90.
32 In the public domain. Full caption: "Women Serving in the Afghan National Police: Women serving in the Afghan National Police wait to be recognized during the Ministry of the Interior International Women's Day celebration in Kabul, Afghanistan, March 13, 2016. At: www.defense.gov/Photos/Photo-Gallery/igphoto/2001480937/.

33 U.S. Government Accountability Office, "Afghanistan: Oversight and Accountability of U.S. Assistance." GAO Highlights (GAO-14-680T), June 10, 2014. At: www.gao.gov/products/GAO-14-680T.
34 UNODC, *The Afghan Opiate Trade and Africa: A Baseline Assessment 2016* (Vienna: UNODC, 2016), 8. At: www.unodc.org/documents/data-and-analysis/Afghanistan/Afghan_Opiate_trade_Africa_2016_web.pdf.
35 Mo Ibrahim Foundation, "Ibrahim Index of African Governance (IIAG)." At: http://mo.ibrahim.foundation/iiag/.
36 World Justice Project, *World Justice Project Rule of Law Index 2016* (Washington, DC: World Justice Project, 2016), 9; and World Justice Project, "About Us" and "What Is the Rule of Law?" At: https://worldjusticeproject.org/.
37 Mo Ibrahim Foundation, *A Decade of African Governance, 2006–2015: Country Insights Collection* (London: Mo Ibrahim Foundation, 2017).
38 *World Justice Project Rule of Law Index 2016*, 4–5.
39 Kenneth Roth, "Ballots and Bullets," review of *War, Guns, and Votes: Democracy in Dangerous Places*, by Paul Collier, *New York Times*, March 22, 2009, at www.nytimes.com/2009/03/22/books/review/Roth-t.html; Larry Diamond, "The Democratic Rollback: The Resurgence of the Predatory State," *Foreign Affairs* vol. 87, no. 2 (2008): 42–43.
40 Samuel Huntington, "The Clash of Civilizations?" *Foreign Affairs* vol. 72, no. 3 (1993), 22–49.
41 Robin Wright, *Rock the Casbah: Rage and Rebellion across the Islamic World* (New York: Simon & Schuster, 2011), 26, 28.
42 In the public domain (Voice of America): "Protesters march on Avenue Habib Bourguiba in downtown Tunis, angry over unemployment, rising prices and corruption, 14 Jan 2011." At: https://commons.wikimedia.org/wiki/File:Tunisia_Unrest_-_VOA_-_Tunis_14_Jan_2011_(2).jpg.
43 Sarah Feuer, "Tunisia, a Success Story? The Troubles Rattling Its Still Fragile Democracy," *Foreign Affairs*, July 6, 2017. At: www.foreignaffairs.com/articles/tunisia/2017-07-06/tunisia-success-story; Transparency International, "Corruption Perceptions Index 2016"; Mo Ibrahim Foundation, *A Decade of African Governance*; *World Justice Project Rule of Law Index 2016;* Human Rights Watch, *World Report 2017.*
44 Human Rights Watch, *World Report 2017*; *World Justice Project Rule of Law Index 2016;* Mo Ibrahim Foundation, *A Decade of African Governance.*
45 Human Rights Watch, "Syria: Events of 2016," and "Yemen: Events of 2016," in *World Report 2017.* At: www.hrw.org/world-report/2017. The actions of external actors against the civilian population, such as Saudi Arabia, have also generated intense criticism.
46 Wright, *Rock the Casbah*, 34.

To Learn More

For an overview of the status of peace and conflict within the world, go to the annual "Global Peace Index" at http://visionofhumanity.org/#/page/indexes/global-peace-index.

The International Security Studies Institute is a highly reputable organization that produces both the annual "Armed Conflict Database" and the "Annual Military Balance," among other surveys and tools. Review their publications and datasets at www.iiss.org/en.

The United Nations Office on Drugs and Crime (UNODC) is the agency with responsibility for assisting member states in fighting crime, terrorism, and illicit drugs. Their website provides research, analysis, and data on related topics at www.unodc.org/unodc/en/about-unodc/index.html?ref=menutop.

To view specific threat assessments related to organized crime throughout the world, visit UNODC's "Transnational Organized Crime Threat Assessments" section at www.unodc.org/unodc/data-and-analysis/TOC-threat-assessments.html.

InSight Crime is a private foundation founded by two journalists; they describe themselves as "a foundation dedicated to the study of the principal threat to national and citizen security in Latin America and the Caribbean: organized crime." Visit their website at www.insightcrime.org to view sobering analysis and data about the magnitude and depth of crime in Latin America and the Caribbean.

Go to https://cpj.org/reports/ to explore the reports of the Committee to Protect Journalists (CPJ), which focuses on the problem of impunity with regard to investigating the murders of journalists around the world.

Examine the detailed methodology and sources that go into producing the annual Transparency International's Corruptions Perception Index, at www.transparency.org/.

The World Justice Project has been steadily increasing the number of countries that it is able to assess through its annual Rule of Law Index, at https://worldjusticeproject.org/.

Go to the Mo Ibrahim Foundation at http://mo.ibrahim.foundation/iiag/ to discover how exhaustively this group assesses over 90 indicators on each African country to arrive at a considered judgment on the quality of governance, a key issue in most of Africa.

The nongovernmental, independent Freedom House has been producing "Freedom in the World" since 1973—its annual assessment of political rights and civil liberties for each country and region of the world, at https://freedomhouse.org/report-types/freedom-world.

Visit the website of Justice in Mexico, a research and public policy program based at the University of San Diego, to download reports on the Mexican drug trade and its effects on Mexico, and to assess the professionalism and effectiveness of actors in the Mexican justice system, at https://justiceinmexico.org/.

In *Illicit: How Smugglers, Traffickers, and Copycats Are Hijacking the Global Economy* (New York: Anchor, 2006), Moisés Naím examines the negative effects of globalization that increasingly enable criminal actors to enrich themselves by breaking the rules and "all the procedures that nations employ to organize commerce, protect their citizens, raise revenues, and enforce moral codes."

For a disturbing chronicle of how globalization has contributed to the carnage of drug-related violence and murder—and the destruction of local government and law enforcement capabilities—read award-winning journalist Charles Bowden's *Murder City: Ciudad Juarez and the Global Economy's New Killing Fields* (New York: Nation Books, 2010).

Chapter 5

Economic Security

Chapter contents

Creating more opportunities in poor places also makes the world more peaceful . . . Our country's modest investment in the well-being of the poorest saves and improves lives, frees up vast amounts of human potential that's been locked away by disease and poverty, and helps prevent global crises before they happen. Generosity is one of our best exports. We are confident that Americans will want their government to continue making strategic investments in a safer, healthier, more prosperous world.

Bill and Melinda Gates, 2017[1]

Considering that Bill Gates is one of the co-founders of Microsoft and was instrumental in the personal computer (PC) revolution (which has made him one of the wealthiest people in the world), his contention that aiding economic growth and opportunity in poorer countries supports U.S. national interests merits serious consideration. In fact, Gates's thesis has been promoted internationally now for some decades, and especially within the United Nations system. Recall from Chapter 2 that the UN Charter proclaimed in 1945 that the organization was founded not only to "maintain international peace and security" but also "with a view to the creation of conditions of stability and well-being which are necessary for peaceful and friendly relations among nations . . . the United Nations shall promote . . . higher standards of living, full employment, and conditions of economic and social progress and development."[2]

The fact that the United Nations was founded with these dual concerns for peace and security, and economic and social development for all peoples, cannot be divorced from the context of the first half of the twentieth century which saw two world wars, worldwide economic depression, impoverishment of millions, and protectionist economic policies which were viewed as partly to blame for the wars. In fact, President Roosevelt's "Four Freedoms" speech in 1941 pointed out that "this is no time for any of us to stop thinking about the social and economic problems which are the root cause of the social revolution which is today a supreme factor in the world" (see Chapter 2). Roosevelt emphasized the importance of "freedom from want—which, translated into world terms, means economic understandings which will secure to every nation a healthy peacetime life for its inhabitants—everywhere in the world."[3]

The assumption of a reciprocal relationship between a peaceful world and a prosperous world was further advanced in the immediate aftermath of World War II. Influential statesmen such as George C. Marshall recognized that the U.S. example of a stable, free market democracy would be easier to emulate for those nations that were able to achieve a certain level of development, and thus were able to provide both peace and prosperity to their citizens.[4] Foreseeing the appeal that socialism and communism posed to the exhausted and desperate societies of war-devastated Europe after years of conflict, Marshall advocated an expansive foreign aid program in 1947 to help rebuild the continent and restore hope in democracy and capitalism. The resulting Marshall Plan is given much of the credit for enabling Western Europe to develop prosperous economies—aid under the plan would amount to more than $500 billion today as a percentage of U.S. national income, which compares to about $30 billion for international assistance in fiscal year 2015.[5] Only a few years after the Marshall Plan, the utility of international assistance as a specific tool to enhance U.S. national security became formalized when the Foreign Assistance Act became law in 1961, and the U.S. Agency for International Development (USAID) was created by executive order.

The larger international concern to accelerate economic and social development around the world soon found its most concrete expression in the United Nations Development Programme (UNDP), established in 1965. International consensus on the importance of economic growth and development to a stable international order are also represented by other UN bodies—such as the United Nations Conference on Trade and Development (UNCTAD)—and specialized and related UN agencies such as the World Bank, the International Monetary Fund (IMF), the International Labor Organization (ILO), and the World Trade Organization (WTO). Diverse regional intergovernmental bodies such as the Economic Commission for Africa (UNECA or ECA) and the African Development Bank are additional important actors in the shared objective of fostering growth and development. And, just as with other human security issue areas, there are many independent, nongovernmental bodies that have emerged that are crucial to providing assistance with better agricultural practices (e.g. Oxfam); microloans and financial services for the poor (e.g. FINCA); and better trading conditions and fair prices for small producers in developing countries (e.g. the Fairtrade Foundation).

This chapter explores the multifaceted issues involved in meeting the economic security needs of all human beings. The goal of attaining prosperity for all people has motivated diverse targeted programs for decades; but in practice it has been very difficult to achieve consensus on what actually works to bring people out of poverty and to provide them with a living wage and a decent lifestyle. While understandably consensus was nearly impossible to achieve in the ideological battleground between democracy and communism in the Cold War years,[6] today there are still honest differences of opinion among economists, development experts, governments, and institutions. This is particularly true in light of the growing issue of inequality in most countries, to include developed countries. Is the answer free trade; and, if so, is that best done nationally, on a regional basis, or globally? Is the answer industrialization, or can some countries rely on commodities and natural resources? Does the answer include foreign aid from the wealthy to the poor, and, if so, under what conditions? Finally, can economic measures be considered separately from political concerns such as good governance (which was examined in the preceding chapter)? After all, if a country is receiving foreign aid but much of that goes to enrich an authoritarian leadership, or if a country possesses a strategic resource such as oil but the ruling class keeps the profits derived at the expense of the majority poor, how can otherwise sound economic policies improve citizens' lives? It is difficult to believe that the all-too-common predatory and corrupt government could offer its people effective development when the majority of the population is deliberately excluded from incorporation in the domestic economy.[7]

In the first section of this chapter we define economic security and its initial conception under the influential 1994 UNDP report which laid out the human security construct. While that report was at pains to emphasize that human security did not equate to development, clearly (economic) development for individuals and communities was the foundation to achieving their economic security interests. Thus, we briefly revisit the concept of development, along with the Sustainable Development Goals (SDGs). We then broaden the discussion to consider poverty more generally, and the critical role that women and gender issues play in this context. Several specific challenges, such as food security and the role of agriculture, are considered here. The chapter then considers how the U.S. perspective on development and economic assistance has evolved in tandem with its perceived link to national security interests. This leads into a discussion of foreign aid and its mixed record. Next, the role of free trade and its complicated relationship to economic growth, sustainable development, and politics are addressed. We conclude this chapter with the observation that it is no exaggeration to claim that inequitable development is a bedrock issue which helps generate national security issues—such as radical populism and extremism—even as it fatally undermines achieving human security.

Defining Economic Security and Development

According to the UNDP report, "economic security requires an assured basic income—usually from productive and remunerative work, or in the last resort from some publicly financed safety net."[8] Unfortunately, as the UNDP points out, income insecurity has very often been the rule, especially in developing countries where unemployment is often high, with many jobs being temporary and/or in the informal sector; plus there may be no social security net provided by the government.[9] Of course, people without an income from any source—or a very limited income—are poor, and may even be classified as living in absolute poverty, as described below. The obvious consequences of poverty are many, ranging from the loss of opportunity to receive education and career opportunities, to the most elemental conditions of homelessness and lack of sufficient food. In fact, the UNDP singled out "food security" as a separate indicator of human security in 1994; but, as explained earlier in this work, we consider access to food to be so inextricably connected to poverty that it is considered here under economic security.

While economic security has clear linkages to human development, development is but one aspect of human security, and human security itself does not equate to human development. According to the UNDP experts: "In defining security, it is important that human security not be equated with human development. Human development is a broader concept—defined in previous Human Development Reports as a process of widening the range of people's choices."[10] Clearly the global understanding of development has continued to change since the UNDP was formed in 1965, just as the concept of human security has evolved into the twenty-first century. In perhaps the ultimate expression of development, Nobel Prize-winning economist Amaryta Sen has conceptualized development as freedom, meaning both that human beings require freedom to develop at the same time as development enables freedom.[11] Development represents both the ends and the means; even the poorest people need to be actively involved in shaping their development and not viewed as merely recipients of programs designed by others, no matter how well intentioned. This emphasis on the need to fully include the poorest, most disadvantaged, and marginalized populations in their own development strategies is reflected in the theme of "universalism" as seen in the UNDP's *Human Development Report 2016*. The first of the five basic messages listed in the report is "Universalism is key to human development, and human development for everyone is attainable."[12] This is a predominant theme in the UN's Sustainable Development Goals (SDGs).

The Sustainable Development Goals

Chapter 2 described how the UN's Millennium Development Goals (MDGs), which were in force from 2000 to 2015, made significant progress in advancing human security needs, particularly in the areas related to economic security. Yet even before 2015 and the conclusion of the MDGs, it was recognized that much more needed to be done, and governments and nongovernmental groups and experts alike worked under UN sponsorship to develop a consensus regarding follow-on goals. This was achieved with the UN Sustainable Development Summit held in September 2015 in New York City, where more than 130 world leaders adopted the 2030 Agenda for Sustainable Development—to include the seventeen specific SDGs, or Global Goals. As the UNDP noted, these goals are more ambitious than the MDGs:

> seeking to eliminate rather than reduce poverty, and include more demanding targets on health, education and gender equality. They are universal, applying to all countries and all

people. The agenda also includes issues that were not in the MDGs such as climate change, sustainable consumption, innovation and the importance of peace and justice for all.[13]

Table 5.1 lists the seventeen SDGs. While these goals might seem quite general, and are clearly meant to be aspirational, each goal has identified specific targets in support of that goal. It is important to emphasize, too, that the MDGs—and now the SDGs—represent literally decades of efforts to understand the mechanics of development, including early attempts to measure development levels through the Human Development Index (HDI).[14] This has been followed by systematic analysis in the UNDP's respected annual *Human Development Reports*. These reports began in 1990, and the UNDP has sponsored and compiled hundreds of other national and regional development reports since that time.

Table 5.1 Sustainable Development Goals (SDGs)

1. No poverty	End poverty in all its forms everywhere
2. Zero hunger	End hunger, achieve food security and improved nutrition, and promote sustainable agriculture
3. Good health and well-being	Ensure healthy lives and promote well-being for all at all ages
4. Quality education	Ensure inclusive and quality education for all and promote lifelong learning
5. Gender equality	Achieve gender equality and empower all women and girls
6. Clean water and sanitation	Ensure access to water and sanitation for all
7. Affordable and clean energy	Ensure access to affordable, reliable, sustainable, and modern energy for all
8. Decent work and economic growth	Promote inclusive and sustainable economic growth, employment, and decent work for all
9. Industry, innovation, and infrastructure	Build resilient infrastructure, promote sustainable industrialization, and foster innovation
10. Reduced inequalities	Reduce inequality within and among countries
11. Sustainable cities and communities	Make cities inclusive, safe, resilient, and sustainable
12. Responsible consumption and production	Ensure sustainable consumption and production patterns
13. Climate action	Take urgent action to combat climate change and its impacts
14. Life below water	Conserve and sustainably use the oceans, seas, and marine resources
15. Life on land	Sustainably manage forests, combat desertification, halt and reverse land degradation, halt biodiversity loss
16. Peace, justice, and strong institutions	Promote just, peaceful, and inclusive societies
17. Partnerships for the goals	Revitalize the global partnership for sustainable development

Source: UNDP, "Sustainable Development Goals," at www.un.org/sustainabledevelopment/sustainable-development-goals/

The *2016 Human Development Report* contains the latest thinking about the HDI, which:

> integrates three basic dimensions of human development. Life expectancy at birth reflects the ability to lead a long and healthy life. Mean years of schooling and expected years of schooling reflect the ability to acquire knowledge. And gross national income per capita reflects the ability to achieve a decent standard of living.[15]

The report ranks almost all countries in groups, ranging from "very high human development" to "low human development." Table 5.2 lists the twenty states with the lowest HDI levels for 2016, although, as the report notes, caution should be exercised because not every indicator was available for each country (and a few countries, such as Somalia, were not assessed for 2016).[16]

Our aim here is not to claim that these indicators and rankings are mathematically precise, but rather to demonstrate the interrelated nature of human security issues. Thus, note that at least ten of the top twenty most at-risk states listed in Table 3.2 are also found in Table 5.2 (and conceivably Somalia would appear in both lists if it had been assessed for HDI purposes). While not in the top twenty for lowest HDI levels, an additional six of the states that are most at risk do fall into the "low development" category (for example, Yemen, Syria, and Nigeria). Some of these same countries also appear in earlier tables depicting the most corrupt states and the states lacking in good governance, which further tend to correlate to highly unequal societies (see Tables 4.1 and 4.2).[17]

The UNDP actually highlights this issue of inequality by calculating "inequality-adjusted HDI" levels that may change an individual country's ranking for better or worse—although for the lowest ranking states, the differences are not significant.[18] What should be evident across all these indicators and rankings is that these countries with immense human security needs are unstable and are either in conflict (usually internal in nature), just coming out of conflict, or in danger of once again falling into conflict. This generates regional instability as their neighbors almost inevitably become embroiled in the

Table 5.2 States Ranked Lowest on Human Development Index (HDI), 2016*

1. Central African Republic**	11. Guinea-Bissau**
2. Niger**	12. Liberia
3. Chad**	13. Democratic Republic of Congo**
4. Burkina Faso	14. Mali
5. Burundi**	15. Ethiopia
6. Guinea**	16. Gambia
7. South Sudan**	17. Djibouti
8. Mozambique	18. Côte d'Ivoire
9. Sierra Leone	19. Malawi
10. Eritrea**	20. Afghanistan**

Source: UNDP, "Overview," *Human Development Report 2016: Human Development for Everyone* (New York: UNDP, 2016), 24–25, available at http://hdr.undp.org/sites/default/files/HDR2016_EN_Overview_Web.pdf; and *The Fund for Peace*, "Fragile States Index 2016," available at http://fsi.fundforpeace.org/.

Note: *Ranked in order with Central African Republic representing the lowest HDI for 2016; ** state also listed in Table 3.2.

conflict, becoming the (often unwilling) hosts for refugees fleeing violence. These points underscore why development, and achieving economic security for communities, is critical to support the national security interests that almost every state has in stability and order, to include the United States. One statistic here demonstrates the enormous implications that conflict has on sustainable development; note that, according to the SDGs, "an estimated 50 per cent of out-of-school children of primary school age live in conflict-affected areas." Without structured education and the accompanying loss of literacy skills and the technologies of the information age for so many of their children, how can these communities ever progress in the globalized economy and move beyond basic human security needs?[19]

Gender Development Issues

One fundamental aspect of development singled out by the UNDP and many other experts is the issue of gender, and what is commonly termed "the gender gap." This refers to the consistently documented fact that, even in the most developed countries, women almost always earn less than men for similar work, and "in most countries [women] earn on average only 60 to 75 per cent of men's wages."[20] But this gap is even more consequential in many lesser-developed countries where, for a variety of reasons (such as the religious and historical-cultural practices noted in Chapter 3), women may be limited in educational opportunities, the right to own property and to inherit, or the right to work freely outside the home. Unfortunately, these limitations are inimical to building higher levels of development for individual women, their families, and their communities.

UN Women, the United Nations body dedicated to gender equality and improving the status of women, cites numerous studies showing that "an increase in female labour force participation—or a reduction in the gap between women's and men's labour force participation—results in faster economic growth."[21] Equally important is the fact that empowering women means better human security results for the entire family, especially children. Already by the 1990s many studies by development economists and respected international organizations and foundations had convincingly demonstrated that educating women had multiplier effects in economic growth for their families and communities. Educated women demonstrably provide better nutrition, health care, and education to their families, while overall women have been found to devote more of their small earnings to food, clothing, and education for their children.[22] As just one instance, "a study using data from 219 countries from 1970 to 2009 found that, for every one additional year of education for women of reproductive age, child mortality decreased by 9.5 per cent"[23] (Image 5.1 demonstrates how strongly a young girl may value education.)

The gender dichotomy continues to be assessed by many economic organizations and institutions that recognize the importance of women to achieve sustainable development. The influential World Economic Forum (WEF)[24] annually compiles comparative data via the "Global Gender Gap Index," which measures the gaps between men's and women's access to resources and opportunities on four critical dimensions in each country: economic participation, education, health, and politics.[25] The index is also constructed so as not to reflect the relative wealth of the economies assessed. In other words, a poorer, less-developed country could score higher than a wealthy country if the poorer country had less of a gap between men and women's access to resources and opportunities. That is why less-developed countries such as Rwanda (in Africa), the Philippines (Asia), and Nicaragua (Central American)—ranked 5, 7, and 10 respectively—can all score as more equal on women's access to resources and opportunities than the United States (ranked 45 in the 2016 index).[26]

Image 5.1 Somali Girl Continues Her Education through Daily, Radio-Based Distance Learning Programs. Photo: USAID

Overall the WEF makes the further point that the global economic gender gap has only narrowed by 2 percent in the ten years since the index was first compiled in 2006.[27] They find this lack of progress puzzling, with "the economic and business case for gender parity becoming ever clearer." Meanwhile, studies by the Organisation for Economic Co-operation and Development (OECD) have estimated that increasing women's participation in the labor force across its member countries by half could increase gross domestic product (GDP) growth levels by 2.5 percent by 2025.[28] The Forum notes a number of other models and empirical studies that estimate how reducing the gender gap would lead to significant economic dividends: for example, "China could see a US$2.5 trillion GDP increase by 2020"; conversely, "East Asia and the Pacific reportedly loses between US$42 billion to [*sic*] US$47 billion annually due to women's limited access to employment opportunities."[29]

The Challenge of Poverty

Incorporating women in every facet of development is clearly vital for countries to make progress out of poverty, and ending poverty is the central goal to achieve economic security for human beings. Ending poverty, especially extreme poverty, was actually the first goal enumerated under the MDGs, and it remains the first goal listed under the currently applicable SDGs. One of the most prominent and consistently cited success stories of the MDGs has been the reduction in absolute, or extreme, poverty (meaning living on less than $2 per day), so that by 2015 "more than 1 billion people have been lifted out of extreme poverty (since 1990)."[30] If we consider that the world's population in 2016 stood at 7.5 billion people, that progress represents a remarkable achievement. Yet at the same time the UNDP noted that 836 million people were still living in extreme poverty, with the overwhelming majority coming from southern Asia and sub-Saharan Africa.[31]

In addition to the UNDP, the World Bank Group plays a critical role in every major area of development and economic security, giving and marshaling financial and technical assistance, analysis, and advice from intergovernmental, governmental, and private investment firms. It has set goals for 2030 related to the SDGs: "End extreme poverty by decreasing the percentage of people living on less than $1.90 a day to no more than 3% [and] Promote shared prosperity by fostering the income growth of the bottom 40% for every country." (The second goal reflects the increased concern of diverse economic and development experts—some of whom work for the World Bank—that the growing level of inequality alongside prosperity in many societies is a serious issue morally, socially, and politically.) In any case there seems to be universal agreement that "helping create sustainable economic growth . . . [is] the surest path out of poverty."[32] This is echoed by the World Economic Forum, acknowledging that, "while economic growth, as measured by GDP, is not an end in itself, it remains a precondition for enhancing human welfare. It provides the resources necessary for improving health, education, and security."[33] However, the dilemma remains—*how* to create this type of growth?

In a 2016 interview Ana Revenga, the senior director of the World Bank's Poverty and Global Equity Practice, stated that the goal of ending extreme poverty could be achieved. She attributed recent success to:

> economic growth—but not *any* kind of economic growth. What's needed is economic growth that improves the income-generating opportunities of the poor. This kind of growth involves either raising the value of the agricultural products that the poor are producing or generating better jobs"[34] (see Image 5.2).

Revenga also noted two other necessary factors—good education systems and social safety nets. Similar themes are reiterated in numerous other studies. But the problem remains: how to feasibly achieve these steps when the most basic poverty-related problems of hunger and malnourishment are still prevalent in much of the world, especially among the rural poor.

Image 5.2 Market Vendors in Sudan. Photo: USAID

Agriculture and Food Security

According to the UNDP:

> one in nine people in the world today (795 million) are undernourished . . . Poor nutrition causes nearly half (45 per cent) of deaths in children under five—3.1 million children each year [and] . . . One in four of the world's children suffer stunted growth [due to lack of adequate nutrition].[35]

In terms of basic economic security needs, food is clearly the number one concern. Achieving food security is the main goal of the UN Food and Agriculture Organization (FAO), which clearly entails eradicating hunger and malnutrition (along with the inevitable accompanying poverty) and ensuring productive and sustainable agriculture, forestry, and fisheries. The FAO agrees with the general consensus that there is enough capacity in the world to feed everyone adequately and into the future; but the problem is that most of the world's poor people live in rural areas, and that is where hunger and food insecurity predominate—so the solution is to work on reducing rural poverty, which in turn means improving agricultural growth and productivity.[36] And the UNDP notes that "agriculture is the single largest employer in the world, providing livelihoods for 40 per cent of today's global population. It is the largest source of income and jobs for poor rural households."[37] A key aspect here would involve more focus on women in agriculture because, as the UNDP also notes, "If women farmers had the same access to resources as men, the number of hungry in the world could be reduced by up to 150 million."[38]

Unfortunately, reliance on the agricultural sector and natural resources such as forestry and fisheries for sustainable income is problematic for a number of reasons. First, these areas are highly susceptible to natural disasters, such as the record-breaking hurricane season that hit much of the Caribbean and the southern United States in 2017; for example, in Puerto Rico, Hurricane Maria is estimated to have wiped out 80 percent of the crop value.[39] But this represents much more than a short-term problem because valuable crops such as coffee trees need at least three to five years to mature before they produce fruit. Manmade disasters can also imperil the ability to sustain a dependable livelihood, as the 2010 Deepwater Horizon (BP) oil spill in the Gulf of Mexico demonstrates; in 2017 adverse effects on marine life and fishing stocks were still being experienced in communities along the Gulf coast.

Note that these examples all pertain to the United States, which has the resources to help its citizens deal with such disasters and to provide a social safety net. But this is not the case for many less-developed countries with large populations of poor citizens who rely heavily on agriculture and fishing for basic survival, and to make a meager living. And, as Chapter 6 on environmental security details, scientists believe that climate change is already increasing the number of natural disasters—such as hurricanes/cyclones, rainstorms and associated flooding, and wildfires—while intensifying their effects. At the same time, climate change is contributing to such events as the desertification that has been occurring in the Sahel region of northern Africa, where drought and crop failures are now common. This region has long experienced cycles of rainfall and drought, with poor grazing practices for herding animals adding to soil depletion, with the result that most of the region's people now face chronic food insecurity.

Tragically, one of the most serious factors enhancing, and sometimes even causing, the loss of agricultural livelihoods is manmade—violent ethnic and religious conflict. Thus, the Director-General of the FAO, José Graziano da Silva, has stated that "about 60 percent of the people suffering from hunger in the world live in areas affected by conflict and the impact of climate change." Specifically, he noted "almost twenty million people facing starvation because of fighting and drought in South Sudan, Nigeria, Somalia and Yemen."[40] Additionally, the head of the UN's World Food Programme (WFP), David Beasley, concluded that ten of the thirteen countries where the WFP spent the most money against food insecurity were in that situation due to man-made crises. Beasley even suggested that "bringing just a few of the world's major conflicts to an end would free enough resources to eradicate hunger"[41] This observation is cited here to highlight again how interrelated the dimensions of human security tend to be, as we find economic security concerns exacerbated by environmental insecurity and conflicts related to identity security concerns.

Assisting starving and malnourished people is a laudable humanitarian goal that motivates not only relevant UN agencies like the FAO and WFP, but also major donor countries like the United States. Yet, as we argue throughout this work, supporting human security needs very often supports national security interests, too. Consider just the four countries noted above of South Sudan, Nigeria, Somalia, and Yemen. Terrorist Islamic State and al Qaeda-allied groups such as al-Shabab are known to shelter in Somalia and Yemen, and Nigeria is home to the militant Islamic group Boko Haram. While experts may disagree about whether poverty and inequitable development actually produce terrorists, they do tend to agree about the destabilizing effects and the unrest these factors can trigger. One of the most serious related factors in both human security and national security terms is the issue of population displacement, both within countries and to neighboring countries, which in turn may cause additional unrest. The initial displacement may be triggered by crop failures or by actual conflict that causes people to flee their homes and abandon their crops and, thus, their food supply and livelihood. But in many cases if the groups have herding animals they will flee with the animals, which puts additional pressure on natural resources in the areas that they flee to—areas that are likely already stressed.[42] This further destabilizes tenuous conditions, and reanimates the cycle of conflict. It is not surprising that extremist groups find it convenient to operate in such areas, and may find support or at least tolerance from struggling communities.

Increasingly, experts are noting the importance of moving beyond immediate and emergency food aid to empowering those in need; to what is termed "food assistance." As the WFP explains:

> Food assistance . . . involves a more complex understanding of people's long-term nutritional needs and of the diverse approaches required to meet them. It implies not just emergency interventions, but tailored, multi-year support programmes designed to lift a whole nation's nutritional indicators.[43]

This type of approach involves such things as giving people cash or vouchers to buy their own food where available, which gives them more choice and helps support the local economy. The rethinking also focuses on the importance of building "resilience" into interventions so as "to lessen the effects of shocks and stressors" and thus mitigate some of the underlying vulnerabilities that poor communities face.[44] Based on this type of approach, the WFP notes that it has been radically rethinking its strategies, methodologies, and approach, and is now transitioning to specific, individual "Country Strategic Plans" for most developing countries, which are expected to cover a period of five years.[45] In effect, the goal is to move even farther away from wealthy countries

Image 5.3 Disaster Assistance in Bangladesh. Photo: U.S. Navy

providing traditional food aid supplies (as depicted in Image 5.3) to long-term technical and related agricultural assistance that enables the hungry to feed themselves by increasing domestic agricultural productivity.

The Challenge of Foreign Aid

The radical rethinking in the WFP about changing its focus to long-term assistance to help the poor develop their own agricultural productivity—versus immediate, short-term food aid—is reflected now in almost every debate about human development and economic progress. This is actually not surprising in light of how thinking about development has evolved in general: the realization today that people must be empowered to make their own choices, which has been increasingly reflected in policies. For example, among government-sponsored programs, the Bolsa Família (Family Stipend or Grant) has been termed "Brazil's antipoverty breakthrough" in an analysis in the widely read *Foreign Affairs* journal. This initiative, begun in 2003, pays families in poverty a small stipend each month to keep their children in school and to ensure that both children and mothers receive periodic health checks. By 2016 the program had benefited more than a quarter of Brazil's 207 million people—including 85 percent of the poor. In just its first three years:

> Bolsa Família cut extreme poverty by 15 percent, and by 2014, the percentage of Brazilians living in indigence had been slashed to less than three percent—a level the World Bank considers equivalent to eradication. At the same time, Bolsa Família has helped lift a total of 36 million people out of general poverty.[46]

While experts point to a number of factors for the success of the program, of particular importance is the fact that it empowers the poor by giving them authority over how the money is to be spent, which occurs within the local community. As it is usually the women of the family who receive the stipend, it has helped empower Brazilian women, too. Equally important is that the direct payment to beneficiaries avoids the use of middlemen and bureaucracy, and the all-too-endemic problem of corruption in a country like Brazil. Many other developing countries have taken note, and as of 2016 at least 40 other countries had initiated similar programs.[47]

This type of empowerment approach is also reflected in the popular practice of providing individuals (predominantly women) with very small loans—often termed "microfinance" loans or ventures—to start their own businesses and to join together to provide their own local community banking services. Bangladeshi economist Muhammad Yunus is given much of the credit for creating this microfinance concept in the 1970s and then in proving its worth through the highly successful Grameen Bank that he originally started in Bangladesh. Yunus (and the Grameen Bank) was awarded the Nobel Peace Prize in 2006 for his work and for arguably helping to remove millions of people from extreme poverty. His approach has inspired not only governments but also non-profit organizations like Finca International, which since 1984 has been helping to create village banking for those who would otherwise be too poor, and lack sufficient collateral, to borrow funds to start or expand businesses within their local communities. The goal is to create sustainable livelihoods for those in poverty.[48] This type of approach, which focuses on enabling the poor to make their own decisions, has gained increasing support internationally, as opposed to programs which rely on expert, but external, analysis to make decisions about what needs to meet or what specific products to provide to a local community.

A larger economic rationale also exists for encouraging this equitable development: the belief that the international economic system will be most prosperous if all states and their citizens are able to participate fully in today's globalized economy. Certainly for the United States, the economic success generated by developing countries is to be encouraged partly because it translates into gains from trade and investment with those countries. Additionally, considering that poor developing countries would never be able to repay the huge debts to the rich states that most have accumulated if they did not experience some level of development, this would further weaken the global financial system and hurt the numerous (often U.S.) banks that hold those countries' loans.[49]

The initial U.S. Foreign Assistance Act of 1961, which authorized legislation for modern foreign aid programs (and created the U.S. Agency for International Development, USAID), was "intended to be a tool for fighting poverty, enhancing bilateral relationships, and/or protecting U.S. security and commercial interests."[50] The act was passed in the wake of the highly successful Marshall Plan, "the largest aid program of the last century . . . acclaimed as a key factor in the post-World War II reconstruction of European states that have gone on to become major strategic and trade partners of the United States."[51] Other key recipients of extensive U.S. foreign assistance, from Japan to Taiwan to South Korea, are often cited as model examples of economic growth and development—and, not incidentally, remain important U.S. trading partners and allies.

The long-established rationale for international assistance and promoting development, based on a combination of U.S. values *and* interests, received renewed impetus as previously unforeseen threats to national security such as terrorism appeared in the twenty-first century. As President George W. Bush pointed out in his administration's 2002 *National Security Strategy*:

> The events of September 11, 2001, taught us that weak states, like Afghanistan, can pose as great a danger to our national interests as strong states. Poverty does not make poor people into terrorists and murderers. Yet poverty, weak institutions, and corruption can make weak states vulnerable to terrorist networks and drug cartels within their borders.[52]

This point was reinforced by Secretary of State Colin Powell in 2005, when he wrote: "Poverty breeds frustration and resentment, which ideological entrepreneurs can turn into support for—or acquiescence to—terrorism, particularly in those countries in which poverty is coupled with a lack of political rights and basic freedoms."[53] Food and nutrition policy scholar Per Pinstrup-Andersen and other experts agree, asserting that:

> widespread poverty, hunger, and inequality contribute to instability at the local, national and international levels and create national security risks for the United States. Failure to deal with these problems will render military efforts ineffective in dealing with the threat of terrorism against the United States and other high-income countries . . . People without hope and with little or nothing to lose have little stake in the status quo. They are susceptible to terrorist appeals."[54]

While some experts still disagree with the contention that poverty helps motivate terrorism, in 2017 the UNDP published a report, *Journey to Extremism in Africa: Drivers, Incentives, and the Tipping Point for Recruitment*, which "unequivocally underscores the relevance of economic factors as drivers of recruitment [to extremist groups]."[55] This significant report is based upon the largest number of interviews ever recorded with individuals who were actually recruited by violent extremist groups; groups which are estimated to have caused 33,000 fatalities in Africa from 2011 to 2016. Survey data reveal that:

> The grievances associated with growing up in contexts where multidimensional poverty is high and far deeper than national averages, with the lived reality of unemployment and underemployment, render "economic factors" a major source of frustration identified by those who joined violent extremist groups . . . employment is the single most frequently cited "immediate need" faced at the time of joining.[56]

Both the Bush and the Obama administrations clearly viewed international aid and assistance as essential for promoting development, democracy, and U.S. security interests—in large part through USAID. According to USAID's own website, it "leads international development and humanitarian efforts to save lives, reduce poverty, strengthen democratic governance and help people progress beyond assistance."[57] Significantly, USAID is expected to perform all these tasks with less than 1 per cent of the U.S. government's budget, and it is not unusual for the agency to find its policies being driven by politics, with specific restrictions on aid, congressional earmarks, and buy-American provisions. At the same time it is worth pointing out that although USAID certainly holds the paramount position for U.S. international assistance; the complex nature of development means that many different U.S. government agencies are involved, besides numerous international and nongovernmental agencies and foundations. And, depending on the security environment where development is taking place, the process may involve the presence of the U.S. military to provide security (Afghanistan), training, and logistics support for other nations' security forces or UN peacekeepers to establish security and law and order (as in much of Africa), or governmental agencies to deliver and organize humanitarian assistance.

In fact, during the George W. Bush administration it was understood that international assistance could be an important catalyst for development in the poorest countries, and official U.S. development assistance grew from $10 billion in 2000 to $22 billion in 2008 as more resources were seen as essential in the battle against terrorism.[58] The U.S. Congress authorized the new Millennium Challenge Corporation (MCC)—an independent U.S. government foreign aid agency—whereby some of the poorest countries would reduce poverty through growth, qualifying for individualized funding compacts only if they agreed to design policies linked to certain requirements. For some critics, this amounted to adding yet more strings to badly needed international assistance. However, decades of development assistance experience had taught the United States that how the money is spent, and accounted for, matters. The MCC was arguably one vehicle to control that process, an example of smart development policy that had strong bipartisan support in U.S. policy circles. In fact, the Obama administration retained the Bush administration's MCC concept, as has the Trump administration. As of 2018 the MCC website noted that it had approved over $13 billion in programs worldwide for individual country-determined projects in "agriculture and irrigation, transportation (roads, bridges, ports), water supply and sanitation, access to health, finance and enterprise development, anticorruption initiatives, land rights and access, [and] access to education."[59]

Under the Obama and Trump administrations the emphasis clearly shifted to supporting programs based on local solutions. For instance, the Obama administration committed to support the international "Feed the Future" initiative, which directed attention and resources to the neglected agricultural sector. Similarly to the MCC concept, the United States focused on public–private partnerships (PPPs) to deliver results that were generally well regarded. The one completely new and "most successfully constructed presidential initiative in the development arena" under the Obama administration was Power Africa, begun in 2013, whose objective was to double access to electricity in sub-Saharan Africa.[60] Here, too, an integral public–private partnership was recognized as important to success.

The above points on the importance of accounting for aid spent, ensuring that governments involved are using the aid for its intended purposes, and the importance of local involvement and public–private partnerships probably all seem like common sense. That may be true, but a key issue is that foreign assistance is a political decision for governments, and the temptation is to provide short-term aid that delivers immediate results and saves lives (such as in a famine). However, short-term aid cannot redress endemic poverty, build strong institutions, or transform weak governments into effective and popular ones; long-term assistance is crucial. In recognition of this, the Organisation for Economic Co-operation and Development (OECD), the influential group representing 35 major developed countries, has long set goals for its members to provide continuing official development assistance (ODA). This assistance is very important because "ODA makes up more than two thirds of external finance for least-developed countries . . . [and] the share of multilateral aid (aid provided via multilateral bodies) to bilateral aid (aid is provided directly by one country to another) is now roughly half to half."[61]

Significantly, for 2016 the United States provided the largest amount of the 29 OECD countries disbursing aid—$33.6 billion—but this represented only 0.18 percent of total U.S. gross national income (GNI). The average given per country was 0.32 percent of GNI, and only six countries met the UN goal of providing assistance at or above 0.7 percent of a country's GNI.[62] In any case it should be noted here that some development experts argue that ultimately "foreign aid may do more harm than good, by reducing recipient government accountability, fueling corruption, damaging export competitiveness, creating dependence, and undermining incentives for adequate taxation."[63] (See Box 5.1 on this topic.)

BOX 5.1 THINK AGAIN: INTERNATIONAL ASSISTANCE DOES NOT WORK

Almost all development experts now acknowledge the limitations of aid or assistance that is provided (and often directed) by outside donors, ranging from lack of adequate planning to inappropriate aid or projects for local conditions and traditions, to lack of incorporation of community needs and desires. Disagreement about the possibility of outside assistance enabling growth and development for poor nations was already present in the 1950s and 1960s. An increasingly vocal minority in the twenty-first century has continued to level critiques at the whole concept of international aid. Among the most well-known critics is economist William Easterly, and the title of his 2006 book, *The White Man's Burden: Why the West's Efforts to Aid the Rest Have Done So Much Ill and So Little Good*, is self-explanatory.[1] So is the title of his later (2014) book, *The Tyranny of Experts: Economists, Dictators, and the Forgotten Rights of the Poor.*[2]

Essentially, Easterly believes that the main problem stems from giving large amounts of aid to bad governments (who may be just weak and ineffective, but often are corrupt, too) with the result that the aid never gets to the poor. Furthermore, the schemes that the aid is meant to support are often far too grandiose and technocratic, and do not consider the individual situations and needs of the poor. As one reviewer of *The White Man's Burden* notes, Easterly believes more progress could be made with piecemeal reforms and supports giving cash transfers or vouchers directly to the poor—acknowledging that "giving vouchers to the poor may be the stupidest idea ever . . . except for all the ideas that have already failed in foreign aid."[3]

In her well-received indictment of aid to Africa in 2009—*Dead Aid: Why Aid Is Not Working and How There Is a Better Way for Africa*—economist Dambisa Moyo points out that, economically, Africa has actually gone backwards rather than forwards since independence in the 1960s and 1970s, in spite of often massive amounts of aid.[4] In her view aid has actually held Africa back, and should be terminated. What reasons do Moyo and other experts give for such a strong critique?[5]

Similarly to Easterly, Moyo believes that bad or weak governance negates the possibility of equitable development, with or without aid. The widespread problem of corruption further distorts the intent of any aid programs, even where a government does have good intentions but weak institutions. Since many of these fragile states also find themselves in post-conflict situations, they may be more focused on the short-term problem of maintaining security and stability of their territory. Also, these are often the states that are threatened by cultural divisions and extremism, whether ethnic or religious in nature. Under these conditions it is extremely important, but also difficult, for any government to allocate assistance fairly to all groups.

Regarding more technical aspects, many weak governments simply cannot absorb large amounts of aid usefully so as to translate that into workable, long-term programs. Indeed, channeling the aid through often rigid, formalized plans and bureaucratic hurdles seems destined to make it ineffective. Conversely, the piecemeal nature of much development aid from many different types of donors may result in duplicative or even conflicting programs in place. Additionally, economists had predicted that countries receiving aid would use sensible policies to encourage their own domestic savings rates, thus reducing aid requirements because eventually they would become self-reliant. But human nature can invalidate economic assumptions; many of these countries realized that once the international community had committed to aid them, donors would continue to do so and that these countries could continue to spend freely and save less.[6]

Finally, another powerful argument against international aid lies in the record of growth and reduction in poverty rates lately achieved by over half a billion people in China and India—according to economist Jagdish Bhagwati, "the greatest and quickest progress in fighting poverty in history."[7] This is significant since these two countries had received negligible amounts of international assistance (India had received aid, but some years before its growth and poverty rates declined) and it clearly did not engender their success.

1 William Easterly, *The White Man's Burden: Why the West's Efforts to Aid the Best Have Done So Much Ill and So Little Good* (New York: Penguin, 2006).
2 William Easterly, *The Tyranny of Experts: Economists, Dictators, and the Forgotten Rights of the Poor* (New York: Basic Books, 2014).
3 Cited by Prakash Loungani (Chief, Policy Communications, IMF), "Foreign Aid Isn't? A Book Review," IMF Views and Commentaries, August 31, 2006, at: www.imf.org/en/News/Articles/2015/09/28/04/54/vc083106.
4 Dambisa Moyo, *Dead Aid: Why Aid Is Not Working and How There Is a Better Way for Africa* (New York: Farrar, Straus, and Giroux, 2009).
5 See also Jagdish Bhagwati, "Banned Aid: Why International Assistance Does Not Alleviate Poverty," *Foreign Affairs* (January/February 2010). At: www.foreignaffairs.com/print/65817.
6 Ibid.
7 Ibid.

The Challenge of (Free) Trade

Regardless of how true criticisms about foreign assistance might be, the central issue remains: how might countries best ensure economic growth and development out of poverty on a sustained basis? Most experts would argue that a large part of the answer has to lie in a country's success in the world economy and its ability to progressively gain increased revenue by exporting products for trade and profit. As a recent *Forbes* commentary argued:

> The last 40 years of globalisation have shown that the finest poverty reduction technique we have is trade. Thus our gift to the poor of the world should be that we tear down the rules that stop them from supplying things to us . . . the best driver of economic growth is to buy things made by poor people in poor countries.[64]

But this equation only works if the terms of trade are favorable to poor countries, which recalls World Bank official Ana Revenga's statement above—that the value of agricultural products must be raised on a sustained basis to progress beyond poverty in less developed countries.

Unfortunately, the fact is that primary commodities such as agricultural products and related natural resource products will almost always be at an economic disadvantage in the global trading system when compared to manufactured items and, increasingly, technologically advanced products. Consider that the terms of trade favor the latter higher-value products over commodities, and these higher-value products' prices also normally rise at higher rates than commodities do. In fact, a huge disadvantage in relying on commodities to spur economic growth is that prices of commodities tend to be quite volatile; they rarely provide for stable, sustained growth (and, as noted above, weather and natural disasters can decimate a country's production of agricultural items). That is why, in its report *The State of Commodity Dependence 2016*, UNCTAD was actually pessimistic about the fact that the revenue from commodity exports for developing countries had increased 25 percent from 2010 to 2015 because this meant even more dependence on commodities, which was not viewed as an effective strategy for ending poverty. As the report noted, dependence on agricultural commodity exports was prevalent in Africa, where 46 out of 55 countries had become commodity-dependent by 2015. In sum, the report found that 41 percent of the developing countries were dependent primarily on agricultural goods, whereas 30 percent were dependent on fuel exports and 23 percent on minerals, ores, and metals (the latter two were predominant in the regions of Asia and Oceania).[65]

This commodity-trading dilemma for developing countries was recognized quite early after the founding of the United Nations, and the first UNCTAD meeting was held in 1964 to address related issues and international actions that could be taken. Reflecting the complexity of the issues (not to mention the inevitable politics) and the importance accorded to assisting developing nations in the global economy, UNCTAD became institutionalized in the UN system with permanent secretariat support. This intergovernmental body's role remains to assist developing nations to flourish in the global economy—and to serve as their voice in formulating consensus policies with the major developed countries. UNCTAD also provides technical assistance and analysis to help developing economies compete in the globalized world economy via sustainable economic growth.[66]

It is logical to assume that reliance on fuel exports and precious minerals, ores, and metals would be more advantageous for developing countries than reliance on agricultural products; there is a reason that the former products are often termed "strategic" commodities. To some extent this is true, and the example of the Organization of Petroleum

Exporting Countries (OPEC) is instructive here. OPEC was founded with five oil-producing nations in 1960, but this intergovernmental group now has fourteen member states that are assessed to hold the majority of reserves of oil in the world. According to the organization's website, OPEC's mission remains:

> to coordinate and unify the petroleum policies of its Member Countries and ensure the stabilization of oil markets in order to secure an efficient, economic and regular supply of petroleum to consumers, a steady income to producers and a fair return on capital for those investing in the petroleum industry.[67]

In the 1970s OPEC really achieved international fame (or infamy), as members "took control of their domestic petroleum industries and acquired a major say in the pricing of crude oil on world markets . . . [in the wake of steep oil prices] Member Countries embarked on ambitious socio-economic development schemes."[68] In the aftermath of the 1973 Arab oil embargo and the 1979 Iranian revolution the United States declared that it had a vital interest in keeping the Persian Gulf open to shipping, primarily to ensure the export of oil to the United States and to its European allies. A commodity does not get more strategic than with this example where oil was explicitly linked to the U.S. national interest. The oil embargo and rise in prices also had negative effects on many developing countries' economies, in addition to the U.S. economy.

Although the OPEC example could thus be cited to demonstrate that some commodities may have trading value similar to higher-tech, manufactured products, the issue of sustainability is still relevant. Scanning OPEC's history in the decades following the 1970s, the organization notes problems such as volatility of prices, weak price levels, and oil gluts (oversupply); and, in the present decade, issues such as overall uncertainty in the international financial markets, unrest in many areas which affected supply and demand, shrinking demand in countries like the United States, and even the growing concern over environmental matters and climate change were affecting stability in the market.[69]

The OPEC example also illustrates how political weaknesses, and the lack of capable and effective governance, may affect the possibility of sustained economic growth for many developing countries, even if they possess a valuable commodity. We are deliberately avoiding the term "good governance" here, which implies democratic, or popular, rule. That is because some of the most successful OPEC member states in terms of steady economic growth and good management of their petroleum industries are authoritarian to varying degrees—namely Saudi Arabia (an absolute monarchy), Kuwait, Qatar, and the United Arab Emirates. While authoritarian rule is not desirable in terms of other human security interests, it may still produce stable economic growth, and the government may even engage in equitable development practices within the country. This is certainly the model that was applied in other countries that are now considered modern economic success stories, from South Korea to Taiwan to Singapore. Here authoritarian governments propelled industrialization and modernization from the top down, but they also supported mass education and equitable provision of social services. Significantly, once a certain level of development was achieved, the citizenry of these countries increasingly demanded, and received, democratic governance, too. An open question today is whether China will follow its economic liberalization and sustained growth with political liberalization as its regional neighbors have done.

Unfortunately, it is quite obvious that other developing countries that do not have effective leadership—or may have predatory and corrupt leadership—cannot manage their economies efficiently, even when possessing strategic commodities like oil. OPEC member countries such as Venezuela, Libya, Iraq, Nigeria, and Angola all demonstrate this tendency. Venezuela and Nigeria in particular have the large population, resources, and oil to build sustainable economic development, but corrupt and authoritarian governments have resulted in impoverished societies and political and social unrest—and in Nigeria's case, these conditions have helped encourage extremist groups like Boko Haram to gain support.

Many economists support free trade schemes as another important avenue to increase economic growth, but it is worth noting that these schemes are just as much political as they are economic. In fact, perhaps the most well-known and established trade scheme was the European Coal and Steel Community (ECSC)—better known today by its ultimate successor, the European Union (EU). The ECSC was established in 1951, just a few years after the end of World War II. While establishing a common market for coal and steel in a key part of Western Europe had an economic rationale, the political rationale was equally—if not more—important. That rationale was to help prevent war between France and (West) Germany once again by making it seem unfeasible by linking the main war-making industries of coal and steel of the two nations (and four others) while building reconciliation. Through the years the original concept became the model that was built upon as economic integration progressed in Europe, eventually taking on greater political and social integration aspects, too, in today's European Union. However, in a sign that politics may still constrain economics within the member states of an organization like the EU, in 2016 citizens of the United Kingdom voted via popular referendum to negotiate withdrawal from the EU (Brexit). The major reasons for the vote appeared to be reluctance to be ruled by external powers, a perception that the UK was not being treated fairly within the EU, and concerns over immigration into the UK—whether based upon perceptions that immigrants were taking jobs from British citizens, or ethnic and religious bias against others.

For the many experts who believe that free trade organizations can spur economic growth and help developing countries, the British example should be carefully examined. In fact, there are numerous other examples of free trade schemes between primarily developing countries in Africa and Latin America which have fallen apart, most often over perceptions that other states were gaining more than one's own state (or due to unrelated economic and political disagreements). This perception has often been reality as the fact is that the most gains will generally accrue initially to the largest member state(s) that possess the larger economies. Unfortunately, when relatively poor developing states are involved in such an arrangement, usually they cannot afford to be patient for promised rewards down the road. This is particularly true when states may already be distrustful due to ethnic or religious differences, or historical conflicts. And, returning to the issue of agricultural commodities, if most of the states produce similar commodities, that is not very beneficial economically. Furthermore, if some of the states are involved in low-level manufacturing assembly operations—a common practice pursued by developing countries to develop some industrialization, diversify exports, and employ the poor—it is all too likely that states will end up competing with one another so that the already low wages earned in these operations are driven down even further.

While the discussion above is focused on developing countries, it also pertains to the North American Free Trade Agreement (NAFTA) between the United States, Canada, and Mexico. This accord came into effect in 1994, with economic and political motivations. Like other free trade agreements, the economic rationale for forming NAFTA was mainly based upon the principle of comparative advantage whereby all countries would gain from trading what resources they possessed naturally, or could produce most efficiently. This economic process in turn would stimulate additional flows of trade and investment between member states. In terms of political rationales, Mexico saw this as endorsement of its ongoing democratic transition and a more important position in Latin America, whereas the United States was interested in preserving stability on its border with Mexico by increasing economic growth there, and ensuring increased access to Mexican oil imports. (Throughout the 1990s there were also hopes that a hemispheric-wide free trade area could be negotiated, but this failed for a number of reasons.)

There is little doubt that NAFTA did increase trade between the three member states; a 2017 Council on Foreign Relations analysis found that economists largely agreed that the accord "encouraged a more than tripling of regional trade and cross-border investment between the three countries also grew significantly." But, as the report also noted, "it has proven difficult to tease out the deal's direct effects from other factors, including rapid technological change, expanded trade with other countries such as China, and unrelated domestic developments in each of the countries."[70] This might not matter so much if it were not the case that perspectives on who gains and who loses in free trade agreements were not so critical to their success and stability. And if NAFTA can be such a polarizing issue as it has become in the United States in 2017–2018—with the Trump administration insisting on renegotiating the agreement—one can understand how these types of ostensibly economic agreements are even more debatable in, and for, poor developing countries.

The unfortunate reality is that there are no clear-cut, easy solutions to attaining economic growth and providing formulas for equitable development. Even if there were definitive, proven economic pathways to achieve economic security, political and other considerations would still complicate the picture. There is a reason why the global World Trade Organization has only evolved very painfully through decades of protracted negotiations, with the primary purpose "to open trade for the benefit of all."[71] Yet there is still discord in achieving consensus on a global system of trade rules, and settling trade disputes between countries is a common occurrence. Scanning the WTO's website gives a sense of the many complex trade topics that complicate even the best-intentioned and well-planned efforts to achieve sustainable growth and development.

Conclusion

Achieving viable economic security, especially for "the bottom billion," is a herculean task. Even well-intentioned experts, governments, and NGOs continue to disagree about the root causes of and optimal paths for achieving development, precisely because the concept is inherently multifaceted and complex. In recognition of this, diverse experts (and the U.S. government) have come to increasingly accept the conclusion that there is no easy, "formulaic" development model. Each country and each region must be analyzed and assessed carefully, with tailored approaches devised. Although this may lead to more successful outcomes, it also increases the time and the expense. Yet, considering the billions of dollars spent by UN agencies globally, and by the United States in the twenty-first century just in Afghanistan and Iraq—and the uncertain results achieved—it is not surprising to find many skeptics.

Unfortunately, as the previous two chapters demonstrated, sustainable human development can seem near impossible to achieve, not only because of poverty but also because of such seemingly intractable issues as cultural extremism, human rights abuses, and terrorist and criminal networks that may become powerful enough to threaten weak, ineffective governments and their economic agendas. If one adds predatory and corrupt governance to that mix, it is obvious why political factors are also critical to consider.

And there are more issues threatening human security, as the next chapters illustrate. Challenges like those posed by public health threats such as pandemics, climate change, and environmental issues, increasing human activities and competition on the oceans, and the ever-accelerating use of cyberspace with all of its risks and rewards will produce consequences that we cannot begin to foresee. But certainly sustainable, equitable development in more of the world's nations would help to deal with those issues, and to provide a more peaceful and stable order which is in every person's, and every state's, interest. Once again we see the interrelatedness of human and national security interests. And finally, on the most basic level, we believe the moral argument to assist the poor has merit, as stated simply by Bill and Melinda Gates: "We have worked in international development for a long time. We started because we believe that what Warren Buffett calls the 'ovarian lottery'—the happenstance of where children are born—shouldn't determine the fate of individuals."[72]

Notes

1 Bill and Melinda Gates, "Comment: Bill and Melinda Gates: Let's Keep Investing in the World's Poor," *Wall Street Journal*, September 16, 2017. At: www.wsj.com/article_email/bill-and-melinda-gates-lets-keep-investing-in-the-worlds-poor-1505300401-lMyQjAxMTI3NjE4NjgxNDY3Wj/.
2 Charter of the United Nations, Chapter 1, "Purposes and Principles," Article 1; Chapter IX, "International Economic and Social Cooperation," Article 55a. At: www.un.org/en/sections/un-charter/chapter-ix/index.html.
3 Franklin D. Roosevelt, "Annual Message to Congress" (the "Four Freedoms" speech), January 6, 1941, Franklin D. Roosevelt Presidential Library and Museum, available at http://docs.fdrlibrary.marist.edu/4free.html.
4 General George C. Marshall was a truly remarkable American, achieving military success as a five-star army general who served as chief of staff to President Franklin D. Roosevelt during World War II, and then civilian policymaking success as both Secretary of Defense and Secretary of State.
5 Hillary Rodham Clinton, "Secretary Clinton's Remarks at Luncheon Honoring Former Secretary of State George C. Marshall," October 16, 2009, available at www.state.gov/secretary/rm/2009a/10/130645.htm. The figure of $30 billion is calculated from the following CRS estimate, omitting the military aid and non-military security assistance figure: "In FY2015, U.S. foreign assistance, defined broadly, was estimated at $48.57 billion, or 1.3% of total federal budget authority. About 43% of this assistance was for bilateral economic development programs, including political/strategic economic assistance; 35% for military aid and non-military security assistance; 16% for humanitarian activities; and 6% to support the work of multilateral institutions." See Curt Tarnoff and Marian L. Lawson, *Foreign Aid: An Introduction to U.S. Programs and Policy* (Washington, DC: Congressional Research Service, 2016), at: https://fas.org/sgp/crs/row/R40213.pdf.
6 It was the developing states emerging out of colonization in the aftermath of World War II that pushed demands for a "New International Economic Order." In the twenty-first century it may be difficult to relate to how issues of poverty, free trade, and development were caught up in the ideological battle between democratic capitalist ideas and socialist-communist economic models. This was especially true for the so-called Third World countries, which constituted themselves as the Group of 77 (Non-Aligned Movement) for negotiating purposes.
7 See Larry Diamond, "The Democratic Rollback: The Resurgence of the Predatory State," *Foreign Affairs* vol. 87, no. 2 (2008): 42–43.
8 UNDP, *Human Development Report 1994* (New York: Oxford University Press, 1994), 25. At: http://hdr.undp.org/sites/default/files/reports/255/hdr_1994_en_complete_nostats.pdf.
9 Ibid., 25–26.
10 Ibid., 23.
11 Amartya Sen, *Development as Freedom* (New York: Knopf, 1999), 53.
12 UNDP, *Human Development Report 2016: Human Development for Everyone* (New York: UNDP, 2016), 1. At: http://hdr.undp.org/sites/default/files/HDR2016_EN_Overview_Web.pdf.

13 UNDP News Centre, "World Leaders Adopt Sustainable Development Goals," September 25, 2015, at: www.undp.org/content/undp/en/home/presscenter/pressreleases/2015/09/24/undp-welcomes-adoption-of-sustainable-development-goals-by-world-leaders.html.
14 The HDI was first created in 1975 and later refined. It was an attempt to more accurately portray a composite picture of the development levels of countries and regions based on combining achievements in the three basic indicators of life expectancy, educational attainment, and income. Yet it was quickly realized that even this composite index needed to be disaggregated for regions and ethnic and gender groups within a country, and to be supplemented by other data and considerations. See UNDP, "Human Development Reports: The Human Development Index," available at http://hdr.undp.org/en/statistics/indices/hdi/.
15 UNDP, "Overview," in *Human Development Report 2016*, 3.
16 Ibid, 24–25.
17 Interestingly, the UNDP report for 2016 cites other indexes that can be helpful for assessing human well-being, such as the Social Progress Index, the Better Life Index, and even the World Happiness Index. See ibid., 9.
18 Ibid., 24–25.
19 UNDP, "Goal 4-Quality Education-Targets," at: www.undp.org/content/undp/en/home/sustainable-development-goals/goal-4-quality-education/targets/.
20 UN Women, "What We Do—Facts and Figures: Economic Empowerment," at www.unwomen.org/en/what-we-do/economic-empowerment/facts-and-figures.
21 Ibid.
22 Isobel Coleman, "The Better Half: Helping Women Help the World," *Foreign Affairs* vol. 89, no. 1 (2010), 126–130, available at www.foreignaffairs.com/print/65880; Melanne Verveer (U.S. Ambassador-at-Large for Global Women's Issues), "Women as Partners in Progress and Prosperity," Keynote Address at the Pathways to Prosperity in the Americas Women's Entrepreneurs' Conference, October 8, 2009, available at www.state.gov/s/gwi/rls/rem/2009/130681.htm.
23 UN Women, "What We Do—Facts and Figures."
24 The World Economic Forum is also known as the International Organization for Public-Private Cooperation, an independent organization headquartered in Switzerland and comprised of government, business, and civil society representatives. See World Economic Forum, "Our Mission," at: www.weforum.org/about/world-economic-forum.
25 World Economic Forum, "The Global Gender Gap Report 2016: The Case for Gender Parity," at: http://reports.weforum.org/global-gender-gap-report-2016/the-case-for-gender-parity/.
26 Of note, the United States scored lowest in the "Political Empowerment" of women indicator, ranking at 73 out of 144 countries evaluated. See ibid., 13.
27 World Economic Forum, "Closing the Gender Gap," at: www.weforum.org/projects/closing-the-gender-gap-gender-parity-task-forces.
28 World Economic Forum, "Global Gender Gap Report 2016," 24; and OECD, "Progress on Gender Equality Far Too Slow," April 10, 2017, at: www.oecd.org/newsroom/progress-on-gender-equality-far-too-slow.htm.
29 World Economic Forum, "Global Gender Gap Report 2016," 26–27.
30 UNDP, "Background on the Sustainable Development Goals: Key MDG Achievements," at: www.undp.org/content/undp/en/home/sustainable-development-goals/background.html.
31 UNDP, Sustainable Development Goals, Goal 1-Targets," at: www.undp.org/content/undp/en/home/sustainable-development-goals/goal-1-no-poverty/targets/.
32 World Bank, "What We Do," at: www.worldbank.org/en/about/what-we-do.
33 World Economic Forum, "The Global Competitiveness Report 2017–2018," Preface, Richard Samans, at: http://reports.weforum.org/global-competitiveness-index-2017-2018/preface/.
34 World Bank· "Ending Extreme Poverty," June 8, 2016 (italics in original). At: www.worldbank.org/en/news/feature/2016/06/08/ending-extreme-poverty.
35 UNDP, "Sustainable Development Goals, Goal 2 Targets: Hunger," at: www.undp.org/content/undp/en/home/sustainable-development-goals/goal-2-zero-hunger/targets/.
36 Food and Agriculture Organization of the United Nations, "About FAO" and "What We Do," at: www.fao.org/about/en/.

37 UNDP, Goal 2 Targets: Food Security, at: www.undp.org/content/undp/en/home/sustainable-development-goals/goal-2-zero-hunger/targets/.
38 Ibid.
39 Frances Robles and Luis Ferré-Sadurní, "Puerto Rico's Agriculture and Farmers Decimated by Maria," *New York Times*, September 24, 2017, at: www.nytimes.com/2017/09/24/us/puerto-rico-hurricane-maria-agriculture-.html?_r=0.
40 Umberto Bacchi, "World Hunger on the Rise Again Due to Conflict and Climate-UN," Thomson Reuters Foundation News, July 3, 2017, at: http://news.trust.org/item/20170703121558-7z5hd/.
41 Ibid.
42 Food and Agriculture Organization, "UN Says More Support Urgently Needed to Tackle Growing Food Insecurity in the Sahel," July 25, 2014, at: www.fao.org/emergencies/fao-in-action/stories/stories-detail/en/c/239860/.
43 World Food Programme, "Food Assistance: Cash and In-Kind," at: http://www1.wfp.org.
44 World Food Programme, "Resilience Building," at: www1.wfp.org/resilience-building.
45 World Food Programme, "Country Strategic Planning," at: www1.wfp.org/country-strategic-planning.
46 Jonathan Tepperman, "Brazil's Anti-Poverty Breakthrough: The Surprising Success of Bolsa Família," *Foreign Affairs*, vol. 95, no. 1 (2016), 34–44.
47 Ibid.
48 "The Nobel Peace Prize 2006," at: www.nobelprize.org/nobel_prizes/peace/laureates/; "Why FINCA?" at www.finca.org/why-finca/.
49 Vincent Ferraro, "Globalizing Weakness: Is Global Poverty a Threat to the Interests of States?" in *Should Global Poverty Be Considered a U.S. National Security Issue?* Commentaries from Woodrow Wilson Center for International Scholars, August 8, 2003, available at www.wilson center.org/index.cfm?fuse action=news.item&news_id=34999.
50 Marian Leonardo Lawson, Does Foreign Aid Work? Efforts to Evaluate U.S. Foreign Assistance," June 23, 2016, CRS Report R42827, Washington, DC, 3, at: https://fas.org/sgp/crs/row/R42827.pdf.
51 Ibid.
52 George W. Bush, *The National Security Strategy of the United States of America* (Washington, DC: White House, September 2002), v. Yet President Bush also noted that "including all the world's poor in an expanding circle of development—and opportunity—is a moral imperative and one of the top priorities of U.S. international policy" (21).
53 Colin L. Powell, "No Country Left Behind," *Foreign Policy* no. 146 (January–February 2005): 30.
54 Per Pinstrup-Andersen, "Eradicating Poverty and Hunger as a National Security Issue for the United States," in *Should Global Poverty Be Considered a U.S. National Security Issue?* Nevertheless, it is important to realize that not all experts posit a direct link among poverty, weak states, and terrorism, with some flatly denying that poverty produces or motivates terrorists. See also Ferraro, "Globalizing Weakness," and Carol Lancaster, "Poverty, Terrorism, and National Security," both in *Should Global Poverty Be Considered a U.S. National Security Issue?*
55 UNDP, *Journey to Extremism in Africa: Drivers, Incentives, and the Tipping Point for Recruitment* (New York: UNDP-Regional Bureau for Africa, 2017), 5, at: http://journey-to-extremism.undp.org/content/downloads/UNDP-JourneyToExtremism-report-2017-english.pdf.
56 Ibid., 5.
57 U.S. Agency for International Development, "Who We Are," at: www.usaid.gov/who-we-are.
58 Brian Atwood, M. Peter McPherson, and Andrew Natsios, "Arrested Development: Making Foreign Aid a More Effective Tool," *Foreign Affairs* vol. 87, no. 6 (2008): 123–132.
59 Millennium Challenge Corporation, "About MCC," at: www.mcc.gov/about.
60 John Norris, "President Obama and His Development Legacy," Global Views: A History of U.S. Foreign Aid, *Devex*, July 12, 2016, at: www.devex.com/news/president-obama-and-his-development-legacy-87853.
61 OECD, Development Co-operation Directorate, "Development Aid Rises Again in 2016 but Flows to Poorest Countries Dip," at: www.oecd.org/dac/development-aid-rises-again-in-2016-but-flows-to-poorest-countries-dip.htm.

62 Ibid.
63 Leonardo Lawson, "Does Foreign Aid Work?", 3.
64 Tim Worstall, "Proof That Government Development Aid Doesn't Produce Economic Growth," *Forbes*, October 18, 2015, at: www.forbes.com/sites/timworstall/2015/10/18/proof-that-government-development-aid-doesnt-produce-economic-growth/#7dacc1ad1cbd.
65 UNCTAD, "Alarm Bells as More Developing Countries Become Commodity-Dependent," at: http://unctad.org/en/pages/newsdetails.aspx?OriginalVersionID=1581&Sitemap_x0020_Taxonomy=UNCTAD%20Home;#2019;#Commodities%20(Special%20Unit).
66 UNCTAD, "About UNCTAD," at: http://unctad.org/en/Pages/aboutus.aspx.
67 OPEC, "Our Mission," at: www.opec.org/opec_web/en/about_us/23.htm.
68 OPEC, "About Us: Brief History," at: www.opec.org/opec_web/en/about_us/24.htm.
69 Ibid.
70 James McBride and Mohammed Aly Sergie, "NAFTA's Economic Impact," October 4, 2017, at: www.cfr.org/backgrounder/naftas-economic-impact.
71 World Trade Organization, "About WTO," at: www.wto.org/english/thewto_e/thewto_e.htm.
72 Gates, "Comment: Bill and Melinda Gates: Let's Keep Investing in the World's Poor."

To Learn More

The World Bank Group offers exceptional analyses of understanding poverty, at www.worldbank.org/en/understanding-poverty.

For a sense of the economic and development issues that are of concern to the more developed (mainly Western) countries, visit the website of the Organisation for Economic Co-operation and Development), at: www.oecd.org.

To view graphically the extent and depth of world hunger, go to the World Food Programme's Hunger Map at: www.wfp.org/content/hunger-map-2015/.

The Famine Early Warning Systems Network (www.fews.net), created by USAID, analyzes weather conditions, food prices, nutrition data, population displacement, and other indicators, pooling information and comparing assessments with other countries and the UN to collectively determine the level of risk.

Scan the U.S. State Department's USAID website (www.usaid.gov/) for a sense of the breadth and depth of U.S. government programs aimed at assisting development in the world, often in conjunction with other governments and NGOs.

Scan the World Trade Organization's website to get a sense of the complex and complicated nature of world trade issues and disputes, at: www.wto.org/index.htm.

Visit the World Economic Forum's website (www.weforum.org) to view the initiatives of an extremely influential non-profit, independent but business-oriented organization that dedicates itself to public–private cooperation to "improve the state of the world."

Go to the Center for Global Development's website (www.cgdev.org/) to get alternative expert viewpoints on development from this independent institution that describes its mission as "a policy crucible" which "work[s] to change the policies and practices of rich countries and powerful institutions to reduce global poverty and inequality."

Visit the Modernizing Foreign Assistance Network (MFAN), "a reform coalition composed of international development and foreign policy practitioners, policy advocates and experts, concerned citizens and private sector organizations," who believe the United States should continue to play a leadership role in promoting growth and reducing poverty in the world, at: http://modernizeaid.net/about-us/.

Chapter 6

Environmental Security

Chapter contents

> Every geo-physical system on which we depend is being affected, from mountains to oceans, from icecaps to forests, and across all the arable lands that provide our food.
>
> Sea ice is at a historic low; sea levels are at a historic high, threatening the existence of low-lying island nations and cities.
>
> The seas are also being affected by warmer temperatures, rapid acidification and coral bleaching, endangering the marine food chain on which so many livelihoods and economies depend.
>
> On land, glaciers are retreating almost everywhere—a risk to the breadbaskets of the world as rivers fed by glaciers run dry.
>
> United Nations Secretary-General António Guterres[1]

Public and scientific concerns about the natural environment and human beings' effects on that environment have been evident since at least 1962, as exemplified by the highly influential work *Silent Spring*, by biologist Rachel Carson, which meticulously documented the dangers of chemical pesticides like DDT on the environment and living beings.[2] If we fast-forward almost sixty years, we now find an increasingly strong global consensus that the phenomenon of climate change is real, fostered at least in part by human activities, which UN Secretary-General Guterres's epigraph suggests will have profound effects on human civilization. What is most significant for our purposes here is the contention that this trend will have profound effects not only on individuals and their local communities, societies, and regions, but also on the national security of states.

Consider that, according to the UN's expert scientists of the Intergovernmental Panel on Climate Change (IPCC):

> By the end of the [twenty-first] century, sea levels may rise twice as much as was predicted two years ago . . . [which] means that the lives of some 600 million people living on low-lying islands, as well as those living in Southeast Asia's populous delta areas, will be put at serious risk.[3]

The implications of relocating literally millions of human beings in areas threatened by climate change are staggering, and people are already internally relocating from low-lying areas in Bangladesh and the Philippines. A 2018 report by the World Bank predicts "climate change will push tens of millions of people to migrate within their countries by 2050. It projects that without concrete climate and development action, just over 143 million people . . . could be forced to move within their own countries" in sub-Saharan Africa, South Asia, and Latin America.[4]

For some island countries, like Kiribati and the Maldives, abandoning low-lying areas is not an option, as their entire countries may become uninhabitable by mid-century. Governments there are now making plans to remove their entire populations to safer landmass areas. Clearly, "ecomigration" is a growing concern, one triggered not only by rising seas for island and coastal nations but also by the opposite phenomenon of desertification and a lack of fresh water in areas like the American Southwest.[5] More ominously, the UN's annual (2018) assessment of the state of the world's water predicts that by 2050:

> between 4.8 billion and 5.7 billion people will live in areas that are water-scarce for at least one month each year, up from 3.6 billion today, while the number of people at risk from floods will increase to 1.6 billion, from 1.2 billion.[6]

It is evident that these environmental conditions create social and economic stress that can enhance and even trigger conflict, disease, and refugees—all factors that may threaten domestic, regional, and ultimately international stability.[7]

Whereas the United States may have the resources to at least mitigate the effects of climate change within its own territory, most developing countries and their populations do not. While wealthy countries can build desalinization plants to increase their drinking water supply and rising insurance costs will push construction away from their flood zones, very poor countries do not have these capacities. Further, climate change threatens important U.S. foreign policy goals of promoting development, good governance, and sustainable agriculture while reducing conflict within and between developing countries. Former UN Secretary-General Ban Ki-moon highlighted the importance of a stable and healthy environment for the entire world community, underscoring the environmental correlation to development and conflict:

> The environment and natural resources are crucial in consolidating peace within and between war-torn societies . . . Lasting peace in Darfur will depend in part on resolving the underlying competition for water and fertile land. And there can be no durable peace in Afghanistan if the natural resources that sustain livelihoods and ecosystems are destroyed. The United Nations attaches great importance to ensuring that action on the environment is part of our approach to peace. Protecting the environment can help countries create employment opportunities, promote development and avoid a relapse into armed conflict.[8]

Consistent with Ban Ki-moon's observation, militaries already respond regularly to environmental and other natural disasters such as the tragic Haitian earthquake in 2010, the tsunami that struck the Philippines in 2013, the African Ebola outbreak in 2014, or the unprecedented hurricane season that hit the Caribbean and United States Gulf Coast in 2017. Military responses are based in part on political culture and values that support a policy of international engagement, humanitarian assistance, and the capacity to deliver food and water wherever needed. This perspective was dramatically illustrated in 2018 by the first visit of a U.S. Navy aircraft carrier to Vietnam since the bitter war between the two countries, for a humanitarian mission in conjunction with the annual Pacific Partnership mission. As Rear Adm. Don Gabrielson, commander of the Task Force acting as the executive agent for the mission, commented: "The challenges we face with natural and man-made disasters do not respect borders or national sovereignty."[9]

Yet at the same time, recognition of the importance of environmental security for global prosperity and stability provides another strategic political rationale for actively managing environmental concerns. R.K. Pachauri, chairman of the IPCC, made this connection clear during his 2007 Nobel Peace Prize acceptance speech:

> Peace can be defined as security and the secure access to resources that are essential for living. A disruption in such access could prove disruptive of peace. In this regard, climate change will have several implications, as numerous adverse impacts are expected for some populations in terms of: access to clean water, access to sufficient food, stable health conditions, ecosystem resources, and security of settlements.[10]

This relationship between the environment and security was amplified some ten years later by UN Secretary-General Guterres's recognition that:

> many conflicts are triggered, exacerbated or prolonged by competition over scarce natural resources; climate change will only make the situation worse. That is why protecting our

> environment is critical to the founding goals of the United Nations to prevent war and sustain peace . . . By helping countries to mitigate and adapt to climate change, we can lower the risk of floods, droughts, famine and instability . . . These are all critical to sustainable development and a peaceful future.[11]

As this chapter explores, the perceived national security implications of environmental security—and particularly climate change—are continuing to gain credence across the spectrum, from scientists to the wider public to national security experts and, increasingly, the U.S. military. In order to understand the current thinking and concerns, this analysis first briefly defines the scope of environmental security, highlighting important events and actors. The bulk of this work then focuses on climate change as the generally acknowledged key environmental issue with implications for human, national, and international security. The evolution of thinking internationally, and within the United States (to include defense and military sectors), is examined. It will be evident that, as with so many other issues at the nexus of national and human security, the role of the United Nations has been key in this area, along with other intergovernmental and nongovernmental organizations (IGOs/NGOs)—including an influential and transnational green, or environmental, movement.

Defining Environmental Security

Concerns about the environment are not original to the twenty-first century. The effects of pesticides, the greenhouse effect, ozone-depleting chlorofluorocarbons (CFCs), and carbon emissions have been debated for decades. But in the earlier decades these discussions tended to be linked more to concerns about the natural environment, and human beings' appropriate place in that environment—often with a focus on conservation of natural resources. In fact, these ecological or environmental concerns gave rise early on to a significant social movement of "green" activists and NGOs advocating environmental causes in North America, Europe, and Japan well prior to the impact of globalization. For example, the Sierra Club was founded as early as 1892, the Natural Resources Defense Council in 1970, Greenpeace in 1971, and Earth First! in 1979.

At the international level, the United Nations' concerted interest in the environment was crystallized in 1972 when the United Nations Environment Programme (UNEP) was created in the wake of the ground-breaking UN Stockholm Conference on the Human Environment. UNEP's mandate is to coordinate the development of environmental policy consensus and to bring important environmental issues such as ozone depletion, biodiversity, and climate change to the attention of governments and the international community for action. Significantly, the organization has consistently been linked to economic development concerns—especially with relation to developing countries—as evidenced by the majority of developing states that sit on its governing council and its headquarters being situated in Nairobi, Kenya. In fact, UNEP is guided by the central tenet of sustainable development, which, as discussed in Chapter 5, is development that meets the needs of the present without compromising the ability of future generations to meet their own needs. Sustainable development suggests that harvesting timber, creating grazing areas for cattle, and preserving wild species must not, and need not, be in conflict. Instead, through careful planning, loggers, ranchers, and environmentalists can work together to promote development and protect the environment. Gro Harlem Brundtland, who has served as a UN special envoy on climate change, maintains that the "environment is where we all live; and development is what we all do in attempting to improve our lot within that abode. The two are inseparable."[12]

This inseparability of development and the environment has been transparent across UN agencies and programs for some time. While UNEP obviously is concerned with environmental issues, the mission of the United Nations Development Programme (UNDP) explicitly states that it "works to eradicate poverty while protecting the planet." Already the 1994 UNDP *Human Development Report* linked environmental security to human security concerns, noting that "the environmental threats countries are facing are a combination of the degradation of local ecosystems and that of the global system."[13] Twenty years later, the UN's Sustainable Development Goals (SDGs) highlighted "climate action" as a specific goal, while many of the other goals relate to sustainable environmental policies, such as "clean water and sanitation" and "affordable and clean energy."[14] Clearly the linkage between the environment and sustainable development, and human and national security, has become increasingly reflected in policy discussions at the international, regional, and domestic levels.

Interestingly, the United States had already established its own domestic Environmental Protection Agency (EPA) in 1970, two years before UNEP was established.[15] But at that time environmental issues were usually couched in the language of concerns about pollution and conservation of natural resources and areas in the wake of what many increasingly saw as uncontrolled population and industrial growth. It was not until the end of the Cold War that key events and steadily accumulating scientific research and empirical evidence on the gravity of environmental concerns would really propel scholars and policymakers to specifically address *(national) security* linkages. For example, in the 1990s Thomas Homer-Dixon and others provided persuasive empirical evidence to show that shortages of agricultural land, forests, water, and fish were already contributing to violent conflict, and they posited that this phenomenon would increase in coming years with a larger world population, unequal resource distribution, and the potential of global warming.[16]

Initially, these studies related to environmental security, resources, and the global warming threat were largely confined to interested scientific, scholarly, and environmental groups; however, a few U.S. policymakers such as former vice president Al Gore came to champion the cause. In Gore's influential 1992 book *Earth in the Balance,* he argued:

> Global warming is also a strategic threat. The concentration of carbon dioxide and other heat-absorbing molecules . . . [poses] a worldwide threat to the earth's ability to regulate the amount of heat from the sun retained in the atmosphere. . . . [H]uman civilization is now the dominant cause of change in the global environment. Yet we resist the truth.[17]

Gore's argument was consistent with views then gaining prominence in many sectors outside of the U.S. government, but it was not as widely accepted among many powerful business, policy, and security sectors. It was also resisted by those developing countries that were most concerned with industrializing and modernizing to support their growing, youthful populations. Economic activity and environmental concerns were perceived to be on opposite sides of policy debates.

In fact, the stark reality of expanding human needs has often meant that governments have found it necessary to accord them priority over conservation or other environmental concerns. This has led to wildlife habitat being destroyed for agriculture and forests being clear-cut for fuel. Nevertheless, in spite of continued resistance in some sectors to acknowledge a link between the environment and conflict or security aspects, an important qualitative and political change has occurred in the twenty-first century with respect to environmental issues and their perceived role in domestic and international politics. This is most clearly seen in the breakthrough Paris Agreement of December 2015, where the vast majority of UN member states—including the largest countries—agreed to work to limit global temperature rise to below two degrees Celsius (this agreement is examined further below). And, where once environmental groups were marginalized and portrayed as fringe groups, environmentalists are now considered part of the political mainstream in many countries. For example, Green Party candidates regularly compete for, and win, public office in Europe and other regions. The "tree-hugger" epithet has given way to an entire green culture that permeates much of government, business, and society. As a symbol of power, the gas-guzzling Hummer has been replaced by the hybrid Prius. And entrepreneur and inventor Elon Musk has become an environmental icon for his part in popularizing electric cars (Tesla), solar energy, and private rocket production and space travel. In short, being green is in vogue in many societies around the world, and this seems to be an enduring trend, despite pushback from nationalist and business sectors, among others.

Several factors have been instrumental in changing perceptions about the environment as a valid policy, and ultimately security, issue. Certainly the committed environmental movement itself with its wide range of actors from individual activists to nongovernmental advocacy groups to the intergovernmental UNEP—and key countries like Sweden—have exercised a growing influence upon public and policymaker opinions alike. This influence has been magnified in our globalized information age, similarly to what has occurred with the transnational human rights movement. Key public figures like Gore and Musk, and committed scientists, have also influenced perceptions, with an excellent demonstration of this influence on display in the award of the 2007 Nobel Peace Prize in equal parts to the UN's authoritative Intergovernmental Panel on Climate Change and to former U.S. vice president Al Gore—specifically for their separate work on publicizing man-made climate change and setting out measures to combat it. Additionally, revered figures such as South African bishop Desmond Tutu, himself a 1984 Nobel Peace Prize Laureate, have framed climate concerns in spiritual terms: "To ignore the challenge of global warming may be criminal. It certainly is disobeying God. It is sin. The future of our fragile, beautiful planet is in our hands. We are stewards of God's creation."[18] These ideas were captured in Gore's acclaimed, Oscar-winning documentary film, *An Inconvenient Truth* (2006), which further increased public awareness of climate change.

At this point, the increasingly prevalent, exhaustively documented phenomenon of climate change is probably the major factor influencing current views on environmental security. Notably, climate change now is given pride of place on UNEP's website (and within other UN agencies and programs, as noted above) and is generally considered to be the most critical environmental security issue of our era. Tellingly, in 2009, U.S. President Barack Obama would proclaim: "climate change poses a grave and growing danger to our people . . . Unchecked, climate change will pose unacceptable risks to our security, our economies, and our planet."[19] Yet, his successor Donald Trump has challenged the science behind climate change, and in 2017 announced that the United States would withdraw from the Paris Climate Accord, a process expected to take three years. Setting presidential politics aside, concern for climate change continues to grow within U.S. military circles and among national security and intelligence professionals, as highlighted below. Yet, if this is the case, why is there still resistance to viewing climate change as a national security threat, as reflected in President Trump's view?

Climate Change, Science, and Perceptions

It is important to underscore first that climate change per se is not a new occurrence, and the notion that the earth's climate does change is not inherently controversial; for example, the conclusion that the last ice age ended 10,000 years ago is widely accepted. However, the current controversy rests on disagreement about the pace, cause, and impact of climate change. How quickly will change occur? Is the change driven mainly by "natural" events or by human activities? What will be the impact of those changes within countries, and on the biosphere as a whole; and what, if anything, should be done about it? The answers to those questions are critical to designing effective national security policies that also take into account human security concerns.

Disagreements over climate change are likely due in part to the fact that given the historically slow pace of climate change, until recently its negative effects have been somewhat obscured from human perception. Yet one can now see dramatic evidence of climate change by comparing recent images of the Arctic to notice the ice melt, the disappearance of snow on Mount Kilimanjaro, or the expansion of deserts in Africa. (Images 6.1 and 6.2 compare ice present on Mount Kilimanjaro in 1993 and 2000.) Each image provides a ready reference that the climate changes, although the pace of change is still disputed. Nevertheless, the prevailing scientific theory predicts that gradual temperature change will produce a 0.2-degree Celsius rise in surface temperatures every decade.[20] Although this is slow, it is already observable in the Arctic and glacial parts of the world—for instance, some evidence suggests that all of the glaciers in Montana's Glacier Park will be gone by 2030. And the trend lines seem clear, as the World Meteorological Organization (WMO) reported that:

> 2016 was the warmest year on record: a remarkable 1.1 [degree] C above the pre-industrial period, which is 0.06 [degree] C above the previous record set in 2015 . . . Globally averaged sea-surface temperatures were also the warmest on record; global sea levels continued to rise; and Arctic sea-ice extent was well below average for most of the year.[21]

Image 6.1 Mount Kilimanjaro in 1993. Photo: NASA

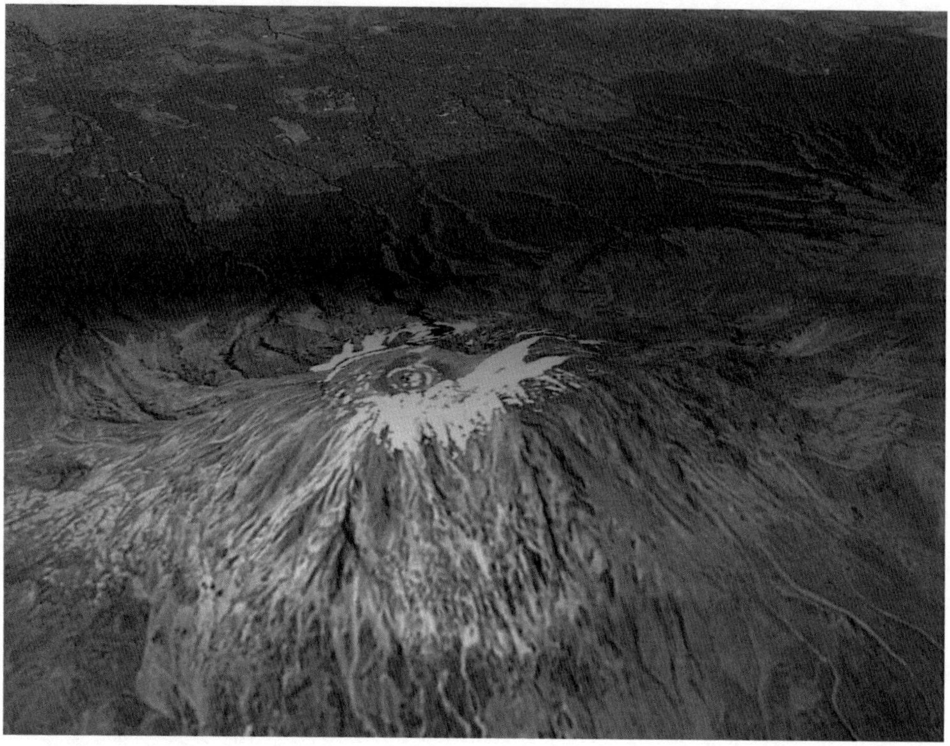

Image 6.2 Mount Kilimanjaro in 2000. Photo: NASA

Yet in spite of these types of statistics, and given the slow, generational pace of climate change, optimists see science and society keeping up with inevitable environmental change. Just as humans adapted to the ice age, optimists argue that we will adapt to climate change again through technology and human migration. People will relocate from low-lying areas to higher ground, new crops will be developed for a new climate, and new types of energy will reduce the use of fossil fuels. At the same time, geo-engineering will draw excess carbon dioxide from the atmosphere or reflect excess light back into space. It is even proposed that some countries like the United States and Canada may actually benefit from climate change as the growing season is extended. Longer growing seasons will enable increased food production and food exports. In short, for optimists time is an ally in coping with climate change, and there is no assumed linkage to increased national security concerns.

❖ BOX 6.1 THINK AGAIN: DISPUTING THE SCIENCE BEHIND CLIMATE CHANGE

In spite of the growing, majority scientific consensus regarding climate change and high-level political support for programs to reduce carbon dioxide emissions around the world, the concept of climate change continues to be attacked. The skepticism ranges along a spectrum, from former Greenpeace activist Bjørn Lomborg—who challenges the most pessimistic assessments of a decaying earth but still sees the need for improvement in how humans interact with the environment—to others who believe that there is no basis to believe human activity is impacting the world's climate detrimentally and that climatic change is a natural, cyclical occurrence.

In the United States, perhaps the most significant skeptic of climate change is Senator James Inhofe (Republican-Oklahoma), who has been leading the campaign against policy that would limit carbon emissions. In 2003 he attracted some support when he declared on the U.S. Senate floor that the notion of global warming was "the greatest hoax ever perpetrated on the American people." He has continued to back up that claim by pointing to instances where certain scientists and popular authors, such as Dr. Michael Crichton, have disputed the majority consensus view expressed by the expert scientists of the UN's Intergovernmental Panel on Climate Change and the University of East Anglia's Climatic Research Unit (UEA CRU) in the UK.

Senator Inhofe received additional support when he released a report in 2010 that addressed a controversy caused by e-mails and documents released from the CRU. (The e-mails suggested that scientific counterevidence against climate change was intentionally stifled, and that the scientists were politically motivated to make a case for global warming being induced by human activity. However, a number of expert panels such as the independent East Anglia review team, found no evidence that the scientists had deliberately manipulated data, or that climate change was a farce).[1] In an opinion piece in *U.S. News and World Report*, the senator wrote:

> Call it the global warming crackup, an unfolding process of contradictory claims about glaciers, weather, and scientists asserting a consensus when none exists. Global warming alarmists can't make up their minds because the entire basis for their energy rationing project has collapsed into a mess of errors, exaggerations, and deceit.
>
> [. . .]
>
> My minority report shows the world's leading climate scientists acting like political scientists, with an agenda disconnected from the principles of good science. And it shows that there is no consensus—except agreement there are significant gaps in what scientists know about the climate system. It's time for the [Obama] administration to recognize this. Its endangerment finding rests on bad science. It should throw out that finding and abandon greenhouse gas regulation under the Clean Air Act—a policy that will mean fewer jobs, higher taxes, and economic decline.[2]

When President Trump withdrew the U.S. from the Paris climate agreement, Senator Inhofe spoke in favor of the decision: "Removing ourselves from the Paris agreement brings us one step closer to removing more harmful Obama-era regulations and commitments."[3]

The impact of climate change skeptics does seem to affect Americans' thinking, although there is more support for the concept in other countries. Some polls have suggested that even a majority of U.S. citizens believe climate change is overrated. This is clearly a contentious political issue that will not be resolved anytime soon.

1 James M. Inhofe, "Climate Change Update: Senate Floor Statement," January 4, 2005, available at www.epw.senate.gov/public/index.cfm/2005/1/subcommittee-on-clean-air-climate-change-and-nuclear-safetymulti-emmissions-legislation.
2 James Inhofe, "Inhofe: Climategate Shows There's No Global Warming Consensus," *U.S. News and World Report*, March 23, 2010, available at https://archive.li/IU40A.
3 "Inhofe Speaks on Senate Floor In Support of Decision to Withdrawal from Paris Climate Agreement," Thursday, June 15, 2017. www.inhofe.senate.gov/newsroom/press-releases/inhofe-speaks-on-senate-floor-in-support-of-decision-to-withdrawal-from-paris-climate-agreement.

An alternative, more pessimistic view predicts that abrupt climate change will occur at a rapid pace, as made notorious by the film *The Day After Tomorrow* (2004). According to the film's scenario, climate change produces cooler temperatures that trigger an ice age, forcing the mass movement of people from the Northern Hemisphere to more tropical climes. As depicted in the film, the greatly accelerated pace of climate change was clearly rooted in fiction, but some scientists believe abrupt climate change will begin with gradual glacial melting that seems to already be happening. The process would alter the ocean's salinity, which slows the warming ocean currents. This could occur over years instead of decades, and would produce colder temperatures instead of warmer ones. The prediction of colder temperatures is counterintuitive to expectations of a warming planet, but Peter Schwartz and Doug Randall have considered the global and national security implications of this possibility:

> Large population movements in this scenario are inevitable. Learning how to manage those populations, border tensions that arise and the resulting refugees will be critical. New forms of security agreements dealing specifically with energy, food and water will also be needed. In short, while the US itself will be relatively better off and with more adaptive capacity, it will find itself in a world where Europe will be struggling internally, large numbers of refugees washing up on its shores and Asia in serious crisis over food and water. Disruption and conflict will be endemic features of life.[22]

Water Scarcity

Worldwide, ongoing climate changes will collectively reduce the amount of fresh water available for drinking and irrigation for food production, negatively impact plant and animal species, and increase societal pressures among already vulnerable populations. A comprehensive 2009 UN water resources study estimates that by 2030, "nearly half of the world's population will be living in areas of high water stress." Furthermore, the United Nations predicts that by 2025, up to 2.4 billion people will be subject to intense water scarcity, which may displace 700 million people by 2030.[23] The distribution of water resources in naturally arid regions has long been recognized as a direct, or contributing, factor to endemic conflict in areas such as the Jordan River basin in the Middle East.[24] Even within the United States, disputes occur; for example, since 1990 the states of Georgia, Florida, and Alabama have continued to quarrel about fair use of the waters from the shared Chattahoochee River.

The growing global awareness of the importance of water is reflected in the fact that, for the first time ever, the UN General Assembly has declared the right to water (and sanitation) to be a basic human right. While non-binding, the UN reminded the world that governments have intentionally undermined human security by creating water scarcity, as evidenced by Iraqi leader Saddam Hussein's draining marshes in southern Iraq in the early 1990s in order to weaken the rival Shiite population there.

The shift to non-carbon fuel sources can also create tensions among governments when rivers are dammed for hydroelectric power and irrigation. Unfortunately, the latter process is particularly prone to cause conflict as many countries in different parts of the world dispute upriver countries' practices that cause stress on countries downstream. For example, Vietnam, Laos, and Cambodia blame China for diverting too much of the shared Mekong River, which provides water for about 60 million people. Developing countries with huge populations like China and India are quite likely to be negatively impacted by climate change as these countries are already stressed by water scarcity and fail to produce enough food for their populations. Recall that this is the type of scenario that Homer-Dixon and his colleagues projected might occur in their work dating back to the early 1990s. In contrast, Wendy Barnaby is optimistic overall, noting that "countries do not go to war over water, they solve their water shortages through trade and international agreements."[25] Clearly, this issue is open to debate, but it seems most likely that wars over water will occur where other stressors between peoples are already present, such as in the Middle East.

In the perpetually unstable Middle East, Syria's conflict has been linked to years of severe drought that led to migration from farms to cities, helping to fuel tensions that led to civil war.[26] On a much larger scale, in Africa, between 75 and 250 million people are projected to be exposed to water stress by 2020, reducing vital agricultural production.[27] Already, millions of Africans suffer from food shortages that lead to regular famines.[28] As noted in Chapter 5, access to food is a precondition for escaping extreme poverty and for improving development, stability, and security, a factor that is already painfully clear in struggling countries in East Africa, Southeast Asia, and Central America. Additionally, some trace the origins of certain conflicts to high food prices or limited access to food.[29] Thus, while some may still dispute that climate change should be considered a national security matter, both the scientific evidence of that phenomenon and the direct, or indirect, effects that climate change may have—such as related to water—in slowing development, stressing societies, and contributing to, or even causing, conflict make it a valid security concern. U.S. and international policymakers and strategists increasingly recognize this linkage; climate change in and of itself can be a source of instability that leads to conflict.

Ecomigration

Sea levels are expected to rise between 0.8 and 2.0 meters by the year 2100. This will have devastating effects on low-lying areas around the world, including Bangladesh, the Netherlands, and the United States' Gulf Coast. Additionally, sea-level rise will literally wash away some existing countries, including Tuvalu, Kiribati (see Image 6.3), the Marshall Islands, Fiji, and the Maldives. President Mohamed Nasheed of the Maldives has been particularly active in raising awareness of his country's plight, with the most spectacular event being holding his cabinet meeting underwater in 2009 while wearing scuba gear.

Located in the Indian Ocean, the highest point in the Maldives is just 2.0 meters, or 6.5 feet, above sea level, but 80 percent of the islands are below 1.0 meter, or 3.0 feet. Because of this, the government has not been waiting to act until sea levels rise, and has

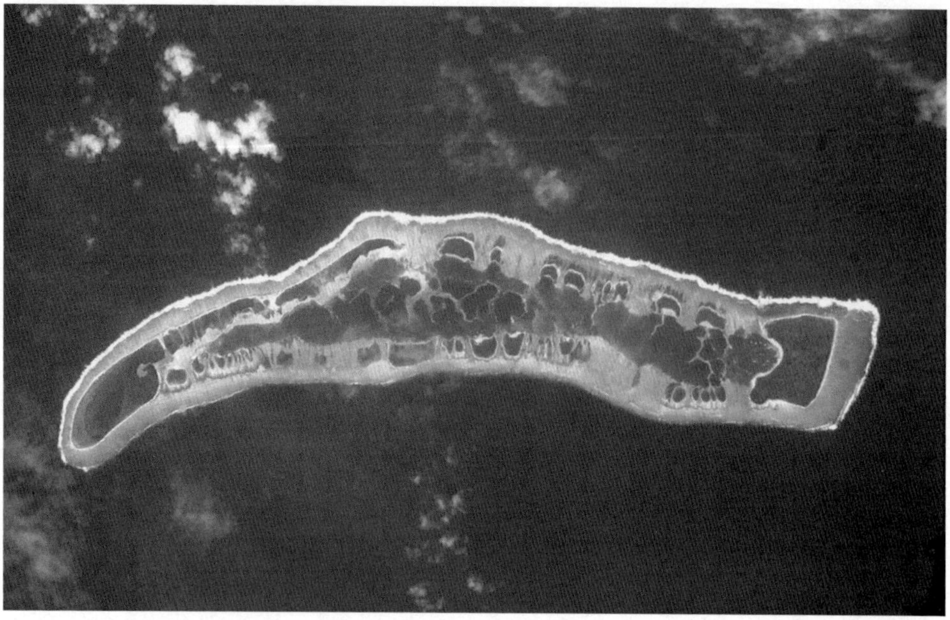

Image 6.3 Uninhabited Millennium Island, South Pacific: one of thirty-two atolls constituting the Republic of Kiribati that are at risk from rising sea levels. Photo: NASA

been searching for a new homeland for the 370,000 Maldivians facing ecodisplacement. Sri Lanka, India, and Australia are potential new homelands, but complex negotiations are just beginning. At least in the modern era, this may be the first instance of a country relocating from its geographic territory. Although the logistics of relocating 370,000 people from the Maldives may be daunting, if we multiply this by the number of states potentially affected, the implications are truly staggering. Many in the U.S. Gulf Coast region experienced some sense of the complexity and cost of this type of scenario as they faced the prospect of having to relocate permanently from coastal areas due to the implications of the 2010 BP oil spill, and more recently in the wake of extremely destructive hurricanes in 2017.

In preparation for the seemingly inevitable sea-level rise, the Maldives and other low-lying countries have formed the Alliance of Small Island States (AOSIS) to serve as an ad hoc lobby and negotiating voice for small-island developing states within the UN system. With at least forty-two members located around the world, the group works to raise awareness of climate change and lobbies for strict controls on the world's temperature. In September 2009, AOSIS issued a declaration that, among many things, called for "urgent, ambitious and decisive action to significantly reduce emissions of all green house gases . . . [and] increased levels of financial and technological resources" for its members. But small states dependent on donors for financial assistance are too limited in what they can accomplish. Thus, at the 2009 Copenhagen climate change summit, these countries pushed for, and received, the promise of access to an international fund to mitigate the impact of climate change. After the 2016 Paris Agreement came into effect, AOSIS warned against complacency since "climate change impacts are transforming our world faster than we can adapt."[30] The group continues to be one of the most vocal in publicizing the urgent nature of climate change for human security.

Climate Change and Inter/National Security

The fact that climate change should be included as a factor in security considerations has captured the attention of strategic thinkers since at least the 1990s. As then-UN Secretary-General Kofi Annan observed:

> Environmental degradation has the potential to destabilize already conflict-prone regions, especially when compounded by inequitable access or politicization of access to scarce resources. I urge Member States to renew their efforts to agree on ways that allow all of us to live sustainably within the planet's means.

His successor, Ban Ki-moon, agreed that "when resources are scarce—whether energy, water or arable land—our fragile ecosystems become strained, as do the coping mechanisms of groups and individuals. This can lead to a breakdown of established codes of conduct, and even outright conflict."[31] With this in mind, Ban envisioned specific threatening scenarios that should stimulate action to reduce the effects of climate change:

- The adverse effects of changing weather patterns, such as floods and droughts, and related economic costs, including compensation for lost land, could risk polarizing society and marginalizing communities. This, in turn, could weaken the institutional capacity of the State to resolve conflict through peaceful and democratic means, to ensure social cohesion, and to safeguard human rights.
- Extreme weather events and natural disasters, such as floods and drought, increase the risk of humanitarian emergencies, and thus the risk of instability and dislocation.
- Migration driven by factors such as climate change could deepen tensions and conflicts, particularly in regions with large numbers of internally displaced persons and refugees.
- Scarce resources, especially water and food, could help transform peaceful competition into violence.
- Limited or threatened access to energy is already known to be a powerful driver of conflict. Our changing planet risk[s] making it more so.[32]

The fact that UN officials had reached some consensus on environmental security concerns at least a generation ago is not entirely surprising in view of the UN's mandate for both peace and security, and development, issues. But it is instructive to note the clear progression of explicit concerns about environmental security, and specifically climate change, in U.S. governmental sectors. For example, the senior government and policy experts of the U.S. National Intelligence Council (NIC) concluded in 2016 that climate change and its resulting effects are likely to pose wide-ranging national security challenges for the United States and other countries over the next 20 years through the following pathways: threats to the stability of countries, heightened social and political tensions, adverse effects on food prices and availability, increased risks to human health, negative impacts on investments and economic competitiveness, and potential climate discontinuities and secondary surprises.[33] In their expanded *Global Trends* report one year later, the NIC again warned of the dangers of climate change, especially for already vulnerable populations:

> Changes in the climate will produce more extreme weather events and put greater stress on humans and critical systems, including oceans, freshwater, and biodiversity. These changes, in turn, will have direct and indirect social, economic, political, and security effects. Extreme

> weather can trigger crop failure, wildfires, energy blackouts, infrastructure breakdown, supply-chain breakdowns, migration, and infectious disease outbreaks. Such events will be more pronounced as people concentrate in climate-vulnerable locations, such as cities, coastal areas, and water-stressed regions.[34]

Significantly, in 2017 the Trump administration published its *U.S. Government Global Water Strategy*, one of the first policy documents of the new administration. That document declared: "There is a growing global water crisis that may increase disease, undermine economic growth, foster insecurity and state failure, and generally reduce the capacity of countries to advance priorities that support U.S. national interests." The document stressed the fact that engagement on water issues was necessary to protect U.S. national security interests.[35]

U.S. Defense and Military Perspective

The importance of environmental security has also been recently influencing strategic defense and military thinking in the United States. As the U.S. government continues to use the military in ways to prevent conflict or stabilize areas, the military has identified climate change as one of the underlying causes of contemporary strife. A group of distinguished retired military officers proclaimed in the report *National Security and the Threat of Climate Change* that it was essential for the military to prepare for natural disasters, pandemic disease events, and other climate change-induced tragedies warranting a response from the United States. These senior officers expected that humanitarian assistance, disaster relief, and stability operations would be persistent features of future military operations.[36] This type of perspective has been increasingly reflected in military journals and in articles, papers, and conference proceedings at major U.S. professional military educational institutions.

Tellingly, the Pentagon now considers gradual warming and abrupt climate changes as important factors, leading to economic malaise, border collapse, and global conflict being commonly expressed in strategic-level guidance. As the 2014 U.S. *Quadrennial Defense Review* declared:

> The pressures caused by climate change will influence resource competition while placing additional burdens on economies, societies, and governance institutions around the world. These effects are threat multipliers that will aggravate stressors abroad such as poverty, environmental degradation, political instability, and social tensions—conditions that can enable terrorist activity and other forms of violence.[37]

Along these lines, "the U.S. should commit to global partnerships that help less developed nations build the capacity and resiliency to better manage climate impacts."[38]

In 2015, the Pentagon specifically required each combatant command to assess the risks of climate change, the ways in which the combatant commands were integrating mitigation of these risks into their planning processes, and a description of the resources required for an effective response.[39] More recently, in unpublished written testimony for the Senate Armed Services Committee on his confirmation to become Secretary of Defense in 2017, retired U.S. Marine Corps general James Mattis stated his belief that climate change is a threat to national security, "impacting stability in areas of the world where our troops are operating today." Furthermore, Mattis noted then that "the military needs to consider the impact that climate change-related outcomes—such as open water in the Arctic and drought in contentious areas of the world—have on military operations."[40]

These U.S. security perspectives on climate change typically focus on the deleterious effects of climate change on weaker states that would complicate achieving U.S. objectives and carrying out military operations in certain regions. In other words, climate change tends to be viewed as an enabler, multiplier, or even trigger of pre-existing stressors, instability, and conflict situations already in play. For instance, countries with traditional border disputes could wage war for control of water or face instability through mass migration of people seeking access to food. Or climate change may aggravate the effects of natural disasters, thus making U.S. humanitarian and military assistance even more necessary to alleviate human suffering (and stem the flow of refugees). This is also a common view among scholarly observers, that:

> the threat to state stability comes not from climate change itself, but rather from how these changes interact with the existing security landscape and with the ability or inability of governments to effectively manage these conditions to ensure that basic resources and prosperity are preserved for their respective publics. Seen through this lens, climate change may present a serious challenge to state sovereignty in a number of places around the world.[41]

At the same time it is important to realize that there is a less obvious and perhaps unexpected role that climate change may play in fostering serious major power competition. For instance, well-known British strategist Colin Gray sees climate change as one potential source of conflict between states in the future, and scholar Michael Klare sees resource competition as a critical factor that could lead to future wars.[42]

> As one example, in 1991, Iraq's invasion of Kuwait was in large part to seek control of Kuwaiti oil production and to gain better access to the Persian Gulf. Nearby, Egypt's ongoing concerns about continued access to adequate Nile River waters have created hostilities with up-stream states which are increasing their use and control of the river.[43]

In line with these perspectives, the United States and China could clash over hydrocarbon resources in the Arctic, Africa, or South America. Of course these assessments are speculative, and there is no way to predict that climate change may produce resource rivalry among states that will lead to war. These perspectives also do not take into account the energy revolution in the United States that is making the country energy self-sufficient. However, as noted above, considering China's enormous population and its requirements, the possibility should not be discounted. In fact, in a 2014 analysis Edward Grumbine expressed concern that China was not adequately considering environmental security concerns in its planning. Grumbine saw this as a critical lack, considering that "after decades of rapid economic growth, major stressors—ecosystem degradation, food, energy, water issues, urbanization, and climate change—are reducing social-ecological resilience within China and across its borders."[44] Furthermore, Grumbine argued that "because China's natural resource base cannot meet growing domestic demand spurred by rapid urbanization, extraction pressures on global resources are increasing."[45] How much of China's creation of manmade islands in the South China Sea—and its apparent determination to control that area—is due to resource concerns is an open question wrapped in nationalism.

Another region that is receiving increasing attention from major powers and the international community at large is the Arctic Ocean. This is not coincidental when assessing climate change because the scientific consensus is that climate change is partly responsible for the melting of Arctic sea ice; in fact, the Arctic may be warming twice as fast as the rest of the world. Thus, "there is concern that melting Arctic sea ice could trigger a new 'great game' of international power politics as nations race to extend their Arctic Ocean territorial shelf claims and extract the abundance of newly accessible natural resources."[46] There is arguably clear incentive to do so as "recent estimates from the United States indicate that about 30 [percent] of the remaining world undiscovered resources of natural gas and some 10 [percent] of the oil are in the Arctic region."[47]

Yet on a more positive note, it is important to emphasize that at the time of this writing diplomacy has predominated among the Arctic nations to include the United States, Russia, Canada, and several European nations. The Arctic Council, a high-level intergovernmental forum, was founded in the 1990s to address issues of concern, including the needs of the indigenous people of the Arctic. Whether this cooperative attitude will prevail into the future is debatable, as "there will be open water seasonally across the Arctic Ocean in the near future allowing for significant increases in marine shipping, easier exploitation of the extensive Arctic reserves of oil, gas and minerals and, consequently, greater environmental threats."[48] Unfortunately, the historical record related to resource competition between states is not promising, as numerous case studies by scholars have shown the prevalence of conflict when it comes to sharing critical resources.

Addressing Climate Change

The warnings about environmental security thus seem increasingly ominous and have prompted a variety of calls for action. However, as noted, a backlash also exists with debate over the causes, severity, and implications of climate change. In particular, climate change has continued to be a contentious economic, and therefore political, issue in countries like the United States. This dates back to the framework adopted at the 1997 climate change summit in Kyoto, Japan, where countries committed to limiting their carbon emissions. As carbon emissions are believed to be a key factor in climate change, it was agreed that they must be reduced. Unsurprisingly, the most developed countries have tended to produce the most carbon emissions because their use is highly correlated to economic activity. The Kyoto Protocol originated in the 1992 United Nations Framework Convention on Climate Change signed in Rio de Janeiro, and it declares in Article 2:

> The ultimate objective [is the] stabilization of greenhouse gas concentrations in the atmosphere at a level that would prevent dangerous anthropogenic interference with the climate system. Such a level should be achieved within a time-frame sufficient to allow ecosystems to adapt naturally to climate change, to ensure that food production is not threatened and to enable economic development to proceed in a sustainable manner.

In principle, the United States initially accepted the goals of climate change treaties such as Kyoto, but domestic concerns and an ingrained belief in the value of the free market system have slowed implementation (see Table 6.1 for a list of major environmental treaties). For example, the United States has tended to favor providing business incentives to reduce carbon emissions, while European governments tend to regulate businesses more heavily. Indicative of this difference is the fact that the U.S. Senate refused to ratify the Kyoto treaty (although President Bill Clinton signed it), and President George W. Bush then withdrew consent for the treaty. For the Bush administration, climate change was considered primarily an economic issue and was still shrouded in scientific uncertainty. However, by the end of the Bush administration's second term in 2008, its leading officials

Table 6.1 Major Environmental Treaties, 1987–2015

1987	Montreal Protocol on Substances that Deplete the Ozone Layer
1987	Agreement Between the Government of the United States of America and the Government of the Republic of Iceland Concerning Icelandic Whaling for Scientific Purposes
1990	International Convention on Oil Pollution Preparedness, Response, and Cooperation
1991	Espoo Convention on Environmental Impact Assessment in a Transboundary Context
1992	United Nations Framework Convention on Climate Change
1992	Convention on Biological Diversity
1992	International Convention on Civil Liability for Oil Pollution Damage
1994	Convention to Combat Desertification
1994	International Tropical Timber Agreement
1996	International Convention on Liability and Compensation for Damage in Connection with the Carriage of Hazardous and Noxious Substances by Sea
1998	Kyoto Protocol
1998	Aarhus Convention on Access to Information, Public Participation in Decision-Making and Access to Justice in Environmental Matters
1998	Protocol on Persistent Organic Pollutants to the Convention on Long-Range Transboundary Air Pollution
2000	Cartagena Protocol on Biosafety
2009	The Convention on the Conservation of Migratory Species of Wild Animals
2009	International Plant Protection Convention
2015	Paris Agreement

Sources: Working Group on Environmental Auditing, www.environmental-auditing.org/Home/FocusonBiodiversity/Internationalagreements/tabid/237/Default.aspx; *Encyclopedia of the New American Nation*, www.americanforeignrelations.com/O-W/Treaties-Environmental-treaties.html; Ronald B. Mitchell, 2002–2018, *International Environmental Agreements Database Project (Version 2018.1)*, https://iea.uoregon.edu/

had accepted the science of climate change. Yet the administration characteristically pursued its own domestic policy to reduce emissions outside the international framework established in Kyoto. For many critics of the United States' perceived unilateral tendencies in the twenty-first century, climate change represented just one more issue dividing the United States from the consensus of international opinion.

Regardless of Washington's official opposition to the climate change treaty, the pace of the transnational environmental movement did not slow appreciably through the 1990s. As noted above, the Nobel Prize Committee made a statement by awarding its Peace Prize to former vice president Al Gore and the Intergovernmental Panel on Climate Change in 2007 for their joint efforts "to build up and disseminate greater knowledge about man-made climate change, and to lay the foundations for the measures that are needed to counteract such change."

Just twelve years after Kyoto, carbon emissions were still the prominent theme at a follow-on global climate change summit in Copenhagen, Denmark. On the eve of the 2009 climate change summit, policy specialist Michael Levi argued that carbon emissions "must be cut deeply in the coming decades if the world is to control the risks of dangerous climate change." If not, experts Jessica Wallack and Veerabhadran Ramanathan predicted, "the earth's temperature stands to careen out of control."[49] The conclusion seemed inescapable to most; for countries to control climate change, they must reduce their carbon emissions.

During the Copenhagen climate change summit, countries focused on carbon emissions from the world's major polluters, including China, the United States, Europe, and India. Debate centered on the size of the cap to emissions, the baseline year for determining it, and the achievability of the cap. Yet in spite of preparatory work and growing public concern about climate change, there remained an unbridgeable chasm between developed and developing countries. Under the earlier Kyoto framework, developed countries had agreed to measure carbon emissions using 1990 as a baseline year, with countries that reduced carbon emissions being allowed to sell their "surplus pollution" on the open market as credits to other countries that could not meet their reduction goals. This new business of trading carbon credits has been valued in the billions of dollars, though the European Union's system has had mixed success to date.

With so much at stake, the baseline year has proved to be critical to discussions, as it favors certain economies. Because the baseline year was set at 1990, it reflected Soviet-era industrial activity, which collapsed in 1992. Since Soviet economic policies were not environmentally friendly, the successor countries in Central and Eastern Europe now have higher than normal carbon emissions quotas relative to the size of their respective economies. Yet with inflated carbon emissions quotas, declining population, and corresponding economic activity, Europe has much to gain from continuing to use the 1990 baseline. Likewise, since China was not a major economy in 1990 when the Kyoto framework was adopted, it is exempt from emissions caps altogether, and is situated in a favorable position.

Logically, as one would expect, the countries that produced high carbon emissions in 1990 or were exempted from caps, like Europe and China, have favored adhering to the Kyoto framework and its baseline. Many of these countries have surplus carbon credits to sell for billions of dollars when using this measure. However, the United States objects to the 1990 baseline and sees 2005 as a more realistic year for emissions since it captures the Soviet demise and China's rise. In support of this change, the United States notes that using 2005 standards, Europe's cuts amount to just 13 percent compared to 17 percent of the United States' cuts. Additionally, China is particularly concerned with the method of determining carbon emissions. Since it is the most populous country and the largest carbon emitter in the world, it does not favor the 1990 or the 2005 benchmark, but instead favors a per capita index or carbon intensity measure. Using this method would place China toward the bottom of polluting countries instead of at the top. It should not be surprising to find that when it comes to carbon emissions, the overall amount seems to matter most in terms of environmental impact, not how the number is calculated. In any case, China is clearly the largest state polluter (see Figure 6.1), resulting in extremely poor air quality and reduced life expectancy in Chinese cities.

Although the 2009 summit attempted to address climate change as a *global* concern for all of humanity, it is apparent that *national* concerns about the economic impact of reducing carbon emissions prevented participants reaching a comprehensive agreement. In Copenhagen, the director of the UN Secretary-General's climate change support team, János Pásztor, captured the challenges of addressing climate change from the United Nations' global perspective: "This is not a climate-change negotiation. It's about something much more fundamental. It's about economic strength. [Countries] just have to slug it out."[50] Of course, countries are mainly guided by national objectives and policies that seek to balance economic growth and pollution and not long-term

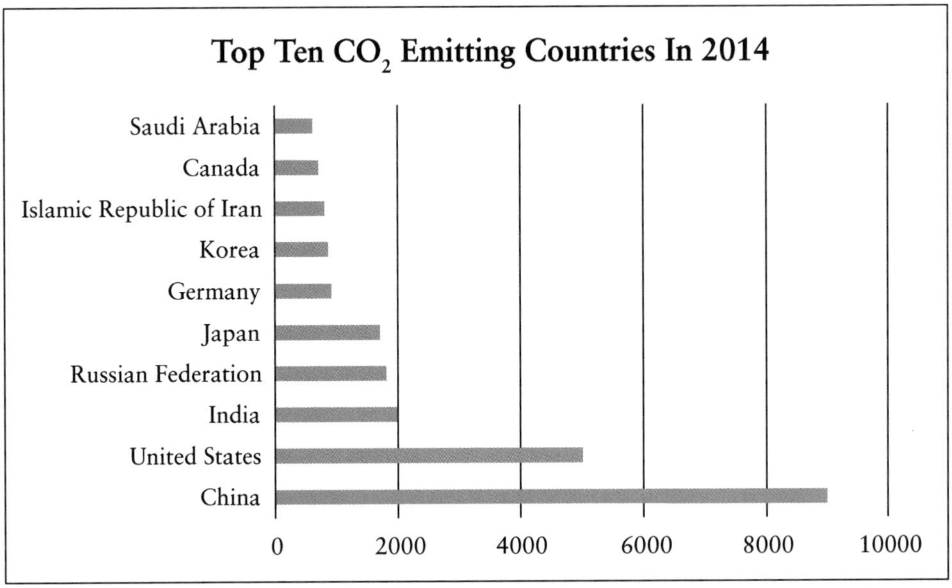

Figure 6.1 Top Ten CO_2 Emitting Countries (gross tons).
Source: International Energy Agency, *CO_2 Emissions from Fuel Combustion Highlights* (Paris: OECD/IEA, 2016). www.iea.org/publications/freepublications/publication/KeyCO2EmissionsTrends.pdf

global human security concerns. China and India have argued, for instance, that their growth should not be curtailed just because the West's industrial revolution began centuries ago.

While the carbon emissions coming from China and India top the world's output, their governments maintain that increased economic activity can actually improve the welfare of human beings. The claims make sense for these developing countries, as economic development is a more pressing concern than climate change. Over the long term, these countries argue, their societies will become stronger through development before the severe effects of climate change are apparent in the latter half of the twenty-first century. For its part, the Obama administration attempted to link the economy and climate change in a positive equation. Through clean energy programs like building wind turbines or solar panels, it asserted that the economy and the environment both could be helped. UN Secretary-General Guterres carried this positive idea forward, declaring that: "The real danger is not the threat to one's economy that comes from acting. It is, instead, the risk to one's economy by failing to act."[51]

Clearly President Obama was personally vested in the issue of climate change and environmental security. Thus, many observers would give him a good share of the credit for energizing international climate change discussions that resulted in the successful 2015 Paris Agreement (Paris Accords), the current global effort to reduce carbon emissions and combat climate change under the United Nations Framework Convention on Climate Change (UNFCCC). The agreement was negotiated at the UNFCCC-associated conference in Paris and adopted by consensus of the conference in December 2015; it went into effect in November 2016. The stated goal is to keep "the global temperature rise in this century well below 2 degrees Celsius above pre-industrial levels and to pursue efforts to limit the temperature increase even further to 1.5 degrees Celsius."[52] Also of note is that the agreement stresses the importance of adaptation to meet climate change effects, and the necessity to help less developed countries in that effort.

The Paris Agreement seemed more palatable to a number of countries because of its dependence on voluntary, "nationally determined contributions" (NDCs):

> The Paris Agreement requires all Parties to put forward their best efforts through "nationally determined contributions" (NDCs) and to strengthen these efforts in the years ahead. This includes requirements that all Parties report regularly on their emissions and on their implementation efforts.[53]

Clearly this is less directive and regimented in nature than earlier attempts, which has given many observers increased optimism about the possibility that states will meet the objectives they have determined. While the United States determined for its goal that it would cut emissions between 26 and 28 percent compared with 2005 levels by 2025, there is concern that the Trump administration's announced withdrawal from the Paris Accords may affect not only U.S. efforts but also the participation of other major powers. In this regard it is notable that the United States and China jointly announced their acceptance of the Paris Accords in September 2016. Significantly, the 2017 U.S. National Intelligence Council assessment proposed that:

> climate change will drive both geopolitical competition and international cooperation as well. China, poised for global leadership on climate change, would likely keep to its Paris commitments but could weaken its support for monitoring mechanisms and gain favor with developing world emitters like India. Tensions over managing climate change could sharpen significantly if some countries pursue geoengineering technologies in an effort to manipulate large-scale climate conditions.[54]

At this point technical and geoengineering solutions to climate change are mainly in the testing phase. According to the NIC:

> early research efforts largely live in computer models to explore techniques to alter temperature and rainfall patterns such as injecting aerosols in the stratosphere, chemically brightening marine clouds, and installing space-mirrors in orbit. Other approaches focus on removing carbon dioxide from the atmosphere. Given the lack of international standards or regulations for such activities, any efforts to test or implement large-scale geoengineering techniques would raise tensions over the risks and potential unintended consequences.[55]

Yet some scholars have found that "there is currently a significant and growing literature on the international politics of climate engineering," pointing to emerging concerns this trend might have for "interstate conflict, militarization, rising tensions between industrialized and developing countries, and governance challenges and opportunities."[56]

At this stage the UN Environment Programme is more concerned with lower-tech and practical approaches for assisting developing countries to meet the challenges of climate change and sustainable development. UNEP identifies three categories of action: climate resilience, low-emission growth, and REDD+, "where we enable countries to capitalize on investment opportunities that reduce greenhouse emissions from deforestation and forest degradation with adequate social and environmental safeguards."[57] UNEP is also particularly concerned with assisting less developed countries to prepare for, and recover from, natural disasters that have become increasingly frequent in the wake of more disruptive, warming weather patterns that are largely attributed to ongoing climate change. This human security-centered environmental approach on the part of a key UN agency should not be surprising in view of the UN priorities highlighted in this work.

In the near term, it seems clear that the U.S. government will continue to be involved in providing emergency humanitarian assistance to populations affected by natural disasters and other long-term crises worsened by global warming; for example, droughts that can impact agriculture and lead to famines. In fact, in 2014, the U.S. Department of Defense (DOD) acknowledged these concerns and published a "Climate Change Adaptation Roadmap" which identified numerous international and domestic security concerns (for example, U.S. coastal installations being vulnerable to rising sea levels) that would require the DOD to adapt across the board, to include "plans, operations, training, infrastructure, and acquisition."[58] The U.S. military's experience in assisting with disaster relief in the wake of flooding and storm damage caused by the powerful hurricanes of 2017 has surely reinforced military concerns.

Finally, it is interesting to note that at the same time the U.S. military responds to environment-induced tragedies, it is also attempting to become more environmentally responsible itself. This is an important change, since militaries have historically treated the environment rather cavalierly as a battle space, testing site, or dumping ground. Yet the U.S. Navy, for example, has committed to deriving 50 percent of its energy needs from alternative sources by 2020.[59] The U.S. Air Force is also continuing to pursue biofuels and other synthetic fuels to power its aircraft for both environmental and renewal energy reasons.[60] The message seems to be that a country can be powerful and also environmentally conscious, contrary to claims made by detractors of climate change.

Conclusion

More so than many other security challenges, environmental security does not discriminate by levels of development and privilege. Instead, all human beings regardless of their citizenship are, or will be, affected by environmental change. Like many of the challenges discussed in this book, climate stress knows no boundary. However, as with so many other globalized security issues, people in developing countries are more vulnerable to environmental change since they lack adequate resources to cope effectively with the problems generated by climate change. They are also the most likely to face already difficult economic and social conditions which climate change may aggravate or serve as the trigger for actual conflict, as noted above. It is this possibility that seems most likely to affect the national security interests of a country like the United States, depending upon the importance of the countr(ies) and region(s) involved.

As this work further demonstrates, addressing climate change from a global perspective will continue to be elusive, as national governments seek either to promote development, thereby increasing use of hydrocarbons, or to sustain high levels of human development without compromising economic activity. Given that the most catastrophic effects of climate change will probably not be evident until later this century, incremental policy solutions may keep pace with environmental change. And if the Paris Agreement is successful overall in terms of marshaling the reduction of carbon emissions—especially for major powers like China, India (and perhaps the United States led by actions by individual state and city governments)—then the effects of climate change may be forestalled and even reversed in the best case. However, frustration with halting changes will doubtless continue to motivate the ever-expanding green social movement around the world, including its growing linkages to the sustainable development movement—as reflected in Al Gore's 2017 environmental documentary, *An Inconvenient Sequel: Truth to Power*. The United Nations will continue to be the major intergovernmental actor supporting this movement, with its many linked agencies and programs focused on human security concerns.

In the short term, existing environmental issues like natural disasters, population density, water scarcity, and desertification will doubtless add to environmental security challenges in many parts of the world. And as developed countries like the United States seek to promote development elsewhere, they must inevitably encounter varied environmental challenges that often involve political issues. This already occurs when the United States supports organizations that dig wells, promote sustainable agricultural practices, and assist with environmental projects. Unfortunately, already struggling governments may be further weakened by the accelerating effects of climate change, which will reduce their capacity to take advantage of international assistance, provide basic services expected of modern governments, or improve human security for their populations. For all these reasons, the U.S. government will need to continue to address the potential for underlying environmental conditions that engender conflict and to study climate change scenarios to understand future implications for national and human security concerns. In turn, all human beings will need to remain sensitive to this issue and to make judgments about how their individual and group actions may impact the environment. As explored in the next chapter, clearly environmental issues are central to many of the security concerns that arise in the context of the maritime domain.

Notes

1 "Address on Climate Action at New York University Stern School of Business," May 30, 2017. Available at www.un.org/sg/en/content/sg/speeches/2017-05-30/secretary-generals-climate-action-address.

2 Rachel Carson, *Silent Spring* (New York: Houghton Mifflin, 2002). *Silent Spring* was first serialized in the *New Yorker* magazine and then published as a book. It was highly influential and popular, not only because of the meticulous documentation and expert evidence that Carson assembled but also due to its fictionalized chapter which told the story of a town that had been "silenced" of all types of life due to the effects of DDT. According to the nongovernmental environmental group Natural Resources Defense Council: "The most important legacy of *Silent Spring*, though, was a new public awareness that nature was vulnerable to human intervention. Carson had made a radical proposal: that, at times, technological progress is so fundamentally at odds with natural processes that it must be curtailed. Conservation had never raised much broad public interest, for few people really worried about the disappearance of wilderness. But the threats Carson had outlined—the contamination of the food chain, cancer, genetic damage, the deaths of entire species—were too frightening to ignore. For the first time, the need to regulate industry in order to protect the environment became widely accepted, and environmentalism was born." At www.nrdc.org.

3 See IPCC at www.ipcc.ch/publications_and_data/ar4/wg1/en/spmsspm-projections-of.html.

4 See World Bank Group, "Groundswell, Preparing for Internal Climate Migration." Open Knowledge Repository Report. https://openknowledge.worldbank.org/handle/10986/29461.

5 Robin Mearns and Andrew Norton (eds.), *Social Dimensions of Climate: Equity and Vulnerability in a Warming World* (Washington, DC: World Bank, 2009). https://issuu.com/world.bank.publications/docs/9780821378878.

6 Jonathan Watts, "Water Shortages Could Affect 5bn People by 2050, UN Report Warns," *The Guardian*, March 19, 2018.

7 Proceedings of the National Academy of Sciences of the United States of America, "Consequences of rapid ice sheet melting on the Sahelian population vulnerability," www.pnas.org/content/early/2017/05/30/1619358114.

8 Ban Ki-moon, "Secretary-General's Message on the International Day for Preventing the Exploitation of the Environment in War and Armed Conflict," November 6, 2008. www.un.org/sg/en/content/sg/statement/2008-11-06/secretary-generals-message-international-day-preventing-exploitation.
9 Mike Yeo, "First US Navy Carrier to Visit Vietnam since War in Wake of Humanitarian Mission," *Defense News*, February 22, 2018. www.defensenews.com/training-sim/2018/02/22/in-a-first-us-navy-carrier-to-visit-vietnam-during-humanitarian-mission/.
10 R. K. Pachauri, "Nobel Peace Prize Lecture," December 10, 2007, available at http://nobelprize.org/nobel_prizes/peace/laureates/2007/ipcc-lecture.html.
11 "Foreword" to "UN Environment Annual Report 2016: Engaging People to Protect the Planet." At: www.unep.org/annualreport/2016/index.php?page=0&lang=en.
12 UN Environment Programme, *Organizational Profile* (Nairobi: UNEP, 2009), 11.
13 UNDP, *Human Development Report 1994* (New York: Oxford University Press, 1994), 28.
14 UNDP. "Our Mission" and "Sustainable Development Goals." At www.undp.org/content/undp/en/home/sustainable-development-goals.html.
15 For an excellent description of the founding of UNEP and its changing environmental concerns over the decades, see Stanley Johnson, *UNEP: The First 40 Years: A Narrative* (Nairobi: UNEP, 2012).
16 Thomas F. Homer-Dixon, "Environmental Scarcities and Violent Conflict: Evidence from Cases," in *Theories of World Peace: An International Security Reader*, ed. Michael E. Brown, Owen R. Coté, Jr, Sean M. Lynne-Jones, and Steven E. Miller (Cambridge, MA: MIT Press, 1998), 501–536.
17 Al Gore, *Earth in the Balance: Ecology and the Human Spirit* (New York: Houghton Mifflin, 1992), 29–30.
18 Al Gore, "Nobel Peace Prize Lecture," December 10, 2007; Desmond Tutu, quoted in presentation speech by Professor Ole Danbolt Mjøs, chairman of the Norwegian Nobel Committee, Oslo, December 10, 2007. At: www.nobelprize.org/nobel_prizes/peace/laureates/2007/.
19 "Remarks by the President at the Morning Plenary Session of the United Nations Climate Change Conference," December 18, 2009. https://obamawhitehouse.archives.gov/the-press-office/remarks-president-morning-plenary-session-united-nations-climate-change-conference.
20 Intergovernmental Panel on Climate Change, *Climate Change, 2007: Synthesis Report* (Valencia: IPCC, 2007).
21 World Meteorological Organization, "WMO Statement on the State of the Global Climate in 2016" (Geneva: WMO, 2017).
22 Peter Schwartz and Doug Randall, "An Abrupt Climate Change Scenario and Its Implications for United States National Security," October 2003, available at www.gbn.com/consulting/article_details.php?id=61, 22.
23 UNCCD, "Desertification: The Invisible Frontline," January 2014. www.unccd.int/Lists/SiteDocumentLibrary/Publications/Desertification_The%20invisible_frontline.pdf.
24 See Munther J. Haddadin. "The Jordan River Basin: A Conflict Like No Other," in *Water and Post-Conflict Peacebuilding*, ed. E. Weinthal, J. Troell, and M. Nakayama (Abingdon: Earthscan, 2014): 243–263.
25 Andrew C. Revkin, "U.N.: Young and Old Boom on the Road to 9 Billion," *New York Times*, March 11, 2009, available at http://dotearth.blogs.nytimes.com/2009/03/11/un-young-old-boom-on-road-to9-billion; Martin Mittelstaedt, "UN Warns of Widespread Water Shortages," *Globe and Mail*, March 12, 2009, available at www.theglobeandmail.com/servelt/story/RTGAM.20090311.wwater0312/BNStory; Steve Lonergan, "Water and War," available at www.unep.org/ourplanet/imgversn/ 154/lonergan.html; Wendy Barnaby, "Do Nations Go to War over Water?" *Nature*, March 19, 2009.
26 Colin P. Kelley, Shahrzad Mohtadi, Mark A. Cane, Richard Seager, and Yochanan Kushnir, "Climate Change in the Fertile Crescent and Implications of the Recent Syrian Drought," *Proceedings of the National Academy of Sciences* vol. 112, no. 11 (2015): 3241–3246.
27 R. K. Pachauri, "Statement at UN Summit on Climate Change," September 22, 2009. www.ipcc.ch/pdf/presentations/rkp-statement-unccs-09.pdf.

28 To be declared a famine, at least 20 per cent of households in an area must face extreme food shortages with a limited ability to cope; acute malnutrition rates must exceed 30 percent; and the death rate must exceed two persons per day per 10,000 persons. See www.un.org/apps/news/story.asp?NewsID=39113#.WPNq3FQpChB.
29 Julie Barbet-Gros and Jose Cuesta, "Food Riots: From Definition to Operationalization," World Bank Guide for the Food Riot Radar, Washington, DC, 2015.
30 Alliance of Small Island States, "Small Islands Call on Marrakech to Live Up To Action COP Billing," November 7, 2016. http://aosis.org/press-release-small-islands-call-on-marrakech-to-live-up-to-action-cop-billing/.
31 Both quoted in Ban Ki-moon, "Statement at the Security Council Debate on Energy, Security, and Climate," April 17, 2007, available at www.un.org/ apps/sg/sgstats.asp?nid=2524.
32 Ibid.
33 National Intelligence Council, "Implications for US National Security of Anticipated Climate Change," NIC Memorandum, September 21, 2016.
34 National Intelligence Council, *Global Trends: Paradox of Progress* (Washington, DC: NIC, 2017), 21. At www.dni.gov/nic/globaltrends.
35 Donald J. Trump, *U.S. Government Global Water Strategy* (Washington, DC: Office of the President, 2017).
36 CNA, "Voices of Experience: On Climate Change and the Conditions for Terrorism," in *National Security and the Threat of Climate Change* (Alexandria, VA: CNA Corporation, 2007), 17. At: www.cna.org/cna_files/pdf/national%20security%20and%20the%20threat%20of%20climate%20change.pdf.
37 Department of Defense, *Quadrennial Defense Review* (Washington, DC: DOD, 2014), 30.
38 See CNA, "Executive Summary," in *National Security and the Threat of Climate Change*, 7.
39 Department of Defense, "National Security Implications of Climate-Related Risks and a Changing Climate," report, Washington, DC, July 23, 2015.
40 Devin Henry, "Trump's Defense Secretary Calls Climate Change a National Security Risk," *The Hill*, March 14, 2017. At: http://thehill.com/policy/energy-environment/323959-trumps-defense-secretary-calls-climate-change-a-national-security.
41 Caitlin E. Werrell and Francesco Femia, "Climate Change, the Erosion of State Sovereignty, and World Order," *Brown Journal of World Affairs*, vol. 22, no. 2 (2016): 221–235, 224.
42 See Colin Gray, *The Future of Strategy* (Hoboken, NJ: Wiley, 2015); and Michael Klare, *The Race for What's Left: The Global Scramble for the World's Last Resources* (London: Macmillan-Picador, 2012).
43 Odelia Funke, "The Role of Biopolitics in Environmental Security Analysis," *Politics and the Life Sciences*, vol. 30, no. 1 (2011): 71–76.
44 R. Edward Grumbine, "Assessing Environmental Security in China," *Frontiers in Ecology and the Environment*, vol. 12, no. 7 (2014): 403–411.
45 Ibid.
46 Kenneth S. Yalowitz, "Arctic Climate Change: Security Challenges and Stewardship Opportunities," in *Environmental Security in the Arctic Ocean*, ed. Paul Arthur Berkman and Aleksandr N. Vylegzhanin (Dordrecht: Springer, 2013), 31–36.
47 Ibid.
48 Ibid.
49 Michael A. Levi, "Copenhagen's Inconvenient Truth: How to Salvage the Climate Conference," *Foreign Affairs* vol. 88, no. 5 (2009): 92–98, 100–104, 92; Jessica Seddon Wallack and Veerabhadran Ramanathan, "The Other Climate Changers," *Foreign Affairs* vol. 88, no. 5 (2009): 105–113, 113.
50 Quoted in Jeffrey Ball, Stephen Power, and Alesandro Torello, "Divisions Persist on Core Questions as Leaders Arrive," *Wall Street Journal*, December 15, 2009.
51 "Address on Climate Action at New York University Stern School of Business," May 30, 2017. Available at www.un.org/sg/en/content/sg/speeches/2017-05-30/secretary-generals-climate-action-address.
52 "United Nations Framework Convention on Climate Change." At http://unfccc.int/paris_agreement/items/9485.php.

53 Ibid.
54 NIC, *Global Trends*, 23.
55 Ibid.
56 Joshua B. Horton and Jesse L. Reynolds, "The International Politics of Climate Engineering: A Review and Prospectus for International Relations," *International Studies Review* vol. 18, no. 3 (2016): 438–461.
57 UN Environment Program, *Annual Report 2016: Engaging People to Protect the Planet*. At: www.unep.org/annualreport/2016/index.php?page=0&lang=en.
58 U.S. Department of Defense, "FY 2014 Climate Change Adaptation Roadmap," Alexandria, VA, June 2014, 4.
59 Secretary of the Navy Ray Mabus, "Remarks at the Naval Energy Forum," McLean, VA, October 14, 2009. At www.navy.mil/navydata/people/secnav/Mabus/Speech/SECNAV%20Energy%20Forum%2014%20Oct%2009%20Rel1.pdf.
60 Marisa Novobilski, "Fueling the Future: AF Works to 'Home-Grow' Biofuels for DOD, Industry," *U.S. Air Force News*, August 29, 2016. At: www.af.mil/News/Article-Display/Article/929168/fueling-the-future-af-works-to-home-grow-biofuels-for-dod-industry/.

To Learn More

The Center for International Earth Science Information Network at Columbia University (www.ciesin.org) works at the intersection of the social, natural, and information sciences, and specializes in online data and information management, spatial data integration and training, and interdisciplinary research related to human interactions in the environment.

Marc Levy asks, "Is the Environment a National Security Issue?" in *International Security* vol. 20, no. 2 (2001): 35–62.

Track global climate patterns through the National Oceanographic and Atmospheric Administration at www.ncdc.noaa.gov/oa/climate/globalwarming.html.

Watch an animation of the planet's snow cover at http://earthobservatory.nasa.gov/GlobalMaps/view.php?d1=MOD10C1_M_SNOW.

Examine the principles of the United Nations Framework Convention on Climate Change at http://unfccc.int/essential_background/convention/back-ground/items/1349.php.

Explore the Alliance of Small Island States to see how they perceive climate change and the approaches they take to lobby carbon emitters at www.sidsnet.org/aosis/.

The World Watch Institute (founded in 1974) is an independent and interdisciplinary nongovernmental research organization that "focuses on the 21st-century challenges of climate change, resource degradation, population growth, and poverty by developing and disseminating solid data and innovative strategies for achieving a sustainable society." Scan their many programs, events, and publications at www.worldwatch.org/.

The Pacific Institute tracks water conflicts over the past 5000 years. Explore the first water-related conflict between the Mesopotamian city-states of Lagash and Umma at http://worldwater.org/conflictchronology.pdf.

World Water Watch (https://worldwaterwatch.org) is a coalition of NGOs, governmental agencies, and local communities involved with the planning, protection, and restoration of water resources.

Scan the website of the Nobel Peace Prize-winning, UN-created Intergovernmental Panel on Climate Change experts from around the world to view their conclusions on global warming: www.ipcc.ch/index.htm.

To read the actual Paris Agreement (climate accord) and chart global progress under that nearly universal compact to address the threat of global warming, go to http://unfccc.int/paris_agreement/items/9485.php.

Review U.S. Senator James Inhofe's explanation about his disputing the evidence of global warming in a Senate speech at www.youtube.com/watch?v=pT9ZeEFDVyM.

Chapter 7

Maritime Security

Chapter contents

> Americans have long looked to the sea as a source of safety and well-being. Bounded by two oceans and the Gulf of Mexico, and crisscrossed by inland waterways, America was destined to be a maritime nation. Our fledgling Republic expanded and became stronger, as our Nation's growing Merchant Marine connected the States and cemented ties among our new allies.
>
> Executive Proclamation on National Maritime Day[1]

When thinking about security, the oceans are often taken for granted, especially in a country like the United States which has long enjoyed the advantages of being protected by vast expanses of ocean on either coast. This has been recognized as "sea blindness." No country governs these waters, no corporation controls them, and no military dominates them. Yet, like the air, the oceans are essential for human life in providing food and oxygen. Beyond this, oceans also provide for human economic and social needs. Oceans offer key resources such as minerals to supply the metals industry and energy to fuel cars and heat homes. Further, the oceans are primarily a transportation resource, facilitating the movement of goods and of people who may improve their human security by emigrating to North America and Europe. At the same time oceans can also undermine human security through naturally occurring events like hurricanes and tsunamis.

Given the global nature of trade, oceans are the vital highways of international commerce. Oceans enable Americans to eat fresh fruit from South America in the middle of winter, allow Europeans to drink coffee from East Africa, and enable Asians to drive their cars with oil from the Persian Gulf. Considering the number of imported goods Americans consume, the international character of the economy is obvious. But unless there is an environmental tragedy—such as an oil spill like the 2010 BP (formerly British Petroleum) event in the Gulf of Mexico, a major natural disaster such as a hurricane, or maritime crime such as piracy that disrupts trade—oceans are often overlooked by policymakers and national security professionals. The United Nations estimates that about 40 percent of the world oceans are heavily affected by human activities, including pollution, depleted fisheries, and loss of coastal habitats.[2]

To better understand concerns about the oceans, this chapter provides a sketch of the global maritime domain, beginning with important definitions about concepts such as territorial waters and key maritime features. Salient human and national security issues affecting the oceans are then examined, ranging from pollution to fishing to piracy to drug trafficking. Maritime disputes between states in various regions of the world—including the South China Sea and the Arctic—are described. In sum, this chapter considers current and future challenges facing policymakers and societies as they attempt to reduce maritime insecurity and encourage collaborative use of the oceans for historically important purposes such as transportation, commerce, and resource extraction.

Defining the Global Maritime Domain

When looking at the earth from space, one fact is obvious: water is the dominant feature. To be precise, 70 percent of the planet is covered by water, and a significant portion of the earth is covered by frozen water in the Arctic and Antarctica. Water is so prevalent that astronomer and writer Carl Sagan dubbed the earth a pale-blue dot, overlooking the brown landmasses that dominate international affairs. Although Sagan meant to evoke how small the earth is in cosmic terms, his accurate description serves as a reminder of how important water is to the planet—80 percent of the world's population lives on or near a coast, and most international commerce travels by sea. Without healthy and safe oceans and access to water in general, human progress is severely limited. As economist

Jeffrey Sachs has argued, "Sea-navigable regions are generally richer than land-locked regions . . . regions easily accessible to sea-based trade almost everywhere have achieved a very high measure of economic development."[3]

Historically, great powers have been those with access to the sea, such as the United States, Britain, France, Germany, Holland, Spain, Portugal, and Japan. Countries forecast to be great powers in the twenty-first century also include seafaring nations like China and India. By contrast, economist Paul Collier has singled out being landlocked as one of the most important development "traps" that characterize the poorest countries of the world.[4] Clearly, this issue of access to the sea is a consequential one for human security concerns. Thus, while this area was not singled out as a human security issue of concern in the landmark UNDP report of 1994—as explained in Chapter 1—we assess the maritime sector separately in this chapter due to its continuing security significance.

In assessing the maritime domain, some key geographic features are obvious, such as the oceans, bays, and straits. Less obvious are those features important for security reasons, such as choke points and ports (Map 7.1 depicts an important choke point,

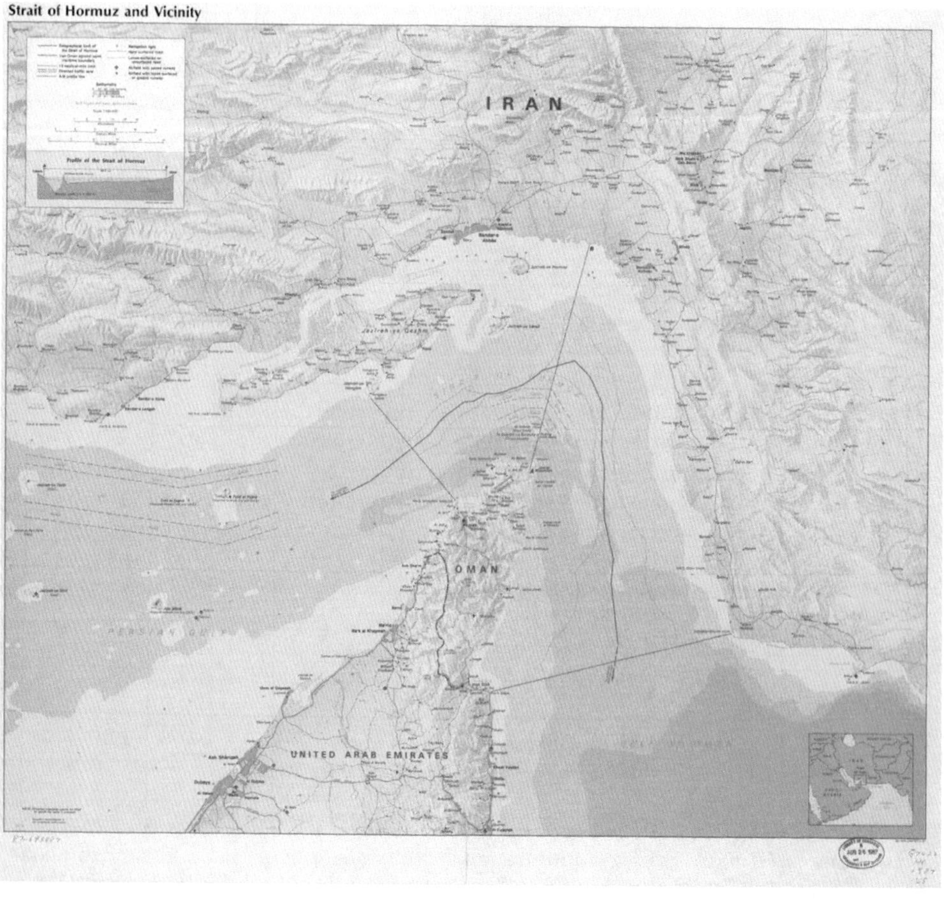

Map 7.1 Strait of Hormuz

The Strait of Hormuz is one of the most important global choke points, where an estimated 40 percent of the world's seaborne oil travels. Map courtesy of the Library of Congress.

the Strait of Hormuz). The U.S. government takes an expansive view of the maritime domain, and includes in its conception "all areas and things of, on, under, relating to, adjacent to, or bordering on a sea, ocean, or other navigable waterway, including all maritime-related activities, infrastructure, people, cargo, and vessels and other conveyances."[5] The U.S. definition of the maritime domain is thus all-encompassing; but it is important to point out three distinct zones reflected in the near-universally accepted 1982 United Nations Convention on the Law of the Sea (UNCLOS).[6] According to UNCLOS, territorial waters are those under government sovereign control, which is legally recognized as 12 nautical miles from the low-water mark of a coastal state. This zone is under the exclusive control of the state, but ships of all nations are allowed innocent passage, which means transit that is "not prejudicial to the peace, good order or security of the coastal State."[7] Beyond 12 nautical miles is the Exclusive Economic Zone (EEZ), which extends seaward to 200 nautical miles. Within an EEZ, the coastal state has special rights to use and exploit marine resources for oil exploration, seabed mining, and fishing. The international community still enjoys the rights and freedom of navigation and overflight in the EEZ, as well as the ability to lay submarine telecommunications cables and other non-resource-related uses of the oceans. Beyond 200 miles is considered the "high seas" or international waters, where all coastal and noncoastal states have equal access and enjoy the freedom of the seas and other activities.

Unless one travels by sea, it is difficult to appreciate how large the oceans are and the role they play in separating the continents. On average, it takes about two weeks to cross the Pacific by sea, or a week to cross the Atlantic. These distances provide natural barriers to war for those countries favorably situated. The United States, for example, has been relatively immune to foreign invasion because of its friendly neighbors in North and South America, with the Atlantic Ocean separating the country from Europe's wars and the Pacific Ocean separating it from Asia's conflicts. Even the previous United States–Soviet Union rivalry, which largely defined U.S. foreign policy in the twentieth century, was predicted to lead to large land battles in Europe and not in North America. To be sure, both countries prepared for great naval battles in the North Atlantic and the Pacific, but land and air warfare tended to dominate their planning. With respect to China's recent rise, air and sea warfare tends to dominate thinking within U.S. and Chinese national security circles since neither ground force envisions they will engage in large-scale clashes.

The Oceans, Trade, and Development

Oceans clearly amplify a country's relative power in the world, enabling competent seafaring countries to have global presence, influence, and disproportionate control of territory, people, and commerce. As Sir Walter Raleigh wrote in the sixteenth century, "For whosoever commands the sea commands the trade; whosoever commands the trade of the world commands the riches of the world, and consequently the world itself."[8] Historically, countries such as the United Kingdom, Portugal, and Oman created networks of ports and trading posts throughout the world that considerably enriched their societies through trade and plunder. At its height, it was said the sun never set on the British Empire due to its control of territory on every inhabited continent, which would not have been possible without the Royal Navy. In fact, the remnants of British and European exploration and colonization are evident in the languages spoken in South America, Asia, and Africa. European languages both form the basis for many cultures in the world and facilitate communication within regions. (In one interesting twist, the African island nation of Madagascar adopted English in 2007 as one of its official languages alongside French and the local Malagasy—not to speak to Americans necessarily but to facilitate interactions with English-speaking countries in East Africa such as Kenya.)

Today, oceans are still essential for economic development: witness China's rapid economic development through large-scale exports that are made possible by containerized shipping and sea transport. In addition to accounting for an amazing 90 percent of international commerce, trade by sea also includes 50 percent of oil movement. Additionally, about 65 percent of the world's oil reserves and 35 percent of the world's gas reserves are located in the oceans. The prevalence of sea-based hydrocarbons not only satisfies global demands to fuel economic activity but also causes friction among states that compete for these resources. Finally, the sea enables intercontinental information flows, with 95 percent of communications traveling via submarine fiber-optic cables that connect the continents. Thus, it is not surprising that economic development and a country's prosperity and ability to provide human security needs are often linked to its proximity to the sea. Knowing this, the African Union has developed a strategy to guide ways to improve development through maritime security. In the strategy, leaders listed its desired end state: "increased wealth creation . . . that positively contributes to socio-economic development, as well as increased national, regional and continental stability, through . . . multilayered efforts to build blocks of maritime sector activities in concert with improving elements of maritime governance."[9]

Countries that are deprived of coastal access must rely on neighboring states, and thus may become partners in promoting regional stability. For example, since Ethiopia and Uganda are landlocked countries, both have been deeply involved in efforts to stabilize Somalia given the importance of the port of Mogadishu, Somalia, to their trade. Likewise, both seek good relations with Kenya because of the port of Mombasa in Kenya. In Latin America, the only two landlocked countries, Paraguay and Bolivia, are less developed than their neighbors and must rely on good neighboring state relations for port access that enables imports and exports, which are important to improving economic development and human security. It is not surprising that their situation has caused conflict in South American in the past. And, as recently as 2016, Russia illegally annexed the Crimean region in order to gain a warm water port. Significantly, countries that control the land adjacent to where oceans meet often sit astride key trade routes. Known as choke points, these narrow straits or canals are considered vital to maritime trade.

The Panama Canal, the Suez Canal, the Strait of Gibraltar, the Strait of Malacca and Singapore, and the Strait of Hormuz are among the most significant choke points in the world (Table 7.1). The small Asian city-state of Singapore's creation and accelerated development were based on its geographic location along one of the most heavily trafficked waterways in the world. Every day, more than 200 ships transit the Strait of Malacca, making Singapore an important transshipment point for global trade. (Malacca is the shortest sea route between Persian Gulf oil and gas suppliers and the Asian markets, which

Table 7.1 Key Maritime Choke Points around the World

Europe	Middle East	Africa	Southeast Asia	Caribbean
Strait of Gibraltar	Suez Canal	Mozambique Channel	Strait of Malacca	Panama Canal
Strait of Dover	Strait of Hormuz	Bab el Mandeb	Lombok Strait	Straits of Florida
Kiel Canal	—	—	Luzon Strait	Windward and Mona Passages

amounts to about 15 million barrels of oil per day.) Or consider the Bab el Mandeb, which connects the Indian Ocean to the Mediterranean Sea via the Red Sea and is a critical route, bringing millions of barrels of oil a day from the Persian Gulf to Europe.[10]

Additionally, as the preceding chapter on environmental security pointed out, as the Arctic ice melts, new trade routes and choke points are expected to open in the High North. It appears that the shorter maritime routes between Europe and Asia that sixteenth-century European explorers searched for may be a reality in the twenty-first century as the Arctic Ocean becomes navigable. This will require the Arctic countries of the U.S., Canada, Denmark, Norway, and Russia to improve maritime infrastructure there. It will also likely divert maritime traffic from countries along existing trade routes such as Egypt, Panama, Kenya, and Yemen. This change will have important economic consequences for those countries.

Challenges to Maritime Security

There is increasing awareness of the shared dangers complicating maritime security and specific human security concerns. In 2009, the United Nations began to annually celebrate June 8 as World Oceans Day. Secretary-General Ban Ki-moon issued a press release on that day, commenting that;

> human activities are taking a terrible toll on the world's oceans and seas. Vulnerable marine ecosystems, such as corals, and important fisheries are being damaged by over-exploitation, illegal, unreported and unregulated fishing (IUU), destructive fishing practices, invasive alien species and marine pollution, especially from land-based sources.[11]

Attention to this issue has continued, and in 2014, Ban declared:

> We have to ensure that oceans continue to meet our needs without compromising those of future generations. They regulate the planet's climate and are a significant source of nutrition. Their surface provides essential passage for global trade, while their depths hold current and future solutions to humanity's energy needs.[12]

Varied international, intergovernmental, and nongovernmental organizations now exist that attempt to deal with issues related to maritime security. Significantly, the inter-agency organization UN Oceans was created by UN resolution in 2003 to "strengthen and promote coordination and coherence of United Nations system activities related to ocean and coastal areas . . . facilitate inter-agency information exchange, including sharing of experiences, best practices, tools and methodologies and lessons learned in ocean-related matters."[13] And, as mentioned earlier, in 2015 the UN adopted its Sustainable Development Goals (SDGs)—"17 goals to transform the world"—with number 14 focused on the oceans (Table 7.2).[14]

Intergovernmental institutions such as the International Maritime Organization (IMO) have a long history (in this case dating back to 1959) of attempting to unify international efforts to improve maritime safety and security. International conventions such as the Safety of Life at Sea (1974) and the associated International Ship and Port Facility Security Code (2002) seek to prevent security incidents on ships and in ports. U.S.-initiated programs such as the Container Security Initiative place U.S. Customs inspectors in international ports to screen cargo, and the Proliferation Security Initiative (2003) aims to prevent trafficking of weapons of mass destruction. And international naval coalitions with countries as diverse as Russia, South Korea, and Denmark are sending warships to combat piracy in East Africa.

Table 7.2 UN Sustainable Development Goals for the Oceans

By 2025, prevent and significantly reduce marine pollution of all kinds, in particular from land-based activities, including marine debris and nutrient pollution
By 2020, sustainably manage and protect marine and coastal ecosystems to avoid significant adverse impacts, including by strengthening their resilience, and take action for their restoration in order to achieve healthy and productive oceans
Minimize and address the impacts of ocean acidification, including through enhanced scientific cooperation at all levels
By 2020, effectively regulate harvesting and end overfishing, illegal, unreported and unregulated (IUU) fishing and destructive fishing practices, and implement science-based management plans in order to restore fish stocks in the shortest time feasible, at least to levels that can produce maximum sustainable yield as determined by their biological characteristics
By 2020, conserve at least 10% of coastal and marine areas, consistent with national and international law and based on the best available scientific information
By 2020, prohibit certain forms of fisheries subsidies which contribute to overcapacity and overfishing; eliminate subsidies that contribute to IUU fishing; and refrain from introducing new such subsidies, recognizing that appropriate and effective special and differential treatment for developing and least developed countries should be an integral part of the World Trade Organization fisheries subsidies negotiation
By 2030, increase the economic benefits to Small Island Developing States (SIDS) and least developed countries from the sustainable use of marine resources, including through sustainable management of fisheries, aquaculture and tourism
Increase scientific knowledge, develop research capacity, and transfer marine technology, taking into account the Intergovernmental Oceanographic Commission Criteria and Guidelines on the Transfer of Marine Technology, in order to improve ocean health and to enhance the contribution of marine biodiversity to the development of developing countries, in particular SIDS and least developed countries
Provide access for small-scale artisanal fishers to marine resources and markets
Enhance the conservation and sustainable use of oceans and their resources by implementing international law as reflected in UNCLOS, which provides the legal framework for the conservation and sustainable use of oceans and their resources

Source: United Nations, "17 Goals to Transform the World," www.un.org/sustainabledevelopment/oceans/

At the same time that governments are sending their navies to conduct stability operations at sea, nongovernmental and pro-environmental groups seek to reduce maritime insecurity, too. For example, Greenpeace and the International Crisis Group identify overfishing as a root cause of piracy and call for better regulation of the world's fishing fleets. And the Sea Shepherd Conservation Society regularly intervenes in whaling activities, which reduced Japan's whale harvest by 50 percent in 2010. More recently, in 2017, Sea Shepherd deployed a former U.S. Coast Guard (USCG) vessel to curb illegal fishing in the Caribbean.[15] Other groups like Friends of the Earth and the Basel Action Network attempt to limit maritime pollution by targeting destructive ship-disposal practices that escape state regulation or provide fuel for cash-strapped militaries to increase patrols of ecologically important areas. The World Wildlife Fund, for example, supports Mozambique's navy through fuel subsidies to reduce poaching.

The changed nature of security is bringing together nontraditional partners like those cited above. Because maritime forces provide necessary presence and logistical capabilities, their governments and various nongovernmental groups are coming together to address the specific sources of maritime insecurity, which include: ocean pollution (plastics); illegal, unreported, and underreported fishing; piracy; and illicit trafficking of people, drugs, and weapons. Clearly all these issues arise from, and have direct consequences on, human security concerns such as access to food, as assessed below.

Ocean Pollution

The United Nations sustainable development goal in the maritime domain is: "By 2025, prevent and significantly reduce marine pollution of all kinds, in particular from land-based activities, including marine debris and nutrient pollution."[16] While globally distributed, scholars estimate there are 5.25 trillion plastic particles in the world's oceans, weighing 268,940 tons.[17] Marine debris is defined by the National Oceanic and Atmospheric Administration (NOAA) and the USCG as any persistent solid material that is manufactured or processed and directly or indirectly, intentionally or unintentionally, disposed of or abandoned into the marine environment or the Great Lakes.[18] It is considered one of the most pervasive pollution problems affecting the world's oceans and waterways."[19] NOAA sees that "debris entering the aquatic environment may have significant impacts on ecology, human health and safety, and the economy."[20] Given the harm plastics cause the environment and the likelihood the materials will impact coastal zones, NOAA tracks marine pollution to include the "Pacific Garbage Patch" (seen in Image 7.1).

The effects of marine pollution are staggering. For example, Merchant Marine Captain Charles J. Moore wrote that "more animals are [likely] killed by vagrant plastic

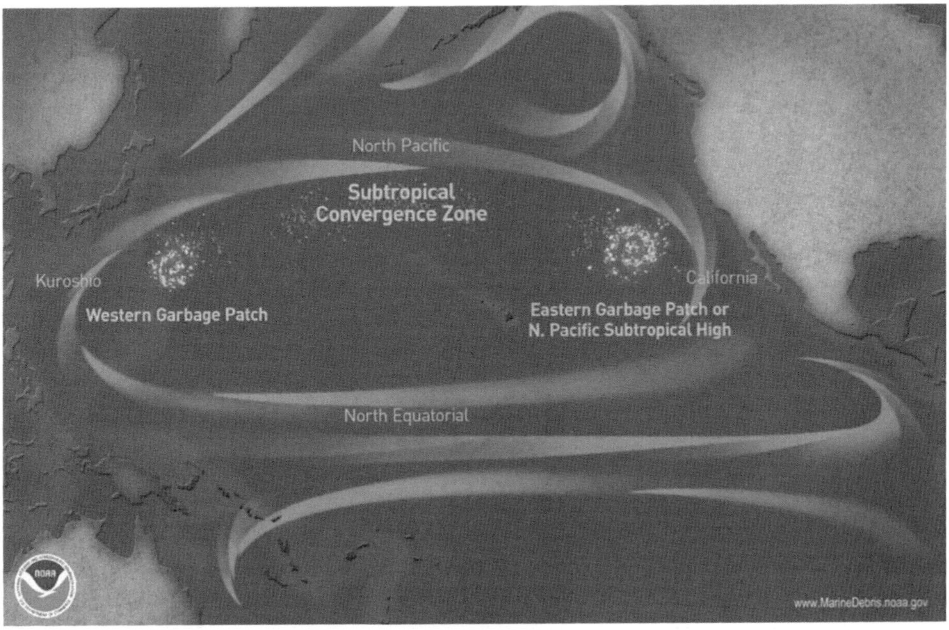

Image 7.1 Pacific Garbage Patch. Photo: NOAA[21]

waste than by even climate change."[22] It is estimated that half of all seabirds and marine mammals have ingested plastic or became entangled in discarded fishing nets.[23] This even extends to creatures living in the deep seas.[24] However, it is important to note that much research is still required to understand the risk that microplastic particles pose to the marine environment.[25]

In an attempt to regulate the impact on the United States, a number of laws guide U.S. efforts to reduce marine pollution. These include:

- the Clean Water Act of 1972, which regulates the amount of trash that cities can discharge into waterways;
- the Coastal Zone Management Act of 1972, which seeks to reduce marine debris entering the coastal and ocean environment;
- the Marine Plastic Pollution Research and Control Act of 1972, which seeks to reduce pollution from ships;
- the Marine Protection, Research, and Sanctuaries Act of 1972, which regulates ocean dumping; and
- the Coral Reef Conservation Act of 2000, which states that NOAA must "provide assistance to states in removing abandoned fishing gear, marine debris, and abandoned vessels from coral reefs to conserve living marine resources."

These laws recognize that pollution comes both from land and sea. Pollution can be intentional (such as illegal dumping at sea) and unintentional (such as hurricanes pulling debris into the ocean).

Illegal, Unreported, and Unregulated (IUU) Fishing

Access to adequate food is obviously essential to human security. In that regard fish are an important resource as they provide more than 3.1 billion people with at least 20 percent of their average per capita animal protein intake.[26] Yet IUU fishing devastates stocks, and undermines developing countries' food supplies and undermines human security. This type of fishing accounts for about one-sixth of all the fish caught at sea, and is worth at least $23 billion; losses are especially significant in developing regions.[27] Greenpeace estimates that illegal fishing costs African countries billions of dollars annually.[28] This represents major income loss and contributes to already low levels of development.

Of course losses to struggling societies have an immediate economic impact, but future fish stocks are jeopardized, too. As a special report concluded:

> The result is the plunder of the world's oceans, threatening not only marine ecosystems, but also the security of human populations. Large-scale IUU fishing endangers food security, threatens livelihoods, undermines the rule of law and deprives states of revenues. It also intersects with other crimes, further amplifying the threat to security.[29]

IUU fishing can also be a flashpoint for conflict among nations competing for fishing grounds. The United Nations has been highlighting this concern for well over a decade. UN General Assembly Resolution 62/177 deplored the fact that "illegal, unreported, and unregulated fishing constitutes a serious threat to fish stocks and marine habitats and ecosystems, to the detriment of sustainable fisheries as well as the food security and the economies of many states, particularly developing states."[30] The UN Food and Agriculture Organization (FAO) declared that IUU fishing constitutes a serious threat to: (a) fisheries, especially those of high value that are already overfished (e.g., cod, tuna, redfish, and swordfish, as seen in Image 7.2); (b) marine habitats, including vulnerable marine

Image 7.2 Illegal Swordfish Catch Seized in West Africa. Photo: U.S. Coast Guard

ecosystems; and (c) food security and the economies of developing countries.[31] Under UN resolutions, states are encouraged to take effective measures to deter illegal activities that undermine fisheries' conservation and management practices.[32]

Given the importance of fish protein, the scope of the problem is global, but it has a disproportionate effect on developing countries that do not have alternate food sources, the income to afford food imports, or the maritime law enforcement forces to reduce IUU fishing. Haibing Ma, the China program manager for the Worldwatch Institute (a non-profit group that researches sustainability), noted how "Overfishing has destroyed the sustainability of China's inshore fisheries," so it harvests fish in other countries' waters.[33] An intergovernmental organization such as the Regional Fisheries Management Organization tackles sustainable fishing by offering countries a venue to manage fishing stocks, but this has not been enough.

Consequently, the FAO has brokered a global treaty to combat IUU fishing. Negotiated in 2009 and ratified by South Korea, the European Union, the United States, and dozens of other countries, the treaty entered into force in summer 2016.[34] While it is too soon to tell if the treaty will be effective, it is a promising approach since boats involved in illegal activities (such as dhows, as seen in Image 7.3) must bring their catch ashore.

By focusing on enforcement in ports, in addition to patrolling vast fishing grounds, this treaty is one more way for states to assert their sovereignty and reduce maritime security deficits. The United Nations sustainable development goal aspires to:

> By 2020, effectively regulate harvesting and end overfishing, illegal, unreported and unregulated fishing and destructive fishing practices and implement science-based management

plans, in order to restore fish stocks in the shortest time feasible, at least to levels that can produce maximum sustainable yield as determined by their biological characteristics.[35]

Additionally, in Asia, several countries are making it a priority to reduce IUU fishing, which creates losses of at least $6 billion annually. Indonesia, which estimates it loses significant revenue annually to IUU fishing, launched the Global Maritime Fulcrum strategy in 2014. The strategy calls for efforts to regain control of its maritime borders and target IUU fishing vessels. Since October 2014, Indonesia has sunk at least eighty-four foreign fishing vessels and confiscated dozens more for alleged poaching.[36] In 2015, the regional intergovernmental Association of Southeast Asian Nations (ASEAN) adopted guidelines to reduce IUU fishing with the objective "to promote regional collaboration among the ASEAN member states (AMs) in strengthening monitoring, control and surveillance systems of fish and fishery products entering in the supply chain."[37]

At the same time that governments are collaborating and sending their maritime forces to confront IUU fishing, pro-environmental, non-state groups are also seeking to reduce maritime insecurity. For example, Greenpeace and the Environmental Justice Foundation have identified overfishing as a contributing factor to piracy.[38] Groups such as Friends of the Earth and the Basel Action Network attempt to limit maritime pollution by targeting destructive ship disposal practices that escape state regulation; they also provide fuel for cash-strapped militaries so that they can increase patrols of ecologically important areas. To protect coral reefs against using poisons, such as cyanide, to stun and harvest tropical fish, the World Resources Institute and other groups are collaborating in the Indo-Pacific Destructive Fishing Reform Program to assist governments in Southeast Asia. To support this effort, developed countries are using their maritime services to help developing

Image 7.3 A Dhow, As Used by Fishermen and Pirates Alike. Photo: U.S. Navy

countries build capacity for fisheries management by monitoring their exclusive economic zones, patrolling their territorial waters, and securing their port facilities. African countries understand the gravity of this issue; the Speaker of Nigeria's House of Representative has noted that "The only way to promote intra-African trade in our water ways is to ensure safety and security of navigation in our waters."[39]

Piracy

Article 101 of the UN Convention Law of the Sea defines piracy as "any illegal acts of violence or detention . . . committed for private ends . . . directed on the high seas, against another ship . . . in a place outside the jurisdiction of any State." It is worth noting that the world has lived with piracy for millennia, and piracy had long been considered largely a nuisance to developed countries since the nineteenth century. When U.S. commerce was threatened, Presidents Jefferson and Madison sent the Navy and the Marines to North Africa to stop the pirate attacks from the Barbary States, and were mainly successful. Yet maritime piracy has recaptured international attention beginning in the late 2000s. What may be different two centuries later after the Barbary pirates is that merchant fleets are mainly private, piracy is no longer state sponsored, and threats to sea-lanes are now thought of as a global rather than a national threat.

Up until 1994, reports of piracy and armed robbery against ships were, more or less, equally distributed around the world. As global trade increased throughout the 1990s, piracy increased in key shipping lanes in the South China Sea, the Strait of Malacca, and the Indian Ocean. Since 2004 there have been about 275 attacks around the world each year (see Figure 7.1); piracy off Somalia spiked in 2008–10, trapping hundreds of Southeast

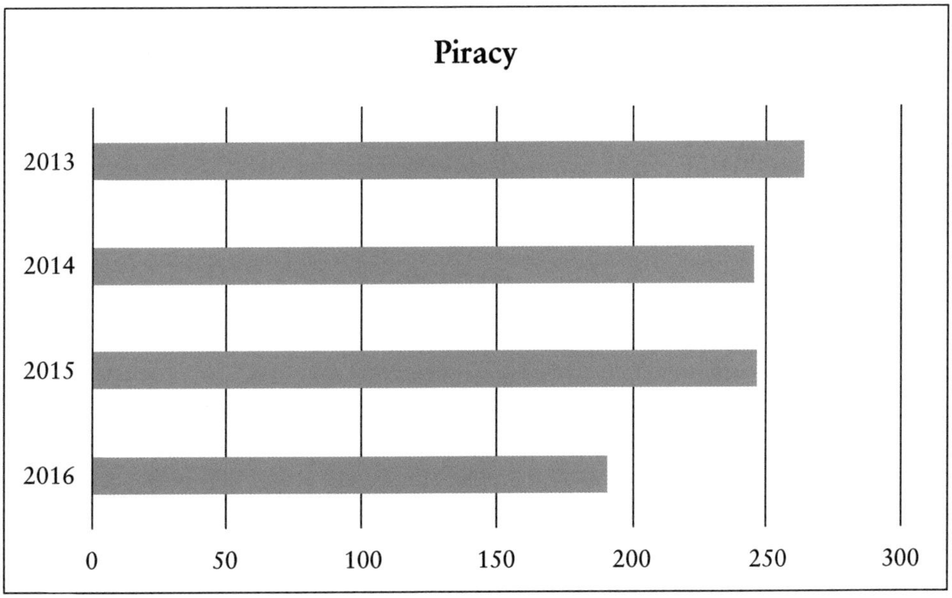

Figure 7.1 Maritime Piracy Incidents, 2013–2016.
Source: ICC Commercial Services, www.hellenicshippingnews.com/wp-content/uploads/2015/01/2014-Annual-IMB-Piracy-Report-ABRIDGED.pdf

Asian merchant mariners in Somalia. From 2011 to 2015, successful and attempted acts of piracy in Southeast Asia more than doubled to about 150 acts, which made the region the hub of global piracy.[40] In 2017, piracy returned to East Africa as attempts to stabilize Somalia struggled to succeed.

Most experts agree that the problem of piracy begins ashore. Martin Murphy explains that the seven factors that enable maritime piracy are basic elements of sanctuary, which provide the conditions ripe for piracy, such as large ungoverned areas, poor governance, and the inability of governments to adequately patrol their territorial waters or defend their seaports.[41] (Many of these factors were addressed in earlier chapters.) Countries are attempting to improve security in ungoverned spaces through maritime security cooperation. Both states and non-state actors have promoted ways to reduce security deficits. For example, Japan has promoted the Regional Agreement on Combating Piracy and Armed Robbery against Ships in Asia (ReCAAP) to support cooperative efforts; the International Chamber of Commerce has sponsored a real-time information-sharing center; and ASEAN has served as a forum to harmonize multinational counter-piracy efforts. The broader effort in the maritime space requires partners with capabilities to protect their territorial waters and exclusive economic zones. There are numerous international agreements to combat piracy; these include: the Djibouti Code of Conduct; and the Code of Conduct Concerning the Repression of Piracy, Armed Robbery against Ships, and Illicit Maritime Activity in West and Central Africa (the Yaoundé Code of Conduct).

Piracy not only affects the commercial shipping industry but also directly affects the most desperate human beings. This can be seen in the efforts of the UN World Food Programme, which delivers 90 percent of the food to Somalia by sea (see Map 7.2 depicting the important Gulf of Aden adjacent to Somalia). In fact, the first U.S.-flagged ship that was almost hijacked in 2009 (and the focal point of the 2013 film *Captain Phillips*) was carrying food aid to alleviate starvation in Somalia.[42] Although East Africans generally show greater concern about illegal fishing than about piracy, international relief efforts to those societies are directly threatened by piracy. To ensure food aid does reach populations in East Africa, naval coalitions are conducting convoy operations. As one would expect, the pirates avoid areas patrolled by naval coalitions, and have extended their range into the Indian Ocean.

Since pirates operate on the sea and hijack seagoing vessels on the world's oceans, it is easy to see piracy as a maritime, primarily national, security issue. Yet pirates also operate from land and thrive in parts of the world where there are human security deficits that allow illegally armed groups (pirates included) to operate. Addressing piracy therefore requires bringing security, stability, and development to countries like Somalia, as outlined in previous chapters. However, given the decades-long civil war there, this is proving to be a significant challenge for Somalis, even with the assistance of the international community. Numerous international attempts since the early 1990s have failed to bring stability to Somalia, and dealing with symptoms of the problem continues to be unsatisfactory. U.S. efforts to improve security in ungoverned spaces that provide sanctuary for illegally armed groups like pirates are captured in the U.S. government's twenty-first-century naval strategy that emphasizes international cooperation:

> naval forces are stronger when we operate jointly and together with allies and partners. Merging our individual capabilities and capacity produces a combined naval effect that is greater than the sum of its parts. By working together in formal and informal networks, we can

> address the threats to our mutual maritime security interests. Maximizing the robust capacity of this global network of navies concept, we are all better postured to face new and emerging challenges.[43]

Unfortunately, piracy is just one of the complicated challenges related to maritime security, as the issue of drug trafficking illustrates.

Map 7.2 Gulf of Aden. Courtesy of CIA

❖ BOX 7.1 THINK AGAIN: PIRATES ARE NOT CRIMINALS

It may be surprising to find that not everyone sees pirates as the scourge of humanity. Some view them as being forced into this way of life due to political and economic misfortune, and others even see pirates as heroes fighting back against illegal dumping and illegal fishing. Perhaps the most prominent person dissenting from a negative view of pirates is Libya's former president, Muammar Gaddafi, who likened them to a navy merely protecting Somali waters. He told the United Nations General Assembly in 2009:

> I am telling you the Somalis are not pirates. The pirates are ourselves because we exploited all the fishing grounds. We undermined their livelihood. We undermined their economies and their regional waters. All the ships of the world, whether from Libya, India, Japan or America exploited Somali waters and we are the aggressors. After the Somali state collapsed we came to pick up the remnants. The Somalis had to defend their marine wealth, which is their food and the food of their children. Then they transformed themselves into pirates to defend themselves. They are not pirates. They only defend their livelihood. And now you are handling it in the wrong way. You are saying let us send warships to strike the Somalis. No. Warships should go to strike the pirates who undermined the Somali wealth and resources. You have to strike the foreign fishing boats.[1]

Gaddafi's defense of pirates has gained little traction, but Africans tend to avoid seeing pirates as a security challenge. This stems from the land-oriented focus of African militaries, an indirect link between maritime commerce and African development, and a romantic view of pirates who secure million-dollar ransoms for foreign ships and foreign crews. For many desperately poor Africans, there may even be a hint of admiration in the fact that such humble individuals can outfox the wealthy and relatively privileged of the world. A pirated vessel can produce exceptional income for the perpetrators of piracy. Acts of piracy, from crimes of opportunity against transiting vessels in the Malacca Strait to ship seizures orchestrated by organized gangs, can earn anywhere from a few thousand dollars in stolen booty to millions of dollars in ransom paid to recover a merchant ship and her crew. To date, pirates have only conducted hijacking for ransom and have not engaged in terrorism. The last decade suggests piracy is more analogous to carjacking than it is to car bombing.

1 Muammar Gaddafi's speech to the United Nations General Assembly, November 23, 2009, provided and translated courtesy of the Jamahiriya News Agency (Jana), available at www.btinternet.com/~davidbeaumont/msf/gadafi.htm.

Drug Trafficking

Illegal fishing and piracy only recaptured international attention in the last decade, but illicit trafficking of drugs by sea has provoked a maritime security response for decades.[44] Criminal groups increasingly benefit from maritime insecurity by exploiting trade routes to traffic drugs, people, and weapons, as referenced in an earlier chapter. And it is the use of the seas by criminal groups that fuels insecurity on land, as also referenced in other chapters. These groups thrive in the vastness of the oceans and relative lack of maritime domain awareness or response capabilities within the developing world. Heroin produced in Afghanistan reaches Europe by sea. Cocaine produced in Colombia reaches Europe and the United States by sea. And methamphetamines produced in Asia reach Africa by sea.

Noncommercial maritime vessels, such as go-fast boats (cigarette boats with large outboard motors) and fishing boats, are the principal conveyances used by traffickers to move cocaine shipments through the eastern Pacific. Go-fast boats and private aircraft are also the most common cocaine transport methods used by traffickers in the western Caribbean, which is an important transshipment corridor. The result is that Mexican and Colombian drug trafficking organizations generate, remove, and launder billions of dollars in wholesale drug proceeds annually.[45] These groups use the profits to equip themselves with the latest weapons, which are often more advanced than their national governments' forces. For example, Colombian drug trafficking organizations increasingly use semisubmersible vehicles to evade detection. Resembling small submarines, semisubmersibles show the traffickers' increasing sophistication that has warranted a military response to detect and interdict these vessels, as police forces lack the capacity to detect submarine-like vehicles (see Image 7.4).

Image 7.4 Captured Semisubmersible Vehicle: USS *McInerney* tows a seized vessel carrying 7 tons of cocaine. Photo: Justin Cooper, U.S. Navy

Since the 1980s national maritime forces have attempted to reduce illicit trafficking by sea. In the twenty-first century, these governmental efforts increased as traffickers used better techniques to get the drugs to market in the United States and Europe. Building on a 1990s' Clinton administration-era initiative, in 2004 the Bush administration declared the Caribbean to be America's third border, which was widely applauded in the Western Hemisphere. At the time, the Caribbean Community (also known as CARICOM):

> recognize[d] our interdependence and the importance of close cooperation to combat new and emerging transnational threats that endanger the very fabric of our societies. By virtue of their small size, geographic configuration and lack of technical and financial resources, Caribbean States are particularly vulnerable and susceptible to these risks and threats. This is especially true for illicit trafficking in persons, drugs, and firearms, terrorism and other transnational criminal activities.[46]

The Third Border Initiative is intended to focus U.S.–Caribbean engagement through targeted programs that comprise both new and ongoing activities designed to enhance cooperation in the diplomatic, security, economic, environmental, health, and education arenas. This includes programs to detect and interdict drug traffickers and dismantle illicit threat networks.

For the U.S. military in general, and U.S. Southern Command in particular (with responsibility for the southern part of the Western Hemisphere), the global illicit drug trade is a significant transnational security threat that undermines democratic governments, terrorizes populations, impedes economic development, and hinders regional stability.[47] These are the true threats to human security. Drug traffickers successfully exploit weak security institutions around the world and use illicit profits to undermine rule of law while taking advantage of political tensions in Latin America created by U.S. drug policy (as examined in Chapter 4). Additional gains made in controlling illicit trafficking from Colombia's Caribbean coast are increasingly offset by drug trafficking occurring from Colombia's Pacific coast or from neighboring Venezuela. The challenge for the United States remains how to build renewed relationships without overwhelming these countries with U.S. military and law enforcement efforts. The challenge for governments in the region is how to protect their populations from violent transnational criminal organizations that rely on political intimidation and assassination to further their aims. Unfortunately, this situation demonstrates the complex and inextricable nature of national and human security.

Maritime Disputes

The preceding discussion highlights how subnational and transnational actors are exploiting the maritime domain, which has facilitated international cooperation among countries (and international organizations) that seek to reduce illicit trafficking and piracy. At the same time, resource exploitation in disputed waters exacerbates tensions among historic state rivals over inhabited and uninhabited islands. For example, in 1982 the United Kingdom and Argentina fought a war over islands in the South Atlantic located 300 miles from South America, 700 miles from Antarctica, and 8,000 miles from the United Kingdom. The islands are about the size of Connecticut, and the dispute stems from competing claims of what the British call the Falklands and the Argentines call the Malvinas. Both claims are rooted in centuries-old colonial claims made by the British and the Argentine governments.

The outcome of the 1982 war that claimed about 1,000 lives proved disastrous for the Argentine military government, which later collapsed, and further set back the country's economic development. Of course the war was successful for the British, who retained control of the islands, where 3,200 people live. Relations between Argentina and the United Kingdom normalized in the 1990s, but with the prospect of new hydrocarbon resources discovered near the South Atlantic islands, the Argentine government challenged the United Kingdom's claims again in 2007. Venezuelan president Hugo Chávez then seized upon the issue to promote South American unity. In February 2010 he told Queen Elizabeth II:

> The time for empires are over, haven't you noticed? Return the Malvinas to the Argentine people. Things have changed. We are no longer in 1982. If conflict breaks out, be sure Argentina will not be alone like it was back then.[48]

In spite of Chávez's statement, both countries lack the military capabilities they once had, and the British seem to have international law on their side. The British first claimed the islands in the sixteenth century, 70 percent of the islands' inhabitants claim British ancestry, and the islands are a self-governing British territory. While the dispute can be viewed through a traditional interstate rivalry lens stemming from early European exploration, the area's rich natural resources—which include fishing stocks and wildlife, and the potential for new hydrocarbon finds—make the Falklands-Malvinas a contentious maritime dispute.

In Asia there are numerous similar competing claims with the potential to spark conflict and adversely affect the livelihood of subsistence fishermen and governments alike. One of the most consequential is over the largely uninhabited Spratly Island chain, which is dispersed over a 600-mile area in the South China Sea. To date, China, Taiwan, Vietnam, the Philippines, and Malaysia have overlapping claims. Brunei also established a fishing zone in the Spratly Islands, but has made no formal claim as of this writing. The islands are little more than exposed reefs, rock outcroppings, and atolls that are barely above sea level and with a total area of about 4 square kilometers. Yet the sea is an important trade route and fishing ground, and contains important hydrocarbon deposits that all five countries seek to claim and develop.

Because of historic rivalries (e.g., China and Vietnam) and political differences among the countries (e.g., China and Taiwan), the Spratly Islands are often characterized as a potential military flash point. Beginning in the 2010s, China's foreign policy has brought the island dispute to the front of international politics. Over the course of several years, China supported its fishing fleet in the region, and significantly transformed atolls and reefs into artificial islands through an ambitious land reclamation program. Once the land was created, it followed suit by developing runways and adding military hardware. These actions were condemned by the international community and resulted in an international arbitration ruling against China that claimed the activities were illegal and "caused severe harm to the coral reef environment and violated its obligation to preserve and protect fragile ecosystems and the habitat of depleted, threatened, or endangered species."[49]

In addition to the Spratly Islands involving a number of significant countries, Japan is embroiled in several island disputes, too. While they resemble traditional territorial disputes, the intractability of these disputes is based on environmental exploitation expectations to meet the food demand within their countries. Japan's northern territories—composed of the islands of Etorofu, Kunashiri, Shikotan, and the Habomai group—are administered by Russia, which calls them the Southern Kuril Islands. The islands were occupied by the Soviet Union in 1945 and remain a roadblock to the formal end of World War II hostilities between Japan and Russia. Additionally, Japan and South Korea jointly claim the Liancourt Rocks (Take-shima/Dokdo), which have been occupied by South Korea since 1954. Finally, China and Taiwan dispute Japan's claims to the Senkaku-shoto (Diaoyu Tai) islands and Japan's economic claims in the East China Sea.

Disputes like these serve as reminders of lingering political challenges, but also show how underwater hydrocarbon exploration can create additional tension among governments. Given the uncertain impact of China's rise on international affairs, maritime disputes like those in the South China Sea also offer a window into Beijing's decision making. So far, China seems to rely on international law to further its claims (though there are clear cases of maritime harassment). As law professor Xinjun Zhang of Tsinghua University explains:

> On balance, international law has come to be seen as a more important and necessary means for China to achieve its foreign policy ends, even though obstacles and uncertainty persist. Moreover, China's turn to international law has been uneven, and unsurprisingly so. International law is more likely to be an appealing instrument for China where the other party to a dispute is a near-peer in political, economic and military power (as is the case, for example, with Japan), or where the other parties are significantly less powerful than China (as is the case, for example, with the ASEAN countries).[50]

The implications of this perspective are clear. International law can be an effective way to peacefully resolve maritime disputes, but perhaps only when the parties have sufficient military capabilities to make war too costly. At the same time what is lost in most of these considerations are how these disputes may disrupt, or adversely affect, the individual human security needs of those peoples native to these areas.

This point is particularly relevant when considering the native people bordering the thawing Arctic Ocean, as referenced in the previous chapter. There are some 165,000 indigenous, specifically Inuit, people living in Canada, Greenland, the Russian Federation, and Alaska, who consider the Arctic to be their home (see Map 7.3). As Okalik Eegeesiak, Chair of the Inuit Circumpolar Council (ICC), noted in 2017:

> Inuit are a maritime people, dependent on the Arctic Ocean for our transportation and its marine resources for food security. Inuit life today also depends on movement, and that movement takes place across Arctic sea ice and on the open ocean. Our entire culture and identity are based on free movement on land, sea ice, and the Arctic Ocean. We rely on free movement in order to eat, to obtain supplies for our traditional clothing, and to preserve our rich cultural heritage . . . It is the Inuit position that any action or intervention that affects our ice, the Arctic Ocean and the lands we live upon must protect the environment, wildlife and, therefore, Inuit, in such a way that we can continue to live off this land. This is the standard of sustainable use that we insist upon. The actions impacting the Arctic, however, are beyond our control.[51]

Of course it is climate change that is impacting the Arctic, as noted in the preceding chapter, and some analysts have compared the Arctic as the new "great game"—analogous to the British and Russian empires competing for influence in Central Asia in the nineteenth century. For example, as maritime expert and scholar Scott Borgerson testified to the U.S. Congress:

> When taking a pan-Arctic view there are also a number of nagging sovereignty disputes. Every single bilateral relationship where Arctic countries share a physical border, except one, Norway and Denmark, has at least one significant point of disagreement. Like previous assumptions that the icecap is melting more slowly than it actually is, it would be a mistake to assume that all these potential flashpoints will remain sleeping dogs. The combination of new shipping routes, trillions of dollars in possible oil and gas resources, and a poorly defined picture of state ownership make for a toxic brew.[52]

Map 7.3 The Arctic. Courtesy of the CIA

In fact, Russia's national security strategy has warned that within a decade, nations could be at war over the Arctic as countries vie for important new maritime trade routes and new economic opportunities for hydrocarbon exploration.

As the Arctic melts, new trade routes connecting the Atlantic to the Pacific across the North Pole may be a reality in the future, albeit for a few weeks during the summer. The expected shipping channel will reduce the transit between Europe and Asia by 10,000 miles. Looking east, German merchant ships proved in 2009 that they could transit from Europe to Asia via a Northeast Passage. By doing so, shipping companies can bypass the dangerous waters of East Africa (with its piracy threat) and Southeast Asia, and save money on fuel and crew days at sea. In fact, 2016 saw the first cruise ship sail through the Arctic. With anticipated commercial and recreational shipping traffic, the navies of Canada, the United States, Norway, Denmark, and Russia expect to map the Arctic sea-lanes, provide search and rescue, and protect their sovereignty claims there. The issue of ownership in this region is already proving to be contentious.[53] The challenge that concerns us here is whether the human security needs of the most vulnerable such as the Inuit will be given appropriate weight when debating, and disputing, the Arctic region.

Conclusion

Although oceans have always been an essential part of human social and commercial activity, there is an increased urgency to protect them. Illegal fishing, overfishing, and illegal dumping threaten a significant food source for many countries. When it comes to the United States specifically, the epigraph at the start of this chapter shows how the U.S.'s rise and prosperity are connected to the seas, yet the oceans and their health continue to be largely taken for granted.

The maritime security deficit has allowed criminal organizations, transnational actors, and pirates to exploit the maritime domain. Given the oceans' size and the complexity of the security environment, no single country can provide security against all threats (not even a superpower's navy). With an emphasis on partnership to fill security gaps, programs that strengthen the maritime capabilities of countries are likely to continue for the foreseeable future. While naval warfare among states is low, we will likely see naval forces attempting to protect the environment; cooperate against illegal fishing, piracy, and criminal trafficking; and respond to maritime-borne natural disasters. At the same time, competing claims on islands, the Arctic, and underwater resources will continue to challenge governments to resolve disputes peacefully. Fortunately, at this stage there appear to be more incentives to cooperate than to contest claims through war. Yet this does not mean that individuals and nongovernmental groups, including the influential environmental movement, will not continue to test the limits of maritime security. Nor does it mean that culturally distinct peoples like the Inuit will accept decisions made by states that ignore their community and human security needs.

In the next chapter we move to examine international and transnational issues that arise in the health sector. As with the maritime sector, there are reasons for countries to cooperate in controlling health issues ranging from HIV/AIDS to potential global pandemic diseases like Ebola. At the same time, other human security issues like poverty and climate change are affecting health issues for many communities, just as is occurring in the maritime domain.

Notes

1 White House, "President Donald J. Trump Proclaims May 22, 2017, as National Maritime Day," May 19, 2017. www.whitehouse.gov/the-press-office/2017/05/19/president-donald-j-trump-proclaims-may-22-2017-national-maritime-day.
2 UNDP, "Goal 14 Targets: Below Water." www.undp.org/content/undp/en/home/sustainable-development-goals/goal-14-life-below-water/targets/.
3 Jeffrey D. Sachs, "Tropical Underdevelopment," CID Working Paper no. 57, December 2000, 1.
4 Collier, *Bottom Billion*.
5 White House, *National Strategy for Maritime Security* (Washington, DC: White House, 2005).
6 The United States signed the UNCLOS convention in 1994 and abides by it, but the Senate has not yet ratified it. Initial concerns about seabed mining prevented ratification, but it remains in limbo due to concerns about how treaties may negatively impact U.S. sovereignty. This occurs in spite of ratification support from President Bush, President Obama, a majority of the U.S. Senate, and the Pentagon. In 2017 the Trump administration was relatively silent about UNCLOS and it is unclear what position they hold on ratification.
7 United Nations, "Law of the Sea, Article 19" December 10, 1982. www.un.org/depts/los/convention_agreements/texts/unclos/part2.htm.
8 Sir Walter Raleigh, "A Discourse of the Invention of Ships, Anchors, Compass," in *The Works of Sir Walter Raleigh, Kt.*, vol. 8 (Oxford: Oxford University Press, 1829, reprinted 1965), 325.
9 African Union, "Africa Integrated Maritime Strategy 2050," 2012. http://cggrps.org/wp-content/uploads/2050-AIM-Strategy_EN.pdf, 11.
10 Energy Information Agency, "World Oil Transit Chokepoints Energy Data," December 2014, available at www.eia.gov/todayinenergy/detail.php?id=18991.
11 UN Secretary-General Ban Ki-moon, "The Secretary-General Message on World Ocean Day," Press Release, June 8, 2009, available at www.un.org/Depts/los/reference_files/worldoceansday.htm.
12 UN Secretary-General Ban Ki-moon, "The Secretary-General Message on World Ocean Day," Press Release, June 8, 2014, available at www.un.org.vn/en/spotlight-articles-press-centre-submenu-253/news-highlights-press-centre-submenu-254/3182-the-secretary-general-s-message-on-world-ocean-s-day.html.
13 UN-Oceans, www.unoceans.org/.
14 United Nations, "Sustainable Development Goals," September 2015, www.un.org/sustainabledevelopment/oceans/.
15 "Sea Shepherd Arrives in Costa Rica with Offer to Help Curb Illegal Fishing Activities in Cocos Island," May 20, 2017. www.seashepherd.org/news-and-commentary/news/sea-shepherd-arrives-in-costa-rica-with-offer-to-help-curb-illegal-fishing-activities-in-cocos-island.html.
16 UNDP, "Goal 14 Targets: Below Water."
17 M. Eriksen, L.C.M. Lebreton, H.S. Carson, M. Thiel, C.J. Moore, J.C. Borerro et al., "Plastic Pollution in the World's Oceans: More than 5 Trillion Plastic Pieces Weighing over 250,000 Tons Afloat at Sea," *PLoS ONE* vol. 9, no. 12 (2014): e111913. https://doi.org/10.1371/journal.pone.0111913.
18 S. Lippiatt, S. Opfer, and C. Arthur, "Marine Debris Monitoring and Assessment." NOAA Technical Memorandum NOS-OR&R-46, 2013.
19 NOAA, "Modeling Oceanic Transport of Floating Marine Debris," May 2016, 2.
20 NOAA, "Programmatic Environmental Assessment for the NOAA Marine Debris Program," March 2013, 14.
21 https://marinedebris.noaa.gov/sites/default/files/GPmap_2012_NOAAMDP.jpg.
22 Charles J. Moore, "Choking the Oceans with Plastic," *New York Times*, August 25, 2014.
23 S. Kühn, E. Bravo Rebolledo, and J. van Franeker, "Deleterious Effects of Litter on Marine Life," in *Marine Anthropogenic Litter*, ed. M. Bergmann, L. Gutow and M. Klages (Cham: Springer, 2015), 75–116.

24 M.L. Taylor, C. Gwinnett, L.F. Robinson, and L.C. Woodall, "Plastic Microfibre Ingestion by Deep-Sea Organisms," *Scientific Reports* vol. **6**, art. 33997 (2016). doi: 10.1038/srep33997.
25 C. Arthur and J. Baker (eds). "Proceedings of the Second Research Workshop on Microplastic Debris," November 5–6, 2010. NOAA Technical Memorandum NOS-OR&R-39.
26 Food and Agriculture Organization of the United Nations, *The State of World Fisheries and Aquaculture (SOFIA)* (Rome: FAO, 2016). www.fao.org/fishery/sofia/en.
27 "Sweden to Provide USD 5.4 Million to FAO to Combat Illegal Fishing," Fish and Information Services, June 12, 2017. www.fis.com/fis/worldnews/worldnews.asp?monthyear=&day=12&id=92191&l=e&special=&ndb=1%20target.
28 Greenpeace, "Hope in West Africa Ship Tour, 2017: Summary of Findings," available at www.greenpeace.org/africa/Global/africa/Oceans/Hope_In_West_Africa_Tour/publications/HopeinWestAfricashiptour_finalbriefing.pdf.
29 Cathy Haenlein, "Below the Surface: How Illegal, Unreported, and Underreported Fishing Threatens our Society," RUSI Occasional Paper, July 2017.
30 UN, "General Assembly, Concerned about World's Marine Ecosystems, Adopts Texts on Law of Sea, Sustainable Fisheries," November 17, 2004, www.un.org/press/en/2004/ga10299.doc.htm.
31 FAO, *SOFIA*, 2014, www.fao.org/fishery/sofia/en.
32 UN General Assembly, Resolution 62/177, "Sustainable Fisheries, Including through the 1995 Agreement for the Implementation of the Provisions of the United Nations Convention on the Law of the Sea of 10 December 1982 Relating to the Conservation and Management of Straddling Fish Stocks and Highly Migratory Fish Stocks, and Related Instruments," February 28, 2008. www.un.org/en/ga/search/view_doc.asp?symbol=A/RES/62/177.
33 Quoted in Salem Solomon, "Chinese Overfishing Threatens West African Economies," Voice of America, July 17, 2017. www.voanews.com/a/chinese-overfishing-threatens-west-african-economies/3947764.html.
34 FAO, "World's First Illegal Fishing Treaty Now in Force," June 5, 2016, www.fao.org/news/story/en/item/417286/icode/.
35 UNDP, "Goal 14 Targets: Below Water."
36 Hongzhou Zhang, "Indonesia's War on Illegal Fishing: Impact on China," RSIS Commentary, Nanyang Technological University, Singapore, September 9, 2015.
37 Southeast Asian Fisheries Development Center/Marine Fishery Resources Development and Management Department, "ASEAN Guidelines for Preventing the Entry of Fish and Fishery Products from IUU Fishing Activities into the Supply Chain," August 24, 2015.
38 "Illegal European Fishing Contributing to Poverty and Piracy in Africa," *Ecologist*, April 20, 2011, www.theecologist.org/News/news_analysis/852417/illegal_european_fishing_contributing_to_poverty_and_piracy_in_africa.html.
39 Quoted in Justice Ilevbare, "Nigeria Loses N7tr to Insecurity in High Seas Annually—Dogara," *The Nation*, July 8, 2017. http://thenationonlineng.net/nigeria-loses-n7tr-insecurity-high-seas-annually-dogara/.
40 ICC International Maritime Bureau, "Piracy and Armed Robbery against Ships: Report for the Period 1 January–31 December," January 2016, Table 1.
41 Martin Murphy, "Piracy and the Exploitation of Sanctuary," in *Armed Groups: Studies in National Security, Counterterrorism, and Counterinsurgency*, ed. Jeffrey H. Norwitz (Newport, RI: U.S. Naval War College, 2008), 160.
42 The temporary seizure of the MV *Maersk Alabama* represented a first in the recent increase in ship hijackings in the vicinity of Somalia.
43 Department of the Navy, *A Cooperative Strategy for 21st Century Seapower* (Washington, DC: Department of the Navy, 2015), 2. available at www.navy.mil/local/maritime/150227-CS21R-Final.pdf.
44 Ethan A. Nadelmann, *Cops Across Borders: The Internationalization of U.S. Criminal Law Enforcement* (University Park: Pennsylvania State University Press, 1993).
45 UNODC, *World Drug Report 2016* (New York: UN, 2016), available at www.unodc.org/wdr2016/index.html.

46 "U.S./CARICOM/Dominican Republic Statement on Third Border Initiative," January 14, 2004. www.america.gov/st/washfile-english/2004/January/20040114144116nesnom0.569256.html#ixzz0AZrjgdVl.

47 Kurt Tidd, "Posture Statement of Admiral Kurt W. Tidd Commander, United States Southern Command before the 115th Congress Senate Armed Services Committee," April 6, 2017. www.armed-services.senate.gov/imo/media/doc/Tidd_04-06-17.pdf.

48 Hugo Chávez quoted in Tom Leonard, "Hugo Chavez Demands Queen Return Falkland Islands to Argentina," *Telegraph*, February 22, 2010, available at www.telegraph.co.uk/news/world news/southamerica/falklandislands/7293985/ Hugo-Chavez-demands-Queen-return-Falkland-Islands-to-Argentina.html.

49 Permanent Court of Arbitration, "The South China Sea Arbitration (*The Republic of the Philippines v. The People's Republic of China*)," July 12, 2016. https://pca-cpa.org/wp-content/uploads/sites/175/2016/07/PH-CN-20160712-Press-Release-No-11-English.pdf.

50 Xinjun Zhang, "China's 'Peaceful Rise,' 'Harmonious' Foreign Relations, and Legal Confrontation—and Lessons from the Sino-Japanese Dispute over the East China Sea," *Foreign Policy Research Institute E-Notes*, April 16, 2010.

51 Okalik Eegeesiak, "The Arctic Ocean and the Sea Ice Is Our Nuna," *UN Chronicle*, vol. 54, nos 1 and 2, May 2017. https://unchronicle.un.org/article/arctic-ocean-and-sea-ice-our-nuna.

52 Scott Borgerson, "Prepared Testimony on U.S. National Security Interests in the Arctic before the House Committee on Foreign Affairs," March 25, 2009, available at www.cfr.org/publication/18922/prepared_testimony_on_us_national_security_interests_in_the_arctic_before_the_house_committee_on_foreign_affairs.html?breadcrumb=%2Fbios%2F13363%2Fscott_g_borgerson.

53 In August 2007 Russia planted its flag on the seafloor at the geographic North Pole. It did so under the United Nations Convention on the Law of the Sea by arguing that the underwater Lomonosov Ridge and North Pole are extensions of its landmass. In 2010 Canada staged its own underwater claim using a remotely piloted submersible vehicle, which it is using to map its claims. The twenty-one-country UNCLOS Commission on the Limits of the Continental Shelf is currently reviewing the claims, but the United States is not represented since it has not ratified UNCLOS. Signed in 1982, UNCLOS "lays down a comprehensive regime of law and order in the world's oceans and seas establishing rules governing all uses of the oceans and their resources. It enshrines the notion that all problems of ocean space are closely interrelated and need to be addressed as a whole." At: www.un.org/Depts/los/convention_agreements/conven tion_overview_convention.htm.

To Learn More

Track marine pollution and ocean debris with the "Marine Debris Tracker" app at www.marined ebris.engr.uga.edu/newmap/.

Get the latest update on global piracy incidents at the International Maritime Bureau Piracy Reporting Centre: www.icc-ccs.org/.

Read the weekly worldwide threats to shipping report prepared by the U.S. Office of Naval Intelligence: www.oni.navy.mil/Intelligence-Community/Piracy/.

Visit the headquarters of the commander, Fifth Fleet—the U.S. admiral responsible for antipiracy operations in the Gulf of Aden, along with other nations' maritime forces—at www.cusnc.navy.mil/.

The non-partisan think tank, Center for International Maritime Security (http://cimsec.org), provides an important venue for wide-ranging maritime discussions.

Martin N. Murphy in *Small Boats, Weak States, Dirty Money: Piracy and Maritime Terrorism in the Modern World* (New York: Columbia University Press, 2009) offers a detailed analysis of modern piracy and the challenges associated with creating maritime security.

Follow journalist John Burns on his personal voyage to understand pirates in *Dangerous Waters: Modern Piracy and Terror on the High Seas* (New York: Dutton, 2002).

Monitor the world's fishing fleets through Global Fishing Watch at http://globalfishingwatch.org/map/; and One Earth Future works to reduce piracy and IUU fishing in East Africa and the Indian Ocean: http://oneearthfuture.org.

Read the latest U.S. Department of State report on major drug-transit or major illicit drug-producing countries at www.state.gov/j/inl/rls/nrcrpt/index.htm.

See how the African Union charted a course to improve maritime security in Africa by 2050 at http://cggrps.org/wp-content/uploads/2050-AIM-Strategy_EN.pdf.

Heather Conley offers "History Lessons for the Arctic: What International Maritime Disputes Tell Us about a New Ocean," December 19, 2016, at www.csis.org/analysis/history-lessons-arctic.

Visit the website of the Arctic Council, the key intergovernmental group promoting cooperation and coordination of the Arctic states (and with indigenous communities), at www.arctic-council.org/.

Chapter 8

Health Security

Chapter contents

People are traveling more. Food and medical product supply chains stretch across the globe. Biological threats (such as Middle East respiratory syndrome coronavirus, or MERS-CoV) and drug-resistant illnesses pose a growing danger to people everywhere, whether diseases are naturally occurring, intentionally produced, or the result of a laboratory accident. In today's interconnected world, poorly treated cases of TB or pneumonia in Asia and Africa have shown up in U.S. hospitals within days.

U.S. Centers for Disease Control and Prevention[1]

Two oceans have kept the United States relatively immune from foreign military invasion. And through the midterm, no country has either the strategic rationale or the military capabilities to attack the United States. Yet homeland security preoccupies strategic thinking. Terrorism, especially the nuclear type, is often assumed to pose an existential threat to the United States, although the combination of homeland security vigilance and terrorist ineptitude has kept the country relatively safe since 2001. However, the United States is not completely immune from harm—sometimes from the most unexpected sources.

Americans are under threat from unseen microbes, bacteria, and viruses, and their prevalence is increasing, in large part due to globalization processes. Robert Cook notes that: "Humanity has become vulnerable to cross-species illnesses, thanks to modern advances such as the rapid transportation of both goods and people, increasing population density around the globe, and a growing dependence on intensified livestock production for food."[2] Further, more bacteria have become antibiotic resistant, which complicates treatment. Infectious disease is still the number-one killer of humans. Globally, millions die from tuberculosis, HIV/AIDS, and malaria, not to mention the more exotic and highly publicized Ebola hemorrhagic fever. In the United States, tens of thousands die each year from seasonal flu, and more than 1 million suffer from HIV/AIDS. There is also concern that terrorists could weaponize diseases and launch biological attacks using substances like anthrax, which occurred in Washington, D.C. in 2001. Fortunately, there have been no successor attacks, and naturally occurring diseases pose a greater threat to human security in the United States and elsewhere. Director of National Intelligence Dan Coats testified to this point in 2017:

> The emergence of a severe global public health emergency is possible in any given year and can have negative impacts on the security and stability of a nation or region. A novel or reemerging microbe that is easily transmissible between humans and is highly pathogenic remains a major threat because such an organism has the potential to spread rapidly and kill millions. Threats such as avian influenza and Middle East Respiratory Syndrome Coronavirus (MERS-CoV) have pandemic potential. The World Bank has estimated that a severe global influenza pandemic could cost the equivalent of 4.8 percent of global GDP, or more than $3 trillion, during the course of an outbreak.[3]

Since disease knows no boundaries, the United States is vulnerable to chronic and infectious diseases prevalent in many other parts of the world. In recent years, epidemiologists have raised concerns about pandemic influenza (see Image 8.1). Commonly known as "bird flu," H5N1 influenza first captured the world's attention in 1997. The impact of H5N1 has been largely limited, but in 2009 another strain of flu demonstrated just how easily influenza crosses borders and impacts all segments of a population.

The initial outbreak of the influenza virus H1N1, formerly known as "swine flu," began in early spring in Mexico; by June the infections were so widespread that the World Health Organization (WHO) declared it a pandemic. Before the first wave of the outbreak was over, it had shuttered Mexico's economy, infected Colombia's president,

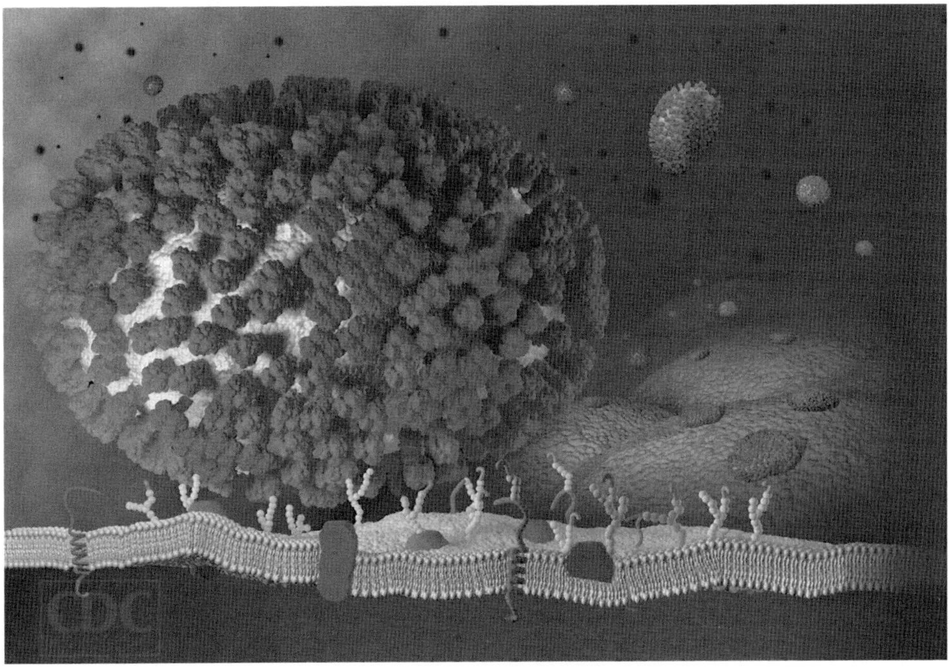

Image 8.1 Graphical Representation of a Generic Influenza Virus. Photo: Centers for Disease Control and Prevention (CDC)[4]

and caused hundreds of millions of infections worldwide. In the fall of 2009 President Barack Obama declared a national emergency to ensure that the government had the necessary authorities to prepare for and react to winter virus infections. And in 2016, the U.S. government issued a decade-long plan through 2027 to improve detection and monitoring of novel influenza viruses; translate research into better diagnostics, therapeutics, and vaccines; and coordinate domestic and international pandemic preparedness and response activities.[5]

In addition to the immediate costs infections have to individuals, disease outbreaks have serious social costs, too. Globally, HIV/AIDS kills millions each year and has devastated numerous African countries. In 2015, "5.9 million children under age five died, a rate of almost 16,000 per day; 83 percent of those deaths were caused by infections, neonatal complications, or nutritional status."[6] This undermines efforts to achieve the United Nations Sustainable Development Goals (SDGs) and more stable, productive societies. By 2030, the UN SDG goal is to "end the epidemics of AIDS, tuberculosis, malaria and neglected tropical diseases and combat hepatitis, water-borne diseases and other communicable diseases."[7] The interconnections created by globalization apply equally to health security as it does to issues like poverty, corruption, and climate change explored earlier in this book. Diseases long since conquered in the West—such as tuberculosis (TB), malaria, and polio—are now making a comeback as international travel, migrating birds, and immigration expose Americans to once-vanquished diseases that are lingering or reemerging in developing countries.

Before further examining trends in key diseases, this chapter first defines health security, which was identified as a human security issue in the 1994 *UNDP Human Development Report*.[8] The chapter then examines how a heretofore public health concern became a question of *national* security for the United States and other countries. Next, some of the most important health issues that could pose security problems for individual countries and the world at large are assessed, particularly disease and pandemic outbreaks of disease. Here we consider the challenges not only of influenza but also of HIV/AIDS, malaria, Ebola, and the Zika virus—along with possibilities for improving health security around the globe.

Health and National Security Defined

In 1994 the landmark UNDP report singled out health security as a human security issue for both developing countries and industrial countries, pointing to the detrimental role of "infectious and parasitic diseases" in developing countries, linked mainly to "poor nutrition and an unsafe environment."[9] At the same time the report noted how the major killer diseases in industrialized countries were often linked to diet, life style, and environmental causes. But the report's focus was on how health security diseases and access to health services were much worse for the poor, living mainly in developing countries, and not on the larger global ramifications.

Twenty years ago, military planners and policymakers were also unlikely to link public health with national security concerns. Instead, health issues were deemed decidedly domestic issues and at odds with traditional foreign policy concerns centered on potential peer competitors, nuclear proliferation, or rogue states. However, after the emergence of avian influenza in Asia in 1997, national security professionals began to reconsider infectious disease as a potential matter of national security. Hypothetical scenarios illustrated that disease could shut down international air traffic as governments would make efforts to limit the scale of a pandemic. Interest heightened again during the 2003 severe acute respiratory syndrome (SARS) outbreak that infected 8,000 and killed 800 globally. And in 2014, an Ebola outbreak in West Africa caused the United States to deploy 3,000 military personnel to prevent widespread outbreaks.

Though these separate outbreaks were unrelated and relatively small, the potential for a regional and even global pandemic is very real. The last three pandemics of the twentieth century killed more than 43 million people. Although medical treatments have improved since the early 1900s, diseases continue to mutate, which challenges pharmaceutical research and development of new medicines. In 2017, President Trump's Director of National Intelligence, Dan Coats, highlighted disease as a concern for national security, as noted at the beginning of this chapter. Further, he testified before Congress that:

> The continued rise of antimicrobial resistance—the ability of pathogens, including viruses, fungi, and bacteria, to resist drug treatment—is likely to outpace development of new antimicrobial drugs. This resistance will result in increasingly difficult or impossible-to-cure infections of previously curable diseases.[10] (Table 8.1 on "superbugs" demonstrates the gravity of this issue.)

Consequently, infectious diseases have the potential to spread rapidly and cause mass casualties, especially with our highly mobile societies. In its 2007 report on future security challenges, the U.S. military noted that "a pandemic in North America would be protracted and pervasive, causing substantial societal impact and persistent economic losses in almost every state."[11] The 2015 *National Security Strategy* saw the U.S. government proclaiming that "America is the world leader in fighting pandemics, including HIV/AIDS, and in improving global health security."[12] In 2017, the acting director of the Defense

Table 8.1 "Superbug" Bacterial Threat Medical Most Wanted List, 2017

Bacterial Threat	Antibiotic Resistance
PRIORITY 1: CRITICAL	
1. *Acinetobacter baumannii*	Carbapenem
2. *Pseudomonas aeruginosa*	Carbapenem
3. *Enterobacteriaceae*	Carbapenem, ESBL-producing
PRIORITY 2: HIGH	
4. *Enterococcus faecium*	Vancomycin
5. *Staphylococcus aureus*	Methicillin, Vancomycin-intermediate and resistant
6. *Helicobacter pylori*	Clarithromycin
7. *Campylobacter spp.*	Fluoroquinolone
8. *Salmonellae*	Fluoroquinolone
9. *Neisseria gonorrhoeae*	Cephalosporin, Fluoroquinolone
PRIORITY 3: MEDIUM	
10. *Streptococcus pneumoniae*	Penicillin-non-susceptible
11. *Haemophilus influenzae*	Ampicillin
12. *Shigella spp.*	Fluoroquinolone

Source: "WHO Publishes List of Bacteria for Which New Antibiotics Are Urgently Needed," at www.who.int/mediacentre/news/releases/2017/bacteria-antibiotics-needed/en/

Threat Reduction Agency (DTRA), which is primarily concerned with countering weapons of mass destruction, testified that: "[The] DTRA addresses the outbreak risk of diseases of concern by promoting best practices in biological safety and security, improving partner countries' abilities to rapidly detect and report dangerous infections, and enhancing partnerships that facilitate information sharing."[13]

In addition to overwhelming hospitals and clinics, commerce would slow as people were quarantined (voluntarily or not), and civil disturbances could overwhelm law enforcement as people's demands increased. The military compares a modern pandemic to the fourteenth-century plague, or "Black Death," which killed about one-third of Europe's population. Because of this, there are fears that future pandemics are capable of producing widespread death, social disorder, and civil disturbances.

Besides the possibility of pandemic influenza in the United States, national security professionals consistently view public health as a security issue in developing countries in sub-Saharan Africa. In his 1996 *National Security Strategy*, President Bill Clinton had already highlighted disease and its harmful impact on development: "New diseases, such as AIDS, and other epidemics which can be spread through environmental degradation, threaten to overwhelm the health facilities of developing countries, disrupt societies and stop economic growth."[14] During President George W. Bush's terms in office, fighting HIV/AIDS became a hallmark of his administration's approach to development assistance in Africa through the President's Emergency Program for AIDS Relief (PEPFAR) program. In many cases, a disease like HIV/AIDS poses a triple tax on poor, developing societies, which must care for the infected, absorb the productivity loss when sick people withdraw from the workforce, and care for the orphans created when millions of parents die every year. Further, these orphans become vulnerable to modern slavery either as domestic, industrial, and sex workers or as child soldiers who can readily take part in Africa's internal wars. Clearly diseases create a much larger burden on poorer, developing countries that do not have the resources to comprehensively address them as can wealthier, developed countries.

Although there are strong humanitarian reasons to be concerned about disease in developing countries, by the end of the twentieth century it was the wide-reaching threat of the effects of disease worldwide that became the focus of security concerns. International travel and migratory birds raised awareness of diseases like West Nile disease and avian influenza. Accordingly, the United States began to articulate strategies that addressed disease as a material threat to Americans, one that is a threat to all Americans' human security. As the 1999 *National Security Strategy* noted, "Diseases and health risks can no longer be viewed solely as a domestic concern."[15] Instead, health was acknowledged to be a legitimate matter of national security.

By recognizing health as a national security issue, the United States affirmed its status as a superpower with global interests because of the potential for disease threats everywhere on the planet. In fact, in his 1998 *National Security Strategy* President Clinton noted that: "Problems that once seemed quite distant—such as resource depletion, rapid population growth, environmental damage, *new infectious diseases* and uncontrolled refugee migration—have important implications for American security."[16] Proximity to a threat has now become irrelevant, as the United States identifies potential threats in every country that lacks strong public health sectors.

President George W. Bush continued the tendency to view disease as a national security challenge in the twenty-first century, stating: "We will also continue to lead the world in efforts to reduce the terrible toll of HIV/AIDS and other infectious diseases." He funded international health programs at unprecedented levels, and issued Homeland Security Presidential Directive 21. Among other things, this directive defined a catastrophic health event as "any natural or manmade incident, including terrorism, that results in a number of ill or injured persons sufficient to overwhelm the capabilities of immediate local and regional emergency response and health care systems."[17]

White House concerns for health security continued apace under the Obama administration in 2009, emphasizing both global and national perspectives, along with the interconnection of many troubling issues. In 2009 a *National Health Security Strategy* was released that outlined ten objectives, including working with global partners to enhance national, continental, and global health security. President Obama told the UN General Assembly:

> Far too many people in far too many places live through the daily crises that challenge our humanity—the despair of an empty stomach; the thirst brought on by dwindling water supplies; the injustice of a child dying from a treatable disease; or a mother losing her life as she gives birth.[18]

Consequently, U.S. health assistance programs now exist in almost every country of the developing world. These efforts are primarily funded through the international assistance account budget of the Department of State, but the Department of Health and Human Services provides important technical information. At the same time, in 2015, the *National Security Strategy* noted: "at home, we are strengthening our ability to prevent outbreaks and ensure sufficient capacity to respond rapidly and manage biological incidents."[19]

It is important to underscore that concerns about public health are not simply a Trojan horse for U.S. expansionism or hegemony, as some critics may warn. Rather, the tendency to view disease as a national security threat is now common to the foreign policies of virtually all developed countries. These nations recognize that along with the benefits of globalization, there are increased vulnerabilities as well. For example, the Netherlands has defined its national security challenges through diverse threats such as SARS, bird flu, floods, and terrorism, acknowledging that through increased interdependencies, what once were relatively minor threats can lead to societal disruption.[20]

Similar sentiments are conveyed in the United Kingdom's national security policy, which sees pandemics as a part of threats and risks that "are driven by a diverse and interconnected set of underlying factors, including climate change, competition for energy, poverty and poor governance, demographic changes and globalization." The British strategy notes that "Disease, particularly pandemic influenza, emerging infectious diseases and growing Antimicrobial Resistance, threatens lives and causes disruption to public services and the economy."[21]

The European Union (EU) reflects these views and includes pandemics as one of several global challenges facing Europe. In this regard, the European Centre for Disease Prevention and Control (ECDC) noted, "Pandemics do not recognise national borders. They affect not only public health but also societies and economies throughout the EU and the world." Finally, the influential World Economic Forum (WEF) includes pandemics as one of the most important risks to global stability. The Forum understands that transnational disease has the potential to slow commerce, and equally development, by interfering with the international movement of goods and people.[22]

Concerns about disease are manifested in international assistance programs that prioritize human security concerns like health issues over traditional security issues. These programs are based on the UN Sustainable Development Goals (described in earlier chapters), which include reducing child mortality, improving maternal health, and combating HIV/AIDS, malaria, and other diseases. In support of these health goals, the United States funded PEPFAR at $15 billion for an HIV/AIDS program and added a $1.2 billion antimalaria program. Europe also launched a €300 million program that targets malaria, tuberculosis, and AIDS. According to the United Nations, 1.5 million babies have been born free of HIV because of programs like these.[23]

Ideas and concerns about health security now transcend the political sphere and in recent years have become integral to national security strategic thinking. The National Intelligence Council of experts affirmed this view as early as 2009 when it linked pandemic disease to conflict: "If a pandemic disease emerges by 2025, internal and cross-border tension and conflict will become more likely as nations struggle—with degraded capabilities—to control the movement of populations seeking to avoid infection or maintain access to resources." Nearly ten years later, the NIC continued to link climate change to disease outbreak that would slow global trade and economic activity.[24] No longer just a fringe national security concern, pandemic disease is now included as a major issue along with terrorism, rogue states, and peer competition over energy. The Department of Defense has explained the rationale for these concerns:

> The United States, our allies, and our partners face a spectrum of challenges, including violent transnational extremist networks, hostile states armed with weapons of mass destruction, rising regional powers, emerging space and cyber threats, natural and *pandemic* disasters, and a growing competition for resources.[25]

When human security is undermined by disease, development efforts fail, which can enhance or even cause political instability and conflict.

Significantly, so important is governmental concern about a future pandemic that the U.S. Secretary of Defense designated responsibility for global pandemic monitoring to Northern Command, which is primarily responsible for U.S. homeland defense, including missile defense. Operating in conjunction with the National Response Plan, Northern Command anticipates natural and manmade disasters to prevent and mitigate crises. Under its charter, Northern Command has responsibility for planning and responding to pandemic influenza. This includes preventive measures and reactive operations if quarantine or civil disturbances exceed state governments' capacities (see Box 8.1).

❖ BOX 8.1 THINK AGAIN: HEALTH SECURITY AND NATIONAL SECURITY

That public health has become a national security concern is surprising to many, and challenges the traditional separations made between domestic and international issues in the United States. On the one hand, the key to health security lies in domestic policy to ensure there are adequate vaccine stocks, trained health professionals, and educational campaigns to promote personal hygiene. (For instance, to prevent the flu, the government reminds us to wash our hands frequently.) On the other hand, the transnational nature of disease requires high levels of international cooperation and coordination to monitor disease outbreaks and coordinate responses. Rebecca Katz and Daniel Singer argue that this approach is not without some risk:

> While health professionals may welcome the higher profile and greater resources given to their issues, characterizing a health issue as a national priority (and particularly as a security issue) may change the understanding of a health threat, put relatively greater emphasis on the views of those outside the health community and potentially alter the approach to solving the problem. Consequently, care should be taken in deciding which health issues should be given priority on par with national security issues and included explicitly in national foreign policy.[1]

As with all human security issues, finding a balance between the policy experts, medical professionals, organizations that deliver services, and government agencies is key to improving human security. Since issues like health do not fall neatly into the national security realm, coordination among many sectors, along with a division of responsibilities, is key. Nongovernmental organizations seem to have the best understanding of local issues. International groups like Doctors Without Borders (Médecins Sans Frontières), the Gates Foundation, or the Carter Center partner with groups in various countries to maximize delivery of health services and work through complicated cultural issues. For example, some leaders in sub-Saharan Africa deny that HIV/AIDS is caused by a virus, and therefore prevent groups from providing care. Local groups may understand how to manage these issues. Likewise, cultural norms may preclude HIV/AIDS preventive measures prescribed by the ABC program of "abstinence, be faithful, and condom use." Groups sensitive to local beliefs may help develop a strategy that can still reduce the incidence of HIV/AIDS. Sadly, in the most unfortunate cases, medical professionals may be restricted from traveling, or even killed, in cases where they are alleged to be pursuing political or religious agendas, as has occurred with nongovernmental medical experts in Afghanistan.

1 Rebecca Katz and Daniel Singer, "Health and Security in Foreign Policy," *Bulletin of the World Health Organization* (March 2007): 85, available at www.who.int/bulletin/volumes/85/3/06-036889.pdf.

The strategic implications of a pandemic are many. First, disease retards and ultimately prevents development. Considering that reducing global poverty is a key U.S. and UN goal, disease is just one of many challenges to overcome in that campaign. The UN seeks to: reduce the global maternal mortality ratio; end preventable deaths of newborns and children under five years; and end the epidemics of AIDS, tuberculosis, malaria, and other diseases.[26] Second, pandemic disease can potentially produce mass casualties greater than traditional warfare. For example, the 1918 influenza outbreak killed more than twice the number of Americans who died fighting during World War I. Third, a pandemic seems inevitable. Since disease is naturally occurring, governments are limited in their ability to prevent pandemics. The best governments can hope to do is minimize their impact through greater awareness, improved public health systems, and vaccination programs. The remainder of the chapter explores these implications by examining disease, especially pandemics and related health threats, to understand their importance for national and human security, along with the challenges to effectively addressing these threats.

Pandemic Disease: Influenza

There are at least 1,500 microbes that cause human illness, but most attention is focused on influenza, which is a highly adaptive virus that produces respiratory disease in humans and animals such as wild waterfowl, and domesticated pigs and poultry. Michael Osterholm has noted that, "Dating back to antiquity, influenza pandemics have posed the greatest threat of a worldwide calamity caused by infectious disease."[27] Influenza is seasonal in temperate climates like the United States and Europe. During a typical year, "seasonal flu" infects millions, but claims the lives of only tens of thousands each year. However, the greatest danger lies in the virus's ability to mutate and to transmit from animals to humans.

On average, three influenza pandemics per century have been documented since the sixteenth century, occurring at intervals of ten to fifty years. Of those in the twentieth century (1918, 1957, and 1968), the 1918 influenza was the most deadly, killing an estimated 50 million people worldwide. The American death toll for the 1918 pandemic was 675,000 lives, or 6 percent of the U.S. population at that time. Unlike seasonal flu, where mortality is greatest in the very young and the very old (a trend seen in the 2017–2018 flu season in the United States, where young children were particularly at risk), pandemic influenza strains tend to be deadliest for young to middle-age adults whose immune systems overcompensate. If a large-scale influenza pandemic were to occur in the United States today, it could produce 75 million hospitalizations and up to 1.5 million deaths.[28] And if history is a guide, then hysteria will also generate security concerns such as rioting and other large-scale civil disturbances. Of greatest concern today are various strains of influenza that have already demonstrated a global reach. The U.S. Department of Health and Human Services cautions: "throughout history, influenza pandemics have led to widespread illness and death. Pandemic influenza is not a theoretical threat; rather, it is a recurring threat."[29]

H5N1 (*hemagglutinin* type 5 and *neuraminidase* type 1) is an influenza variant that is commonly referred to as "bird flu." First appearing in southern China, H5N1 originated in aquatic birds such as ducks and geese and then passed to chickens and other domesticated birds. The virus occasionally passes from bird to human, and people living in developing countries who tend to live close to their livestock are especially vulnerable. Though transmission from bird to human is relatively rare, these zoonotic events are very serious. Once in the lung cells of a mammalian host, the virus can "reassort," or mix genes with

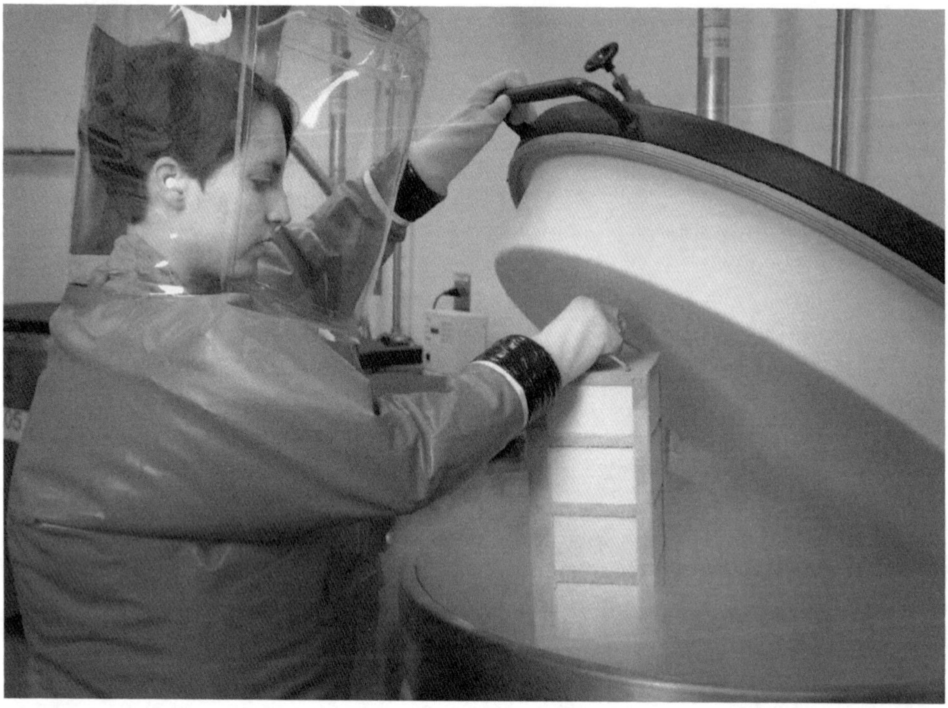

Image 8.2 A CDC Scientist Inserts Biological Stocks into Liquid Nitrogen for Storage. Photo: James Gathany, CDC[30]

already existing human influenza strains. Once adapted, this newly reassorted influenza can more easily transmit from human to human. An influenza variant with components from a previously nonhuman strain is considered a "novel" influenza, and as such it poses a unique threat. First, the virulence of such an influenza strain is unknown, and potentially more deadly. Second, there would be no human resistance to such a variant, as humans have not had exposure to it before. These reassortments, when highly contagious, are the beginnings of what could become a pandemic (Image 8.2 demonstrates continuing research at the CDC).

It is not possible to predict how or when a virus will mutate in such a way that it poses a threat to humans, but once it does, the results can be deadly. When the H5N1 virus infects domestic poultry, there is a100 percent chicken mortality rate within forty-eight hours. It is unclear how humans affected by the virus would react, but prediction models suggest many casualties. This is based both on the nature of the virus and on inadequate emergency health care facilities. Dr. Steven Phillips and Rear Adm. George R. Worthington have argued that "on any given day, the emergency rooms of most U.S. hospitals are at or near capacity, and it is unrealistic to expect them to respond effectively to sudden large-scale needs."[31] In an effort for the health care system to become more efficient, a substantial number of hospital closures occurred over the past two decades. Largely driven by business concerns of profitability or sustainability in public hospitals, this has created a vulnerability, since overcapacity is a virtue when it comes to a public health crisis. Adding to these concerns in the developed world, the poorer regions of the world are characterized by a lack of medical capacity to meet even routine health needs.

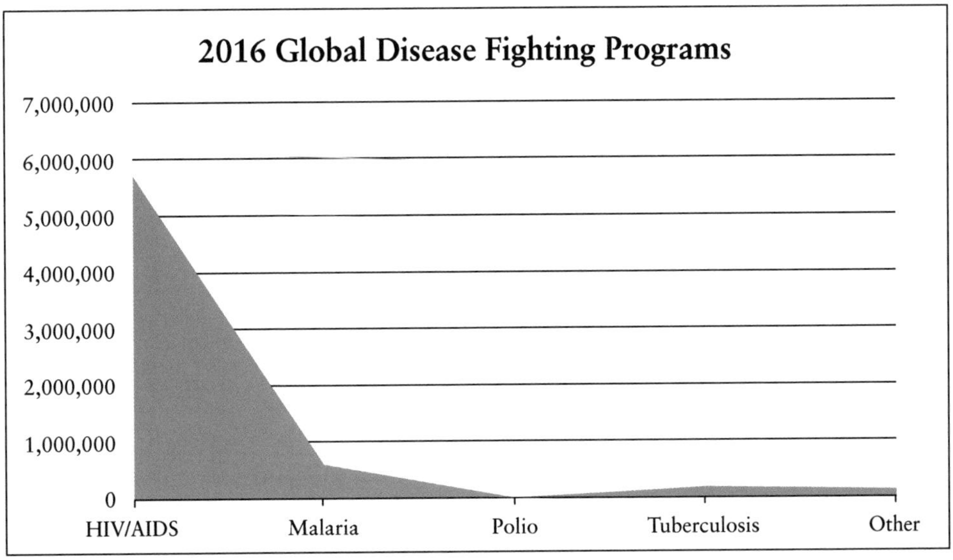

Figure 8.1 Programs to Fight Global Diseases.
Source: Adapted from U.S. Agency for International Development, *Congressional Budget Justification Foreign Assistance Summary Tables Fiscal Year 2016*, www.state.gov/documents/organization/238223.pdf

As one example, in 2009 a novel influenza strain captured the world's attention when what became known as "swine flu," or H1N1 (*hemagglutinin* type 1 and *neuraminidase* type 1), emerged in La Gloria, Mexico. In February 2009 five-year-old Édgar Enrique Hernández suffered from a flu virus that had mutated from pigs. Édgar recovered, but the mutated virus gave rise to a global pandemic. Just five months after the first case, there were 300,000 laboratory-confirmed cases, 4,000 deaths, and infections in 191 countries and territories. At the end of 2009, up to 67 million Americans were infected.[32] Given the pace of infections, the World Health Organization declared a pandemic, and many governments increased their preparedness measures (Figure 8.1 shows spending on global programs).

Given the relative speed with which influenza can mutate and infect humans, it has recently been given priority by the U.S. national security establishment. In 2005, for example, the federal government developed a *National Strategy for Pandemic Influenza*, and later created a website to inform and prepare Americans. Under the national strategy, the Department of State is the lead federal agency for international influenza issues. The government has raised the profile of influenza to something historically bigger than seasonal flu, but admits that primary responsibility lies with individuals, as with so many human security issues. Yet the strategy does rest on three pillars and addresses the full spectrum of events that link a farmyard overseas to a living room in America. Although the circumstances that connect these environments are very different, the strategic principles remain relevant. The pillars of the strategy are:

- Preparedness and Communication: activities that should be undertaken before a pandemic to ensure preparedness, and the communication of roles and responsibilities to all levels of government, segments of society, and individuals.

- Surveillance and Detection: domestic and international systems that provide continuous "situational awareness" to ensure the earliest warning possible to protect the population.
- Response and Containment: actions to limit the spread of the outbreak and to mitigate the health, social, and economic impacts of a pandemic.[33]

The national pandemic strategy has survived two presidential administrations and the H1N1 pandemic. However, the U.S. government has not yet been able to generate a civil defense-type mentality with pandemics—but it keeps trying. This may be because conventional wisdom sees the government's role as limited to providing information and sponsoring vaccine development.

HIV/AIDS

Whereas the influenza virus is considered potentially the deadliest across all demographic groups, HIV/AIDS already claims millions of lives each year around the globe. Unlike influenza, the human immunodeficiency virus (HIV) is transmitted through behavior that results in the sharing of infected bodily fluids. HIV is a retrovirus that infects cells of the human immune system, destroying or impairing cellular function (Image 8.3 depicts HIV-1). The most advanced stage of HIV infection is acquired immunodeficiency syndrome, or AIDS. It can take ten to fifteen years for an HIV-infected person to develop AIDS, a process that can be slowed by antiretroviral drugs. Like influenza, treatment is limited to antiviral drugs, which can slow immune system degeneration and protect an infected person from secondary infections. Yet eventually, as the

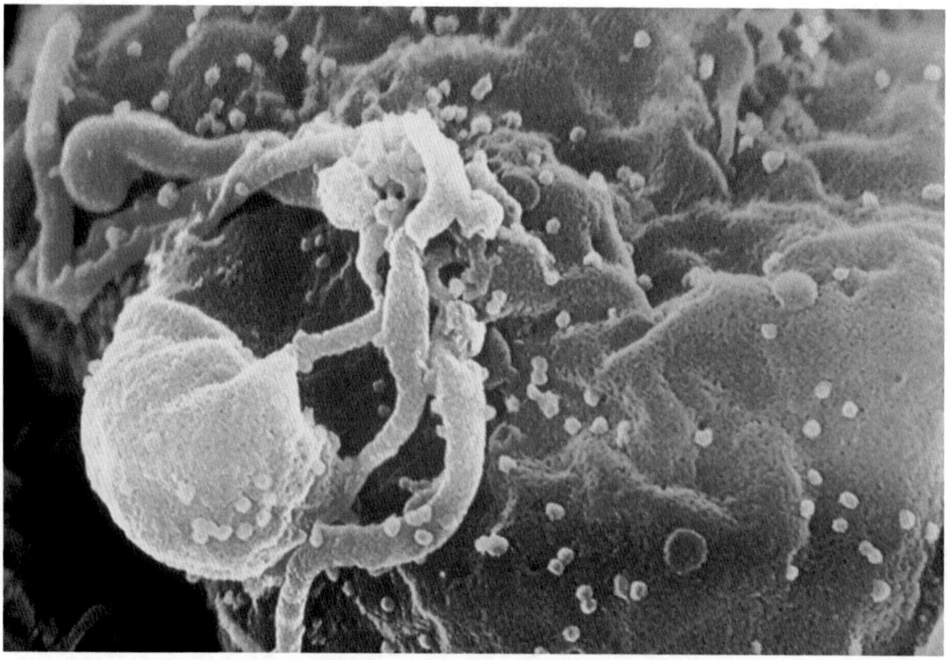

Image 8.3 Scanning Electron Micrograph of HIV-1. Photo: Cynthia Goldsmith, CDC

virus destroys a person's immune system, death often comes from a secondary infection such as TB or influenza.

Approximately 37 million people live with HIV/AIDS.[34] The geographic distribution of those infected with HIV/AIDS is not random. Instead, there are high concentrations of infected people in sub-Saharan Africa, with southern African societies being primarily infected. In the West infections are highest among intravenous drug users and those who engage in homosexual behavior. But in Africa women are infected (through heterosexual behavior) at the highest rates. Incredibly, in Botswana and South Africa, nearly 1 in 5 people are infected.[35] Cultural norms in sub-Saharan Africa tend to prevent condom usage, resulting in the faster spread of HIV/AIDS. Despite substantial gains in mitigating the impact of HIV/AIDS, 19 million Africans still live with the virus.[36] This poses a serious challenge for promoting future economic development and stable, productive societies in many African countries. To date, there is no cure for HIV/AIDS. The complexity of the virus and limits of medical research have kept researchers focused on vaccine development since 1984. Fortunately, recent work in Southeast Asia is pointing the way to a vaccine which has shown a 30 percent success rate in vulnerable populations. However, much more work remains to be done, and prevention efforts still dominate policy actions.

The transformation into viewing HIV/AIDS as a national security threat rather than a sexual disease has not been easy. Some religious leaders have viewed HIV/AIDS as the supreme punishment for immoral acts.[37] Yet many experts have recognized that the disease does not discriminate, and that absolute infection rates are highest among heterosexual women who may receive it from their spouses. Furthermore, the destabilizing effects on societies in Africa and the observed link between sick and absent parents and the increase in child soldiers have helped move the issue to the forefront of international security. Former World Bank president James Wolfensohn captured the challenges of AIDS as a health security issue when he commented:

> Many of us used to think of AIDS as a health issue. We were wrong . . . Nothing we have seen is a greater challenge to the peace and stability of African societies than the epidemic of AIDS . . . We face a major development crisis, and more than that, a security crisis.[38]

Analyst Laurie Garrett has examined the linkage between HIV and security, concluding that "the stability of states with high rates of HIV infection may well be threatened, but more likely through a process of erosion of its elite populations, its political leadership, its college-trained professionals, and its skilled labor forces."[39] There are additional effects on security forces in states with high infection rates. Already, an alarming 25 percent of African military personnel are HIV positive. This not only further debilitates weak states but also subjects civilian populations to infection, given that military personnel are important vectors. In recognition of this fact, HIV testing among UN peacekeepers is now common to prevent future spread of the disease by soldiers deploying to various regions of the world.

In recognition of this fact, as early as 2000 the United Nations Security Council declared HIV/AIDS to be a threat to international peace and security. The associated UN resolution stressed that the HIV/AIDS pandemic, if unchecked, may pose a risk to stability and security.[40] In response, the UN's overall goal is to ensure that "all people, regardless of their identity, choices or circumstances, have access to relevant HIV prevention services, voluntary HIV testing and a affordable treatment and high-quality care and support services—including psychosocial, financial and legal services."[41]

Malaria

In contrast to influenza and HIV/AIDS, malaria is insect-borne, making prevention seem easier. Yet it remains one of the most challenging diseases in the world, with 300 to 500 million persons infected annually, producing about 1 million deaths each year. Malaria is a bloodborne infection transmitted by mosquitoes. The parasites destroy red blood cells, which leads to anemia and lung and kidney failure and can result in death. And, in contrast to influenza and HIV/AIDS, the vast majority of those killed are children. In fact, 90 percent of fatalities are children under the age of five, a fact that has clear implications for retarding future development in affected countries.[42]

Preventing malaria is not as simple as it might appear. More than half the world's population lives in areas where malaria infection is possible. There is generally less risk of infection at altitudes greater than 4,000 feet, but climate is the main determinant. Tropical climates offer ideal conditions for mosquito breeding, and the political instability often prevalent in developing countries complicates control and treatment. This includes parts of South America, sub-Saharan Africa, South Asia, and Southeast Asia. Additionally, it is worth noting the connection to environmental security here in that a number of experts believe that the rise of global temperatures may increase the range of such traditionally tropical diseases as malaria and yellow fever into areas such as Europe.[43]

Given the scope of the malaria challenge, governments that prioritize development assistance increasingly include antimalarial programs in an effort to reduce the disease's impact. The U.S. government, for example, has been aiding anti-malaria efforts since the 1950s through USAID programs, recognizing that that this is "a critical component of the U.S. Government's national security strategy with investments in global health and malaria contributing to economic and political stability." In 2017 the "U.S. President's Malaria Initiative" was focused on 24 sub-Saharan African countries and several countries in the Greater Mekong Subregion in Asia, in addition to various other programs.[44]

The U.S. global malaria coordinator, advised by representatives of USAID, the Centers for Disease Control and Prevention (CDC) and the Department of Health and Human Services, the Department of State, the Department of Defense, the National Security Council, and the Office of Management and Budget, oversees the U.S. program. Since prevention is the primary objective, the program focuses on distributing mosquito nets, antimalarial drugs, and insecticide. At the same time, the program also seeks to strengthen partner countries' health services through education, training, and resources.

This is consistent with economist Jeffrey Sachs's advice that economic development in tropical ecozones would benefit from a concerted international effort to develop health technologies specific to the needs of tropical climates. Logically, a healthy workforce can be a much more productive workforce. As former World Bank president Robert Zoellick has observed, "Malaria is not only a disease of poverty; it's also a cause of poverty."[45]

Zika

An unfortunate recent illustration of how disease impacts U.S. populations was the unforeseen 2016 Zika virus outbreak. Like malaria, the Zika virus is mosquito-borne, but produces "severe birth defects in about 10 percent of babies born to mothers who were infected while pregnant, and is likely causing neurological symptoms for a small number of infected adults. A separate strain of the virus will likely continue to affect Southeast Asia, where scientists believe it has circulated since the 1960s.[46] By March 2018 the CDC reported that since 2016 there had been well over 40,000 symptomatic cases of the Zika virus disease reported in the United States and its territories.[47] A virus like Zika illustrates how once isolated diseases can affect large populations worldwide and threaten a pandemic.

Conclusion

Pandemics have long been a part of human civilization. More recently, the threat of pandemics was crystallized in the three influenza pandemics of the twentieth century that killed tens of millions. The 2009–2010 influenza and HIV/AIDS pandemics, coupled with malaria, cripple societies, stifle development, and cause millions of deaths every year. When thinking about pandemics and societies like the United States, it is not a question of if but when the next pandemic will produce millions of deaths. Given the potential for an enormous loss of life and socioeconomic instability, pandemics are now included on the national security agenda of many countries. Thus, health security is not just a public health issue in today's globalized world.

As this chapter demonstrates, disease seldom discriminates; it impacts both rich and poor societies. Realistically, as Laurie Garrett argues: "In the event of a deadly influenza pandemic, it is doubtful that any of the world's wealthiest nations would be able to meet the needs of their own citizenry—much less those of other countries."[48] Diseases can no longer escape notice since large-scale, quick-moving infections have the ability to upset social stability, even necessitating a military response to support civil authorities, as occurred during the 2014 Ebola outbreak in West Africa, through the UN Mission for Ebola Emergency Response, and the 2016 Zika outbreak in the Western Hemisphere. Further, disease undermines the key development goals established by the United Nations and supported by the United States as serious health issues complicate any strategies devised to decrease poverty and increase economic growth.

Most challenging for the United States is pandemic influenza. As previous discussions make clear, influenza strains cannot be contained by borders or robust prevention. Pandemics, by their very nature, are international in scope and have become a key feature of the national and human security landscape. Fortunately, pandemics do facilitate international cooperation since all people are vulnerable regardless of nationality, ideology, or geography. The United States and China are at the forefront of this struggle and cooperate at bilateral, global, and regional levels to prevent and respond to pandemic influenza. Ironically, whereas traditional security concerns like military modernization can cause friction between great powers, human security concerns such as diseases can create trust. And, whereas fear can cause conflict, shared insecurity can generate peace.

The inevitability of pandemics need not lead to complacency or overreaction. Environmental monitoring and prevention measures can reduce the impact of the next pandemic. Although no single vaccine can provide broad-spectrum immunity for future diseases, governments and other groups can manage the impact of the next pandemic, if they remain prepared. The relatively quick response to the H1N1 pandemic that included vaccine production illustrates how negative effects can be minimized. Yet, even though fatalities were limited in 2009, then-director general of the World Health Organization, Dr. Margaret Chan, had earlier warned the world:

> Pandemic influenza is . . . looming on the horizon. The threat has by no means receded and we would be very unwise to let down our guard, or slacken our preparedness measures. As with climate change, all countries will be affected, though in a far more rapid and sweeping way.[49]

Thus, health security remains a crucial component of ensuring each nation's security and every individual's human security.

In the next chapter we turn to an issue that is arguably even more complex and ambiguous than health in terms of the private–public mix: the virtual information world. This new cyber domain, which is inextricably tied to globalization processes, demonstrates how quickly new technological innovations can change individual, national, and international perspectives on what is private versus what is public; and critically, on what constitutes national and human security concerns.

Notes

1 Centers for Disease Control and Prevention (CDC), "Why Global Health Security Matters," www.cdc.gov/globalhealth/security/why.htm.

2 William B. Karesh and Robert A. Cook, "The Human-Animal Link," *Foreign Affairs* (July–August 2006): 38–50, 59.

3 Daniel R. Coats, "Statement for the Record Worldwide Threat Assessment of the US Intelligence Community Senate Armed Services Committee," May 23, 2017. www.dni.gov/files/documents/Newsroom/Testimonies/SASC%202017%20ATA%20SFR%20-%20FINAL.PDF.

4 www.cdc.gov/flu/images/influenza-virus-nolabels.jpg.

5 U.S. Department of Health and Human Services, "Pandemic Influenza Plan 2017 Update."

6 National Intelligence Council (NIC), *Global Trends*, 2017, 120.

7 UN, "Sustainable Development Goals," www.un.org/sustainabledevelopment/health/.

8 UNDP, *Human Development Report, 1994*, 27–28.

9 Ibid., 27.

10 Coats, "Statement for the Record Worldwide Threat Assessment."

11 Joint Forces Command, *Joint Operating Environment: Trends and Challenges for the Future Joint Force through 2030* (Norfolk, VA: Joint Forces Command, 2007), 53.

12 White House, *National Security Strategy*, 2015, 14.

13 House Armed Services Committee, "Statement of Ms. Shari Durand Acting Director, Defense Threat Reduction Agency Countering Weapons of Mass Destruction Posture Hearing Before the Emerging Threats and Capabilities Subcommittee Committee on Armed Services United States House of Representatives," March 23, 2017. http://docs.house.gov/meetings/AS/AS26/20170323/105748/HHRG-115-AS26-Wstate-DurandS-20170323.pdf.

14 White House, *A National Security Strategy for Enlargement and Engagement* (Washington, DC: White House, 1996).

15 White House, *A National Security Strategy for a New Century* (Washington, DC: White House, 1999), 13.

16 White House, *A National Security Strategy for a New Century* (Washington, DC: White House, 1998), 1 (emphasis added).

17 Bush, *National Security Strategy*, 2002, ii; Homeland Security Presidential Directive 21: Public Health and Medical Preparedness", Washington, DC, White House, October 18, 2007.

18 Barack Obama, "Remarks by the President to the United Nations General Assembly," September 23, 2009.

19 White House, *National Security Strategy*, 2015, 14.

20 The Netherlands Ministry of the Interior and Kingdom Relations, *National Security Strategy and Work Programme, 2007–2008* (The Hague: The Hague Center for Strategic Studies, 2007), available at www.hcss.nl/en/ publication/689/Dutch-National-Security-Strategy.html.

21 HM Government, "National Security Strategy and Strategic Defence and Security Review," Cm 9161, November 2015, 86; Cabinet Office, "National Security Strategy of the United Kingdom: Security in an Interdependent World," Cm 7291, March 2008), 3, available at www.gov.uk/government/uploads/system/uploads/attachment_data/file/228539/7291.pdf.

22 European Centre for Disease Prevention and Control, "Influenza," at: http://ec.europa.eu/health/ph_threats/com/Influenza/novelflu_en.htm; World Economic Forum, *Global Risks, 2007: A Global Risk Network Report* (Geneva: WEF, 2007), available at www.weforum.org/en/media/publications/GlobalRiskReports/index.htm.

23 UN Department of Economic and Social Affairs, *World Population Prospects: The 2015 Revision* (New York: UN DESA, 2015).

24 NIC, *Global Trends*, 2017, 21; National Intelligence Council, *Global Trends, 2025: A World Transformed* (Washington, DC: NIC, 2009), 95.

25 Department of Defense, *National Defense Strategy*, 1 (emphasis added) (see chap. 4, n. 15); Department of Defense, *National Military Strategy*, 2015.

26 UN, "Sustainable Development Goals: Good Health and Well-Being," www.un.org/sustainabledevelopment/health/#7e9fb9b0ec8c8e6e6.

27 Michael T. Osterholm, "Preparing for the Next Pandemic," *Foreign Affairs* (July–August 2006): 25.

28 Joint Forces Command, *Joint Operating Environment*.

29 Department of Health and Human Services, "Pandemic Influenza Plan 2017 Update," 3.

30 www.cdc.gov/media/subtopic/library/LabsScientists/10724.tif.

31 Steven J. Phillips and George R. Worthington, "When Disaster Strikes," *Naval Institute Proceedings*, October 2009, 33. See also House Oversight and Government Reform Committee, 111th Congress, "Committee Holds Hearings on the Lack of Hospital Emergency Surge Capacity," May 2008, available at http://oversight.house.gov/index.php?option=com_content&task=view&id=35 13&Itemid=2.

32 CDC, "CDC Estimates of 2009 H1N1 Influenza Cases, Hospitalizations, and Deaths in the United States, April–November 14, 2009," December 10, 2009, available at www.cdc.gov/h1n1flu/estimates/April_December_12.htm.

33 White House, *National Strategy for Pandemic Influenza* (Washington, DC: White House, 2005), 3.

34 UNAIDS, "AIDS Data," 2016. www.unaids.org/sites/default/files/media_asset/2016-AIDS-data_en.pdf.

35 Ibid.

36 NIC, *Global Trends*, 2017, 120.

37 For example, Reverend Jerry Falwell reportedly said, "AIDS is the wrath of a just God against homosexuals. To oppose it would be like an Israelite jumping in the Red Sea to save one of Pharaoh's charioteers." Cited in Timothy Noah, "Jerry Fallwell's Hit Parade," *Slate.com*, May 15, 2007, available at www.slate.com/id/2166220.

38 James Wolfensohn, "Speech Delivered to the UN Security Council," New York, January 10, 2000; United Nations, Security Council Resolution 1308, July 17, 2000.

39 Laurie Garrett, *HIV and National Security: Where Are the Links?* (New York: Council on Foreign Relations, 2005), 10.

40 UN, Security Council Resolution 1308, July 17, 2000.

41 UNAIDS, *2016–2021 AIDS Strategy: On the Fast-Track to End AIDS* (Geneva: UNAIDS, 2015), 7.

42 USAID, *The President's Malaria Initiative: Third Annual Report* (Washington, DC: USAID, 2009).

43 Andrea Swalec, "Climate Already Helping Disease Spread North: Study," Reuters Alertnet, June 10, 2010, available at www.alertnet.org/thenews/news desk/LDE65918G.htm.

44 USAID, "What We Do—Global Health: Fighting Malaria," at: www.usaid.gov/what-we-do/global-health/malaria.

45 Robert Zoellick, "World Bank Group President Robert Zoellick's Remarks at the 2008 Millennium Development Goals Malaria Summit," UN Headquarters, New York, September 25, 2008, available at http://siteresources.worldbank.org/INTAFRBOOPRO/Resources/RBZ_remarks_at_MDG_Forum_2008-malaria.pdf.

46 Coats, "Statement for the Record Worldwide Threat Assessment," 14.

47 CDC, "Zika Virus: Reporting and Surveillance," at: www.cdc.gov/zika/reporting/case-counts.html.

48 White House, *National Security Strategy for a New Century*, 1999, 5; Laurie Garrett, "The Next Pandemic?," *Foreign Affairs* (July–August 2006): 3–23, 17.

49 Quoted in U.S. Department of State, "Avian and Pandemic Influenza: The Global Response," Avian Influenza Action Group, Washington, DC, October 2008, available at http://2001-2009.state.gov/documents/organization/111559.pdf.

To Learn More

John M. Barry details the twentieth-century pandemic that claimed tens of millions of lives in *The Great Influenza: The Story of the Deadliest Pandemic in History* (New York: Penguin, 2005).

Laurie Garrett examines trends and forecasts in *The Coming Plague: Newly Emerging Diseases in a World Out of Balance* (New York: Penguin, 1995); and focuses on Ebola in *Ebola: Story of an Outbreak* (New York: Hachette, 2014).

In *Guns, Germs, and Steel: The Fates of Human Societies* (New York: Norton, 1999), Jared Diamond considers how disease has shaped human societies.

Track pandemics and other global health concerns through the World Health Organization at www.who.int/gho/en/.

Read the Center for Disease Control and Prevention's current assessment of flu activity and their advice on protecting yourself from the H1N1 influenza at www.cdc.gov/flu/weekly/fluactivitysurv.htm.

Given the U.S. military's global presence and the role it plays in strengthening other countries' militaries, health has become a key component of security assistance. Examine how the Department of Defense is assisting allied militaries and uniformed services with international public health issues at https://health.mil/Military-Health-Topics/Health-Readiness/Global-Health-Engagement.

Explore various facets of health security in the *Routledge Handbook of Global Health Security* edited by Simon Rushton and Jeremy Youde (New York: Routledge, 2015).

Chapter 9

Information Security

Chapter contents

> Rarely has something been so important and so talked about with less clarity and less apparent understanding [than information security]. . . . I have sat in *very* small group meetings in Washington . . . unable (along with my colleagues) to decide on a course of action because we lacked a clear picture of the long-term legal and policy implications of *any* decision we might make.
>
> General Michael Hayden, USAF (retired), former head of the CIA and the National Security Agency (NSA)[1]

General Hayden's concerns highlight the critical nature of information security and the challenges associated with grasping the importance of this concept for national security. The challenge is not too dissimilar from previous ones discussed in this book, which can be characterized as a human security challenge created when government cannot meet citizens' needs, albeit in this case in the virtual world. As the preceding chapters suggest, intra-state, transnational, and regional actors challenge a sovereign government's ability to provide a secure environment for its citizens. Yet, unlike other challenges such as the development, health and maritime sectors, where the U.S. government has well-established programs, the same is not true in cyberspace. In the information environment, Americans' privacy is challenged by both states and non-state actors; Americans' livelihoods are challenged by malicious code and intellectual property theft; and Americans' freedoms are challenged by threats to their privacy.

The array of threats to information security is broad. Transnational organized criminal groups harness the power of the Internet to steal identities and conduct financial crimes; terrorist organizations use cyberspace to recruit fighters and promote their destructive deeds; countries employ cyber tools for espionage while laying the groundwork for military operations in cyberspace; and nations worry about disruptions to their critical infrastructure such as electricity distribution and water purification. Cyber challenges like these cut across all dimensions and simultaneously cross into political, economic, and social realms. More than ever, citizens, regardless of nationality, are exposed to risks created by cyber *insecurity* in the information environment. Reinforced by intelligence assessments, polling in the United States places cyber insecurity as a leading national security challenge and a pressing concern for citizens and policymakers alike. This chapter considers these challenges to information security facing billions of people online. After defining the genesis, scope, and scale of the information environment, the chapter considers the benefits, but equally the rapidly evolving threats in the information environment, to individuals, and to nations. The increasing linkages to national security are examined—especially for the United States—to include the possibility of cyber war. Finally, possible strategies and norms for addressing security concerns in this domain are addressed.

Defining the Information Environment

The Internet was originally conceived of and funded by one of the Defense Department's research organizations, then known as the Advanced Research Projects Agency (ARPA). Given the state of telecommunications and the non-networked computer systems that existed in the 1960s, researchers wanted to create a reliable network where a user's system or location was unimportant to his or her ability to participate on the network. Charles Herzfeld, ARPA director from 1965 to 1967, explains the genesis of the network:

> The ARPANET was not started to create a Command and Control System that would survive a nuclear attack, as many now claim. To build such a system was clearly a major military

> need, but it was not ARPA's mission to do this; in fact, we would have been severely criticized had we tried. Rather, the ARPANET came out of our frustration that there were only a limited number of large, powerful research computers in the country, and that many research investigators who should have access to them were geographically separated from them.[2]

This vision of a network became a reality in 1969 when a computer link was established between the University of California-Los Angeles, the University of California-Santa Barbara, Stanford University, and the University of Utah. At the time, the connection was called "internetworking," which was shortened to Internet (Image 9.1 portrays a small part of the Internet). For thirty years, the Internet was largely the domain of universities, colleges, and research institutes. But when Tim Berners-Lee and his colleagues created the World Wide Web (WWW) in 1990, commercial and social applications exploded. Within a few short years, companies like Amazon.com and eBay (1995), Wikipedia

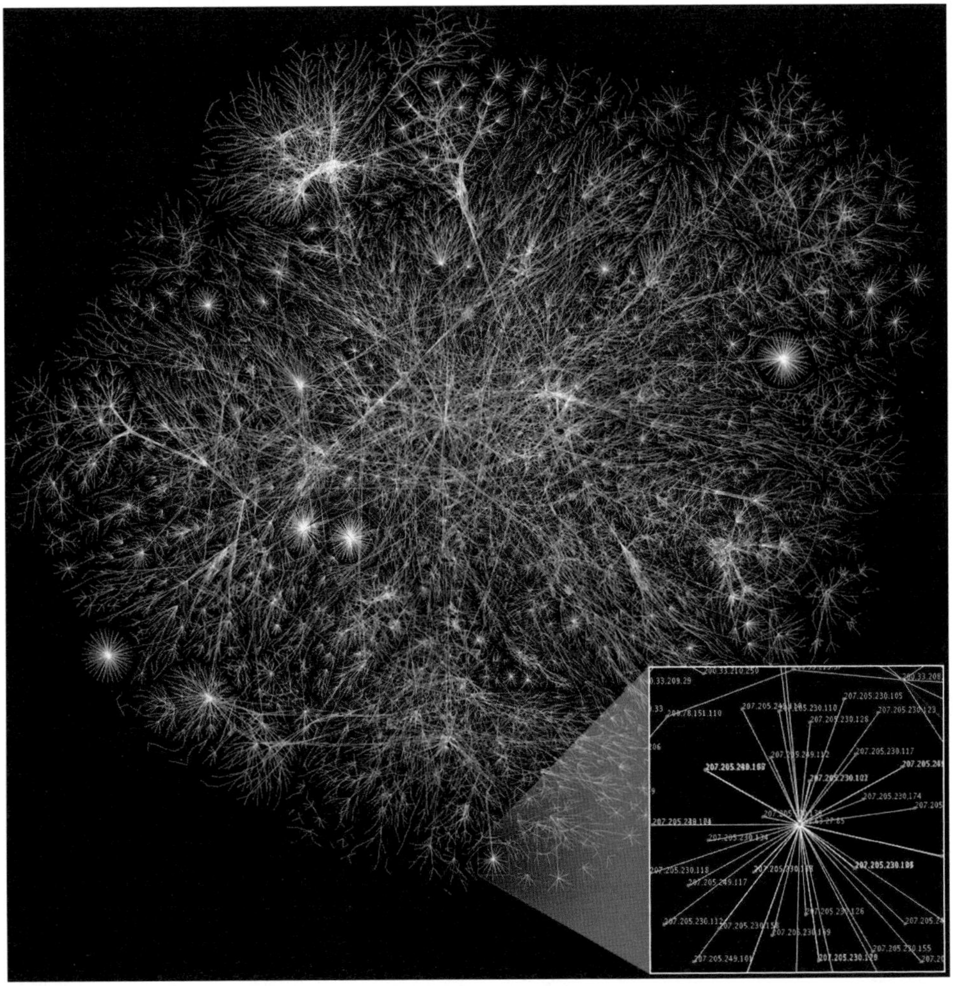

Image 9.1 Partial Map of the Internet by the Opte Project. CC BY 2.5[3]

(2001), Facebook (2004), Twitter (2006), and Snapchat (2011) founded a new industry and changed the way we live and work.

The development of the information environment has been influenced by science fiction, which offers both inspiration and anxiety for thinking about technological change. Writer William Gibson coined the term "cyberspace" in a short story published in 1982. Once confined to the cyberpunk literature and science fiction like the movie *The Matrix* (1999), the information environment entered the real world in the late 1990s, and in 2003 the Bush administration defined cyberspace as the "nervous system—the control system of our country. Cyberspace is composed of hundreds of thousands of interconnected computers, servers, routers, switches, and fiber optic cables that allow our critical infrastructures to work." The U.S. Defense Department later defined cyberspace as "a global domain within the information environment consisting of the interdependent network of information technology infrastructures, including the Internet, telecommunications network, computer systems, and embedded processors and controllers."[4] When we add people and the decisions they make to the cyberspace definition, we have the information environment.

Like the physical environment, the information environment is all-encompassing. It includes: physical hardware such as networks and machines (or even contact lenses, as shown in Image 9.2); information such as data and media; the cognitive realm such as the mental processes people use to comprehend their experiences; and the virtual world where people connect socially through avatars. When aggregated, what we think of as cyberspace serves as a fifth dimension where people can exist through alternate personae on blogs, social networking sites, and virtual reality (VR) games. Larry Johnson, chief executive officer of the New Media Consortium, predicts that over the next fifteen years we will experience the virtual world as an extension of the real one. He concludes:

> Virtual worlds are already bridging borders across the globe to bring people of many cultures and languages together in ways very nearly as rich as face-to-face interactions; they are already allowing the visualization of ideas and concepts in three dimensions that is leading to new insights and deeper learning; and they are already allowing people to work, learn, conduct business, shop, and interact in ways that promise to redefine how we think about these activities—and even what we regard as possible.[5]

It is incredible to think that this new dimension was still barely conceivable when the UNDP published its landmark *Human Development Report 1994*, so that the cyber domain was not considered to be a human security concern, let alone a national security concern.[6]

Within just the past decade, people everywhere have become as dependent on the virtual world for their daily activities as they are dependent on the physical world for human activities. Consider the implications for yourself when the network is down, cell phone calls are dropped, or a virus crashes your device. In many cases, daily routines are broken, frustrations rise, and work stops. There are clear benefits to information technology, which we now embrace as essential to our lives, our economy, and, ultimately, our national security. Information technology connects people in unique ways. Global fiber-optic networks have also enabled communication in an unprecedented manner, propelling the emergence of India as the world's "back office," allowing companies to move offshore, giving consumers access to a variety of data from around the planet, and linking developing countries to the global market.

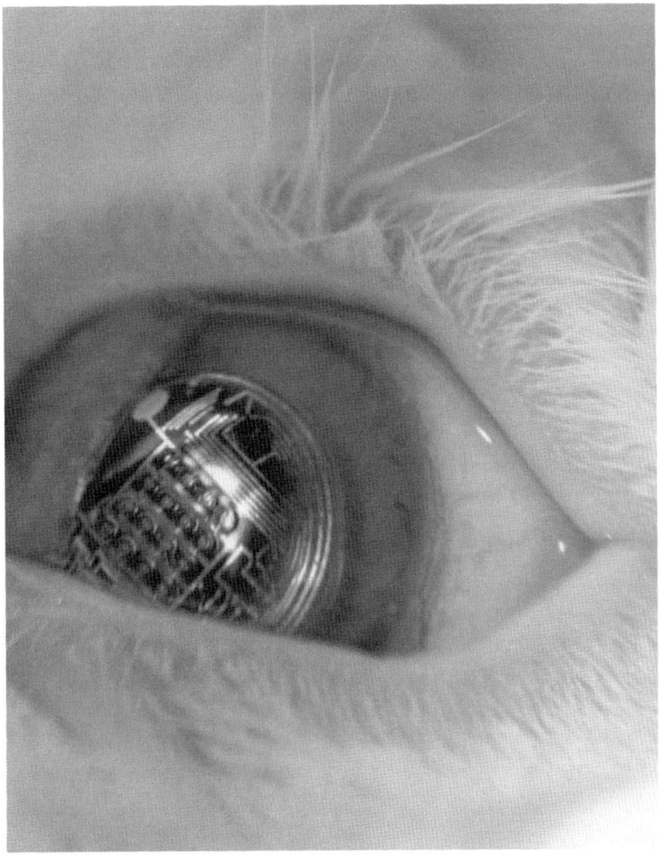

Image 9.2 Contact Lenses with Metal Connectors for Electronic Circuits: virtual display for potential use by drivers, pilots, video-game companies, communications workers, and others. Photo: Babak Parviz, University of Washington[7]

More than one-half of the world's population uses the Internet (Figure 9.1 depicts the use of the internet by region, and Table 9.1 lists the worldwide distribution of internet users). This interconnection of the world's population within and across societies holds tremendous positive implications for economic growth and development, particularly for impoverished areas. UN Secretary-General António Guterres sees information technology as socially transforming and as integral to human security since "farmers can monitor prices, refugees can let their families know they are safe, and health workers can check a patient's status or respond to emergencies."[8]

It also gives countries the potential to overcome the challenges of being landlocked or geographically isolated from the developed core countries in North America, Europe, and North Asia. Yet, at the same time, this interconnection has the potential to trigger a culturally based backlash in traditional societies against perceived attempts to impose an alien culture and mores, as examination of the issue of globalization and identity security earlier in this book revealed. Inasmuch as the Internet can share culture, it can also homogenize or even destroy culture—or at least be perceived as doing so.

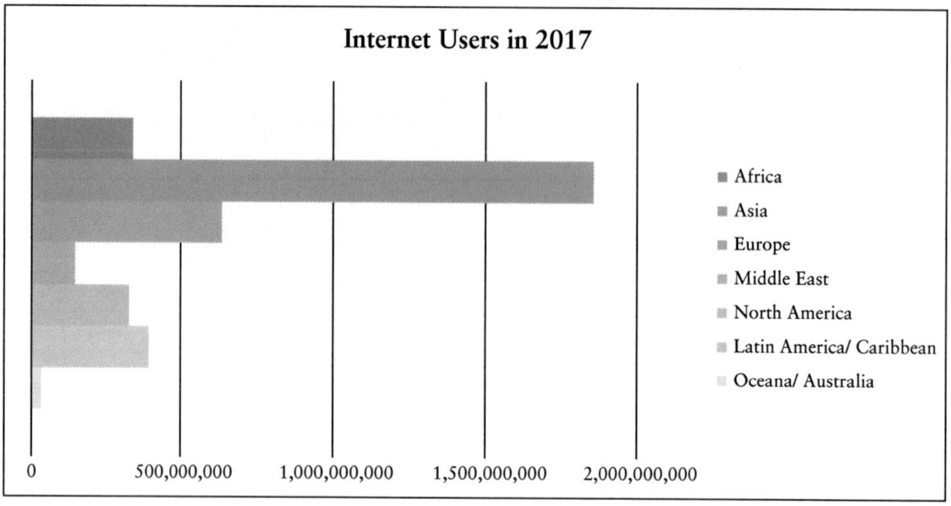

Figure 9.1 Internet Users by Region, 2017.
Source: www.internetworldstats.com/stats.htm

Table 9.1 Geographic Distribution of Internet Users

World Internet Usage and Population Statistics, March 31, 2017 (Update)						
Region	Population (2017 est.)	Population (% world)	Users (no.)	Penetration (% pop.)	% Growth (2000–17)	Users (%)
Africa	1,246,504,865	16.6	353,121,578	28.3	7,722.1	9.4
Asia	4,148,177,672	55.2	1,874,136,654	45.2	1,539.6	50.1
Europe	822,710,362	10.9	636,971,824	77.4	506.1	17.0
Latin America/ Caribbean	647,604,645	8.6	385,919,382	59.6	2,035.8	10.3
Middle East	250,327,574	3.3	141,931,765	56.7	4,220.9	3.8
North America	363,224,006	4.8	320,068,243	88.1	196.1	8.6
Oceania/ Australia	40,479,846	0.5	27,549,054	68.1	261.5	0.7
World Total	7,519,028,970	100	3,739,698,500	49.7	936.0	100

Source: Internet World Stats, "Usage and Population Statistics," www.internetworldstats.com/stats.htm

Threats to the Information Environment

Cyber threats can take a number of forms, with the major ones defined as follows:

- Virus: Malicious code that can self-replicate and cause damage to the systems it infects. The code can delete information, infect programs, change the directory structure to run undesirable programs, and infect the vital part of the operating system that ties together how files are stored.
- Worm: Similar to a virus, a worm is distinctive for its ability to self-replicate without infecting other files in order to reproduce.

- Trojan horse: A stealthy code that executes under the guise of a useful program but performs malicious acts such as the destruction of files, the transmission of private data, and the opening of a back door to allow third-party control of a machine.
- Logic bomb: Camouflaged segments of programs that destroy data when certain conditions are met.
- Zombie: A computer that has been covertly compromised and is controlled by a third party.
- Botnet: A network of zombie machines used by hackers for massive coordinated system attacks.
- Denial-of-service: Attack employing a botnet to send massive simultaneous requests to servers, preventing legitimate use of the servers.

Kenneth Geers reminds us that the "internet today is merely a reflection of what came before—including crime, espionage, and warfare—and that the international security environment is still closer to Pandemonium."[9] Table 9.2 captures these sources of cyber insecurity with the same actors and similar behaviors in the information environment that can be observed in the physical one.

Table 9.2 Sources of Cyber Insecurity

Threat Source	Motivation
Foreign nations	Foreign intelligence services use cyber tools as part of their information-gathering and espionage activities. These include exploitation and potential disruption or destruction of information infrastructure.
Criminal groups	Criminal groups use cyber intrusions for monetary gain.
Hackers	Hackers sometimes crack into networks for the thrill of the challenge or for bragging rights in the hacker community. While remote cracking once required a fair amount of skill or computer knowledge, hackers can now download attack scripts and protocols from the Internet and launch them against victim sites. Thus, attack tools have become more sophisticated and easier to use.
Hacktivists	These groups and individuals conduct politically motivated attacks, overload e-mail servers, and hack into Web sites to send a political message.
Disgruntled insiders	The disgruntled insider, working from within an organization, is a principal source of computer crimes. Insiders may not need a great deal of knowledge about computer intrusions because their knowledge of a victim's system often allows them to gain unrestricted access to cause damage to the system or to steal data.
Terrorists	Terrorists seek to destroy, incapacitate, or exploit critical infrastructures to threaten national security, cause mass casualties, weaken the U.S. economy, and damage public morale and confidence. The Central Intelligence Agency (CIA) believes terrorists will stay focused on traditional attack methods, but it anticipates growing cyber threats as a more technically competent generation enters the ranks.

Source: Government Accountability Office (GAO), "Cybersecurity: Continued Efforts are Needed to Protect Information Systems from Evolving Threats," Statement for the Record to the Subcommittee on Terrorism and Homeland Security, Committee on the Judiciary, U.S. Senate, November 17, 2009. Available at www.dtic.mil/dtic/tr/fulltext/u2/a516401.pdf.

Apart from the potentially harmful cultural impacts of technology, there is also a dark side of the cyber world wherein hackers, phishing scam artists, and transnational criminal groups harness the technology, too. Through phishing, criminals and spies gain access to government and private computer networks. Through viruses and denial-of-service attacks, individuals and groups can disrupt governments and corporations. And through spyware or government surveillance programs, the cherished civil liberty of privacy is subverted. No longer only in fiction, the personal, professional, and financial records of one's life can be erased or stolen for malevolent purposes. Thus, for many in the United States and other citizens of developed countries, the ultimate threat to their individual human security comes from cyberspace.

Yet cyber security is not just a personal issue but a national security issue, too. A former U.S. Director of National Intelligence testified to this point: "The growing connectivity between information systems, the Internet, and other infrastructures creates opportunities for attackers to disrupt telecommunications, electrical power, energy pipelines, refineries, financial networks, and other critical infrastructure."[10] The Trump administration's Director of National Intelligence extended the ideas linking to a human security construct: "Cyber threats also pose an increasing risk to public health, safety, and prosperity as cyber technologies are integrated with critical infrastructure in key sectors."[11]

In the cyber world, individual hackers tend to pose the greatest danger to information security, but governments are now concerned enough to include cyber warfare in their military planning and operations. An example that demonstrates why governments should be concerned was the cyber attack that accompanied Russia's invasion of Ukraine in 2014. As Russian tanks and aircraft were entering Ukrainian territory, cyber warriors attacked government websites and advanced Russian interests through the information sphere. In a subsequent attack in December 2015, the nightmare scenario became real as a cyber attack shut down power for some 200,000 Ukrainians.[12] Though it had a temporary effect, the attack was a harbinger; future conflicts will have both a physical dimension and a virtual dimension. The reality is that as governments and militaries embrace technology for efficiency and effect, they also become vulnerable to cyber attacks. And as more of society, government, and the economy move online, individuals in developed countries can no longer be isolated from the effects of war. Americans have become accustomed to seeing their military fight wars abroad with little impact on the homeland; cyber war has the potential to change this perception (see Box 9.1). Adversaries may disrupt Americans' access to such fundamental necessities as electricity, telecommunications, and water. And, as we saw in the 2016 presidential election, a foreign power can even shape U.S. voters' views and undermine democracy.

❖ BOX 9.1 THINK AGAIN: BYTES ARE NOT BOMBS

Much like civilian organizations and governments, militaries are increasingly dependent on cyberspace for their operations. Information technology connects ships, aircraft, and ground vehicles to harmonize operations and avoid fratricide. Commanders rely on computer networks to maintain situational awareness and facilitate decision making. Given this dependence, the U.S. military identifies its cyber infrastructure as a critical vulnerability it must protect during war and peace. With very little imagination, it is possible to envision cyber war; that is, using cyber attacks to advance and defend state interests.

Yet this does not mean that the military can or should protect cyberspace. The aim of cyber threat differs substantially from physical warfare; data loss is not the same as human loss. Defacing a website is not the functional equivalent of bombing a country's capital. Along these lines, Bruce Schneier sees the United States going down a dangerous path, since:

> cybersecurity isn't a military problem, or even a government problem—it's a universal problem. All networks, military, government, civilian and commercial, use the same computers, the same networking hardware, the same Internet protocols and the same software packages. We all are the targets of the same attack tools and tactics. It's not even that government targets are somehow more important; these days, most of our nation's critical IT [information technology] infrastructure is in commercial hands.[1]

As noted in this chapter, the U.S. government currently places responsibility for the protection of the U.S. Internet infrastructure and its critical sectors under the Department of Homeland Security, via such measures as the Computer Emergency Readiness Team. But, just as with other homeland security threats or natural disasters, this department can call upon the Defense Department for support in an emergency. In that case the involvement of DOD would need to be carefully constrained so as to intrude as little as possible into traditionally sacrosanct areas such as citizens' private information and civil liberties.

1 Bruce Schneier, "Who Should Be in Charge of Cybersecurity?" *Wall Street Journal*, March 31, 2009.

In any case, virtual war need not have physical attack characteristics, which dominates Western conceptions of warfare. While physical destruction through a cyber attack is possible, countries increasingly employ cyber operations as a unique tool of power. As Herb Lin wrote, "Cyber attacks are particularly well suited for attacks on the psychology of adversary decision makers who rely on the affected computers, and in this case such effects can be regarded as indirect effects."[13] On any given day, foreign governments sponsor regular intrusions into U.S. government networks, hackers steal financial data from banks, foreign intelligence services conduct cyber espionage, and foreign governments influence individuals' perceptions of events. Given the importance of information technology networks and the threats posed to them, there is a growing linkage to national security.

When attempting to examine cyber threats, the point of origin is very difficult to determine. Unlike a missile launch that has a discrete signature and geographic location, those who employ cyber tactics can easily hide their origin, which makes attribution extremely difficult. James Lewis has argued that "Uncertainty is the most prominent aspect of cyber conflict—in attribution of the attackers [*sic*] identity, the scope of collateral damage, and the potential effect on the intended target from cyber attack."[14] Thus, when trying to analyze the threats to the cyber domain, it is best to take a comprehensive approach. Accordingly, we can classify threats: by *actor*, such as individual and government; by *target*, such as financial sector or defense department; or by *means*, such as virus, bot, or denial-of-service.

In terms of the actor, those who use cyber tactics for nefarious purposes range from individual hackers and organized criminal groups to intelligence services and other agencies of governments. As the diversity of actors illustrates, the barriers to entry for cyberspace are low, which helps explain why cyber attacks have become commonplace. The head of the United Nations International Telecommunication Union (ITU) noted:

> There is no such thing anymore as a superpower in the cyberspace because every individual is one superpower in itself because it's a human brain that makes a difference in this field. And this is one natural resource that is equally distributed everywhere in the globe.[15]

This fundamentally changes thinking about national security, which is no longer the exclusive domain of governments. To be sure, governments are still leading efforts to seek advantage in cyberspace, but now multinational companies, nongovernmental organizations (NGOs), and transnational organized criminal groups are important actors in cyberspace. The Defense Department predicts that "Strategic attacks will likely focus on disrupting elements of the U.S. financial infrastructure, where trust and data integrity are paramount."[16]

Web-based attacks are the common source of malicious activity, which often happens by exploiting a vulnerable Web application or exploiting some vulnerability present in the underlying host operating system. In general, attackers concentrate their attacks for financial gain by stealing online banking credentials and credit card information. Phishing has become a common way to steal financial information by soliciting confidential information from an individual, group, or organization by mimicking (or spoofing) a specific brand. So far, criminals constitute the majority of bad actors as they take advantage of the Internet for their illicit purposes. This creates genuine disagreement on whether cyberspace should be treated as a war-fighting domain—equivalent to air, space, land, and sea—or as an off-limits civilian space. A human security paradigm helps make sense of how threats in cyberspace constitute national security concerns for information security.

Information Environment and National Security

The link between national security and the information environment has been developing since the Clinton administration in the 1990s. Yet there are significant differences between cyberspace and traditional domains like airspace that make protecting the former difficult. To begin with, no single entity owns the Internet, but individuals, companies, and governments use it. Governments also do not have a monopoly on operating in cyberspace. Anyone with a phone, tablet, or computer with an Internet connection can operate there. And, making it more challenging for governments, most of the information technology expertise resides in the commercial sector. According to Israeli Defense Force Cyber Chief of Staff Brig. Gen. Yaron Rozen:

> This whole front resides in the civilian world, not in the military one. Look how long it took nations across the globe to sign the Kyoto Treaty, which deals with global warming and affects everyone. The Cyber nations are not just the superpowers, but huge international corporations like Google, Facebook and Kaspersky.[17]

When they were senior leaders at the Department of Homeland Security (DHS) Jane Holl Lute and Bruce McConnell emphasized that "Cyberspace is fundamentally a civilian space—a neighborhood, a library, a marketplace, a school yard, a workshop."[18] Yet all sectors are affected equally by disruptions in the information environment: a computer virus disruption that occurs through a commercial website can slow down the Internet for government and military users as well as for corporations and private citizens.

As it relates to war, the Internet is both a means and a target for militaries. U.S. Deputy Defense Secretary William Lynn underscored how important the information infrastructure is to national defense in 2009:

> Just like our national dependence [on the Internet], there is simply no exaggerating our military dependence on our information networks: the command and control of our forces, the intelligence and logistics on which they depend, the weapons technologies we develop and field—they all depend on our computer systems and networks. Indeed, our 21st century military simply cannot function without them.[19]

Offense tends to dominate in the information environment since: there is an open architecture and protocol; a wired society offers many vulnerabilities; speed of attack is beyond human perception; and malicious actors take advantage of human vulnerabilities through social engineering to elicit network access. Consequently, Kenneth Geers argues:

> Nations today use computer network operations to defend sovereignty and to project power, and cyber conflicts may soon become the rule rather than the exception. Most cyber attacks do not rise to the level of a national security threat, but in the post-Stuxnet era [a malicious worm], the notion of "cyber war" has moved closer to reality.[20]

Erik Gartzke, however, maintains that "the need to follow virtual force with physical force to achieve lasting political consequences suggests that the application of cyberwarfare independent of conventional forms of warfare will be of tertiary importance in strategic and grand strategic terms."[21] This approach was on display when Russia invaded Georgia in 2008 and Ukraine in 2014. And it is important to realize that governments could use cyber attacks similarly to the way they use drone strikes to meet immediate security needs.

Additionally, governments use the Internet to shape their messages through media outlets hosted throughout the Web. U.S. military commanders use public blogs, operational units post videos to YouTube, and military members share ideas on Twitter. This gives both the military and citizens unprecedented insight from pilots after they bomb a target or from Marines as they conduct humanitarian assistance. The transparency is intended to reduce suspicion, counter deceptive claims made by adversaries, and improve the image of the military. The United States sees its center of gravity or vulnerability as popular support, so connecting the military directly to the people is important. Yet there are limits to these potential advantages; the Pentagon is concerned that its personnel can also project a bad image through Facebook or YouTube (as has occurred), which runs counter to its efforts.

In contrast to traditional war-fighting domains like land, air, or sea, governments are not the only actors in the information environment. Rather, individuals can readily harness technology to compete on a global scale. And it is worth noting that virtualization will continue this trend of democratizing the Internet, giving individuals tremendous power unthinkable even ten years ago. Satellite imagery used to be highly classified and limited by the intelligence community, but now anyone can access imagery from an iPhone using Google Earth. Likewise, the complexity and cost of building nuclear weapons limit their production to governments, but the same cannot be said for the virtual weapon of mass destruction that can destroy data and networks, undermine international credibility, and disrupt commerce. Malicious activity through worms, viruses, and zombies regularly disrupts Internet activity. And there are already many examples of virtual activities impacting the physical world, such as: terrorists being recruited, radicalized, and trained on the Internet; communications being severed; or power production being disrupted. Illegally armed groups use cyberspace to move money, conceal identities, and plan operations, which makes it extremely difficult for governments to compete with them. Consequently, governments are increasingly concerned with the cyber domain as a new feature within the national security landscape as individuals are exposed to the dangers of being connected.

Cyber and War

As early as 1993 John Arquilla and David Ronfeldt had forecast that cyber war in the twenty-first century would be the equivalent of Nazi Germany's highly successful and near-revolutionary blitzkrieg operations in the twentieth century. And, according to Keith Alexander, benefiting from this "revolution in military affairs," militaries would use "cyberspace (by operating within or through it) to attack personnel, facilities, or equipment with the intent of degrading, neutralizing, or destroying enemy combat capability, while protecting our own."[22] This prediction has been validated by Russian interference in the 2016 U.S. elections, North Korea's hack of Sony Entertainment in 2014, and China's decade-long espionage campaign against the United States.

Many analysts have framed these violations as representing an era of ever more sophisticated and dangerous cyber conflict.[23] But others dispute the meaning of these types of attacks, and there is a robust scholarly debate on the value of fighting in the information environment and the very existence of cyber war. For example, Thomas Rid has declared that "cyber war will not take place."[24] Data collected by Ryan Maness and colleagues found that 87 of 164 successful cyber incidents (53 percent) could be classified as cyber espionage (but not war) during 2001 to 2014.[25] These exploits sought information or served to spread disinformation; on the other hand, coercive actions like Stuxnet are much rarer to date.[26] Further, cyber effects are often temporary given backups and the ability to create security patches.

At the time of writing, there has not been a cyber attack that satisfies a conventional Clausewitzian definition of war that relies on violence, has produced significant damage, or has resulted in political coercion (Table 9.3 shows evidence of malicious cyber activities by country). Instead, cyber attacks have accompanied traditional warfare with limited impact. Defacement of government websites, denial-of-service attacks, and data stealing have been conducted over the Internet but do not constitute warfare. Yet senior military leaders worry about U.S. vulnerabilities and potential irrelevance of current capabilities to cyber threats. The U.S. Joint Staff has forecast that "the next decades will see the further emergence of state-sponsored actors and associated organizations with more advanced cyber warfare capabilities. The doctrine and capabilities for cyber war are still developing.[27] But this may not be true for long: "Like strategic airpower before it, state-based cyber advocates will develop strategies that attempt to 'leap over' traditional U.S. military forces and directly influence the decision calculations of political and military leadership."[28]

Although cyber war has not yet occurred, the U.S. military services have recognized the importance of cyberspace both in peace and in war.[29] For example, the air force has claimed cyberspace as one of its three operating domains (air and space are the others).[30]

Table 9.3 Malicious Cyber Activity by Country

Country	2015 Rank	2014 Rank	2015 Overall %	2014 Overall %	Malicious Code Rank	Spam Zombies Rank	Phishing Websites Host Rank	Bot Rank	Attack-Origin Rank
China	1	2	24	11	3	1	9	1	2
United States	2	1	19	21	1	2	1	2	1
India	3	3	3	4	2	—	—	—	4
Netherlands	4	4	3	4	4	—	5	—	3
Taiwan	5	6	2	3	—	3	—	3	—
Turkey	6	20	2	1	—	4	—	4	—
United Kingdom	7	7	2	3	9	—	3	—	—
Germany	8	5	2	3	—	7	2	7	10
France	9	14	2	2	—	9	6	9	—
Brazil	10	10	2	2	7	8	10	8	5

Source: *Symantec Global Internet Security Threat Report: Appendices*, vol. 21, April 2016. Available at www.symantec.com/content/dam/symantec/docs/reports/istr-21-2016-appendices-en.pdf

The navy created the Fleet Cyber Command (Tenth Fleet), while the Director of National Intelligence created the Joint Interagency Cyber Task Force. At the same time, service capabilities are aggregated under U.S. Cyber Command—which is responsible for developing and implementing integrated operations for defense and attack in the cyber domain. Yet in thinking about the future, the U.S. military sees itself as uncomfortably vulnerable in the cyber domain and expects other countries to exploit it. Wesley Clark and Peter Levin argue:

> There is no form of military combat more irregular than an electronic attack; it is extremely cheap, is very fast, can be carried out anonymously, and can disrupt or deny critical services precisely at the moment of maximum peril. Everything about the subtlety, complexity, and effectiveness of the assaults already inflicted on the United States' electronic defense indicates that other nations have thought carefully about this form of combat.[31]

Like other countries that face these interrelated national and human security challenges, the domestic and international divide narrows when it comes to the information environment; cyberspace knows no boundaries. Then-director of the NSA Michael Hayden agreed: "[I]n the cyber domain the technical and operational aspects of defense, espionage, and cyberattack are frankly indistinguishable—they are all the same thing."[32] This complicates how governments attempt to protect citizens in the information environment.

China is often identified as a likely opponent in a cyber war. This has as much to do with realist scholars' predictions about the inevitability of war between great powers as it does with Chinese cyber behavior. As the Chinese military newspaper *PLA* [People's Liberation Army] *Daily* stated, "Internet warfare is of equal significance to land, sea, and air power and requires its own military branch," and "it is essential to have an all-conquering offensive technology and to develop software and technology for net offensives . . . able to launch attacks and countermeasures."[33] The PLA seem impressed and inspired by U.S. cyber capabilities and are closely following events. Ming Zhou, a China specialist, noted that "information warfare is not just a theology, they can integrate it into nation-state interests."[34] Ironically, while China simultaneously exploits cyberspace for its national security benefits, it is increasingly vulnerable to cyber exploitation itself.

Beyond China, a number of countries that have sophisticated cyber national security capabilities include both allies and competitors: Russia, Israel, India, and France. Accordingly, the U.S. military is wrestling over the implications of this as it relates to warfare, and views cyberspace as critical to its operations, which requires defensive and very probably offensive measures. Current doctrine, which guides how the military acts, is organized along five lines: computer network attack; computer network defense; computer network exploitation; information assurance to guarantee data integrity; and information operations that includes deception.

At this stage it is clear that the global security implications of developing cyber capabilities for militaries are profound. In recognition of this, Hamadoun Touré, Secretary General of the ITU, has warned:

> The next world war could take place in the cyberspace and this needs to be avoided. The conventional wars have shown us that first of all, there is no winner in any war and second, the best way to win a war is to avoid it in the first place. So we need to plant the seeds for a safer cyberspace together. And it can only be done at the global level because the criminal needs no longer to be on the crime scene and you can attack many places at the same time in the cyberspace.[35]

With these concerns in mind, the United Nations is working on a no-first-strike policy for its members, which is reminiscent of the policy for nuclear weapons use. This approach certainly makes sense given that the United Nations is organized around the nation-state concept; but it can have little effect on contemporary vulnerabilities of the Internet, where many threats emanate not from states but from small groups and other non-state actors.

Information Security and Strategy

The U.S. government actually came late to recognizing cyberspace as a national concern. It first emerged as a distinct national security policy area in 1998 when President Clinton signed Presidential Decision Directive 63, which established a White House structure to coordinate government and private action to "eliminate any significant vulnerability to both physical and cyber attacks on our critical infrastructures, including especially our cyber systems." To establish redlines against such attacks, President George W. Bush declared in 2003 that it would be the policy of the United States to protect against the debilitating disruption of the operation of information systems for critical infrastructures and, thereby, help to protect the people, economy, and national security of the United States.[36] The 2005 *National Defense Strategy* identified cyberspace as a new theater of operations and assessed cyberspace operations as a potentially disruptive challenge, concluding that in "rare instances, revolutionary technology and associated military innovation can fundamentally alter long-established concepts of warfare." The 2008 *National Defense Strategy* explored these implications further, assessing that small groups or individuals "can attack vulnerable points in cyberspace and disrupt commerce and daily life in the United States, causing economic damage, compromising sensitive information and materials, and interrupting critical services such as power and information networks."[37]

In spite of recognized vulnerabilities and threats to cyberspace, there are clear gaps in how policy and law address these concerns. International law and national security policy offer no clear answers on important issues such as how to respond to cyber intrusions, whether computer network attacks constitute a form of warfare, and whether the UN conception of self-defense applies in cyberspace. Yet the threat remains. Deputy Defense Secretary William Lynn admitted in 2009 that the Defense Department's culture regarding cybersecurity issues must change because "we're seeing assaults come at an astonishing speed—not hours, minutes or even seconds—but in milliseconds at network speed."[38] And, as early as 2010, DOD officials admitted that their systems were being probed by unknown users some 250,000 times an hour, or a staggering 6 million times a day.[39]

However, whereas the Pentagon has a plan to stop an air attack against the United States, there is no corresponding plan to reduce malicious activity. In an effort to understand these challenges and raise awareness of cyberspace, the respected Center for Strategic and International Studies (CSIS) think tank bluntly warned in 2008: "America's failure to protect cyberspace is one of the most urgent national security problems facing the new administration." In recognition of this, President Obama declared October 2009 to be National Cybersecurity Awareness Month due to "our Nation's growing dependence on cyber and information-related technologies, coupled with an increasing threat of malicious cyber attacks and loss of privacy."[40] Just a month later, a former NATO commander declared: "The cybersecurity threat is real. Adversaries target networks, application software, operating systems, and even the ubiquitous silicon chips inside computers, which are the bedrock of the United States' public and private infrastructure." Retired army general Wesley Clark and analyst Peter Levin argued:

> All evidence indicates that the country's defenses are already being pounded, and the need to extend protection from computer networks and software to computer hardware is urgent. The U.S. government can no longer afford to ignore the threat from computer-savvy rivals or technologically advanced terrorist groups, because the consequences of a major breach would be catastrophic.[41]

The U.S. government is not waiting for "cybergeddon" as it has become more proactive in cyberspace. As noted, the Secretary of Homeland Security is responsible for coordinating critical infrastructure protection, including cyber infrastructure. Homeland Security Presidential Directive 7 assigned the DHS as the lead for sharing threat information, assessing vulnerabilities, encouraging appropriate protective action, and developing contingency plans. This necessitates high levels of cooperation among many actors. As the White House's Cyberspace Policy Review Committee made plain in 2009:

> The Federal government should work with the private sector to define public–private partnership roles and responsibilities for the defense of privately owned critical infrastructure and key resources. The common defense of privately-owned critical infrastructures from armed attack or from physical intrusion or sabotage by foreign military forces or international terrorists is a core responsibility of the Federal government. Similarly, government plays an important role in protecting these infrastructures from criminals or domestic terrorists. The question remains unresolved as to what extent protection of these same infrastructures from the same harms by the same actors should be a government responsibility if the attacks were carried out remotely via computer networks rather than by direct physical action.[42]

Image 9.3 U.S. Air Force Operations Center, Joint Base San Antonio-Lackland: cyber operations support the Air Force network and U.S. Cyber Command. Photo: U.S. Air Force/ William Belcher

The emerging strategic approach is one that views cyber as a larger piece of national power that includes diplomacy, foreign assistance, sanctions, and conventional military power. The 2015 DOD cyber strategy captured this approach: "As a matter of principle, the United States will seek to exhaust all network defense and law enforcement options to mitigate any potential cyber risk to the U.S. homeland or U.S. interests before conducting a cyberspace operation."[43] At the same time, the entire U.S. government is attempting to make its systems more secure and resilient.[44] One of the key challenges to doing this is the cross-cutting nature of the information environment. In recognition of this fact, the U.S. Congress has given authority to improve information security to many different entities; Defense, Homeland Security, and Justice dominate the efforts. The Defense Department defends the nation from attack and supports national efforts to recover from a major incident (see Image 9.3 illustrating U.S. Air Force personnel supporting cyber activities). The Department of Homeland Security protects critical infrastructure and coordinates national responses. And the Department of Justice investigates cyber crimes, leads domestic national security operations, and coordinates cyber threat investigations.

Path to International Norms

Individuals, regardless of nationality or location, are exposed to dangers in the information environment. The commander of U.S. Cyber Command and director of the NSA, Admiral Michael S. Rogers, has noted: "It is only a matter of the 'when,' not the 'if'—we're going to see a nation-state, group or actor engage in destructive behavior against critical infrastructure in the United States."[45]

With persistent vulnerabilities in the software and the relative impunity with which states, groups, and individuals operate in cyberspace, data breaches will continue resulting in fraud, intellectual property theft, and other disruptions in our IT-reliant society. Consequently, governments and corporations have been promoting international norms to guide state behavior, to harmonize relations among governments, and to coordinate action against shared cyber threats. For example, in September 2015, the United States and China agreed not to target commercial entities for economic value as a way to slow down intellectual property theft. At the November 2015 G20 summit in Belek, Turkey, governments agreed that nation-state conduct in cyberspace should conform to international law and the UN charter. This may be significant considering that the G20 group represents the 19 wealthiest countries in the world, along with the European Union (EU).

These types of evolving norms grew out of the work of the UN's Group of Governmental Experts (GGE), which is a set of cyber security experts from a small number of nation-states. The group has agreed that no country should intentionally damage the critical infrastructure of another state or impair infrastructure that serves the public and would undermine the human rights guaranteed by the UN Declaration. At the 2016 G7 summit in Ise-Shima, Japan, member governments there recognized that cybersecurity is a key component of the global economy and trade, development, and quality infrastructure investment. This group of the seven most advanced economies in the world declared: "We will take decisive and robust measures in close cooperation against malicious use of cyberspace, both by states and non-state actors, including terrorists."[46]

At the same time, corporations that develop information technology hardware and software are promoting norms, too. The executive chairman of Google's parent company, Alphabet, thinks that "getting the governments to agree that we are better off collectively by having a more open internet with less attacking—especially at nation state level—would be a clear improvement for everybody."[47] Microsoft has promulgated a set of norms "to detect, contain, respond to, and recover from events in cyberspace."[48] Furthermore, Microsoft's president and chief legal officer, Brad Smith, thinks the world actually needs a Digital Geneva Convention:

> that will commit governments to protecting civilians from nation-state attacks in times of peace . . . [and the tech sector] should commit ourselves to collective action that will make the internet a safer place, affirming a role as a neutral Digital Switzerland that assists customers everywhere and retains the world's trust.[49]

Conclusion

In its short history, the Internet has been harnessed by individuals and companies to create a new industry, a new social sphere, and a new battle space. At the same time, criminals, other non-state actors, and intelligence services have benefited as well. As the virtual and physical worlds continue to merge, new threats will develop that take advantage of the vulnerabilities inherent in a relatively open system. When it comes to security, there is tension between the common free space that is the Internet and a government's attempt to police it. This fact was recognized in the 1996 Telecommunications Act:

> The policy of the United States [is] . . . to promote the continued development of the Internet and other interactive computer services and other interactive media . . . [and] preserve the

vibrant and competitive free market that presently exists for the Internet and other interactive computer services, unfettered by Federal or State regulation."

Thirteen years later, however, growing security concerns led President Obama to declare: "Cyber attacks and their viral ability to infect networks, devices, and software must be the concern of all Americans."[50] This might produce the type of regulation that the 1996 law sought to forestall, and ultimately stifle Internet activity. As the United States is the hub for the informational realm, its actions will affect human beings around the world and their access to information.

Now that information security is a focus for national security, a key challenge is to understand "who is in charge." The private sector primarily designs, builds, owns, and operates the Internet, but there is a growing expectation that the U.S. government will protect it. The Defense Department is responsible for ensuring the ".mil" domain remains safe, while the Department of Homeland Security oversees security of the ".gov" domain. But the ".com" domain is entrusted to the companies that operate there. In recognition of this reality, Richard Harknett and James Stever call for cyber security to rest on a balanced triad of intergovernmental relations, private corporate involvement, and active cyber citizenship as a model.[51] Yet it is unclear how the Department of Defense, Google, and individual users would manage this complicated relationship.

In reality, for U.S. citizens and people around the world, the question of who owns what, or who is responsible for what, is probably unimportant. An individual depending on the Internet to do banking just wants secure transactions in the .com domain; an individual trying to find information on charities just wants reliable information in the .org domain; someone trying to find information about driver's license requirements only wants access to timely, accurate data in the .gov domain; and the student trying to pursue education online wants an effective system in the .edu domain. In other words, most individuals want the cyber world to enhance their human security needs without causing additional vulnerabilities.

Yet there are a myriad of challenges as documented in this chapter. Attacks may come from such varied bad actors as a foreign intelligence service, a terrorist group, a criminal group, hacktivists, individual hackers, or disgruntled insiders. As the virtual and physical worlds become closer over the next twenty years, new and unforeseen challenges will emerge. But one fact is certain: information security will remain a key feature of the national and human security landscape; and all governments will struggle to keep pace, just as all citizens will feel compelled to protect their individual, private human security online. This overarching cyber, or informational, dimension clearly enables human security as much as it may disrupt it, which aptly reflects the realities of globalization processes continuing to transform our world. Continued controversy regarding the vulnerability of personal information of millions of users of the popular Facebook social media platform is just one example of the dilemma. In the final chapter of the book we reflect this mixed evaluation as we consider some specific aspects of protecting and promoting human security in a borderless world.

Notes

1 Michael Hayden, "The Future of Things 'Cyber,'" *Strategic Studies Quarterly*, vol. 5, no. 1 (2011), 3–7, 3 (emphasis in original), at: www.files.ethz.ch/isn/153779/spring11.pdf.

2 http://inventors.about.com/library/inventors/bl_Charles_Herzfeld.htm.

3 http://creativecommons.org/licenses/by/2.5, via Wikimedia Commons, https://commons.wikimedia.org/wiki/File:Internet_map_1024.jpg.
4 George W. Bush, *The National Strategy to Secure Cyberspace* (Washington, DC: White House, February 2003), 1; Christopher J. Castelli, "Defense Department Adopts New Definition of 'Cyberspace,'" *Inside the Air Force*, May 23, 2008, available at http://integrator.hanscom.af.mil/2008/May/ 05292008/05292008-24.htm.
5 Larry Johnson, "Thru the Looking Glass: Why Virtual Worlds Matter, Where They Are Heading, and Why We Are All Here," Keynote Address to the Federal Consortium on Virtual Worlds, Washington, DC, April 24, 2008.
6 UNDP, *Human Development Report 1994*.
7 These lenses were safely worn by rabbits in laboratory tests at the University of Washington, A virtual display like this could be used by drivers or pilots to see a vehicle's speed projected onto the windshield; by video-game companies who could use the lenses to completely immerse players in a virtual world without restricting their range of motion; or, in the field of communications, by people on the go who could surf the Internet on a midair virtual display screen that only they would be able to see.
8 Quoted in UN, "Fast Forward Progress: Leveraging Tech to Achieve the Global Goals," www.itu.int/en/sustainable-world/Documents/Fast-forward_progress_report_414709%20FINAL.pdf.
9 Kenneth Geers, "Pandemonium: Nation States, National Security, and the Internet," NATO Cooperative Cyber Defense Centre of Excellence, *Tallinn Papers* vol. 1, no. 1 (2014), 1. https://ccdcoe.org/publications/TP_Vol1No1_Geers.pdf.
10 Director of National Intelligence, "Annual Threat Assessment of the Intelligence Community for the Senate Armed Services Committee: Statement for the Record, March 10, 2009, 39–40.
11 Daniel R. Coats, "Statement for the Record Worldwide Threat Assessment of the US Intelligence Community Senate Armed Services Committee," May 23, 2017.
12 Kim Zetter, "Inside the Cunning, Unprecedented Cyber Hack of Ukraine's Power Grid," *Wired*, March 3, 2016. www.wired.com/2016/03/inside-cunning-unprecedented-hack-ukraines-power-grid/.
13 Herb Lin, "Operational Considerations in Cyber Attack and Cyber Exploitation," in *Cyberspace and National Security*, ed. Derek S. Reveron (Washington, DC: Georgetown University Press, 2012), 41.
14 James Lewis, "The 'Korean' Cyber Attacks and Their Implications for Cyber Conflict," Center for Strategic and International Studies, October 2009, 1, available at http://csis.org/files/publications/091023_Korean_Cyber_Attacks_And_Their_Implications_For_Cyber_Conflict.pdf.
15 Derek S. Reveron, "An Introduction to National Security and Cyberspace," in Reveron, *Cyberspace and National Security*, 17, note 25, quoting ITU chief from October 6, 2009.
16 Joint Staff, "Joint Operating Environment 2035," Washington, DC, July 14, 2016, 7.
17 Quoted in Yoav Zitun, "Head of IDF's new Cyber Division: It's a world with no rules," *Y Net News*, April 16, 2017. http://www.ynetnews.com/articles/0,7340,L-4949752,00.html.
18 Jane Holl Lute and Bruce McDonnell, "A Civil Perspective on Cybersecurity," *Wired*, February 14, 2011.
19 Quoted in Donna Miles, "Gates Establishes New Cyber Subcommand," *American Forces Press Service*, June 24, 2009.
20 Kenneth Geers, "Pandemonium: Nation States, National Security, and the Internet," 12.
21 Erik Gartzke, "The Myth of Cyberwar: Bringing War in Cyberspace Back Down to Earth," *International Security*, Vol. 38, No. 2 (Fall 2013), 59.
22 John Arquilla and David Ronfeldt, "Cyberwar is Coming!" (Santa Monica, CA: RAND Corporation, 1993), at: www.rand.org/pubs/reprints/RP223.html; and Keith B. Alexander, "Warfighting in Cyberspace," *Joint Force Quarterly*, no. 46 (3rd Quarter 2007), 60.
23 Ian Bremmer. "These 5 Facts Explain the Threat of Cyberwar." *Time* 6/19/15, Accessed 8/12/15, http://time.com/3928086/these-5-facts-explain-the-threat-of-cyber-warfare/.
24 Thomas Rid, *Cyber War will not Take Place,"* (New York: Oxford University Press, 2013).

25 Maness, Ryan C., Brandon Valeriano, and Benjamin Jensen. 2016. Coding Manual for v1.5 of the Dyadic Cyber Incident and Dispute Dataset, 2000–2014, Available at drryanmaness.wix.com/irprof, 2016.

26 Maness, Ryan C. and Brandon Valeriano. "The Impact of Cyber Conflict on International Interactions." *Armed Forces and Society* 42 (2, 2016), 301–323.

27 Head of the National Security Agency Gen. Keith Alexander has claimed, "We have yet to translate these strategies into operational art through development of joint doctrine for cyberspace." In Alexander, "Warfighting in Cyberspace," 59.

28 Joint Staff, "Joint Operating Environment 2035: The Joint Force in a Contested and Disordered World," Distribution Statement A, Washington, DC, July 14, 2016, 7.

29 Eric Schmitt and Thom Shanker, "U.S. Debated Cyberwarfare in Attack Plan on Libya," *New York Times,* October 17, 2011. www.nytimes.com/2011/10/18/world/africa/cyber-warfare-against-libya-was-debated-by-us.html.

30 U.S. Air Force officials converted more than 43,000 enlisted airmen from former communications career fields to cyberspace support on November 1, 2009. The new specialty is made up of three former career fields: communications-electronics, knowledge operations management, and communications-computer systems. The new cyberspace support career field is broken into eleven new air force specialties: knowledge operations management; cybersystems operations; cyber surety; computer systems programming; client systems; cybertransport systems; radio frequency (RF) transmission systems; spectrum operations; ground radar systems; airfield systems; and cable and antenna systems. The navy did something similar on October 1, 2009, when it created the Fleet Cyber Command (Tenth Fleet) and consolidated several career fields into information dominance.

31 Wesley K. Clark and Peter L. Levin, "Securing the Information Highway: How to Enhance the United States' Electronic Defenses," *Foreign Affairs* vol. 88, no. 6 (2009): 2–10, 2.

32 Michael Hayden, "Cutting Cyber Command's Umbilical Cord to the NSA," July 17, 2017. www.thecipherbrief.com/article/tech/cutting-cyber-commands-umbilical-cord-nsa-1092.

33 Robert K. Knake quoted in Ellen Nakashima and John Pomfret, "China Proves to Be an Aggressive Foe in Cyberspace," *Washington Post*, November 11, 2009, available at www.washingtonpost.com/wp-dyn/content/article/2009/11/10/AR2009111017588.html; *PLA Daily* quoted in Alexander, "Warfighting in Cyberspace," 59.

34 Nakashima and Pomfret, "China Proves to Be an Aggressive Foe."

35 "ITU Chief Stresses Need for Cooperation to Protect Cyberspace," United Nations Radio, October 6, 2009.

36 White House, *National Strategy to Secure Cyberspace*, 2003.

37 Presidential Decision Directive 63, "Critical Infrastructure Protection," May 22, 1998, sec. 2; U.S. Department of Defense, *The National Defense Strategy of the United States of America* (Washington, DC: DOD, 2005), 3; Secretary of Defense, *National Defense Strategy*; DOD, *National Defense Strategy*, 2008, 7.

38 Jim Garamone, "Lynn Calls for Collaboration in Establishing Cyber Security," American Forces Press Service, October 1, 2009.

39 Ben Bain, "Military Wrestles with Cyber War Battle Planning," *Federal Computer Week*, July 26, 2010, available at http://fcw.com/articles/2010/07/ 26/feat-cyber-command-tackles-cyber-war.aspx.

40 CSIS Commission on Cybersecurity for the 44th Presidency, *Securing Cyberspace for the 44th Presidency* (Washington, DC: CSIS, 2008), 11, available at http://csis.org/files/ media/csis/pubs/081208_securingcyberspace_44.pdf; White House, "National Cybersecurity Awareness Month." Press release, October 1, 2009, available at www.whitehouse.gov/the_press_office/Presidential-Proclamation-National- Cybersecurity-Awareness-Month/.

41 Clark and Levin, "Securing the Information Highway," 10.

42 White House, *Cyberspace Policy Review: Assuring a Trusted and Resilient Information and Communications Infrastructure* (Washington, DC: White House, 2009), 28, available at www.whitehouse.gov/assets/documents/Cyberspace_Policy_Review_final.pdf.

43 U.S. Department of Defense, "The Department of Defense Cyber Strategy" (Washington, DC: Secretary of Defense, April 2015), 5; at: www.defense.gov/Portals/1/features/2015/0415_cyber-strategy/Final_2015_DoD_CYBER_STRATEGY_for_web.pdf.

44 White House, "Presidential Executive Order on Strengthening the Cybersecurity of Federal Networks and Critical Infrastructure," May 11, 2017. www.whitehouse.gov/the-press-office/2017/05/11/presidential-executive-order-strengthening-cybersecurity-federal.

45 Quoted in AFP, "NSA Chief Worries About Cyber Attack on US Infrastructure," *Security Week*, March 2, 2016. www.securityweek.com/nsa-chief-worries-about-cyber-attack-us-infrastructure.

46 G7, "Ise-Shima Leaders' Declaration," 26–27 May, 2016. www.mofa.go.jp/files/000160266.pdf.

47 Quoted in Elain Edwards, "Research into Artificial Intelligence Should Not Be Left to Military, Says Google Exec," *Irish Times*, February 16, 2017. www.irishtimes.com/business/technology/research-into-artificial-intelligence-should-not-be-left-to-military-says-google-exec-1.2977720#sst.

48 Microsoft, "International Cyber Security Norms: Reducing Conflict in an Internet-Dependent World" 2014. http://download.microsoft.com/download/7/6/0/7605D861-C57A-4E23-B823-568CFC36FD44/International_Cybersecurity_%20Norms.pdf.

49 Brad Smith, "The Need for a Digital Geneva Convention." Microsoft blog, February 14, 2017. https://blogs.microsoft.com/on-the-issues/2017/02/14/need-digital-geneva-convention/#PjWhiTaH9aZ2eg3I.99.

50 47 USC, Section 230 (b); White House, "National Cybersecurity Awareness Month."

51 Richard J. Harknett and James A. Stever, "The Cybersecurity Triad: Government, Private Sector Partners, and the Engaged Cybersecurity Citizen," *Journal of Homeland Security and Emergency Management* vol. 6, no. 1 (2009).

To Learn More

Brandon Valeriano and Ryan C. Maness explore interstate rivalry in cyberspace in *Cyber War versus Cyber Realities: Cyber Conflict in the International System* (New York: Oxford University Press, 2015).

Adam Segal examines global cyber issues in *The Hacked World Order: How Nations Fight, Trade, Maneuver, and Manipulate in the Digital Age* (New York: Public Affairs, 2016).

Jason Healey and Karl Grindal (eds) offer a history of cyber conflict in *A Fierce Domain: Conflict in Cyberspace, 1986 to 2012* (Vienna, VA: Cyber Conflict Studies Association, 2013).

To track the growth of Internet usage by country, see www.internetworldstats.com.

Examine current malicious cyber activity and the latest national threat advisory level assessed by the United States Computer Emergency Readiness Team (US-CERT), at www.us-cert.gov/.

The International Telecommunication Union (dating to 1865!) is the leading UN agency for information and communication technology issues, and the global focal point for governments and the private sector in developing networks and services. Explore how the ITU is connecting the world at www.itu.int/en/pages/default.aspx.

The acclaimed PBS *Frontline* series explores cyber vulnerabilities at www.pbs.org/wgbh/pages/frontline/shows/cyberwar/.

According to the Electronic Frontier Foundation, EFF "is the leading nonprofit organization defending civil liberties in the digital world. Founded in 1990, EFF champions user privacy, free expression, and innovation." Scan its ongoing efforts at: www.eff.org/.

Chapter 10

Protecting and Promoting Human Security

Chapter contents

> In Syria, Afghanistan, South Sudan and elsewhere, a generation of children have known nothing but conflict for their entire lives. Every civilian has a right to safety and protection. We must all do everything we can to deliver on this right. We must enhance respect for international humanitarian and human rights law. We must protect humanitarian and medical missions and prioritize the protection of civilians in United Nations peace operations. And we must prevent forced displacement and respect the rights of people who have fled violence, by pursuing durable solutions for all those who have been displaced, both inside their own countries and across borders.
>
> UN Secretary-General António Guterres, World Humanitarian Day, 2017[1]

It is not surprising that the Secretary-General of the United Nations (who was the UN High Commissioner for Refugees for the previous ten years) would be so concerned about peace, human rights, and refugees—that goes with the job description. But it may be surprising to find that twelve years earlier the vast majority of sovereign states agreed that where "national authorities are manifestly failing to protect their populations from genocide, war crimes, ethnic cleansing and crimes against humanity" the member states of the United Nations were "prepared to take collective action, in a timely and decisive manner, through the Security Council, in accordance with the Charter, including Chapter VII."[2] The reference to Chapter VII is significant because Chapter VII allows for the Security Council to take enforcement measures to restore international peace and stability. Whereas in the past this authority was reserved for interstate conflict where one state threatened another state's sovereignty (such as when Iraq invaded Kuwait in 1990), there was increasing recognition that a state's actions (or inactions) against its own citizens could also threaten international peace and stability.

This recognition was encapsulated in the Responsibility to Protect (R2P) concept, and it effectively illustrates the theme of this last chapter—protecting and promoting human security. These two elements have actually been part of the discussion throughout the text, as we have considered policy options in each chapter for improving human security issues; whether encouraging good governance, expanding economic opportunity, planning for climate change and natural disasters, collaborating to halt pandemic disease spread, or protecting the cyber realm. Protecting and promoting human security also relates to our thesis that national security for states cannot be achieved on a sustainable basis unless human security concerns are addressed. As then-UN Secretary-General Ban Ki-moon declared in his 2009 report:

> The responsibility to protect is an ally of sovereignty, not an adversary. It grows from the positive and affirmative notion of sovereignty as responsibility, rather than from the narrower idea of humanitarian intervention. By helping States to meet their core protection responsibilities, the responsibility to protect seeks to strengthen sovereignty, not weaken it. It seeks to help States to succeed."[3]

The Secretary-General's perspective highlights another critical fact—that many states today do not have the capability to protect their national security or the capacity to meet pressing human security issues exacerbated by nationalism, poverty, famine, disease, and environmental change. Whereas in the past powerful and expansionist states threatening military actions tended to pose the most serious challenges to the world community, today the greatest threats tend to emerge from, and are enabled by, the least developed and poorly governed states, as we have discussed throughout this book. In weak countries that lack effective and stable institutions, bad actors can find refuge: groups from terrorists to extreme nationalists intent on genocide, to drug traffickers and criminal gangs, to cyber hackers who use these countries as bases of operation. Undoubtedly, impoverished states are more prone to internal conflict, which in turn further impoverishes these societies. And typically the conflict may spill over legal borders to cause greater regional instability due to ethnic and religious ties between populations. At the same time, problems that can become global concerns, such as pandemic diseases, are more likely in undeveloped states with weak public health systems and poor living conditions where people and livestock frequently commune. Environmental tragedies can more easily occur where governments are corrupt and the majority of the population is not well educated so public scrutiny is minimal. Maritime piracy, too, originates in weak states or essentially ungoverned areas, where individuals may find no other lucrative economic opportunity or effective law enforcement agency to restrain them.

We have highlighted how the forces of globalization may foster many of these challenges, sometimes transforming them into clear and immediate security threats to the United States and its citizens. No less a figure than Mark Zuckerberg, founder of Facebook—the immensely influential, global social media platform—has acknowledged the interconnected nature of threats:

> Today's threats are increasingly global, but the infrastructure to protect us is not. Problems like terrorism, natural disasters, disease, refugee crises, and climate change need coordinated responses from a worldwide vantage point. No nation can solve them alone. A virus in one nation can quickly spread to others. A conflict in one country can create a refugee crisis across continents. Pollution in one place can affect the environment around the world. Humanity's current systems are insufficient to address these issues.[4]

Yet the picture we have attempted to portray in this work is not entirely grim. Globalization has equally demonstrated the potential to improve human security, as Zuckerberg also stressed in his comments which encouraged building a global community, noting "our greatest opportunities are now global—like spreading prosperity and freedom, promoting peace and understanding, lifting people out of poverty, and accelerating science."[5] We have argued that the increasingly integrated global economy is proving productive enough to help the poorest states develop out of extreme poverty; that technologies allow the spread of information and education among citizens everywhere and put pressure on ineffective governments to make necessary reforms; and that the Internet enables nongovernmental groups and activists across state borders to cooperate in publicizing problems and creating novel solutions. For instance, there is absolutely no doubt that the human rights protections that U.S. citizens take for granted would not be as widely accepted around the world today without the sustained campaign of the transnational human rights movement, including groups such as Amnesty International and Human Rights Watch. Without the persistent efforts of the global coalition of experts in Transparency International, many more governments would be able to hide their corruption—one of the principal problems hamstringing good governance and economic development. And with no network of scientists, policy experts, and environmental activists, major corporations would be at liberty to pollute and deplete scarce animal and mineral resources without consequence for future generations.

In this concluding chapter we reflect upon key features of the many challenges that have been presented throughout the book, integrating them through the construct of protecting and promoting human security. This integration is essential because of the sobering fact that so many of these transnational challenges are inextricably linked and dependent on one another, as they lie across the seams of issue and policy areas (recall Figure 1.1, Spectrum of Challenges, which illustrates these seam areas). Additionally, these challenges meet at the juncture of domestic and foreign policy bureaucracies, further complicating

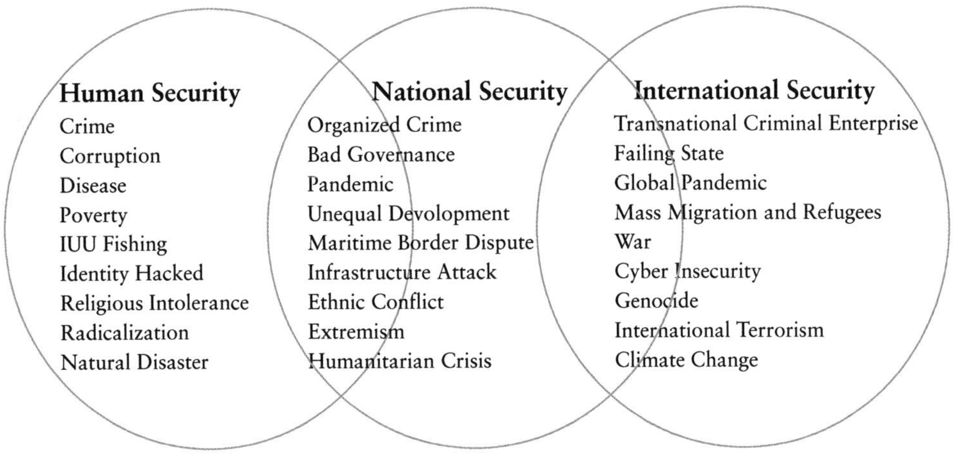

Figure 10.1 Relationship of Human, National, and International Security.
Source: Based on "Securing an Open Society: Canada's National Security Policy," April 2004. http://publications.gc.ca/collections/Collection/CP22-77-2004E.pdf

individual government efforts to alleviate human suffering and improve national security. Figure 10.1 depicts how individual security threats to human beings can quickly translate into national security concerns, and ultimately to global security issues. For example, criminal violence within a community harms individuals' human security; this activity may evolve into large-scale organized crime that poses a threat to security and good governance at the state level (Guatemala, Mexico); and powerful criminal networks may then spread the violence across state borders (Central America–Mexico–United States).

The complexity of human security issues can seem overwhelming, and it makes proposing policy recommendations particularly difficult. As professor and former senior national security official Sarah Sewell wrote, "The most formidable challenge, therefore, remains convincing officials to think about security in unfamiliar ways and to take actions that do not appear to be in their traditional or immediate self-interest."[6] In this regard the international community, led by the United Nations (through its Human Security Unit), is attempting to operationalize the human security construct as a policy tool through its framework of "protection and empowerment." This framework includes a comprehensive, hybrid approach which is meant to assist with developing human security policies and specific programs and projects.[7]

Yet, as the United Nations has recognized, even with sound policies and programs, achieving success will require the combined efforts of intergovernmental organizations (IGOs), nongovernmental organizations (NGOs), individual governments, civil society, and the business sector, among others. Certainly the U.S. government's active involvement will be crucial. To withdraw from this effort is to jeopardize human security for individuals everywhere and, ultimately, the national security of the United States and its citizens. Christopher Hitchens phrases this warning very effectively in reviewing Gary Bass's 2008 book *Freedom's Battle: The Origins of Humanitarian Intervention*, concluding:

> [Bass] makes a sensible case that everyone has a self-interest in the strivings and sufferings of others because the borders between societies are necessarily porous and contingent and are, when one factors in considerations such as the velocity of modern travel, easy access

> to weaponry, and the spread of disease, becoming ever more so. . . . Afghanistan's internal affairs are now the United States'—in fact, they were already so before Americans understood that. A failed state may not trouble Americans' sleep, but a rogue one can, and the transition from failed state to rogue can be alarmingly abrupt.[8]

To make sense of this, we assess the concept of humanitarian intervention and the more specific R2P framework and its elements. The 2011 humanitarian intervention in Libya is then examined in order to illustrate key lessons about interventions and R2P. The Libyan case also provides an important link to the increasingly prevalent issue of refugees, internally displaced persons (IDPs), and migrants, which falls under both protecting and promoting human security. While refugees and IDPs usually flee to escape violence, the reality is that they may still face violence in refugee camps or other temporary living situations, and thus require protection from the country of refuge, or from international peacekeepers. At the same time, individuals or groups may flee areas of famine or lack of employment to support their families, and what these migrants most need is international assistance and promotion of opportunities to thrive in the long term. Here sustainable development is seen as key to promoting human security—a concept that has become enshrined not only in UN agencies but also within many other IGOs and NGOs.

Humanitarian and developmental assistance to other countries has long been considered to be an important aspect of U.S. foreign policy efforts, as we found when examining the U.S. Agency for International Development (USAID) in Chapter 5 (Image 10.1 illustrates this nexus of security and humanitarian motives). As we conclude this work, we look beyond the pragmatic and self-serving reasons for American citizens to give aid and

Image 10.1 USNS Hospital Ship *Mercy*: regular provider of medical care and supplies throughout the world. Photo: Hank Gettys, U.S. Navy

to be concerned about human security issues to philosophical reasons as well. As Irish rock star and humanitarian activist Bono has commented, "America is not just a country but an idea, a great idea about opportunity for all and responsibility to your fellow man. . . . In dangerous, clamorous times, the idea of America rings like a bell."[9] We believe that U.S. leadership is necessary—indeed, imperative!—around the world to protect and promote human security, thus supporting both U.S. national security interests and U.S. values.

Protecting Human Security and R2P

Diplomat and human rights advocate Gareth Evans points out that massacres and horrific crimes against civilians have occurred since the birth of mankind; yet only in the wake of the widespread genocide and atrocities of World War II did a sustained movement emerge to protect human rights and, eventually, to support humanitarian intervention on behalf of threatened populations.[10] Today a global consensus exists that never again should there be genocide in Yugoslavia or Rwanda, or any other area of the world. In fact, these cases from the 1990s really cemented the growing support for the R2P norm; a norm that was formally accepted by more than 150 heads of state at the United Nations Sixtieth Anniversary World Summit in September 2005.

In his special report in 2009, Secretary-General Ban Ki-moon outlined the three key elements of R2P. First, states have the primary responsibility to protect their populations against genocide, war crimes, ethnic cleansing, and crimes against humanity. Second, the international community should provide assistance to states in building capacity to protect their populations from catastrophe by addressing underlying conditions. Third, the international community should take timely action when states fail to protect their populations. As the report declared, "The strategy stresses the value of prevention, and, when it fails, of early and flexible response tailored to the specific circumstances of each case."[11]

Based on these elements, Gareth Evans insists that it is "absolutely not the case" that R2P is just another version of humanitarian intervention—"coercive military intervention for humanitarian purposes."[12] Similarly, two veteran U.S. diplomats have stressed that "R2P was intended less as a guide for reacting to crises than as a road map to prevent humanitarian catastrophes from evolving."[13] R2P is first predicated on self-help; that the state in question attempts to help itself with tailored, preventive international assistance across the range of the political-diplomatic, economic, legal, or security sectors. The R2P focus is on identifying states at risk and helping to strengthen these preventive, positive actions—to improve development and standards of living—so as to avoid the possibility of intervention because of adverse conditions generating genocide or other massive violations of human rights (such as the use of rape as a weapon of war). Significantly, Evans doubtless felt compelled to make this case because many developing countries continue to be leery about providing a pretext for more powerful countries to intervene in their internal affairs, no matter how praiseworthy their motivations.

At the same time, this focus on prevention does not mean that coercive military action would never be considered in the case of another genocide where the government manifestly cannot, or will not, prevent mass killings—such as Rwanda endured in 1994. The U.S. government has stated as much; as early as 2006 the Bush administration's *National Security Strategy* explicitly acknowledged that armed intervention might be necessary on the part of the world community to stop mass atrocities and genocide.[14] In 2010 the U.S. Defense Department's *Quadrennial Defense Review* strategy included the responsibility for the U.S. military to be ready to intervene to end mass atrocities causing large-scale human suffering.[15] Then in 2011, President Obama declared mass atrocities prevention to be a core national security interest and a core moral responsibility for the United States, although that did not mean the United States would use its military to intervene in each case. Rather, he stressed the non-military tools that the U.S. should employ (diplomacy, financial, etc.) in order to forestall and prevent mass atrocities from ever occurring.[16] This echoes the R2P focus on prevention first.

Of course, it is always a political judgment to decide whether, and when, international coercive action is required. Additionally, national interests, domestic politics, and capabilities help explain which external actors may intervene, and where. The tragedy of Syria in the wake of the 2011 "Arab Spring" illustrates how political considerations and foreign policy concerns can dictate UN actions and individual state policies, to include the specific scope of U.S. actions in Syria. As the diversity of experts who formed the U.S. Working Group on the Responsibility to Protect noted:

> The terrible carnage in Syria illustrates that the international community's embrace of R2P is not sufficient, in itself, to prevent a ruthless dictator from inflicting grievous harm on his own citizens, especially when the permanent members of the Security Council are divided and external military intervention is difficult.[17]

With regard to the Democratic Republic of the Congo, where over 5 million people are believed to have died in over twenty years of political and economic-related civil conflict, the Working Group essentially concluded that "until the country has a government worthy of the name," the violence was bound to continue and the international community could not accomplish much (in spite of the near-continuous presence of UN peacekeepers in parts of the country). However, it is worth noting that the Group assessed that "in some respects, the international action in Libya was a textbook application of R2P principles."[18] Thus, it is worth examining the Libyan intervention for useful lessons.

R2P and The Libyan Intervention

It is not surprising to find that by 2011 the increasingly dysfunctional Libyan regime under Muammar al-Qaddafi had cemented its image, in the words of one commentator, as "a society long traumatized by the Middle East's most Orwellian regime."[19] Some experts would probably express surprise that the mercurial Colonel Qaddafi had been able to remain in power for some forty years, constantly shifting the balance of power and economic resources among various sectors ranging from the military to tribal leaders and militias. While many might argue about whether this vast desert territory with long-established historical cleavages between groups ever could have had a reasonable chance of "nationhood" after Italian colonial rule ended, certainly under Qaddafi and his sons those opportunities were not only squandered but also deliberately sabotaged. In 2011 the NGO Human Rights Watch labeled Qaddafi "a dictator who had amassed a deplorable human rights record over 42 years."[20]

As the "Arab Spring" unfolded in early 2011, peaceful anti-government protests emerged in Libya's largest cities, mainly in response to arrests of many government critics. The government responded with massive repression and excessive use of force against the protests, to include "lethal use of live fire on peaceful protesters, as well as the arrest and disappearance of hundreds of people suspected of involvement in anti-government demonstrations."[21] In later months details would emerge about the large-scale human rights violations committed by the Qaddafi regime (and by some rebel groups) from February to August, to include summary executions, torture, gang rape, and indiscriminate use of mortars against civilian populations. In response, the UN Security Council agreed to tighten economic sanctions put in place against Libya earlier that month. Most importantly, the Council, concerned about possible "crimes against humanity" (attacks on civilians), adopted Resolution 1973, which:

> authorized Member States, acting nationally or through regional organizations or arrangements, to take all necessary measures to protect civilians under threat of attack in the country, including Benghazi, while excluding a foreign occupation force of any form on any part of Libyan territory.[22]

The consideration of R2P principles and the primary responsibility of governments are clearly evident in the actual text of the Security Council resolution, "*Reiterating* the responsibility of the Libyan authorities to protect the Libyan population and *reaffirming* that parties to armed conflicts bear the primary responsibility to take all feasible steps to ensure the protection of civilians." However, since the Libyan authorities had failed in their responsibilities, the Council concluded that the situation constituted a threat to international peace and security, and thus acted under their Chapter VII (enforcement authority) to authorize member states to take appropriate and necessary measures.[23] This is significant because it was the first *use of force* authorized under the R2P construct. NATO member countries—principally France, the United States, and the United Kingdom—chose to enforce the no-fly zone against the Qaddafi regime under "Operation Unified Protector." But it was the expansion of the NATO mission to give support to anti-Qaddafi forces beyond this stated UN mandate—and ultimately to remove Qaddafi from power (he was killed in October 2011)—that created controversy over the Libyan intervention.

There is no doubt that the actions of the Libyan regime in early 2011 were horrifying, but the Qaddafi government had committed serious human rights violations for decades; and there were (and are) equally other reprehensible regimes that did not receive swift UN condemnation and authorization for military action as occurred in Libya. Why was Libya singled out under R2P principles? The U.S.-centered Working Group on the R2P offers a convincing rationale:

> Three facts help explain the robust international response to Qadhafi's threats of mass violence. First, the modest capacity of Libya's armed forces, the open desert landscape, and the country's proximity to Europe and allied military bases aided the military aspects of the operation. Second, the Arab League, including Libya's neighbors, endorsed the action—a testament to Qadhafi's political isolation. Third, the governments of Russia and China, often reluctant to support intervention, chose to abstain rather than veto crucial UN Security Council resolutions. The absence of any one of these conditions—a favorable military balance, regional support, and Security Council authorization—might have led to a different result.[24]

In any case, the Libyan intervention remains contentious. Even at the time of the intervention noted scholar Michael Doyle was pointing out that "imposing democracy from the outside tends to fail" as it needs to be built by the citizens themselves. A different tyranny or a client state may result, or continuing civil conflict.[25] In that regard, it is instructive to note the situation in Libya some six years later, as summarized by Human Rights Watch in September 2017:

> Libya's political and security crisis continues as three authorities, including the Tripoli based UN-backed Government of National Accord, compete for legitimacy, control of territory and of vital institutions. Continuing armed clashes have displaced hundreds of thousands of people and interrupted access to basic services, including fuel and electrical power. Forces engaged

in the conflict are guilty of arbitrary detention, torture, unlawful killings, indiscriminate attacks, disappearances, and the forceful displacement of people.[26]

Finally, one of the most tragic consequences of the continuing conflict in Libya concerns its relationship to the plight of the tens of thousands of refugees and migrants attempting to reach Europe via Libya and the Mediterranean Sea (in addition to the estimated half-million Libyans who are internally displaced within the country due to the instability). Again, according to Human Rights Watch, the UN's International Office for Migration (IOM) "estimated that 771,146 migrants and asylum seekers were in Libya as of November [2016]." Furthermore, the human rights organization documented that "while in Libya, armed groups and guards at migrant detention facilities subjected many to forced labor, torture, sexual abuse, and extortion."[27] There were even reports from NGOs that Libyan coast guard units were actively shooting at aid workers and refugees in the Mediterranean Sea, as the Libyans cooperated with European Union efforts to shut down migration routes into Europe.[28] Considering that it was European NATO members, along with the United States, who had decided to intervene in Libya and remove its leadership, it might be wise to remember the colloquial saying, "If you break it, you own it" (variously attributed to columnist Tom Friedman and former Secretary of State Colin Powell, the latter with regard to the 2003 invasion of Iraq).

Promoting Human Security

As the Libyan intervention should illustrate, carrying out the R2P mandate to assist governments and vulnerable populations—to include perhaps the most vulnerable of all, refugees and displaced peoples—can be successful only with a deep understanding of the issues and the context, which naturally includes sensitivity to cultural beliefs and practices. If this is ignored, external efforts are unlikely to be productive, and even well-intentioned and well-funded development strategies to promote the human security needs of the most threatened can fail. In the worst case, intervention efforts—military, political, economic, or some combination of the three—might actually cause conditions to deteriorate further, as the United States and the United Nations have learned at great cost in a number of cases.

Refugees and Internally Displaced Persons

The UN Refugee Agency (UNHCR) 2009 annual report placed the number of refugees at 15.2 million, IDPs at 27.1 million, and 43.3 million persons forcibly displaced overall.[29] While those numbers are sobering, the comparable UN statistics in 2017 are staggeringly higher: 22.5 million refugees (over half under 18), 38 million IDPs, and 65 million forcibly displaced overall.[30] Additionally, some 10 million people are "stateless" persons, meaning they have no claim to nationality or the protection and services of a national government. This is the situation for most Roma throughout Europe, and describes the desperate situation of the Rohingya people who have been persecuted and deliberately excluded from citizenship in Myanmar (Burma).

It is important to understand the different terminology in this area. The differences amount to more than semantics because, under international law, the status of *refugee* provides more protection and possibility of international assistance than does being a migrant or an IDP, where the host government still bears the major responsibility.

In the wake of the destruction of World War II and deliberate displacement of many European peoples, the 1951 Refugee Convention was established; today it has been ratified by almost 150 states. The Convention is the only global legal document pertaining to refugees (along with the 1967 Protocol, which expanded its scope beyond the initial European refugees), who are considered to be people who have been forced to leave their countries because of persecution or armed conflict.

The office of the UNHCR was also established at that time with a mandate to protect and find solutions for refugees. The Convention outlines the rights of refugees and displaced persons and the responsibilities of states, which are supposed to cooperate with UNHCR in carrying out its responsibilities. According to UNHCR, "the core principle is non-refoulement, which asserts that a refugee should not be returned to a country where they face serious threats to their life or freedom. This is now considered a rule of customary international law."[31] Those individuals officially deemed refugees are entitled to at least some protections under international law and assistance from the United Nations. To date that assistance has often amounted to families literally spending generations in refugee camps with no hope of returning home due to continuing conflict, such as the hundreds of thousands of Palestinians still living in camps since the 1948 war which created the state of Israel, along with later conflicts. The sad fact is that probably a third of refugees worldwide are in camps, and well over two-thirds of African refugees make their homes in camps.[32] Many of these camps are located in areas subject to endemic conflict, often in impoverished neighboring countries, as is the case with refugees from Sudan who have fled to Chad, or the Rohingya who have had little choice but to escape to already densely populated and poor Bangladesh.

But as unfortunate as these situations may be, acknowledged refugees do have legal rights and a claim to international assistance. Such is not the case with *internally displaced persons*, who by definition are supposed to receive protection and support from their national government, even if that government is responsible for the forced displacement of its citizens. Examples ranging from Syria to Sudan are relevant here. Finally, *migrants* are not entitled to international legal protection and assistance (see Image 10.2 depicting migrants at sea). The IOM—the leading intergovernmental organization dealing with migration—defines a migrant as:

> Any person who is moving or has moved across an international border or within a State away from his/her habitual place of residence, regardless of (1) the person's legal status; (2) whether the movement is voluntary or involuntary; (3) what the causes for the movement are; or (4) what the length of the stay is.[33]

The IOM assessed that for 2015, "the number of international migrants worldwide—people residing in a country other than their country of birth—was the highest ever recorded, having reached 244 million (from 232 million in 2013)." According to the IOM, "over 1 billion people in the world are migrants, or more than 1 in 7 people globally," but this figure includes international and internal migrants.[34] Obviously this category is very broad and contains what many might consider economic migrants or "immigrants," such as people from Africa and the Middle East who have been trying to attain a better life in Europe and so have been willing to risk their lives through dangerous voyages across the Mediterranean Sea. In fact, at least 15,000 refugees and migrants had lost their lives in the Mediterranean in the four years since these journeys became frequent in 2013 (October 2013–September 2017). As dramatically publicized by the media, many of these people were abandoned by smugglers who left them adrift in unsafe boats with little, if any, water.

Image 10.2 Migrants Aboard an Inflatable Vessel: the destroyer USS *Carney* provided them with food and water before coordinating with a nearby merchant vessel to take them to safety. Photo: Wesley R. Dickey, U.S. Navy

In recognition of the global magnitude of the refugee and migrant crisis, in 2016 United Nations member states unanimously adopted the New York Declaration for Refugees and Migrants, calling for increased international cooperation on this issue. More concretely, the declaration set in motion plans for two compacts to be adopted in 2018:

> The global compact on refugees [which] will help the global community find more equitable ways to share the responsibility for refugees, including support to the countries and communities who host them [. . .]

The global compact for safe, orderly and regular migration [which] will seek to enhance international cooperation in governing migration and focus attention on migrants . . . aim to protect the vulnerable; leverage the many benefits migrants bring to their host and home countries; and tackle the drivers of irregular and forced migration.[35]

One year after the New York Declaration, UN Secretary-General Guterres emphasized the need for continued progress on refugee protection and an understanding that orderly migration in and of itself was not a threat but a normal occurrence historically, and one that benefitted countries. Rather, his concern was for "unregulated and forced migration that creates problems especially for migrants, who take life-threatening risks and are exploited by traffickers and smugglers, but also for host countries who are concerned about the control over their borders."[36]

Concerns over their borders had led almost all European countries and the United States to greatly restrict the numbers of refugees and migrants allowed into their countries by 2017, in spite of their endorsement of the New York Declaration. In the European case this essentially closed several of the most popular routes across the Mediterranean and Aegean Seas, which in turn increased the dangers and resort to smugglers by desperate refugees and migrants mostly coming from the Middle East (such as from Syria), Asia (Afghanistan and Bangladesh), and Africa. For the United States under the Trump administration this has resulted in various controversial executive acts meant to curb all immigration, and limit refugees—especially from countries with a majority Islamic population. In September 2017 the administration announced plans to admit no more than 45,000 refugees in 2018, less than half what the Obama administration had been recommending. These plans also included regional caps ranging from 17,500 for the Near East and South Asia—which includes most Middle Eastern countries—to 1,500 for the entire region of Latin America and the Caribbean.[37] If we consider that Syria alone had generated some 5 million refugees by September 2017 (with over 6 million internally displaced) and that Central American refugees/immigrants numbered close to 2 million for just 2015–2016, the extremely limited nature of U.S. immigration allowances is obvious. (At the time of this writing the actual refugee and immigration numbers for the United States in 2018 were not clear as legal challenges and political bargaining were complicating policymaking.)

It is important to point out that this trend represents a dramatic reversal from established U.S. policy on migrants, and especially refugees. The United States has long prided itself on playing a leading role in offering asylum and welcoming refugees and immigrants. In the aftermath of the Vietnam War, as large numbers of people were dying at sea as they fled communist regimes, the United States accepted nearly half of those 2.5 million refugees who had been U.S. allies or displaced by the Southeast Asian conflict. And the country "has annually resettled around 60,000 refugees at the recommendation of UNHCR . . . the United States has accepted more people from UNHCR lists than any other country."[38]

While the United States has cited humanitarian and moral reasons for accepting large numbers of people, there have also been political reasons (anti-communism, for example). And cooperation to forestall large numbers of refugees in the world has generally been seen as benefiting U.S. national security interests in a stable international order. However, as Professor Martin Schain has argued, under the Trump administration perceptions have changed, with refugees generally being relegated to the status of immigrants who are viewed as trying to get into the United States to benefit themselves (or, in the case of Syrians particularly, to pose a threat to the United States). For Schain, this reflects more fundamental "questions of integration and identity. And the problem with the politics of identity is that it's not entirely rational."[39] UN Secretary-General Guterres echoed this theme when he observed: "Many of the negative perceptions about so-called 'economic migrants' fuel xenophobia and intolerance, but are based on false assumptions and poor analysis."[40] Recall that in Chapter 3 we saw how these identity security interests can fuel conflict, both domestically and across state borders.

Regardless of one's views about the morality of refugee and immigrant policies—and their implications for human security concerns—it is not difficult to understand the national security case for assisting refugees. Since at least World War II the United States has had a vital interest in helping to maintain a stable, peaceful, and productive world order as this benefits the United States militarily, politically, and economically. Large flows of refugees, and even large numbers of IDPs within countries and regions that are already unstable and at risk of conflict, threaten regional and even global stability. To illustrate this concern, one need only consider that the vast majority of Syrian refugees have fled to neighboring Jordan, a small country with limited resources; to Lebanon, an equally small country with a long history of internal conflict, due in part to hosting Palestinian refugees for decades; to Turkey, which has exacerbated already acrimonious relations with the Syrian government and other neighboring countries; and even to troubled Iraq. In fact, the UNHCR terms the Iraqi refugee situation itself an "emergency" and cites 220,000 Iraqi refugees in other countries, in addition to nearly 3 million displaced within Iraq. Note, too, that most of the Syrian refugees do not live in camps that the UN or other aid groups have established: in Lebanon about 70 percent live below the poverty line, whereas in Jordan 93 percent live below the poverty line.[41]

In sum, most refugees are hosted by developing countries which can ill afford to sustain them or meet their very real human security needs, enhancing the chances of more instability and conflict which can easily draw in outside powers. This is nowhere more obvious than in the Middle East. Table 10.1 gives some key data about the numbers of refugees (and migrants), their origin, their current residence, and other aspects. One fact in particular stands out: of some 22 million refugees worldwide in 2016, a mere 189,300 were resettled, which equates to less than 1 percent.[42]

Refugees and forcibly displaced persons clearly need protection of their most basic human security needs first, including the right to live. As noted, bona fide refugees have internationally recognized rights, and arguably so do displaced persons within their own countries if we recall the R2P mandate placed upon individual governments. Clearly states, and IGOs like the UN, play the main role—or should play the main role—in protecting vulnerable populations. But how do these millions of individuals move beyond basic human security protections to actual empowerment? Who promotes their other human security

Table 10.1 Refugees, Displaced/Stateless Persons

Category: number	Major Place of Origin (recent)	Major Host or Destination
*Refugees:** 22.5 million Under UNCHR mandate: 17.2 million; 5.3 million Palestinians In refugee camps: 2.6 million Resettled (2016): 189,300	Syria Afghanistan South Sudan	Ethiopia Uganda Iran Lebanon Jordan Pakistan Turkey Europe (Italy, Greece)
*Forcibly Displaced Persons:** 65.6 million 21.3 million across state borders	Africa: Democratic Republic of Congo, Nigeria, South Sudan Middle East: Syria, Iraq South Asia	Africa Middle East South Asia
*Stateless Persons:** 10 million	Roma (Europe) Rohingya (Burma/Myanmar) Côte d'Ivoire	Europe Bangladesh Côte d'Ivoire
*Migrants:*** 244 million	Africa Middle East Asia Central America, Mexico	Europe (via Italy, Greece) Germany United States United Kingdom Russian Federation

Sources: UN High Commissioner for Refugees, at www.unhcr.org/en-us/figures-at-a-glance.html (for 2017); IOM, "Global Migration Trends Factsheet, 2015," at http://gmdac.iom.int/global-migration-trends-factsheet (for 2015).

Note: * Figures as of 2017; ** figure for 2015.

needs? In that regard the UN Refugee Agency is quite forthright that, while it depends upon governments, the agency is only able to accomplish its mission and provide protection and solutions to refugees by working with a wide variety of other governmental and nongovernmental organizations. According to UNHCR, it has relationships with more than 900 partners, governmental and nongovernmental alike, and the agency entrusts 40 percent of its budget to these partners. In particular, UNHCR relies "heavily on NGOs to implement a wide range of projects, including aid distribution, protection, logistics, shelter, health, water, sanitation, nutrition and education projects."[43] Additionally, the agency emphasizes the assistance it derives from "UN Sister Organizations," singling out the World Food Programme, UNICEF, the World Health Organization, the Office for the Coordination of Humanitarian Affairs, the UN High Commissioner for Human Rights, the Joint UN Programme on HIV/AIDS, and the UNDP.[44]

As we have referenced in earlier chapters, the UNDP's role is integral to improving human development worldwide by empowering individuals and communities in almost every aspect of human security (Image 10.3 reminds us that governments can only provide part of the equation for improving human security.) Recall that the initial Millennium Development Goals (2000–2015), which were focused in areas ranging from poverty to education to gender equality to combating diseases to environmental sustainability, achieved some remarkable progress under the UNDP's coordination and assistance. This type of success provided the impetus for UN member states to agree in 2012 to move ahead, beginning in 2015 with the even more ambitious and comprehensive Sustainable Development Goals, which run until 2030. These goals were described in Chapter 5 and outlined in Table 5.1.

Image 10.3 New Road in Madagascar: even after governments build roads like this one, it still takes time for modern transportation to arrive. Photo: Jennifer Doyle

In Conclusion

The individual human security issue chapters in this book (Chapters 3–9) assessed what we consider to be the key threats and challenges related to human security, especially in the context of national security concerns. In those chapters we also considered some of the most important policy initiatives at the global, regional, and national levels, along with transnational efforts that are often waged by nongovernmental groups—from human rights to indigenous peoples to green movements. One theme that we believe has been clearly demonstrated throughout this consideration of various dimensions of human security is the inextricable nature of human security, often abetted by the processes of globalization, as reiterated below.

We have seen that identity security concerns are often enabled, or aggravated, under conditions of poverty and inequitable development. Poverty and inequitable development trigger communities and their leaders to find scapegoats. Poverty and lack of opportunity also help attract people to support or at least tolerate extremist groups, who may cause conflict and instability in their own countries, or equally to export it to other places via transnational terrorism. Poverty also enables criminal groups to find recruits among the dispossessed to prey upon their own communities, or to engage in transnational crime across borders. The immense profits to be found in illicit trafficking of drugs, people, natural resources, and weapons fuel both criminal gangs and facilitate public corruption and violence. The ability to use the maritime domain to traffic drugs and commit acts of piracy is linked in turn to the willingness of communities to cooperate because of their lack of opportunity and stable governance—particularly in certain regions of Africa. And many of these actors are further empowered by the fact that information technologies can be abused by criminal groups and extremist elements to support their activities.

We have also pointed out that one of the central factors aggravating poverty and lack of opportunity in many developing areas is environmental stresses that have increased the incidence of droughts and desertification, thus reducing the possibility to make a living via agriculture or herding. It is not surprising that families and communities would migrate in search of a way to make a living in these circumstances; but, as noted above, this often causes strain in those regions where they relocate. In this case even well-intentioned but poor governments will often face unrest and internal conflict, which again may be aggravated by cultural or religious differences between groups.

But, as we have seen, the incidence of good governance is not that common in certain regions of the world. It is thus difficult to envision that an equitable development path out of poverty, which is in critical need across the globe today to support human security needs, is possible where the government is predatory and not committed to its citizens. In fact, among the four factors that respected economist Paul Collier identifies as being central to extreme poverty for the bottom billion is bad governance.[45] This relationship between bad governance, extreme poverty, and hunger is reinforced by Amaryta Sen, who notes that:

> no substantial famine has ever occurred in a democratic country—no matter how poor. . . . This is because famines are extremely easy to prevent if the government tries to prevent them, and a government in a multiparty democracy with elections and free media has strong political incentives to undertake famine prevention.[46]

While hopefully Sen's prediction continues to hold true, it is also the case as we enter the third decade of the twenty-first century that human security issues related to identity concerns and economic inequities can enflame nationalist populism even in established democratic and relatively prosperous societies. It is sobering indeed to read the warnings in 2017 of prominent scholar Robert Keohane, who, along with his colleague Joseph S. Nye, had laid the foundations forty years earlier of the transnational relations approach, previewing the accelerated globalization processes to come:

> Those of us who have not only analyzed globalization and the liberal order but also celebrated them share some responsibility for the rise of populism. We did not pay enough attention as capitalism hijacked globalization. Economic elites designed international institutions to serve their own interests and to create further links between themselves and governments. Ordinary people were left out. The time has come to acknowledge this reality and push for policies that can save the liberal order before it is too late.[47]

For Keohane, the answer lies in developing the type of sustainable policies that "will make globalization serve the interest of middle- and working-class citizens."[48] While this prescription is aimed specifically at the United States and developed countries with similar issues, it sounds remarkably like the type of policies and goals contained in the global SDGs.

Nevertheless, as we conclude this work, on balance we are still optimists. Recall the reality of the low incidence of interstate war, as pointed out in the first chapter. Consider that nearly all of the world's governments have been able to agree recently on compacts so foundational to improving human security as the Sustainable Development Goals, the Responsibility to Protect doctrine, the New York Declaration for Refugees and Migrants, and the Paris Accords to protect and promote environmental security. Of course, these only represent governmental efforts ongoing at the state level. Intergovernmental organizations, especially the extensive United Nations system of agencies, and major regional organizations such as the Organization for Security and Cooperation in Europe and the Inter-American Commission for Human Rights, are all key actors consistently working to improve human security.

Since this text is concerned with *human* security, we tend to believe that the most promising actors for meeting the many security challenges and devising innovative solutions lie in the nongovernmental sector: whether global social movements dedicated to improving human rights or finding solutions to poverty; independent institutions and foundations researching peaceful resolution of historical enmities and technological fixes for energy consumption; national groups dedicated to exposing injustices and abuses of governance; or individual activists who refuse to be intimidated in the campaign to educate girls equitably. In fact, many of these groups, institutions, and individuals are most powerful when they join with intergovernmental organizations and receptive states to advance human security interests—that is certainly the lesson of the green environmental movement to date.

It is also encouraging to realize that promoting human security is not really a novel idea, although the linkages now made between human security and national security are no longer ignored as they often were in the past. Traditionally, states would provide international assistance to buy influence, even if short-lived and haphazard in nature. Although this is still true in some parts of the world, over the past twenty-five years there has been an increased urgency to reach out directly to people in need in every region. This is happening for both humanitarian and security reasons. For example, the individual child vulnerable to polio in Afghanistan certainly needs the vaccine, but the children in the rest of the world need polio to be eradicated, too. And whereas states may be motivated at least in part to give assistance because of security concerns, the actions of thousands of citizen-activists across the world who give their time, effort, and money to causes ranging from eliminating landmines and providing microfinance loans for women's groups to writing letters to protest political prisoners and demanding the tropical rainforests be protected must be accounted for, too. Traditional international relations theories such as realism cannot explain the shift or the important roles that non-state actors play in international security today, although constructivism (and liberalism to some extent) can help to engender thoughtful consideration of these issues.

What should be evident from the nontraditional security issues and cases presented in this book is that the current era of globalization links people, organizations, and countries across many heretofore dividing seams in unprecedented ways. In contrast to previous eras, when different regions or ideologies could be ignored with little effect on U.S. national security, that is increasingly untrue. What happens in countries that range from Afghanistan to Zimbabwe does impact security in the United States, whether it triggers an incidence of terrorism or generates a pandemic or allows cyber criminals to hack into banks unhindered. One consequence of Thomas Friedman's flat world is that U.S. security is dependent on security in nearly every country of the world; as was evidenced in the 2015 Zika virus outbreak that began in Brazil, but quickly migrated to the southern United States.

Given the changed nature of the security environment, no single solution or policy can address decades of neglect; clearly, long-term international and transnational cooperation is essential. In view of the insecurity present in the maritime domain, the environment, and cyberspace, it is unrealistic to think that a single country can provide for its own security today. For example, any environmental gains made in developed countries can be offset by environmental calamities in developing countries. Likewise, disease prevention and eradication in developed countries can be undermined by poor public health practices and the misuse of antibiotics in developing countries. The international criminal gang that steals the credit card number of a U.S. college student may be based in Nigeria. And the lack of governance in failing states and resulting ineffective maritime security in East Africa will continue to weaken international commerce through piracy. Though none of these challenges is equivalent to the nuclear threat facing much of the world in the aftermath of World War II, these challenges threaten state sovereignty and regularly undermine everyone's human security. Fortunately, recognition of this is occurring, albeit slowly.

From our perspective, one of the most promising indications of transforming attitudes that will ultimately strengthen the ability to address human security concerns is visible in the approach of the U.S. Defense Department and its military forces. Secretary of Defense Robert Gates—a highly respected public servant under both George W. Bush and Barack Obama—consistently voiced his support for the State Department and its development mission, including support to increase the latter's budget. In a representative speech to midlevel army officers in 2010, he commented:

> When I left the government in 1993 when I retired for the first time . . . there were 16,000 people in the Agency for International Development (AID). It was an expeditionary agency. Those people, most of them expected and wanted to be deployed overseas in developing countries, in harsh circumstances, often with imperfect security. And they were experts in agronomy and rule of law and building water systems and building schools and so on. Now, AID has 3,000 people and is basically a contracting agency. So we have to reestablish, we have to—AID, USIA, these civilian institutions that play such a huge role in our success in the Cold War have to be recreated in some way with the same scale for the 21st century. And we're a long way from being there yet.[49]

In a similar vein, Secretary of Defense Jim Mattis stated while he was still a four-star U.S. Marine Corps general: "If you don't fully fund the State Department, then I need to buy more ammunition."[50] For many of us, if traditionally conservative and security-conscious defense sectors are concerned not just with the military budget and forces but equally with supporting civilian agencies and their development mission, there should indeed be optimism!

Notes

1 António Guterres, "UNSG Remarks at 'Stand Together' Event to Mark World Humanitarian Day 2017." At: www.un.org/sg/en/content/sg/speeches/2017-08-18/secretary-generals-world-humanitarian-day-2017-remarks.
2 UN General Assembly, "Implementing the Responsibility to Protect: Report of the Secretary-General" (A/63/677), January 12, 2009, 4. At: www.globalr2p.org/media/files/implementing_the_responsibility_to_protect.pdf.
3 Ibid., 7–8.
4 Mark Zuckerberg, "Building Global Community," Facebook, February 16, 2017. At: www.facebook.com/notes/mark-zuckerberg/building-global-community/10154544292806634/.
5 Ibid.
6 Sarah Sewall, "Do the Right Thing: A Genocide Policy that Works," *Boston Review*, September/October 2009. http://bostonreview.net/archives/BR34.5/sewall.php.
7 United Nations Trust Fund for Human Security and Human Security Unit, *Human Security in Theory and Practice: An Overview of the Human Security Concept and the United Nations Trust Fund for Human Security* (New York: UN, 2009), 15. At: www.un.org/humansecurity/sites/www.un.org.humansecurity/files/human_security_in_theory_and_practice_english.pdf.
8 Christopher Hitchens, "Just Causes: The Case for Humanitarian Intervention." Review of *Freedom's Battle: The Origins of Humanitarian Intervention*, by Gary J. Bass, *Foreign Affairs* 87, no. 5 (2008): 162.
9 Bono, "Rebranding America," *New York Times*, October 18, 2009, available at www.nytimes.com/2009/10/18/opinion/18bono.html.
10 Gareth Evans, *The Responsibility to Protect: Ending Mass Atrocity Crimes Once and for All* (Washington, DC: Brookings Institution, 2008).
11 UN General Assembly, "Implementing the Responsibility to Protect."
12 Evans, *Responsibility to Protect*, 56. Evans was at pains to make this case because of the fact that this type of activity had become unpopular among many UN members, to include the United States.
13 Madeline K. Albright and Richard S. Williamson, *The United States and R2P: From Words to Action* (Washington, DC: United States Institute of Peace, 2013), 9. At: www.brookings.edu/wp-content/uploads/2016/06/23-united-states-responsibility-protect-albright-williamson.pdf.
14 Bush, *The National Security Strategy of the United States of America*, 2006, 17.
15 Robert M. Gates, *Quadrennial Defense Review Report* (Washington, DC: U.S. Department of Defense, 2010), vi.
16 The White House, Office of the Press Secretary, "FACT SHEET: President Obama Directs New Steps to Prevent Mass Atrocities and Impose Consequences on Serious Human Rights Violators," August 4, 2011. At: https://obamawhitehouse.archives.gov/the-press-office/2011/08/04/fact-sheet-president-obama-directs-new-steps-prevent-mass-atrocities.
17 Quoted in Donald Steinberg, "Responsibility to Protect in the Real World: A Tale of Two Countries," World Learning at the U.S. Institute of Peace, www.worldlearning.org/media/press-room/speeches/responsibility-to-protect-in-the-real-world-a-tale-of-two-countries/.
18 Albright and Williamson, *The United States and R2P*, 16–18.
19 Frederic Wehrey, "Libya's Terra Incognita: Who and What Will Follow Qaddafi?" *Foreign Affairs*, February 28, 2011. At: www.foreignaffairs.com/articles/north-africa/2011-02-28/libyas-terra-incognita.
20 Human Rights Watch, *World Report 2012: Libya-Events of 2011*. At: www.hrw.org/world-report/2012/country-chapters/libya.
21 Ibid.

22 UN Security Council, "Security Council Approves 'No-Fly Zone' over Libya, Authorizing 'All Necessary Measures' to Protect Civilians, by Vote of 10 in Favour with 5 Abstentions," March 17, 2011. At: www.un.org/press/en/2011/sc10200.doc.htm.
23 Ibid.
24 Albright and Williamson, *The United States and R2P*, 16.
25 Michael W. Doyle, "The Folly of Protection: Is Intervention against Qaddafi's Regime Legal and Legitimate?" *Foreign Affairs*, March 20, 2011. At: www.foreignaffairs.com/articles/africa/2011-03-20/folly-protection.
26 Human Rights Watch, "Countries: Libya," September 2017. At: www.hrw.org/middle-east/n-africa/libya.
27 Human Rights Watch, *World Report 2017: Libya*.
28 Anealla Safdar, "IOM: Refugees Dying at Quicker Rate in Mediterranean," *Al Jazeera*, September 17, 2017. At: www.aljazeera.com/indepth/features/2017/09/iom-refugees-dying-quicker-rate-mediterranean-170917035605080.html.
29 UN Refugee Agency, *2009 Global Trends: Refugees, Asylum-Seekers, Returnees, Internally Displaced, and Stateless Persons* (Geneva: UNHCR, 2010). At: www.unhcr.org/.
30 UN High Commissioner for Refugees, "Figures at a Glance," at: www.unhcr.org/en-us/figures-at-a-glance.html. Also IOM, "Global Migration Trends Factsheet, 2015," at: http://gmdac.iom.int/global-migration-trends-factsheet.
31 UN High Commissioner for Refugees, "The 1951 Refugee Convention," at: www.unhcr.org/en-us/1951-refugee-convention.html.
32 "Lost in Limbo," *Economist*, August 27, 2009. At: www.economist.com/world/international/story_id=14302845.
33 IOM, "Who Is a Migrant?" at: www.iom.int/who-is-a-migrant.
34 IOM, "Global Migration Trends Factsheet, 2015." Of note, the IOM was also founded in 1951, as of 2017 had 166 member states, and in 2017 became a related UN agency.
35 António Guterres, "Remarks to General Assembly Side Event on Refugees and Migrants 'Follow-up to the New York Declaration: One Year On,'" September 20, 2017. At: www.un.org/sg/en/content/sg/speeches/2017-09-20/sgs-follow-new-york-declaration-remarks.
36 Ibid.
37 Laura Koran, "Trump Administration Dramatically Scales Back Refugee Admissions," *CNN Politics*, September 27, 2017. At: www.cnn.com/2017/09/27/politics/us-trump-refugee-admissions/index.html.
38 Kavitha Surana, "Why Do Some Countries Get Away with Taking Fewer Refugees?" Interview with Yun Sun and Martin Schain, *Foreign Policy*, September–October 2017, 15.
39 Ibid.
40 Guterres, "Remarks to General Assembly Side Event on Refugees and Migrants."
41 UNHCR, "Syria Emergency;" at: www.unhcr.org/en-us/syria-emergency.html; and UNHCR, "Iraq Emergency," at: www.unhcr.org/en-us/iraq-emergency.html.
42 UN High Commissioner for Refugees, "Figures at a Glance."
43 UNHCR, "Governments and Partners: Non-Governmental Organizations." At: www.unhcr.org/en-us/non-governmental-organizations.html.
44 UNHCR, "Governments and Partners: UN Sister Organizations." At www.unhcr.org/en-us/un-sister-organizations.html.
45 Collier, *The Bottom Billion*. Incredibly, Collier places nearly 1 billion people (or one-seventh of the world's population) in fifty-eight countries as being at risk of failure.
46 Sen, *Development as Freedom*, 51–52.
47 Jeff D. Colgan and Robert O. Keohane, "The Liberal Order Is Rigged: Fix It Now or Watch It Wither," *Foreign Affairs* vol. 96, no. 3 (2017), 36–44, 37. See also Robert O. Keohane and Joseph S. Nye, *Power and Interdependence: World Politics in Transition* (New York: Little, Brown and Co., 1977).
48 Colgan and Keohane, "The Liberal Order Is Rigged," 44.
49 Robert Gates, "Remarks by Secretary Gates at the Command and General Staff College," Fort Leavenworth, KS, May 7, 2010, available at www.defense.gov/transcripts/transcript.aspx?transcriptid=4623.

50 Quoted in Dan Lamothe, "Retired Generals Cite Past Comments from Mattis while Opposing Trump's Proposed Foreign Aid Cuts," *Washington Post*, February 27, 2017. www.washingtonpost.com/news/checkpoint/wp/2017/02/27/retired-generals-cite-past-comments-from-mattis-while-opposing-trumps-proposed-foreign-aid-cuts/?utm_term=.b0c307281915.

To Learn More

Gareth Evans offers a comprehensive examination of changing international norms and sovereignty in *The Responsibility to Protect: Ending Mass Atrocity Crimes Once and for All* (Washington, DC: Brookings Institution, 2008).

Listen to former Chairman of the Joint Chiefs of Staff and U.S. Secretary of State Colin Powell's characterization of security as he discusses the role of international cooperation to facilitate security at https://www.theatlantic.com/magazine/archive/2007/04/a-conversation-with-colin-powell/305873/.

The journal *Prism* publishes articles on efforts to improve governmental coordination during complex operations, which includes humanitarian assistance and development. See http://cco.ndu.edu/Publications/PRISM/.

The U.S. Institute of Peace is a nonpartisan, independent institution established and funded by the U.S. Congress to help prevent and resolve violent conflict around the world and to help build post-conflict stability, development, and peace-building experts. View their many projects at www.usip.org/.

Visit the website of the United Nations High Commissioner for Refugees to get a sense of the immensity of the numbers, problems, and challenges facing refugees, internally displaced persons, and other stateless persons at www.unhcr.org/en-us/.

Visit the International Organization for Migration website for the latest figures on migrants/refugees and for a very helpful guide defining terms in this area. At: www.iom.int/key-migration-terms.

In *Refuge: Rethinking Refugee Policy in a Changing World* (Oxford: Oxford University Press, 2017), Oxford professors Alexander Betts and Paul Collier explore the refugee crisis and propose practical, workable solutions that take into account the concerns of host communities while providing refugees with the ability to find autonomy and dignity in their lives.

The International Coalition for the Responsibility to Protect, founded in 2009, "brings together NGOs from all regions of the world to strengthen normative consensus for RtoP." Scan their informative website at http://responsibilitytoprotect.org/index.php/about-coalition.

The nongovernmental International Crisis Group was founded in 1995 by former high-level government officials and policy experts who saw the tragedies of Somalia, Rwanda, and Bosnia as demonstrating the need for better prediction and international response to impending conflicts. View their website at www.crisisgroup.org to see why the group's analysis, policy recommendations, and advocacy efforts are so highly regarded.

In *A Path Appears: Transforming Lives, Creating Opportunity* (New York: Alfred A. Knopf, 2014), Pulitzer Prize-winning journalists Nicholas D. Kristoff and Sheryl WuDunn describe local and global initiatives which have actually proved successful in bettering people's lives around the world.

Glossary

Balance of power: a realist theory that predicts equilibrium in the international system where two or more opposing states constrain one another's actions due to fear of escalation leading to a major war.

Bipolarity: a stage in international affairs where two opposing states dominate the international system (e.g., the United States and the Soviet Union in the Cold War era).

Botnet: a network of zombie machines used by hackers for massive coordinated system attacks.

Choke point: a narrow waterway of strategic value that separates two larger bodies of water.

Civic security: protection of an individual's physical safety and integrity, along with respect for one's rights as a citizen—the right to be a political participant in decisions about how one will be governed.

Civil society: the sector of society not controlled by the government or corporations but by citizens, who may form private, voluntary groups for social, economic, educational, humanitarian, and religious purposes, among others.

Climate change: a perspective that maintains that the earth is currently undergoing a slow warming process due primarily to human activity; this process is viewed as generating mainly negative and even catastrophic effects for human beings.

Constructivism: a newer school of international relations that holds that the international system is constantly being shaped ("constructed") by shared ideas and interactions between peoples and their societies, and that this process can result in shared values for better or worse.

Corruption: the abuse of entrusted power for private gain.

Culture: the beliefs, values, norms, and practices that a society holds as meaningful to define itself through generations (normally linked to ethnicity, language, religion, and a common history).

Cyberspace: the information environment characterized by computers and their networks, information flowing on the networks, and the interpretations of the information by users.

Democratic peace theory: the belief (seemingly validated by numerous data-supported studies) that as democracies do not go to war with another, establishing more democratic states in the international system would eventually lead to stable peace.

Denial-of-service attack: employing a botnet to send massive simultaneous requests to servers, thus preventing legitimate use of the servers.

Development: a process that traditionally meant achieving economic growth and progress for societies but has been consistently broadened into a more comprehensive process including the concepts of sustainability, equity, and capacity (and even social and cultural aspects).

Ecomigration: the movement of people primarily due to environmental conditions such as drought, rising sea levels, or desertification.

Economic security: the right of all human beings to adequate resources necessary for survival such as food, shelter, and employment; often conceptualized as the right of human beings to equitable and sustainable development.

Exclusive Economic Zone (EEZ): waters that extend seaward from the low-water mark of a coastal state to 200 nautical miles.

Failing state: a state at risk of collapse into anarchy because its very weak government, economy, and other institutions cannot effectively protect the state's borders and the citizenry, or provide necessary services and resources.

Food security: the right of all human beings to have access to safe and nutritious food and to be free from hunger.

Four Freedoms: freedom of speech, freedom of worship, freedom from want, and freedom from fear, as popularized in President Franklin Delano Roosevelt's 1941 State of the Union address.

Globalization: a common term used to describe the seemingly dominant trend in the international system that is characterized by constantly accelerating transnational economic, cultural, and information flows, resulting in an increasingly integrated (but sometimes conflicted) world community.

Green revolution: the technological transformation of agricultural practices after World War II into the 1970s which vastly increased agricultural production in developing countries, allowing them to feed their rapidly growing populations.

Hegemony: a stage of international affairs where one state dominates the international system.

Human rights: the belief that all human beings are inherently entitled to certain rights because they are human beings. There is disagreement about whether human rights should be considered universal or relative (affected by cultural and religious values), but almost all would agree that each person has the right to life and respect for their person and dignity.

Human security: a people-centered approach focused on individual human beings and their rights and needs; specifically, freedom from fear, freedom from want, and freedom to live in dignity.

Human trafficking: the practice of illegally transporting and employing mostly poor women and children (usually by force or trickery) for illicit purposes such as forced labor, debt peonage, and prostitution.

Identity security: respect for a human being's personal beliefs and dignity.

Illegally armed groups: subnational or transnational groups that use violence to fulfill their objectives outside of state control.

Internally displaced person (IDP): a person who has moved within a state away from his/her habitual place of residence, usually for involuntary reasons. The person is supposed to receive protection and support from their national government, even if that government is responsible for the forced displacement of the citizen.

Liberalism: a dominant school of international relations that holds that the international system is progressing into a peaceful, just, and prosperous community of (democratic) states and non-state actors as education and learning influence cooperation for the betterment of all.

Logic bomb: camouflaged segments of programs that destroy data when certain conditions are met.

Microfinance: the practice of providing very small loans to generally poor and marginalized populations (mostly women) so they can establish productive small businesses and escape extreme poverty; it often includes the concept of village-level banks and cooperatives.

Migrant: a person who is moving or has moved across an international border or within a state away from his/her habitual place of residence, for voluntary or involuntary reasons. A migrant is not entitled to international legal protection and assistance.

Millennium Development Goals (MDGs): a set of eight interrelated and comprehensive development goals—to include twenty-one quantifiable targets and sixty indicators—that member states of the United Nations agreed to achieve by 2015 to address the main development challenges facing the world's peoples.

Multipolarity: a stage in international affairs where more than two opposing states dominate the international system, particularly at the regional level.

Narcotrafficking: the shipment of illegal drugs across national boundaries.

National security: traditional focus on protecting the state's perceived vital and important national interests through integrating military, diplomatic, and economic means.

Nationalism: the belief that people sharing a significant heritage such as a language and/or other important characteristics and traditions should live in a single state.

Nongovernmental organization (NGO): private non-state actors that develop and implement social, political, and economic policies. These can be solely domestic or international in scope; if international, they are termed INGOs.

Non-state actor: an individual, group, organization, or company that influences the social, political, economic, or security dimensions of society.

Paris Agreement/Paris Accords: the current global agreement between states to reduce carbon emissions and combat climate change under the United Nations Framework Convention on Climate Change.

Piracy: an act of boarding or attempting to board any ship in international waters with apparent intent to commit theft or any other crime, and with apparent intent or capability to use force in the furtherance of that act.

Populism: the belief among a group that it represents ordinary, "patriotic" people in society who have been taken advantage of by the elite, usually privileged, mainstream politicians, governmental officials, and established institutions. It may be left-wing or right-wing in nature.

Predatory state: a state where the government's purpose (even if elected) is to rule in such a fashion as to enrich the leadership and its cronies, and not to provide services and resources to the majority of the citizens.

Realism: a dominant school of international relations that holds that in an international system characterized by anarchy and insecurity, states will constantly seek military and other forms of power to protect themselves and to dominate weaker states.

Refugee: a person who has been forced to leave his/her state because of persecution or armed conflict. Under international law, a refugee has international legal rights, including non-refoulement (no forced return to the home country) and international protection and assistance.

Responsibility to Protect (R2P): as outlined by the United Nations, it includes three principles. First, states must protect their populations against genocide, war crimes, ethnic cleansing, and crimes against humanity. Second, the international community should provide assistance to states in building capacity to protect their populations from catastrophe by addressing underlying conditions. Third, the international community should take timely action when states fail to protect their populations.

Rogue state: a term used to refer to states that do not follow conventional, widely accepted norms of state behavior such as respect for diplomatic conventions.

Security assistance: a form of military cooperation that includes education, training, and equipping other countries' militaries.

Social movements: decentralized, usually transnational networks of activists and nongovernmental groups (and sometimes intergovernmental groups) motivated to work together for a cause, often a perceived injustice such as abuse of human rights.

Sovereignty: international legal concept established by the Treaty of Westphalia of 1648 that recognizes the supreme authority of a government within its own defined territory.

Sustainable development: development that meets the needs of the present without compromising the ability of future generations to meet their own needs.

Sustainable Development Goals (SDGs): a set of seventeen interrelated and comprehensive development goals—to include specific targets—that member states of the United Nations have agreed to achieve by 2030 to address the main development challenges facing the world's peoples. The SDGs followed upon completion of the MDGs.

Territorial waters: those waters under government sovereign control and legally recognized as 12 nautical miles from the low-water mark of a coastal state.

Terrorism: acts (or threatened acts) of political and related violence deliberately directed against civilians or civilian targets to instill fear.

Transnational challenge: a challenge that crosses national boundaries and cannot be controlled solely, if at all, by individual states.

Trojan horse: stealthy computer code that executes under the guise of a useful program but performs malicious acts such as the destruction of files, the transmission of private data, and the opening of a back door to allow third-party control of a machine.

Unipolarity: a stage in international affairs where a single state can dominate the international system.

Virus: a malicious computer code that can self-replicate and cause damage to the systems it infects. The code can delete information, infect programs, change the directory structure to run undesirable programs, and infect the vital part of the operating system that ties together how files are stored.

Weak state: a state characterized by the government's inability to effectively control its borders, provide security for its citizens, and generate sufficient economic opportunities to improve living standards.

Worm: similar to a virus, a worm is distinctive for its ability to self-replicate without infecting other files in order to reproduce.

Zombie: a computer that has been covertly compromised and is controlled by a third party.

Index